Unlocking the *Treasury*

ELEMENTARY LEARNING FOR BOYS IN QING CHINA

Katherine Ngo

LEVER
PRESS

ASIANetwork Books

Series Editors:
Erin McCarthy (St. Lawrence University)
Lisa Trivedi (Hamilton College)

ASIANetwork Books strives to publish high-quality, original monographs, edited collections, and translations that embody a rigorous liberal arts approach to Asian Studies. A collaboration with ASIANetwork, a consortium of Asian Studies faculty at 160 colleges, the series seeks to fill a space between works that address the critical pedagogical strategies of the Asian Studies classroom and works of specialized scholarship that engage a broad readership outside higher education. Manuscripts published in the ASIANetwork Books series, no matter how narrowly focused, are expected to raise broad questions of interest for the public and demonstrate classroom utility for Asian Studies.

Titles in the Series

Vikash Yadav and Jason Kirk, *The Politics of India under Modi: An Introduction to India's Democracy, Economy, and Foreign Policy*

Kelly Ngo, *Ordering Tang China: Cultural Memory, Emperor Taizong, and the* Essentials

A complete list of titles in the series can be found at www.leverpress.org

Lever Press (leverpress.org) is a publisher of pathbreaking scholarship. Supported by a consortium of higher education institutions focused on, and renowned for, excellence in both research and teaching, our press is grounded on three essential commitments: to be a digitally native press, to be a peer-reviewed, open access press that charges no fees to either authors or their institutions, and to be a press aligned with the liberal arts ethos.

The complete manuscript of this work was subjected to a fully closed ("double-blind") review process. For more information, please see our Peer Review Commitments and Guidelines at https://www.leverpress.org/peerreview

DOI: https://doi.org/10.3998/mpub.14506576
Print ISBN: 978-1-64315-074-1
Open access ISBN: 978-1-64315-075-8

Library of Congress Control Number: 2024940788

Published in the United States of America by Lever Press, in partnership with Michigan Publishing.

This book is dedicated to my parents,
the late Venerable Master Chin Kung AM
and Clayton Chou.

Table of Contents

Member Institution Acknowledgments

Lever Press is a collective effort. This work was made possible by the generous support of Lever Press member libraries from the following institutions:

Amherst College
Atlanta University Center Consortium
Berea College
Bowdoin College
Carleton College
Central Washington University
Claremont Colleges
Claremont Graduate University
Claremont McKenna College
Clark Atlanta University
College of Saint Benedict & Saint John's University
The College of Wooster
Davidson College
Denison University
DePauw University
Grinnell College
Hamilton College
Hampshire College
Harvey Mudd College
Hollins University
Iowa State University
Keck Graduate Institute
Knox College
Lafayette College
Macalester College
Middlebury College
Morehouse College
Morehouse School of Medicine
Norwich University
Occidental College
Penn State University
Pitzer College
Pomona College
Randolph-Macon College

Rollins College
Santa Clara University
Scripps College
Skidmore College
Smith College
Spelman College
Susquehanna University
Swarthmore College
Trinity University
UCLA Library
Union College
University of Delaware
University of Idaho
University of Northern Colorado
University of Puget Sound
University of Rhode Island
University of San Francisco
University of Sheffield
University of Vermont
Vassar College
Washington and Lee University
Whitman College
Whittier College
Willamette University
Williams College

Acknowledgments

I am eternally indebted to the late Venerable Master Chin Kung AM, who introduced me to the traditions of Chinese education and inspired me to embark on this path into Sinology. He was a towering international leader in intercultural and interfaith harmony who remained tireless in his efforts to foster world peace into his nineties, and I feel humbled to have personally learned from his wisdom, compassion, and vision for a better world.

This study would not have been possible without the kind guidance and support of Thomas Jansen, who selflessly imparted his extensive scholarship experience; Rebekah Humphreys, for her expertise in normative and applied ethics and moral philosophy and encouragement in realizing cross-cultural dialogue; and Chang Ching-Chuan, who contributed his specialist knowledge of the premodern elementary primers. I pay tribute to the Academy of Sinology at the University of Wales Trinity Saint David and its founding provost, the late Clayton Chou, who taught me the spirit of Sinology through his words and through his example. Provost Venerable Shengmiao has been a source of unfailing support and guidance. I am grateful to all the past and present staff of the Academy for their amazing work and wonderful friendship, as well as my students, who continue to be a source of invaluable insight.

I would also like to acknowledge Christopher Foster, Anne Kinney, Christopher Nugent, Li Ren-Yuan, and Federico Valenti for generously furnishing me with their conference papers and manuscripts. Throughout this work, I have benefitted from the help and advice of librarians around the world. My research has been generously sponsored by a scholarship from the Chin Kung Multicultural Education Foundation.

That this monograph is a reality owes largely to the fine team at Lever Press, and the anonymous reviewers for their constructive reading and their immensely helpful comments.

And as ever, my boundless gratitude to my parents and my sister for their blessed love and enduring inspiration.

Technical Notes

- Chinese names, concepts, place names and book titles are transliterated in Hanyu pinyin without tone marks.
- Chinese characters are provided with the transliteration the first time Chinese terms are encountered, excluding place names and contemporary Chinese scholars whose names can be identified in the bibliography.
- All Chinese names begin with the family name.
- Dates for dynasties and personages of premodern and early modern China are also provided on initial mention.
- The Chinese text for quotes from primary sources has been provided.
- When referring to Chinese education, ages will be based on the traditional concept of *sui* 歲 (years old) with the child considered aged one *sui* at birth; in this system the western "age of eight" would be considered nine years old.
- All translations are my own unless otherwise noted.

INTRODUCTION

As early as the second century BCE, the first phases of education were considered foundational for human development.[1] The earliest writing on educational theory entitled "*Xue ji* 學記" (On learning and teaching) from the same period employs a metaphor of unpolished jade for the uneducated:

> 玉不琢，不成器；人不學，不知道。
> A piece of jade that remains uncut will never become a sacred vessel, and a person that does not learn will never realize the proper way.[2]

As the raw jade mineral must undergo refinement to realize its worth as a precious object, human beings have an innate potential that requires education to be fully realized. Over a thousand years later, this sentence was included almost verbatim in the late imperial primer *Sanzi jing* 三字經 (Three character classic),[3] which was recited by children throughout the empire.[4] As the first stages in jade processing mold its shape before the later stages of polishing creates detail, the philosopher and educator Zhu Xi 朱熹 (1130–1200) explained that for the human, the mold of a sage is created in these elementary years:

> 古者，小學已自暗養成了，到長來，已自有聖賢坯模，只就上面加光飾。

> In antiquity, elementary learning nurtured people without their even knowing it. So that as they got older, they were naturally molded as a sage or worthy and simply added some finishing touches.[5]

The concept of a crucial period of early education was ingrained in the mindset of parents and teachers and underpinned the compilation of children's texts known as *mengshu* 蒙書 (beginners' books). Akin to classical scholarship being based on the textual tradition,[6] elementary education also depended on children's textbooks. The elementary textbook in imperial China was a unique genre designed for primary education. These textbooks were generally taught to children under the age of fifteen in family homes or village schools. The texts were repeatedly read aloud until they could be recited by the students. The significance of these texts can be deduced through two aspects: the texts engaged the reader in the formative years of their life and for a prolonged period to the point of committing them to memory. Despite this, in the long-established, rich, and hierarchical tradition of Chinese literature, with canonical works being most researched,[7] the genre of elementary textbooks has long been neglected.

Bibliographies offer the earliest record of primary education texts. The *Hanshu* 漢書 (History of the Former Han) mentions that elementary texts were used by official scribes to teach the young.[8] The first text, the *Shi zhou pian* 史籀篇 (Historian Zhou's primer), written during the time of King Xuan of Zhou 周宣王 (r. 827–782 BCE), predates the essay "On Learning and Teaching." Subsequent Qin dynasty (221–206 BCE) texts were based on *Historian Zhou's Primer*, including the *Cang jie pian* 倉頡篇 (Cang jie primer), the *Yuan li pian* 爰歷篇 (Yuanli primer), and the *Boxue pian* 博學篇 (Scholarly primer), which have been traditionally attributed to the most senior government ministers of the time—Chancellor Li Si 李斯 (d. 208 BCE), Zhao Gao 趙高 (d. 207 BCE), and Hu Wujing 胡毋敬 (fl. 221–206 BCE), respectively. These early primers were used primarily for teaching Chinese literacy.[9] However, the function of children's textbooks evolved as they proliferated in late imperial China, reaching their zenith in the Ming (1368–1644) and Qing (1644–1912) dynasties. Notwithstanding their authorship, elementary texts were traditionally confined to the ranks of popular literature and were not well researched in imperial China.[10] Children's literature around the world shared a similar fate, as Peter Hunt explains:

> To some, "children's literature" might well be a contradiction in terms: the values and qualities which constitute "literariness" naturally cannot be sustained either by books designed for an audience of limited experience, knowledge, skill, and sophistication or by the readers.[11]

The rich commentarial tradition and layers of textual analysis afforded to works of the Confucian canon were largely absent from primary education texts that were meant to be accessible in style, instruction, and language. In the 1960s, modern Chinese educator and linguist Zhang Zhigong lamented:

> Elementary education was rarely recorded. Book collectors did not value elementary textbooks and many are now lost, such that it is challenging to acquire texts nowadays. The texts were seldom documented and even bibliographic details are difficult to find today.[12]

For the imperial scholar, it was difficult to justify annotating a book that even children could read or writing a commentary on texts that were merely stepping stones to advanced learning texts that were the subjects of more formal study. For the modern scholar, the purpose of analyzing a book that was simply memorized for classical Chinese literacy was equally elusive. These common though unfounded assumptions meant that important questions of education have remained largely unresearched until recent years.

The final dynasty of imperial China, the Qing dynasty, represented the culmination of premodern educational thought, including elementary education. The Qing period was characterized by shifting intellectual attitudes, and primary educators accommodated various strands of thinking. An elementary textbook that was popular throughout the Qing dynasty, the *Youxue qionglin* 幼學瓊林 ("Treasury of elementary learning," hereafter referred to as the *Treasury*) forms the focus of this study in understanding the theoretical foundations of educational literature. The *Treasury,* one of the longest children's primers used in the Qing dynasty, integrated many of the strengths of its predecessors in a creative form. Written in prose with parallel sentences, the lines were rich in classical allusions and idioms. The text provided a children's encyclopedia of knowledge covering a diversity of topics including geography, etiquette, parents, and poverty. The *Treasury* struck a chord with the masses after it was published, which lasted for over a hundred years. In Cai Dongfan's 蔡東藩 (1877–1945) foreword to the revised edition of the *Treasury* published in 1924, he recollects:

> When walking through the streets in my youth, I could hear reciting voices emanating from the village school. Listening closely, they were not reciting the Four Books but the *Treasury*. When educational reforms were enacted, there was a transient phase during which the Four Books were no longer taught but the teaching of the *Treasury* continued unabated.[13]

The Four Books (*sishu* 四書) were no longer compulsory learning following the abolition of the civil service examinations in 1905.[14] However, one may plausibly infer from Cai's observation of the enduring popularity of the *Treasury* that it fulfilled certain primary educational needs beyond examination preparation. Indeed, there was a common saying:

> 讀了《增廣》會說話，讀了《幼學》會讀書。
> Children will know how to speak after reading the *Zengguan xianwen* 增廣賢文 [Extended collection of wise words], and they will know how to read books after reading the *Treasury*.[15]

Another version of the saying went like this:

> 讀了《增廣》會說話，讀了《幼學》走天下。
> Children will know how to speak after reading the *Extended Collection of Wise Words,* and they will be able to make their way in the world after studying the *Treasury*.[16]

Although there was not a stipulated national curriculum for primary education before 1904,[17] many sources have highlighted the widespread use of the *Treasury*.[18] As the title suggests, the text presented a treasure trove of knowledge and learning strategies. Different orientations of developmental theory and curricular thought intersect on the pages of the *Treasury* for two main reasons. First, the likely age of the *Treasury*'s reader was approximately ten years, and by this stage, they were beginning to make the transition into mature forms of cognitive and moral understanding.[19] Second, the *Treasury* trained its readers to navigate the diverse schools of thought in the Qing dynasty, schools that offered varying views on living the good life and becoming a sage. The content and structure of the *Treasury* mirror how the readership was at the center of complex educational concerns at both the individual and cultural levels. This book focuses on the Qing dynasty primary educational theory and practices that manifested in the *Treasury*, unlocking the strategies and illuminating its riches for the reader.

THE LIFE OF THE *TREASURY OF ELEMENTARY LEARNING*

The period of the Ming dynasty to the high Qing (1683–1799) was characterized by economic expansion at both the domestic and foreign levels.[20] The economic achievements supported unprecedented growth in population. Demographically, the population more than doubled during the Ming dynasty and continued to increase to 1850, despite a slight interruption during the seventeenth century due to the Manchu conquest.[21] The eighteenth century saw a tripling of the population, which in turn stimulated the migration and colonization of new lands.[22] Since the start of the sixteenth century, there was a commercial publishing boom that was attributed to a number of factors, including the reduced cost of paper and woodblock carving.[23] Although the publishers were initially concentrated in south China due to its abundant production of bamboo paper, the migrations of the high Qing geographically broadened the supply and demand of publishing.[24] From a political perspective, recommendations and referrals from associates were the primary method of securing a government position in the early Ming, but by the second half of the fifteenth century, the examination system became the primary recruitment channel.[25] Increasing numbers of examination candidates from the late fifteenth century coupled with the declaration of the highly formulaic essay style, the eight-legged essay (*baguwen* 八股文),[26] as the official examination style during the Chenghua 成化 period (1464–1487) resulted in a lively market for examination manuals.[27] The growth of examination aids and also new categories of texts, such as encyclopedias, were undoubtedly fueled by authors who were failed examinees and the rise in commercial printing.[28] These multiple and interrelated geographic and historical dimensions created fertile ground for the production and demand of educational texts like the *Treasury*.

The authorship of the *Treasury* has been questioned, although there is a broad consensus that the original text was compiled during the Ming dynasty.[29] The original text is traditionally attributed to Cheng Dengji 程登吉 (1601–1648), who wrote the *Youxue xuzhi* 幼學須知 (Required knowledge for elementary learning), also titled *Chengyu kao* 成語考 (Study of idioms) and *Gushi xun yuan* 故事尋源 (Seeking the origins of classical allusions). Some have mentioned Qiu Jun 邱浚 (1419–1495) as authoring a text entitled *Chengyu kao*.[30] Qiu had passed the highest level of civil service examinations, attaining the title of "presented scholar" (*jinshi* 進士), during the Jingtai 景泰 period (1450–1456) of the Ming dynasty and compiled several works, including the *Daxue yanyi bu* 大學衍義補 (Supplement to the extensive meaning of the *Great Learning*). However, compilation of the text is not recorded in Qiu's biography in the *Ming shi* 明史 (History of the Ming dynasty). Moreover, false attribution to a famous scholar was a common promotional strategy and cannot be ruled out in this case.[31]

Biographical information on Cheng is limited; the main source is the *Jiangxi lishi mingren yanjiu* 江西歷史名人研究 (Research on historical figures of Jiangxi).[32] According to this record, Cheng Dengji (formal name Boyi 伯禩, *alias* Yunsheng 允昇) was born into a scholar-official family in Nanchang, Jiangxi. Despite his brothers attending the civil service examinations, Cheng felt that the eight-legged essays had no relevance to governance or administrative ability and allegedly preferred a simple life over bureaucracy. He was known for his erudition, particularly enjoying rare books and the writings of the masters. Consequently, he was employed as a private teacher for the elementary education of many families. He wrote the *Required Knowledge for Elementary Learning* after several decades of professional experience. Lacking funds to publish the text, manuscript copies were circulated by students until Provincial

Administration Commissioner Song Luo 宋犖 (1634–1713) published the work in 1688 as part of his efforts to disseminate educational works. This brief summary of the life of Cheng Dengji foregrounds his familiarity with the needs of elementary students. As a private teacher, he was likely tutoring budding examination candidates, and so the *Required Knowledge for Elementary Learning* would certainly have been compiled with this readership in mind.

The original edition and the 1688 edition no longer exist. The date of first publication has been challenged by an edition likely dating to the Chongzhen 崇禎 reign (1627–1644). This edition is titled *Jiantang chongding Youxue xuzhi biandu gushi* 簡堂重訂幼學須知便讀故事 (A concise reader of allusions in the *Required Knowledge for Elementary Learning*, revised by the Bamboo Slip Studio, hereafter referred to as the "Jianyang edition"), and the sole author noted is Cheng Dengji. Several features of this edition suggest circulation of the text during the late Ming, including Cheng's foreword, dated 1637; an appendix of dynastic reign periods with the final entry referring to the Chongzhen reign as the "current period"; and a reverential statement about the Ming monarch ("The first year of the Chongzhen reign is *wu chen*, lasting thousands of years" 崇禎元年戊辰乞萬萬歲).[33] While this copy may be the earliest extant edition of the *Treasury*, it presents a "revised" (*chongding* 重訂) edition, and the extent of changes made by the publisher remains unclear.[34] Certainly, the title, the increase in the number of topical categories, and the positioning of further annotations in an upper register indicate at least three revisions. The inside cover names "Yang Xiaomin, Shulin" 書林楊小閩, who was a commercial publisher of the Ming dynasty in Jianyang, Fujian province, indicating that the text had already spread beyond the geographically proximal Jiangxi province.[35] However, the exact date of this printing is not known.

The text seems to have resonated with readers as it was subsequently supplemented, revised, and annotated, resulting in the development of multiple editions during the Qing dynasty and even after the fall of the imperial government. It can also be argued that the new editions helped ensure relevance and maintain readability for the evolving needs of the contemporary readership. Li Ren-Yuan has analyzed the layout, paratexts, and physical appearance of the various extant *Treasury* editions up to the early twentieth century. Moreover, he has evaluated how the changing appearance of the textbook reflected strategies employed by publishers for different readers.[36] He highlights five stages in the evolution of the text: (1) the early to mid-seventeenth century, in which the *Treasury* was compiled as an advanced textbook for children; (2) the late-seventeenth to mid-eighteenth-century editions, which saw the addition of scholarly annotations; (3) the mid-eighteenth-century editions, which were supplemented with various elements to produce an "encyclopedic" reference work; (4) the nineteenth and early twentieth centuries, which saw further annotated versions and the popular circulation of reprints; and (5) the late nineteenth and early twentieth centuries, in which lithographic editions reflected shifting intellectual paradigms and educational reforms.

From the late seventeenth century to the mid-eighteenth century, at least two annotated editions appeared. As they no longer exist, we can only guess at their contents based on evidence from later reprints. A reprint of the *Youxue xuzhi ju jie* 幼學須知句解 (*Required Knowledge for Elementary Learning* explained phrase by phrase) published in 1757 is credited to Huang Wangruo 黃汪若, whose background is unknown. However, the publisher and editor Qian Yuanlong 錢元龍 writes in the foreword that he read the text as a child, indicating the existence of a former edition.[37] The earliest extant copy of the *Youxue xuzhi zhi jie* 幼學須知直解 (Fully annotated *Required Knowledge for Elementary Learning*) was printed in 1818 with a supplement attributed to Wang Xiang 王相 (fl. 1662–1722). Wang was active during the Kangxi 康熙 period (1662–1722) in annotating other primers, including the *Sanzi jing xungu* 三字經訓詁 (Exegesis of the *Three Character Classic*) and the *Baijiaxing kao lüe* 百家姓考略 (Summary of evidential research on the *Hundred Surnames*). Distinctive changes in the page layout of these two editions have been noted; longer annotations in the format of "inserted double-column annotations" (*shuanghang jiazhu* 雙行夾註) and entries of author names and source titles relating to information in the couplets are placed in boxes.[38] These changes notably correspond to the expansion of evidential learning, which is covered in Chapter 2.[39] However, it remains unclear whether these editions occurred in the early Qing or high Qing period; the extent of the revisions in the reprint compared to that of Wang and Huang is also not known.

Zou Shengmai's edition, entitled the *Youxue gushi qionglin* 幼學故事瓊林 (Treasury of literary allusions for elementary learning), commonly abbreviated as "*Youxue qionglin*" 幼學瓊林 (Treasury of elementary learning), includes his foreword dated to the year 1760. His edition became more popular than the original book as well as other versions during the Qing dynasty; this volume is the focus of this book.[40] In many ways, Zou's profile exemplifies the compiler of such primers, which arguably contributed to the book's success. Zou Shengmai (formal name Yiyan 宜彥, *alias* Wu Gang 梧岡) was born into a merchant family in Sibao, Fujian Province. His father, Zou Funan 鄒撫南 (1653–1738), established a publishing business in the late seventeenth century and collated, proofread, and published canonical and historical works.[41] Hoping that his son would attain a government position, he constructed a room dedicated to study and appointed renowned teachers. Zou Shengmai commenced schooling at the age of six at home. He was studious and became known for his erudition as a young adult. However, he never became a government official. Different explanations have been recorded. One account notes that he consistently failed the imperial examinations,[42] with local lore explaining that this was due to his aversion to the compulsory eight-legged essays.[43] Li Fengrui writes that Zou Shengmai was highly gifted but was "born proud and unwilling to compose the vulgar eight-legged essays,"[44] which destroyed any chance he had of examination success. Other biographies paint the young Zou Shengmai as an upright, virtuous, and talented scholar who was infuriated by the Manchu government's literary inquisition.[45] Determined to dissociate himself from this regime, he rejected the civil service examinations and dedicated his life to publishing, writing, and editing.

According to the *Liancheng xianzhi* 連城縣志 (Liancheng gazetteer):

> 資質忠直，言行一致，好學深思。在青年時期，他認識到讀經能立德，為公毋私，為眾毋貪，為人毋晦，為己毋隱；剛毅正直，坦蕩如砥，有助人之行，無盜世之心；學史可明智，辨是非，分曲直，明原委，知興衰，別正反，善對應，服人以理，化人以德；習詩詞能養性，識比興，擅詞令，知含蓄，能大度，冶性情，闊胸襟，嚴己寬人，豁達容物。

> [Zou Shengmai] was a person of integrity, his actions were consistent with his words, and he was studious and thoughtful. In his youth, he became aware that reading the canonical works would help establish one's moral qualities—to act in the best interests of the public without greed, to interact without ulterior motives, to be clear of one's faults, to be resolute, upright, sincere, helpful and to not take advantage of society. He realized that studying historical works would help one to become astute: discern right from wrong, distinguish the wicked from the honest; see the full picture; understand the rise and fall of dynasties; discriminate between correct and contrary; be adept at interpersonal interactions; convince others through reasoning, and inspire them to cultivate their character. Moreover, learning poetry could nurture one's character by understanding the use of analogies and rhetoric, knowing to be reserved, capable of being magnanimous, improving one's temperament, broadening the mind, disciplining oneself and being accommodating toward others.[46]

Zou's awareness of the importance of book learning was arguably a key theme in his life. As a publisher, Zou was credited with advancing publishing technologies to the extent of leading the Sibao industry—the Sibao township being one of the four largest publishing centers during the Qing period. However, he later retired at the age of fifty to focus on writing—building a residence at a remote location with an abundant book collection. It was during this time that he wrote the *Ji ao shan fang shi wenji* 寄傲山房詩文集 (Anthology of poems and prose from the noble mountain residence), compiled the *Zengbu Wujing bei zhi cui jing* 增補五經備旨萃精 (Supplemented essentials of the Five Classics) and revised the *Treasury*.[47] Zou added 360 couplets and detailed annotations to the *Treasury,* catering to a readership beyond that of the Ming dynasty editions.

Multiple paratexts were included in the extant *Xinzeng Youxue gushi qionglin* 新增幼學故事瓊林 (Newly expanded *Treasury of Elementary Learning*, hereafter referred to as the "Expanded Treasury") (Figure 1). However, those paratexts are not mentioned in Zou's foreword, and it is unknown whether they formed part of the 1760 edition. Zou Shengmai's son, Zou Tingyou 鄒廷猷 (1715–1803), and Tingyou's father-in-law, Xie Meilin 謝梅林 (fl. 1760), are credited as collators, and they may have added this new material. An introductory section (*juan* 卷, literally "scroll") includes illustrations of an astrological chart, Chinese provinces, the Luo River, the Yellow River, the Five Mountains, Confucius, and dynastic founders, and details of the texts used in various rites such as the capping ceremony,[48] weddings, and funerals. The upper register of each scroll consists of secondary texts. The first section includes a list of rulers throughout Chinese history and a dictionary of legal terms; the second section has a manual of terms of address for different social relations; the third section contains a dictionary of various categorized terms, and the fourth section has a manual of letter-writing. The Zou family was renowned for compiling various popular household encyclopedias and compendia, for example the *Choushi jinnang* 酬世錦囊 (Precious guide to social exchange), which might well have been the source material for these paratexts.[49]

Who was the market for the *Treasury*? First, the text could be used in a traditional sense as an aid in examination knowledge and composition. Historical studies of Taiwan primary schools during the Qing dynasty have recorded that the *Treasury* was read from the third to the fifth years of school, when the children were nine to eleven years old.[50] The aspiring official began their educational journey with word-recognition primers like the *Three Character Classic*, the *Baijiaxing* 百家姓 (Hundred surnames), and the *Qianzi wen* 千字文 (Thousand character essay); these were collectively known as the "*San bai qian.*" The next stage involved advanced primers like the *Treasury* as a transition to the classical texts (discussed in Chapter 4). Such study of the *Treasury* is well documented among autobiographical sources. For example, Lu Xun 魯迅 (1881–1936) records that some used the *Treasury* to teach students literary Chinese;[51] Hu Shih 胡適 (1891–1962) noted that students at his primary school would read the *Treasury* and the Four Books after mastering the rhyming texts;[52] Cai Yuanpei 蔡元培 (1867–1940) and Feng Youlan 馮友蘭 (1895–1990) both document that schools in their time generally taught using textbooks with classical allusions and terms, such as the *Treasury*, in training students to write poetry and the examination essay.[53] Like the large group of model essays, commentaries, and other educational texts churned out by publishers, the primers were an aid to examination preparation.

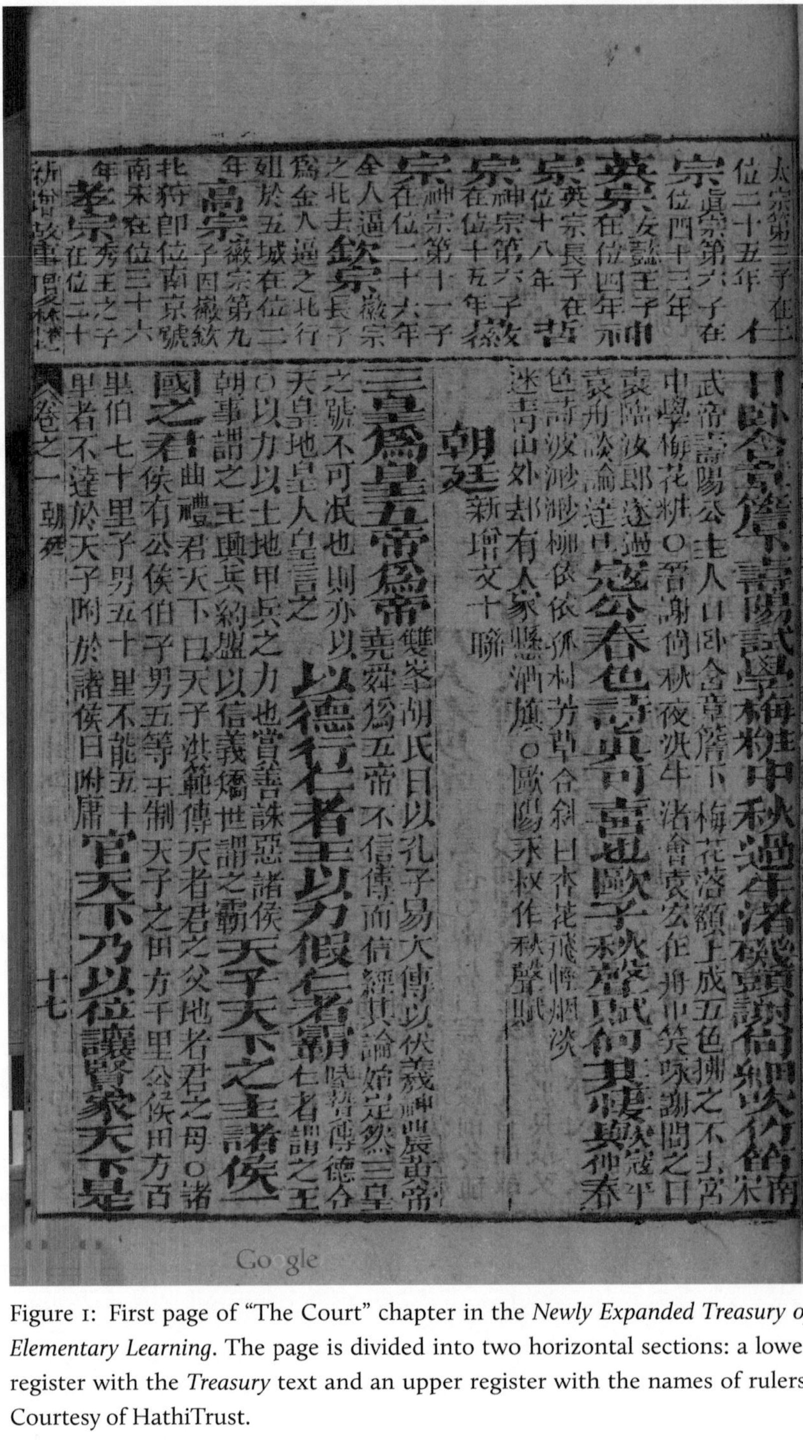

Figure 1: First page of "The Court" chapter in the *Newly Expanded Treasury of Elementary Learning*. The page is divided into two horizontal sections: a lower register with the *Treasury* text and an upper register with the names of rulers. Courtesy of HathiTrust.

An analysis of the title of Zou's revised edition provides evidence of such authorial intent. The full title, *Youxue gushi qionglin* 幼學故事瓊林, is composed of three disyllabic words: *youxue* 幼學, *gushi* 故事, and *qionglin* 瓊林. The term *you* 幼 means "the young," which generally refers to children up to the age of ten. *Xue* 學 means "to learn" or "school," according to the *Records on Ritual*.[54] In the Han dynasty, children aged ten had already commenced schooling, so the term *youxue* 幼學 refers to elementary learning in general.[55] Given that Cheng Dengji and Zou Shengmai included *youxue* in their respective titles, they would have had elementary students in mind as the target readership. *Gushi* 故事 does not denote fictional stories in the modern context but refers to "literary allusions" and "historical anecdotes." For example, Sima Qian 司馬遷 (c. 145–c. 86 BCE) in the foreword to the *Shiji* 史記 (Records of the historian) explains that the *gushi* he documents are narratives that have been transmitted throughout the generations and are not of his own creation.[56] In the title of the *Treasury*, *gushi* signals the predominant use of classical allusions and historical anecdotes throughout the text. Finally, *qionglin* 瓊林 has two connotations. *Qiong* 瓊 originally denoted a type of jade and later took on the derived meaning of "beautiful jadestone," according to the *Shuowen jiezi* 說文解字 (Explaining simple graphs and analyzing complex graphs).[57] The *Xin Tangshu* 新唐書 (New history of the Tang dynasty) notes that *qionglin* was the name of one of the two state treasuries for rare valuables during the reign of Emperor Xuanzong 唐玄宗 (r. 713–756) of the Tang dynasty (618–907).[58] It is therefore not surprising that *qionglin* designates "a treasury of knowledge" in light of the scope and detail of topics covered by the text. The second connotation of the term originates in the Song dynasty. Emperor Taizong 宋太宗 (r. 976–997) of the Song dynasty began the tradition of holding a reception for newly awarded presented scholars in his "Qionglin Garden" (*Qionglin yuan* 瓊林苑), so *qionglin* later became an analogy for attaining the presented scholar degree.[59] In this way, the book's title is associated with its target audience of young students, its main content of literary allusions, and its purpose of providing the extensive learning considered to be essential for excelling in the civil service examinations.

By the high Qing, growing prosperity and a demographic explosion led to increased social mobility and educational opportunities. Literati lineages no longer held a monopoly over elite status.[60] Mercantile households could also afford to invest in the resources necessary for the protracted period of examination studies. For example, the commercial Huizhou prefecture, Anhui, and the silk-producing town of Nanxun, Jiangsu, were known for their successful candidates.[61] Certainly, the heightened competition from increased numbers of candidates for limited positions would have fueled demand for examination cribs. However, those aiming for the civil service were in the minority of the schoolchildren.[62] The *Treasury* would have also found a market in those seeking a basic education in the fundamentals of cultural literacy.

Commercialization and urbanization stimulated a need for the rudimentary education that was generally required for social, business, and religious activities and interactions. Functional literacy was useful for the practical demands of urban life, such as keeping records and signing contracts. Functional literacy at this time, defined as mastery of fewer than two-thousand Chinese characters, included those who were schooled in the elementary curriculum but did not undertake further studies.[63] Indeed, Rawski estimates that 30 to 45 percent of men and 2 to 10 percent of women had some level of literacy in the nineteenth century—from functional to examination level.[64] Although the market ranged from those seeking basic cultural literacy to aspiring licentiates, publishers appealed to the largest market in the lower levels of literacy. Indeed, texts typically read by aspiring presented scholar candidates, such as dynastic histories or literary collectanea, were absent among the Sibao booklists.[65] Beyond the vocabulary of the "*San bai qian*" primers, the *Treasury* helped children who were not considering a civil service career to develop familiarity with elite values, ritual expressions, etiquette, and moral instruction. Indeed, it has been argued that education in Confucian values, which was important for commercial success and social respectability, formed an integral part of late imperial merchant culture.[66]

The rise of woodblock publishing also supported and supplied an unprecedented expansion of state-run and private schools throughout the Qing empire in the eighteenth and nineteenth centuries. The Qing dynasty inherited the community school system (*shexue* 社學) from the Ming period and decreed the establishment of charity schools (*yixue* 義學) to provide free education for disadvantaged or peasant children from 1652 on. In the Kangxi era, a 1713 decree expanded the mandate, ordering that "every province, prefecture, department and county establish charitable schools, and recruit intelligent teachers and assemble orphaned or impoverished youths, so that they may exert themselves in study."[67] Cynthia J. Brokaw writes that the development of schools to "civilize" the frontier areas, such as Guangxi, Yunan, and Guizhou, were all sites with healthy Sibao book sales.[68] Officials and merchants also supported the Confucian agenda to improve social mores through the ethical teachings inherent in primary education. In addition to the charitable schools, there were other types of private elementary schools: those founded by the teacher in their home for children of the neighborhood or local community, those established by the village for children in the area, and clan schools for children of wealthy families.[69] Universality of primary education was far from achieved,[70] but an extended network of elementary schools served to provide a functional and cultural literacy, predominantly through the use of primers.

Beyond the established examination system, these texts provided another avenue for upward mobility. Failed examinees like Zou Shengmai acquired wealth and social respectability through the writing, editing, copying, and publishing of reading materials. Some of the publisher-booksellers were so profitable that they earned the designation of "untitled nobility" (*su feng* 素封).[71] Indeed, markers of elite status were broadened in the eighteenth century, as Susan Naquin and Evelyn Rawski argue: "any concentration of education, political influence, social status, or wealth tended to be used to attain similar power in the other spheres."[72] Household encyclopedias with manuals for letter writing, social etiquette, family rituals, and other manners were compiled for those with insufficient education. Broad appeal and practical utility for all classes of readers were common claims in the prefaces of such texts.[73] This is also evidenced by the blurb on the front cover of the *Expanded Treasury*:

> 此書廣博已久，不但為士林所需，即農工商亦無不展覽 ... 載事即謂酬世全書也可。[74]
>
> This book has been widely circulated for a long time. Not only is it read by the literati, but it is also commonly read among farmers, craftspersons, and merchants . . . this book can be regarded as the complete book for social exchanges.[75]

The readership could thus include non-scholar adults and merchants who, like the printers, required practical skills and knowledge. In effect, a new elite stratum demanded and even developed new forms of literature. To this end, revisions to the *Treasury* can be seen to cater to a variety of readers and their learning and teaching strategies.

The diverse aims of the reading public intersect with the eclectic intellectual ideas on education of the period. Indeed, the rise of evidential research following the fall of the Ming was closely linked with the accessibility of printing and book collection.[76] An understanding of the backgrounds of Cheng Dengji and Zou Shengmai integrated with the sociohistorical circumstances shed light on the context in which the *Treasury* flourished. Brokaw's study of late imperial print culture shows that reading primers, including the *Treasury*, were staples of the Sibao publishers.[77] The Sibao textbooks were also bestsellers throughout southern China in the nineteenth century.[78]

Later editions of the *Treasury* highlight the cultural importance of the text beyond the high Qing. The addition of paratexts to the *Expanded Treasury* created a multifunctional text that could serve as an elementary primer, a scholarly reference, and a household encyclopedia that continued to flourish in the nineteenth century. Like other commercially successful educational volumes during the period, existing editions of the *Treasury* were reprinted by different publishers with various revisions under new titles, although most included the word *youxue* 幼學.[79] It was common publishing practice to slightly edit or supplement an earlier edition and market the revised version as being the most "new and improved" one. In Yang Yung-chih's research on *Treasury* editions discovered in Taiwan dating from the late Qing to the present day, he lists eighteen versions from the late nineteenth century; twenty-eight out of twenty-nine lithographic editions from the twentieth century were based on Zou Shengmai's version.[80] Additionally, at least two new highly annotated editions appeared: *Youxue qiu yuan* 幼學求源 (Seeking the origins of elementary learning) and *Youxue xun yuan* 幼學尋源 (Searching for the origins of elementary learning). Both are noted to have such detailed annotations that most pages only cover two sentences of the main text, which would suggest that they functioned as reference books for erudition rather than children's primers.[81] *Youxue qiu yuan* was supplemented by Dong Cheng 董成, who was a teacher in Huizhou and was likely shaped by the evidential scholarship community of southern Anhui.[82] Interestingly, an English translation of the *Treasury* by James Stewart Lockhart was printed in 1893 in Hong Kong, indicating the spread and popularity of the text. In his foreword, Lockhart observes the challenges of learning literary allusions for writing and states:

> To meet this difficulty, works of a special class have been compiled treating solely of quotations. Of this class the work, of which for the first time a complete English translation is now offered to the public, is one of the most common, being generally known and widely used throughout the whole of China.[83]

Lockhart's intended readers were not only foreigners learning Chinese, a group that increased after Hong Kong became a British colony in 1842, but also Chinese students learning English.

Critical acclaim is underscored by further recensions of Zou's edition after the fall of imperial China and the adoption of educational reforms. At least five different main editions were published during the Republic of China (1912–1949). Kuizhao Lou 奎照樓 (fl. 1897), who printed the first lithographic version of the *Treasury,* issued a revised edition in the 1910s with material for the new era.[84] The editions by Cai Dongfan and Dong Jianzhi 董堅志 include forewords written in 1918 (despite being printed in 1924) and 1928, respectively, as well as further paratexts and addenda at the end of every chapter.[85] Ma Ziyi 馬自毅 notes that Fei Yourong's 費有容 (1874–1931) version supplemented new terms related to the Republic of China, e.g., "The law has three freedoms" 法律有三大自由, and Ye Puxun 葉浦遜 (1876–1958) later added supplements regarding historical figures and anecdotes.[86] As I have not been able to access copies of the latter two editions, the following discussion is limited to the Cai and Dong recensions.

The main text of Zou Shengmai's edition remains largely unchanged except for occasional adjusted phrasings and the addition of new material and paratexts. In Cai's edition, the introductory section also includes an updated map of China, templates of invitations for different occasions, diagrams of the five degrees of relations for mourning rites, various terms of address, and a list of counties. In the main sections, Cai added couplets at the end of each chapter, a total of 291, supplementing those by Zou Shengmai. The top margin of each page includes text in the English language detailing the months of the year, the days of the week, the alphabet, and the names of Chinese cities and official titles. The Chinese words generally precede the English definition and their Chinese transliteration. Below the top margin, each page is divided into three registers. The upper register has anecdotes of moral exemplars for the young (*qingnian mofan* 青年模範) with the text of the story set out on the left side and illustrations on the right. The middle register provides model correspondence (*chidu* 尺牘) from a textbook with questions and answers about learning. The lower register provides the main text. Kuizhao Lou's edition of the 1910s similarly had three registers and included a letter-writing manual and the *Yingwen jiejue* 英文捷訣 (Mnemonic chant for studying English).[87] Dong's edition contains comparatively less content in the introductory section with only the illustrations of dynastic founders, a list of rulers throughout history, and a list of counties. The paratexts are also simpler, as the page is divided into only two registers. The top register has illustrated anecdotes for family instruction in the first section and famous Chinese and Western adages written in Chinese in the later sections. Dong also includes supplementary couplets for each chapter, 255 in total.

The additional information plausibly responded to the needs of students following educational reforms in the early twentieth century. First, the Western influence seems manifest—Cai's edition includes English vocabulary, while Dong provides foreign adages. This is not present in the Zou Shengmai edition, as Western subjects were introduced into school curriculums in the late Qing period.[88] However, Chinese learning remained the substance while Western learning was adopted for practical purposes, expressed in the *ti yong* 體用 (substance-function) dictum.[89] For example, foreign languages were to be taught from the age of eleven but no earlier.[90] This attitude is exemplified by a new conclusion to the "Literary Matters" (*wen shi* 文事) chapter in Cai's edition: "Chinese and foreign learning are mutually different, comprehend the Western studies, forget not the Chinese studies" 學術則中外互殊，通西學毋忘中學.[91] Moreover, the lack of English in Dong's later published version provides evidence of foreign language training being less of a priority at the time.

Although policies increasing Western mathematics and science content in the school curriculum were promulgated starting in 1902, few teachers were available to teach such subjects.[92] Moreover, during the first half of the twentieth century there was ambivalence in political circles regarding the transition to a modern educational system.[93] Such attitudes toward educational transformation explains the continued, albeit diminishing, market for traditional primers and new editions of the *Treasury*. As an attempt to enhance relevance to the revised curriculum, new editions of the *Treasury* provided supplemented couplets pertaining to Western scientific knowledge. However, ambivalence to change was also reflected by further historical anecdotes from the early modern and even premodern period being included. Practical guides for ritual practice continued to target a broader readership beyond schoolchildren. Despite these revisions, demand for the traditional primers plummeted.

Vernacular translations and annotated commentaries of the *Treasury* reemerged in the late 1980s with China's renewed interest in New Confucianism and research on traditional education.[94] Comic and storybook editions of the *Treasury* appeared in the 1990s.[95] Since the turn of this century, there have been increasingly positive references to Confucianism in political and popular discourse, which have emphasized the inclusion of classical literature in school.[96] Increasing research on late imperial primers in recent decades reflects Chinese Ministry of Education directives to explore the revival of traditional culture in schools.[97] In the current context, there has been renewed interest in elementary educational materials such as the *Treasury*.

The *Treasury*'s complex textual history with myriad revisions and supplements at the hands of different authors attests to its popularity during the Ming-Qing period. This discussion raises many interesting questions on the functions of the *Treasury* relating to the different readers and their reading practices in Qing China. Moreover, the later interpretation and significance of the text after the end of imperial China remain to be explored. This study has chosen to analyze primary educational thought in Zou Shengmai's edition to address how the *Treasury* resonated with and reflected elementary learning in the high Qing.[98] Specifically, the Shanghai Classics Publishing House 2018 edition will be used, as it preserves Zou's annotations without the later paratexts or modern commentary.

ELEMENTARY EDUCATION: WHAT'S IN A NAME?

What was meant by primary education in premodern and early modern China? The modern definition of "primary education" is the first stage of compulsory formal education characterized by systematic studies, such as reading, writing, and mathematics, beginning at the age of five or six and lasting for four to six years.[99] However, there are key differences in the concept of primary education before China's adoption of the three-tiered educational system of primary school, secondary school, and tertiary education in 1902. Prior to 1902, formal schooling was simply divided into two stages: primary education (*xiaoxue* 小學) and advanced education (*daxue* 大學). Throughout history, the terms *xiaoxue* and *mengxue* 蒙學 were used interchangeably to refer to the first stage of formal schooling, and both may be translated as "primary education." Exploring these terms and the respective connotations used in the Qing dynasty highlights the different aims of this educational phase.

Mengxue

The term *mengxue* 蒙學 sheds light on the philosophical thought underpinning primary education. The canonical reference for this term is the fourth hexagram entitled *Meng* 蒙in the *Yijing* 易經 (Changes), also known as the *Zhouyi* 周易. The wording from the text and the first appendix of the *Meng* hexagram appears regularly in later educational discourse, including that of the Qing dynasty, it being common practice to cite the authority of canonical writings associated with classicist scholarship. It is important to note that the *Changes,* having originated as a divination text, uses wording that is manifestly enigmatic and symbolic. The commentarial tradition is also complex and difficult for modern readers to understand. However, focusing on Qing period interpretations provides a necessary context for this study. In reprinting the *Shisan jing zhushu* 十三經注疏 (Exegeses of thirteen canonical works) in 1815, Ruan Yuan 阮元 (1764–1849) included the *Zhouyi zheng yi* 周易正義 (Orthodox exegesis of the *Changes*) with commentary by Wang Bi 王弼 (226–249) and sub-commentary by Kong Yingda 孔穎達 (574–648).[100] The *Meng* hexagram is composed of the trigrams *Gen* 艮 (mountain) above *Kan* 坎

(water). According to Wang Bi, the water represents a dangerous abyss, while the mountains present an obstacle; the *Meng* hexagram thus conveys perplexity in the face of peril—a depiction of juvenile ignorance.[101] This interpretation is corroborated by Zhu Xi's commentary *Zhouyi benyi* 周易本義 (The original interpretation of the *Changes*) endorsed by the Qing regime.[102] The first appendix then concludes: "(The method of dealing with) the young and ignorant is to nourish the correct (nature belonging to them);—this accomplishes the service of the sage" 蒙以養正，乃聖功也.[103] Kong Yingda further adds that an ignorant child needed to be taught the proper way of living to recover their innate nature, thereby becoming a sage. This was the goal of education for the ancient sages.[104]

Indeed, Qing philologist Duan Yucai 段玉裁 (1735–1815), who is best known for his annotated edition of *Explaining Simple Graphs and Analyzing Complex Graphs*, glosses the character *meng* 蒙 as consistent with the concept in the *Changes*. Duan states that *meng* 蒙 was originally written as *meng* 冡, composed of the graph for "cover" (*mao* 冃) above the graph for "pig" (*shi* 豕).[105] The extended meaning of *meng* was "unknowing." Children were referred to as *mengtong* 蒙童 or *tongmeng* 童蒙, both of which can be parsed as "the ignorant child." The term for elementary education also alludes to overcoming the ignorance of childhood through the word *meng*, for example *tongmeng jiaoyu* 童蒙教育 (literally, education for the ignorant child), *qimeng jiaoyu* 啟蒙教育 (education for enlightening the ignorant), and *mengxue* 蒙學 (studies for the ignorant child). The term *meng* is also used to describe primary school textbooks, such as *mengshu* 蒙書 (beginners' books, literally "books for the ignorant") and *qimeng jiaocai* 啟蒙教材 (educational resources for enlightening the ignorant).

In one of the earliest studies on the history of Chinese elementary education in 1989, Qiao Weiping and Cheng Peijie claim that the aim of childhood education as set out by the *Changes,* to "nourish the correct nature" (*meng yi yang zheng* 蒙以養正), remained largely consistent throughout imperial China.[106] A decade later, several works in the field maintained that moral development was the foremost priority of primary education.[107] The grounding of educational thought in the wider philosophy of "becoming a sage" through the term *meng* may lead to reductionist views of elementary education as merely tasked with moralization and discipline of students. It is thus important to clarify the concept of "moral education" in the premodern Chinese context.

The Chinese view of "morality" is not commensurate with the notions of right or wrong in Western ethics.[108] While the Western ethical tradition deliberates on the questions of "what is good" and "how to know the good," Chinese thinkers have instead focused on "how to become good."[109] Hence, the definition of morality is based on how Chinese philosophers have defined the "good." To clarify the "good" in Chinese thought, we naturally turn to Confucius (551–479 BCE), the first Chinese thinker to articulate a system of thought on the "good life" for human beings—the Way (*dao* 道). The Way is a governing rule or cosmic pattern for all existence in the universe and is also the life-giving force that creates all things.[110] The Way dictating the proper workings of the universe also represented the right way of human living. In Chinese cosmology, the human world and the natural world are united as an organic whole.[111] The relationship between humans and nature has been likened to a hall of mirrors in which every mirror reflects and is reflected by all other mirrors; one is in all and all is in one.[112] Similarly, each individual has the potential to manifest the Way through their actions, to realize harmony within the family and community. Hence, the Way provides "the highest moral precept for human beings."[113] Teaching or learning to live according to the Way is "moral education," and this was a key concern from the stage of primary education. The connotations of the term *xiaoxue* point to further considerations on the educational agenda.

Xiaoxue

In his monograph on the history of traditional Chinese education, Thomas Lee explains three meanings of *xiaoxue*.[114] The term *xiaoxue* first appeared in the *History of the Former Han,* where it denoted, depending on the context, the first stage of formal schooling or its associated textbooks. The chapter "*Yiwen zhi* 藝文志" (Treatise on arts and literature) states:

> 古者八歲入小學，故周官保氏掌養國子，教之六書。
>
> In ancient times, children started elementary school at the age of eight. Thus, according to the *Rituals of Zhou*, the Guardian who was

> responsible for raising the scions of noble families, taught the six principles of writing.[115]

The curriculum for primary education is further elaborated upon in the "*Shi huo zhi* 食貨志" (Treatise on foods and commodities) chapter:

> 八歲入小學，學六甲五方書計之事，始知室家長幼之節。
> At eight they entered elementary school, studying such subjects as calendric changes, geography, writing, and arithmetic. They began to know the etiquette between marital partners, and between young and old within the family.[116]

In the above excerpts, *xiaoxue* refers to the first level of schooling for nobility in the Zhou dynasty. State-sponsored primary schools emerged in the Han dynasty (202 BCE–220 CE) for children from the ages of eight to fifteen.[117] At fifteen, students could then continue to advanced education.[118] There was clearly a breadth of subjects in elementary learning, and it seems that the term *xiaoxue* was closely associated with literacy training in the Han period. Indeed, the "Treatise on Arts and Literature" refers to a category of texts for teaching literacy as *xiaoxue*, such as the *Cang Jie Primer* compiled in the Qin dynasty.[119]

Xiaoxue developed a third connotation during the Song dynasty (960–1279) based on Zhu Xi's writings on primary educational thoughts in his recorded teachings the *Zhuzi yulei* 朱子語類 (Classified sayings of Master Zhu) and encapsulated by his textbook *Xiaoxue* 小學 (Elementary learning). Zhu Xi redefined the roles of primary and advanced education. The elementary stage emphasized moral education; students would learn to perform and understand the rudiments of common tasks (*shi* 事). On the other hand, students undertaking advanced learning "were instructed in the Way of probing principle (*li* 理), cultivating oneself, and governing others" 教之以窮理、正心、修己、治人之道.[120] In other words, they would learn the principles and reasoning behind what they had been taught. Since the Song dynasty, *xiaoxue* thus also referred to the primer by Zhu Xi and its prescribed curriculum.

The concept of *xiaoxue* developed a fourth meaning during the Qing dynasty. The Han dynasty texts used for the exegesis of Confucian canonical works and ancient books were later brought to the forefront in the school of evidential learning (*kaoju xue* 考據學 or *kaozheng xue* 考證學) in the eighteenth century to form the foundation of the field of modern Chinese linguistics (*yuyan xue* 語言學).[121] As the linguistic subjects of philology, phonology, and semantics were considered prerequisites for the exegesis of texts in advanced learning, this foundational learning also came to be known as *xiaoxue*. Thus, the term *xiaoxue* was extended to denote the subjects of textual exegesis and their related texts.

These four interrelated meanings of *xiaoxue* were all used during the Qing dynasty: the first stage of formal schooling, the elementary textbooks used in that stage, the textbook for primary education by Zhu Xi and its emphasis on moral education, and the foundational subjects for textual exegesis. The first three of these connotations are directly relevant to this volume. In this book, the term "primary education" will be used synonymously with "elementary education" and "elementary learning" to refer to the phase of formal schooling before advanced learning in early modern and premodern China. During the Qing dynasty, the enrollment age for primary education ranged from six to twenty,[122] and advanced education generally began at the age of fifteen.[123]

This brief survey of the complexity of the different Chinese terms for "primary education" accounts for the distinctive research areas in the literature on primary education in Qing China.[124] There have been five main approaches: the exploration of historical educational discourse by scholars and officials, the subjects taught, the textbooks used, educational theory, and primers as a transnational genre. In one of the earliest studies on the history of elementary education, Qiao Weiping and Cheng Peijie argue that Qing dynasty pedagogy was more systematic than prior eras, as it drew on the accumulated experiential and theoretical discourse to that point.[125] Chi Xiaofang's monograph on *xiaoxue* education directly summarizes the key teaching principles from various Qing educators,[126] while Jacques Gernet and Giulia Falato discuss the history of primary education pedagogy from the eleventh to seventeenth centuries through key thinkers and their representative works.[127]

Subjects of premodern and early modern elementary learning have been covered by the "History of Chinese Primary Education Subjects" series from Shandong Education Press.[128] However, the subjects of literacy (*yuwen jiaoxue* 語文教學), mathematics (*shuxue jiaoxue* 數學教學), moral learning (*sixiang pinde jiaoxue* 思想品德教學), and general knowledge (*changshi jiaoxue* 常識教學) have been defined from the perspective of modern Chinese education. Each volume covers a significant time period from the pre-Qin through to the Republic period, with specific chapters devoted to Qing dynasty theories and pedagogy. Within the scope of moral education, Gao Qianmin also summarizes the ideas of Ming-Qing scholars such as Lu Shiyi 陸世儀 (1611–1672) and Zhang Lüxiang 張履祥 (1611–1674), although their discourse is not integrated with his main arguments. Rather than subject titles, Angela Leung uses "acquisition of knowledge" to refer to language learning and "moralization and discipline" for character development in discussing the content of primary education in the seventeenth and eighteenth centuries.[129] The educational system and the form and content of learning are outlined using statistics and linked to the sociohistorical context. Western scholarship in this area has been largely related to literacy—literacy training having been a central focus of elementary schooling from the earliest reference in the *History of the Former Han*. In Evelyn Rawski's pioneering study in 1979 on popular literacy in China, she demonstrates the existence of a continuum in literacy from the barely literate to the highly educated scholar during the eighteenth and nineteenth centuries, drawing from a wide range of sources including local gazetteers, genealogies, and traditional textbooks.[130] This highlights the significance of primary education and its textbooks for popular education. Beyond the stage of literacy was learning composition for examinations. Charles Ridley's doctoral thesis remains a seminal work on the link between social context, theories of moral and intellectual development, and educational practices in teaching literary composition during late imperial China.[131] His views of traditional pedagogy are informed by the works of three Ming-Qing intellectuals—Lu Shiyi, Zhang Xuecheng 章學誠 (1738–1801), and Wang Yun 王筠 (1784–1854)—and analyzed under Western educational concepts as a frame of reference.

Explorations of elementary education have also been structured by the textbooks used. Following the cessation of the civil service examinations in the late Qing dynasty, traditional primers were more likely to be researched than read.[132] However, these papers reflected the evidential scholarship popular in the Qing period identifying issues of authorship and different recensions.[133] Numerous cross-sectional historical reviews of the primers have proposed different stages of development. In the first classification, Ju Junong proposed three periods in the development of these texts.

1. From the Zhou dynasty (1046–256 BCE) to the Tang dynasty: Mainly literacy primers with some also providing moral instruction and general knowledge.
2. Song dynasty to the mid-Qing dynasty: Elementary primers proliferated, which Ju classified as textbooks for literacy, moral education, learning history, poetry, classical allusions, and general knowledge.
3. Mid-Qing dynasty to the Republic of China: Traditional primers were published in revised forms.[134]

Although these stages have since been reevaluated by recent scholars,[135] Ju's discussion set in motion analysis of different subgenres based on the learning aims. The classifications are limited by simplistic assessments of the content, particularly as the primers often have multiple educational functions.[136] For example, the *Three Character Classic* is a preliminary primer for character recognition that also presents cultural and historical knowledge. A further research perspective has been to understand the primers based on a single subject area. Zhang Zhigong's monograph in 1962 discussed elementary primers within the discourse of language acquisition.[137] The textual features of primers were analyzed based on traditional pedagogical theories and practices for language learning, such as the use of rhyme and rhythm to improve readability and facilitate memorization. Confucian moral development through traditional primary educational texts formed the topic of Limin Bai's monograph.[138] While it is a key work on Chinese primers in the English literature, the textual analysis is limited to the unique characteristics of the textbooks due to the broad historical scope from the pre-Han era to the end of the nineteenth century.

Primers have also been evaluated primarily from the perspective of educational theory and learning technique.[139] Theresa Kelleher's chapter on Zhu Xi's *Elementary Learning* provides a detailed analysis of the content and structure as grounded in Zhu's educational theories and is the first essay of the text in a Western language.[140] Although Kelleher provides historical evidence of the text's use by both children and adults, the teaching pedagogy is not elaborated upon. Christopher Nugent's research has focused on literary culture and how pedagogical practices assisted the learning of poetry, encyclopedia works, and educational primers in medieval China.[141] His recent monograph explores elite literary training through the material and textual features of Dunhuang manuscripts of five literary primers.[142] The research calls attention to mnemotechnics through analysis of the use of parallelism, textual organization, paratexts, and other techniques. Nugent argues that the content and structure of such works provides evidence of a sophisticated understanding of memory in medieval China.

Studies on Chinese primers as a transnational genre have raised questions on how their educational functions have evolved or shifted in different cultural and historical contexts. As the Chinese script (called "Sinitic") was commonly used throughout East Asia from the eighth century to the mid-twentieth century, the primers were studied beyond the Chinese empire. For example, the *Thousand Character Essay* was also popular as a primer in Japan and Korea.[143] Peter Kornicki provides a brief overview of the transmission and vernacularization of Chinese primers in premodern East Asia, including the *Thousand Character Essay*, the *Three Character Classic*, and the *Mengqiu* 蒙求 (Inquiries of the young).[144] Beyond Sinitic literacy, the Chinese primers provided a new genre for literacy in target cultures, such as Tangut translations of Chinese primers used as teaching material predominantly for the Tangut language rather than for Sinitic.[145] The familiar format of the *Three Character Classic* was also appropriated for the transmission of faith traditions including Buddhism, Islam, and Christianity.[146] Recent monographs have further discussed Western missionary influences on children's textbooks in China during the late nineteenth to the early twentieth century.[147]

This brief overview demonstrates that there is increasing recognition of the significance of primary education textbooks among scholars. But many questions regarding their historical, cultural, philosophical, and educational themes have yet to be answered. How did learning occur through the text? Why were the texts structured the way they were? How did the child engage with the text to achieve the stated educational aims? What were the educational concerns of the textbooks? How did the text reflect or shape primary educational thought at the time? There is clearly a research gap in the analysis of elementary textbooks in a way that contextualizes and historicizes their use.

AN INTERPRETIVE COMMUNITIES APPROACH: INTELLECTUAL SCHOOLS IN THE QING

To read the *Treasury* from the modern educational perspective of an elementary textbook on language learning would be anachronistic. To assess the text on its own merits, we need to analyze the elementary curriculum as derived from Qing dynasty educational prescriptive discourse[148] and engage in a process of reverse-engineering from viewing the *Treasury* as a "textbook" to its educational "theory." The reconstruction of the Qing dynasty intellectual milieu is, however, challenging, as the period saw the emergence of differing educational views. Moreover, primary education occurred in a variety of public and private settings and was conducted by a heterogeneous group of teachers without a standardized curriculum. All of these issues are to be taken into consideration when attempting to understand how the curriculum was delivered and, importantly for this study, how the elementary textbook was taught to the individual learner.

Rather than ignoring these challenges and focusing on a single approach to the text, this study borrows from the reader-response concept of "interpretive communities." First advocated by Stanley Fish, this theory of literary criticism departed from not only the formalist perspective of locating meaning within the text but also the unbridled subjectivity of situating meaning entirely with the reader.[149] Fish argued that the formal structures of the text only acquire significance in the context of the reader's experience—meaning emerges gradually in the dynamic interaction between the linguistic facts (the text) and the reader's expectations, judgments, and assumptions. Such concerns of the reader exist prior to their engagement with the text and ultimately give rise to the interpretation. Fish strikingly illustrated this through a story of English religious poetry students who convincingly interpreted a list of surnames of linguists as a religious poem—the list had in fact been an assignment left on the blackboard from his previous class on linguistics and literary criticism.[150] In other words, the reading act proceeds based on interpretive decisions, which gives rise to interpretive strategies—a predisposition to "find" themes, confer significances, mark out textual structures, and assign intentions. Hence, the determinacy of meaning lies in predetermined interpretive strategies rather than in the text or reader.

The strategy executed by different readers will determine which aspects of the text they focus on and thereby produce different readings. Those who share the same interpretive strategies constitute an "interpretive community." The "community" is not defined as a collective of individuals but rather a "bundle of strategies or norms of interpretation that we hold in common and which regulate the way we think and perceive."[151] However, those who have learned and share the same interpretive principles will agree on similar readings and disagree with those who hold other interpretive strategies, that is, other "interpretive communities."

The theory of interpretive communities has been widely applied in the field of Sinology, resonating with Chinese intellectual history and its diverse schools of thought. This is particularly manifest in the scholarship of canonical works that have been afforded a rich commentarial tradition.[152] Such a hermeneutic approach is arguably necessitated by the indefinite authorship (and hence authorial intent), dating, and historical circumstances surrounding the compilation of early Chinese canonical works.[153] In analyzing the commentaries of the *Analects*, Daniel K. Gardner argues:

> . . . in addressing a classic, commentators have a range of interpretive options from which they make choices. The choice the commentator makes evolves out of a complex dialectic in which the words of the text, pregnant with possible meanings, interact with the commentator's intellectual concerns and assumptions, which themselves develop out of the contemporary zeitgeist. This interaction between text and commentator results in the particular commentary, which thus may serve as a window on the intellectual disposition of the commentator—as well as that of his age.[154]

The interpretive strategies for Chinese intellectuals were steeped in the state of the tradition and the historical circumstances. Similar to Fish's observation, Gardner also explains that the Confucian interpretive community was ever-changing, as reflected in the analysis of various commentaries.

In my research, the interpretive strategies within the context of Qing dynasty's intellectual schools of thought, as related to elementary education, constrains the possibility of an infinite plurality of readings. The intellectual schools of thought at the time can be conceived of as "interpretive communities." The "community" in this context is not a tangible, quantifiable group within the Qing population but rather the identified modes of interpretation in primary educational pedagogical literature discussed in Chapter 1, which offered relevant interpretive strategies for a variety of readers. This would include annotators, publishers, teachers, and students, particularly as teachers guided their students in developing the requisite interpretive strategies. The teacher's disposition toward one school of thought or another, and their educational philosophy and principles, would have been a defining influence on how the text was explicated for their student.[155] The child's reading of the text was necessarily directed by the classroom tutor given their limited knowledge. In other words, the student's interpretive strategies and learning experiences are guided by their teacher and the "interpretive community" their teacher subscribed to.

This book seeks to advance understanding on the early modern elementary pedagogy inherent in the *Treasury* as linked to the educational aims and approaches at the time through various intellectual schools of thought conceptualized as "interpretive communities."[156] The questions that drive the investigation are: How can we understand the main philosophical and intellectual trends identifiable in Qing dynasty elementary education? How are these early modern Chinese elementary educational theories and practices expressed in the textual information and literary structures of the *Treasury*? How does the *Treasury* mediate the child's learning process and how is this significant for modern education scholars? It should be noted that the demographic group in this study is the primary school student, excluding the children of the imperial court and household. While women's education was likely in elite families, there was no typical program or standard curriculum in the seventeenth and eighteenth centuries.[157] As this paper explores primary education through the *Treasury* in late imperial China, female education is beyond its scope.

The first chapter is a study on primary educational thought in the Qing dynasty through the different dominant intellectual trends and their associated educational philosophy. There are three main propositions in this chapter. First, Neo-Confucian thought dominated the high Qing intellectual milieu due to patronage by the Manchu government and the institution of the civil service examination.[158] Second, Neo-Confucianism was represented by different schools of thought with varying educational emphases, namely the school of principle (*lixue* 理學), the school of heart-mind (*xinxue* 心學),[159] and the school of practical learning (*shixue* 實學). These streams of academic thought formed the basis of elementary learning as reflected in the prescriptive educational discourse. Third, Qing dynasty elementary theory and practice were eclectic in nature despite the underlying focus on the Cheng-Zhu school philosophy.

After an exploration of the heterogeneous nature of Qing primary education, the following chapters provide close readings of the *Treasury* based on different educational concerns. The chapters address interpretive strategies through the textual features to understand how learning may have been mediated. Educational aims are derived from the schools of thought and the social demand for examination training.

The influence of practical statecraft learning with its emphasis on empirical inquiry will be explored in Chapter 2. The categorization and order of the chapters in the *Treasury* will be evaluated as to their consistency with the traditional ethical framework. A translation of the twenty-third chapter, "Gems and Treasures," will then be used to demonstrate evolving educational ideas through the micro-structures of the main text. Attention is drawn to the wider literary tradition through glosses of literary terms and allusions coupled with annotations. It will be argued that these features aided the young reader in training for the interpretive strategies of evidential scholarship.

Chapter 3 will analyze moral development through the *Treasury*, particularly honing in on the functions of the literary allusions. Education in the Qing period continued to emphasize "nourishing the correct," as per the Cheng-Zhu school, however the use of allusions reflects fresh ideas of the child-oriented approach espoused by Wang Yangming. This chapter explores how Wang's encouragement of reflection finds application through the text: allusions facilitated metaphoric learning; ritual language employing allusions required the child to consider contextual issues; and the presentation of exemplars helped the child to develop a moral sense.

Chapter 4 assesses how the *Treasury* catered to the sociopolitical demands of education, namely preparation for the civil service examinations. Memorization as the first step in the premodern and early modern learning process provided a key consideration in the construction of elementary texts. How the powers of memory are engaged through the textual features will be explored based on findings from contemporary memory research. It will be demonstrated that the *Treasury* familiarized the student with the examination essay form and cultural literacy.

The concluding chapter will discuss the significance of the research for contemporary education scholars. The various arguments and evidence for Qing primary educational thought reflected in the *Treasury* will be rearticulated through curricular concerns common to educators. Such a reframing of early modern Chinese educational ideas is forward-looking—as preliminary steps to enhance cross-cultural dialogue.

CHAPTER ONE

THE ECLECTIC NATURE OF QING PRIMARY EDUCATIONAL THOUGHT

Traditional Chinese elementary textbooks were authored not simply for the child's amusement but were shaped by myriad educational concerns. These include inherited theories about the aims of education and the nature of the child's development. Although the "philosophy of education" is an interdisciplinary field of research in the West, the field of Chinese educational theory can be considered a part of Chinese traditional philosophy itself. Primary educational thought is an integral part of this field. To elucidate the theory behind the textbook, there is a need to first understand the factors that influenced the curriculum. Robin Barrow argues that tradition "ranks high as an influence," but ultimately the school curriculum is the product of various competing individuals and institutions.[1] Early modern China was no different. The interests of the Manchu-led imperial court and the Chinese scholar-officials, the views of the literati serving as teachers, and pressures stemming from the family and the civil service examinations were some of the factors that affected educational theory.

The Cheng-Zhu school remained the predominant educational thought, particularly in the high Qing dynasty. Following the conquest of the empire, the Manchus faced multiple challenges in consolidating their power. In particular, the Manchus were an ethnic minority ruling a

Chinese population. Education became a key strategy in exerting authority over the Chinese literati.[2] It was through the regulation of scholarship that both the general population and the intellectuals would have a common ideology. First, the Manchus reaffirmed the school of principle as state orthodoxy through a series of policies. Despite receiving imperial endorsement starting in the Yuan dynasty as the basis of the civil service examinations, Zhu Xi's exegeses had been increasingly undermined and criticized by advocates of the school of heart-mind in the late Ming period.[3] Hence, an edict issued in 1653 stated that "discussions of the classics ought to be based on the editions and interpretations of the Song dynasty; bookstores should be allowed to print and circulate only books of [the school of] principle, works on government and those books which contributed to the literary enterprise."[4]

Emperor Kangxi fashioned himself as the patron of Zhu's school of principle, and starting in his reign, only scholars of the school of principle were selected to be royal tutors and lecturers.[5] The imperial court also sponsored the publication of over thirty scholarly works, particularly of the Cheng-Zhu school.[6] For example, a Manchu-Chinese bilingual edition of the *Daxue* 大學 (Great learning) was reissued in 1672 and distributed to every official, a complete text of the emperor's lessons on the Four Books published in 1678, and a compilation of Zhu Xi's complete works (*Yu zuan Zhuzi quanshu* 御纂朱子全書) in 1713.[7] These acts effectively defined a "canon" of orthodox textbooks—compulsory learning for aspiring officials that also set the philosophical agenda for schooling in general.

In the Kangxi, Yongzheng 雍正 (r. 1722–1735) and Qianlong 乾隆 (r. 1735–1795) eras, attempts were made to collect and standardize the literary heritage while simultaneously destroying writings with an anti-Manchurian sentiment.[8] To this end, voluminous encyclopedias, including *Gujin tushu jicheng* 古今圖書集成 (Collection of books past and present), *Qing tongdian* 清通典 (Comprehensive statutes of the Qing dynasty), and *Siku quanshu* 四庫全書 (Complete library of the four branches); and dictionaries such as the *Kangxi zidian* 康熙字典 (Kangxi dictionary) and *Peiwen yunfu* 佩文韻府 (Repository of esteemed phrases arranged by rime) were compiled. The collection of books for the *Complete Library of the Four Branches of Literature* and the general literary inquisition destroying "seditious" material were "inseparably linked," according to Luther

Carrington Goodrich.[9] From 1774 to 1782, an estimated 13,862 books were destroyed; the figure is considered conservative.[10] The high Qing period strictly censored written works—the writer of anti-Manchurian or pro-Ming sentiments and associated scholars or their family was at risk of being persecuted and could even be sentenced to death. For example, proceedings against literati engaged in compiling a private history of the Ming Dynasty began under the first Manchu emperor.[11] These literary inquisitions constrained intellectuals and were considered a contributing factor in the rise of evidential research.[12] Willard Peterson concludes that the Qing government was "taking control of texts and tools that would serve in the future as the imperially endorsed foundation for learning."[13]

The Manchus did not fully adopt all the Neo-Confucian doctrines but were selective in the beliefs that they supported.[14] Hence, Benjamin A. Elman distinguishes the state "ideology" from the state "orthodoxy":

> "Orthodoxy" is that which the late imperial state, represented by the overlapping but asymmetrical interest of the bureaucracy and the throne, publicly authorized and which became the core of the civil service examinations curriculum. . . . When moral philosophy entered the political arena of state examinations, however, its intellectual life was constricted into a system of concepts, arguments and beliefs endorsed by the state for larger political purposes. The educational content of civil examinations resulting from that process of restrictive manipulation, by which concepts, arguments and beliefs selectively served to legitimate political sovereignty and create a Confucian mind-set, is what this chapter refers to as imperial "ideology."[15]

Education for the civil service examinations was politicized such that all civil servants understood and shared the imperial ideology. Relatedly, Wing-tsit Chan analyzed the evolution of Song learning by comparing the Qing government-sponsored *Xingli jingyi* 性理精義 (Essential ideas on human nature and principle) with the original *Xingli quanshu* 性理全書 (Complete works on human nature and principle) published in 1415.[16] The *Xingli jingyi* was a reedited compendium of passages from Song Neo-Confucian thinkers intended to be circulated to all schools as a standard reference book.[17] Chan indicates that compared to the Ming edition, metaphysical elements were downplayed, which was largely a response to the intellectual climate of vacuous philosophical discourse and the neglect of state affairs in the late Ming. Instead, social engagement elements were emphasized, changing the focus of education to more practical purposes.

The state ideology was propagated through the educational system and government recruitment. In their analysis of Qing dynasty education, Liu Xiusheng and Yang Yuqing argue that the two goals of education were political: improving social mores and creating talent, with the latter being the priority.[18] In the project of developing political talent, schools were the training ground for the required political knowledge and attitudes. The civil service examinations selected candidates who subscribed to the state ideology, and the appointment of officials was the desired outcome of education. As the examinations established the selection criteria for officialdom, the school was a mere handmaid to the civil service examinations. Elman corroborates this view by highlighting that the imperial state committed itself financially to support an empire-wide school network.[19] Liu and Yang also claim that primary schools were already part of the government training in which developing officials was the ultimate objective.[20] However, it must be questioned to what extent the state controlled the content of the examinations and ultimately the curriculum of advanced learning. Chow argues that the examination system was "an arena where no single group could establish absolute dominance."[21] For example, the Chinese gentry had a vested interest in preserving the status quo. There was considerable resistance to various changes in examination questions made by the Manchu regime, such as the repudiation of Emperor Kangxi's decree to abolish the eight-legged essay and restructure the examination.[22] Elman has described the dynasty as functioning in a "dynamic partnership" between the court and the literati.[23] Indeed, lineage-based academies sought to consolidate their power and other educators such as Huang Zongxi 黃宗羲 (1610–1695) proposed that schools should be the center of authority with political leaders learning and constrained by academics.[24] Therefore, the intellectual influence of the literati on the curriculum was significant, but the civil service examination as a cultural tradition was also critical.

The merits and failings of the examination system are beyond the scope of this research, but it is important to understand the content of the examinations, as they were such a key influence on the primary school curriculum.[25] The Qing government adopted the Cheng-Zhu interpretation of the Four Books and Five Classics,[26] and the essay questions were based on these texts. From 1756, questions based on evidential learning and poetry were also included. Extensive intellectual training, such as developing skills in prosody and the eight-legged essay and knowledge of the Confucian classics including their commentaries and history, was required for even the lowest level of examinations (*tongshi* 童試). Adding to the pressure were the limited quotas on successful examination candidates.[27] The civil service examinations provided crucial motivation for education and were a primary means of promoting state ideals. The skills required for the civil service examinations were a significant influence on the content and structure of the elementary textbook.

As previously discussed, increased social mobility from the improved economic conditions during the Ming-Qing period meant even merchants, artisans, and peasants wished for their children to be well educated.[28] At least a functional literacy was necessary for the practical demands of life—a trend stimulated and aided by the publishing boom. Through the Qing dynasty's educational system, both its state-run and private aspects, arguably more people gained functional literacy than at any other time in the past. From a sociohistorical perspective, primary education enabled the attainment of basic literacy, served as preparation for the civil service examinations, and was part of the national strategy to instill cultural values. The political, social, and cultural aspects of education are arguably derived from the distinct educational theories and assumptions of the time. I turn now to the key theories that were influential in the child's learning in the Qing.

1.2 THEORETICAL BASIS OF PRIMARY EDUCATION

While much ink has been spilt in Chinese and Western languages on the intellectual trends of the Qing dynasty, this is largely related to advanced learning. For example, the late Qing intellectual Liang Qichao 梁啟超 (1873–1929) argues:

> Over the two-hundred-year history of Qing scholarship, its influence and the general academic trend can be summarised in one phrase: "returning to ancient ways as a form of emancipation". The first phase was being freed from the shackles of Wang Yangming's school of heart-mind by restoring Song dynasty scholarship. The second phase was returning to Han and Tang dynasty intellectual thought to be liberated from the Cheng-Zhu school. The third phase was to recover Western Han learning thereby rejecting Xu Shen 許慎 and Zheng Xuan 鄭玄thought. The fourth stage was to return to pre-Qin ancient learning and be freed from all commentaries and sub-commentaries. However, having restored pre-Qin ancient scholarship, they did not continue to the extent of dismissing Confucius and Mencius' thought.[29]

Being a reform-movement intellectual, Liang's perspective persuasively justifies the need for revolution in educational policy. However, these traditional interpretations of the rejection of Song-Ming Confucianism by Qing scholars have been debated. Indeed, Qian Mu 錢穆 argues that Song learning remained the dominant tradition,[30] while Yu Ying-shih explains that the Qing intellectualist pursuit of the canonical texts derived from the "inner logic" of Neo-Confucianism.[31] The extent to which these trends influenced primary education at the time has received limited discussion.

While acknowledging that the conventional classification of "schools" of scholarship in the Qing does not accurately represent the complex realities of local and regional intellectual development,[32] discussing primary educational thought through school divisions does offer a constructive framework. There are various reasons. First, each scholarly group advocated for different emphases in the content of the examination, and it is this general direction rather than the specific activities of the group that influenced the elementary curriculum for potential examination candidates. Second, heterogeneity within each school is further complicated by the difficulty in assigning Qing educators to these schools. The fusion of traditions in their essays on elementary learning means that teasing out the origins of such thoughts is vital in analysis. Third, the compilers of the *Treasury* were not manifestly associated with any specific intellectual trend. Not only was educational thought in the text implicit but there was also likely the intent to market to a wide readership rather than a certain lineage. Consequently, the beliefs of distinct geographical schools, individual educators, and the compilers themselves are unreliable in directing this investigation. Ultimately, the teachers of the child reader were the major determinant in the educational values learned. The teacher's partiality toward a school of thought would have led to distinct interpretive strategies in reading the textbook. As such, the approaches of the teachers can be approximated through the traditional schools of thought and analyzed as "interpretive communities."

This overview will explore the main tenets of the school of principle (also known as the Cheng-Zhu school), the school of heart-mind (also known as the Lu-Wang school), and practical learning (also known as "solid learning") as related to primary education. More detail on the Cheng-Zhu school will be provided, as it was the established orthodoxy compared to the other schools—it could be argued that these schools evolved and reformulated the Neo-Confucian tradition. This is not intended to be a full account of the rich theories of the different schools. Indeed, from an analytic philosophical point of view, it is worth bearing in mind that there were many political and ideological objections springing from the conceptual understandings tied to these schools, which later provided grounds for contention and rejection. The many internal inconsistencies have been widely debated in the literature on these schools of thought. The analysis here will instead focus on the educational aims and the methods of learning and teaching in primary education. This will provide a useful background to prescriptive theories on primary schooling in the high Qing period as expressed through the writings of prominent elementary educators including Lu Shiyi, Tang Biao 唐彪 (1640–1713), Zhang Boxing 張伯行 (1651–1725), Chen Hongmou 陳宏謀 (1696–1771), Wang Yun, and Zhang Xingjian 張行簡 (fl. 1813). How to achieve a flourishing life is a philosophical topic that has interested laypersons and academia alike for millennia. As such, there are striking parallels and points of similarity between traditional Chinese and ancient Greek philosophy in terms of educational discourse.[33] While comparisons of Neo-Confucian and Western primary educational thought are limited in the secondary literature, such analysis is beyond the scope of the current discussion. Moreover, as the impact of Western primary educational thought was limited in the high Qing period and thus the Zou Shengmai edition of the *Treasury* to be studied, Western educational thought will not be discussed in this volume.

1.2.1 Zhu Xi and the School of Principle

Since the Yuan dynasty, the imperial government had adopted Zhu Xi's philosophy as state orthodoxy. The Qing dynasty continued this endorsement, which significantly influenced primary educational thought during the period.[34] The adoption of Zhu's commentaries to the Four Books as orthodox interpretation for the civil service examinations from the fourteenth century to the early years of the twentieth century was certainly not an insignificant ramification.[35] In the *Qingdai tongshi* 清代通史 (Comprehensive history of the Qing dynasty), Xiao Yishan provides a comprehensive list of school of principle officials and scholars. He then concludes that 90 percent of the literati of the high Qing period greatly esteemed the Cheng-Zhu philosophy.[36] Indeed, the *Qing xue'an xiaozhi* 清學案小識 (Small records of the cases of learning in the Qing) recorded: "All scholars today follow Zhu's tradition. Those who do are considered orthodox, those who do not are considered heterodox" 今之學者無他，亦宗朱子而已，宗朱子者為正學，不宗朱子者即非正學.[37] Rejection of radical liberalism in Wang Yangming's school of heart-mind was a major factor in the revival of the school of principle from the beginning of the Qing dynasty.[38] Despite evidential learning or Han learning (*Hanxue* 漢學) later becoming the hallmark of Qing scholarship, Feng Youlan considers that "adherents of the Han Learning who concentrated on philosophy should, despite their outward opposition to the school of principle, properly be regarded as its perpetuators and developers, rather than as the founders of a completely new school."[39] Hence the Cheng-Zhu school continued to hold sway over the intellectual landscape of the high Qing.

Zhu Xi's original ideas on education will be briefly covered before delving into their interpretation in primary education. The early Song Confucian masters reemphasized the cultivation of the moral self as the central vision of the Confucian mission, and this shift in thinking initiated the Neo-Confucian movement.[40] However, it was Zhu Xi who synthesized the work of his predecessors in creating a comprehensive agenda encompassing such diverse concerns as literature, education, and politics, all with self-cultivation as the axis.

There are several key tenets in Zhu's educational philosophy. First, education aimed to recover one's natural human propensities. Consistent with Mencius' (391–308 BCE) position, Zhu stated that native human propensities are good—in his recorded teachings, compiled in the *Classified Sayings of Master Zhu*, he states: "Native human propensities are purely good" 性則純是善底.[41] The innate moral "goodness" proposed here is not a value-based judgment but was considered an absolute based on the concept of the Way. The educational aim is evident in the *Great Learning*, the text Zhu designated as first to be studied in his reworked core Confucian curriculum of the Four Books. The *Great Learning* states:

> 大學之道，在明明德，在親民，在止於至善。
> The Way of learning to be great consists in manifesting the clear character, loving the people, and abiding in the highest good.[42]

Zhu's commentary to the Four Books elaborates on Neo-Confucian metaphysics. In this first sentence of the *Great Learning*, he explains that humans are born with a "clear character" (*mingde* 明德); this is the native human propensity (*xing* 性) that is common to all.[43] Our innate inclinations are suffused with the "principle" (*li* 理) that is the original entity of all things.[44] According to Zhu, principle is manifest through the natural process of events and the innate properties and function of matter in the natural world.[45] In humans, principle is exemplified through the moral qualities of humanity (*ren* 仁), rightness (*yi* 義), ritual propriety (*li* 禮), and wisdom (*zhi* 智).[46] In other words, humans have innate moral dispositions.

Zhu also explains that humans are born with a psychophysical endowment (*qi* 氣) that differs between individuals and is the matter and energy that constitutes all things.[47] In contrast to the innate human propensities, the *qi* varies in clarity or refinement, which leads to different dispositions, such as a person being born kind or unkind, wise or ignorant. Zhu uses water as an analogy for native propensities and colored bowls for the endowment. All water is clear, as native propensities are virtuous in all. However, the clear water appears to be colored when held in different bowls, just as humans have dissimilar dispositions.[48] When this imperfect endowment is exposed to temptations in the external environment, the consequent inordinate desires draw one further away from the "clear character."[49] Hence, it is this endowment that prevents the complete manifestation of the innate propensities.[50]

Education is the way to recover our native human propensities and become a sage (*shengren* 聖人). According to Zhu through his explication of the *Great Learning*, the aim of education is first, to cultivate one's psychophysical endowment such that native human propensities are realized ("manifesting the clear character"); second, to help others realize their native human propensities through one's example ("loving the people"); and third, to eradicate all selfish desire and completely accord with principle ("abiding in the highest good"). Learning was primarily for moral self-development. With education, a person could become virtuous, but without education, they might become a mean person.[51] In discussing the history of primary education in China, Chi Xiaofang believes that Zhu's school of thought established education as the pivotal factor in recovering one's innate morality. Other schools of Confucianism may not have articulated the association between learning moral conduct and native human propensities, resulting in passive compliance with externally imposed moral codes of conduct according to humanity, rightness, ritual propriety, and wisdom. In contrast, the school of principle proposed that these qualities were inherent in our native inclinations and could be realized and lived out through education.[52]

Realizing the clear character was not for a self-centered purpose but was linked to practical ends. Manifesting one's innate character was inextricably linked to "loving the people"—helping others realize their moral dispositions through a logical process. This is further described in the *Great Learning*:

> 古之欲明明德於天下者，先治其國；欲治其國者，先齊其家；欲齊其家者，先修其身；欲修其身者，先正其心；欲正其心者，先誠其意；欲誠其意者，先致其知，致知在格物。物格而後知至，知至而後意誠，意誠而後心正，心正而後身修，身修而後家齊，家齊而後國治，國治而後天下平。

> The ancients who wished to manifest their clear character to the world would first bring order to their states. Those who wished to bring order to their states would first regulate their families. Those who wished to regulate their families would first cultivate their personal lives. Those who wished to cultivate their personal lives would first rectify their heart-minds. Those who wished to rectify their heart-minds would first make their wills sincere. Those who wished to make their wills sincere would first extend their knowledge. The extension of knowledge consists in the investigation of things. When things are investigated, knowledge is extended; when knowledge is extended, the will becomes sincere; when the will is sincere, the heart-mind is rectified; when the heart-mind is rectified, the personal life is cultivated; when the personal life is cultivated, the family will be regulated; when the family is regulated, the state will be in order; and when the state is in order, there will be peace throughout the world.[53]

Here, the emphasis is again on personal cultivation as the foundation of learning, and such learning is the basis of familial, political, and universal harmony and flourishing. The outward transformation of others in ever-expanding social circles was grounded in inner moral learning. A person who achieved this was considered a sage. Han Zhongwen believes that Zhu continued the cultural tradition of Confucius and the Southern Song dynasty (1127–1279) masters in advocating that the educational objective was to become a sage.[54] Who was a sage? The *Doctrine of the Mean* explains:

> 唯天下至誠，為能盡其性；能盡其性，則能盡人之性；能盡人之性，則能盡物之性；能盡物之性，則可以贊天地之化育；可以贊天地之化育，則可以與天地參矣。
>
> Only those who are absolutely sincere (*cheng* 誠)[55] can fully develop their nature. If they can fully develop their nature, they can then fully develop the nature of others. If they can fully develop the nature of others, they can then fully develop the nature of things. If they can fully develop the nature of things, they can then assist in the transforming and nourishing process of Heaven and Earth. If they can assist in the transforming and nourishing process of Heaven and Earth, they can thus form a trinity with Heaven and Earth.[56]

In his annotated commentary, Zhu explains that this paragraph is a description of the sage.[57] The description here is similar to the *Great Learning* but further elucidates that the sage is a human who has achieved unity with all other beings and the universe. As Tu Wei-ming aptly explains in his monograph on the *Doctrine of the Mean*: "By realizing humanity in its all-encompassing wholeness, the sage transforms others as well as himself because he also is without any doubleness. The Way of the sage, therefore, is centered on the commonality of human nature."[58] A sage is "an authentic manifestation of our nature" as they have realized the native human propensities—the same moral inclinations that all humans and the universe possess.[59]

How does one learn to become a sage? There was a certain curriculum and educational method. The main objective was to exhaustively investigate all things (*gewu* 格物) to realize their underlying principle. The sages recorded their experiences on understanding principle in the canonical texts, so the main method was through book reading.[60] According to Zhu, learning the Confucian canonical works was to learn from the experience of the sages themselves. He states:

> 夫天下之物，莫不有理，而其精蘊，則已具於聖賢之書，故必由是而求之。然欲其簡而易知，約而易守，則莫若《大學》、《中庸》、《論語》、《孟子》之篇也。
>
> All things in the world have principle, but its essence is embodied in the works of the sages and worthies. Hence in seeking principle we must turn to these works. For ease, brevity, simplicity and immediacy, the writings of the *Great Learning*, the *Analects*, the *Doctrine of the Mean* and the *Mencius* are unsurpassed.[61]

The sages realized the principle was constant in all things. Their thoughts, words, and deeds abided by the principle and were recorded in the texts. Hence, learning these canonical texts involved emulating the examples of the sages. Although the Five Classics remained the focus, Zhu selected the *Great Learning*, the *Analects*, the *Doctrine of the Mean*, and the *Mencius* as the first four texts to be studied for their comprehensibility,[62] these texts were later known as the "Four Books." Moreover, historical works were also necessary to understand how the principle was manifested in affairs and to learn how to respond in various situations.

While the content of these texts would help the learner investigate principle, reading would be ineffective without the correct method. Zhu explains:

> 為學之道，莫先於窮理。窮理之要，必在乎讀書。讀書之法，莫貴乎循序而致精。而致精之本，則又在於居敬而持志。此不易之理也。
> The first priority in the process of engaging in learning is to investigate principle fully. The key to investigating principle is reading books. Nothing is more valuable in the method of reading books than following the sequence [of the text] and concentrating. The basis of concentration in turn lies in residing in seriousness and maintaining commitment. This is an unchanging principle.[63]

Zhu's teachings on book learning were compiled in the *Zhuzi dushufa* 朱子讀書法 (Master Zhu's method of reading) by his students.[64] There are six principles: follow the sequence, attain familiarity and apprehension, keep an open mind, experience the principles, dedicate oneself, and maintain respect and commitment. First, read one book at a time and read the text in the order presented. Second, be familiar with the text by reading repeatedly until the text is memorized and such that the meanings are internalized. Third, read with a humble and open mind to apprehend the meaning of the sages. Fourth, the principles should be implemented in daily life to experience the teachings firsthand. Fifth, be conscientious in learning, even to the extent of forgetting to eat. Sixth, always be respectful, particularly through one's concentration in the process of reading. In his discussion of Zhu's philosophy, Qian Mu concludes that for Zhu, the process of reading was itself moral cultivation.[65] For this reason Zhu proposed an innovative curriculum and learning strategy for becoming a sage.

The formative influence of primary education was crucial for developing the habits necessary for investigating principle. The *Zhongguo jiaoyu tongshi* 中國教育通史 (Comprehensive history of Chinese education) asserts that educational discourse prior to the Southern Song dynasty was largely directed at advanced learning for governance and that Zhu was instrumental in bringing elementary education to the forefront of intellectual thinking.[66] This resulted in an increased compilation of children's textbooks and the establishment of primary schools. Zhu's thoughts on elementary education were recorded by his students in the *Collected Conversations of Master Zhu* and disseminated in his other writings. Zhu viewed moral and intellectual learning as divided into two stages—elementary and advanced learning:

> 小學者，學其事；大學者，學其小學所學之事之所以。
> Elementary education is the learning of tasks. Advanced education is the learning of the principle behind the tasks studied in primary education.[67]

> 小學是事，如事君、事父、事兄、處友等事，只是教他依此規矩做去。大學是發明此事之理。
> Elementary education is the learning of tasks—such as serving one's ruler, serving one's father, serving one's brother, and dealing with one's friends. It teaches one to behave according to certain rules. Advanced education illuminates the principle behind these tasks.[68]

Tasks were concrete activities in daily life, which included table etiquette and how to walk, talk, sit, address elders, read, and write.[69] Children were first to learn by "doing"—practicing these everyday tasks and interpersonal interactions with a basic understanding of the concepts and attitudes to be acquired. For example, the concept of family reverence (*xiao* 孝) was explained as being "skillful in serving parents 善事父母"[70] and "children should empathize with parents 人子當曲體父母之心."[71] Implementation of family reverence was expressed through instructions such as these:

> 若父母長上有所召喚，卻當疾走而前。
> When summoned by parents or elders, one must walk swiftly to come before them.[72]

> 凡出外，及歸，必於長上前作揖。
> Before leaving the home and upon returning, one must bow before elders.[73]

Limin Bai uses the term "ritualizing the body" to describe Zhu's notion of self-disciplined behavior, abiding by rules of deportment and demeanor derived from the *Records on Ritual* and other ritual texts.[74] Children were to practice norms of behavior, which would become second nature over time. This reflected Confucius' notion that "habits formed in childhood become as if innate and such habits are like second nature" 少成若天性，習慣如自然.[75] The observation of these social rites was a "ritualizing" process believed to shape one's personality by learning and internalizing the values that the rituals embodied. Mastering the elementary learning tasks would prepare the student for the deeper intellectual inquiry of advanced education, such as understanding how the moral value of family reverence was the basis of humanity, as stated in the *Analects*.[76] Through a thorough understanding of the principles, they could pursue the goals in advanced learning expressed in the *Great Learning*: cultivating the personal life, regulating the family, ordering the state, and advancing peace throughout the world.

Zhu's two compilations intended as elementary textbooks—*Elementary Learning* and *Tongmeng xuzhi* 童蒙須知 (What youngsters should know)—embody his approach to elementary education. The foreword outlines two main content areas.[77] First, tasks of daily living and skills were to be learned, as disciplining the physical body was believed to facilitate rectification of moral character. Second, the child was defined within a network of five fundamental human relationships (*wulun* 五倫) relating to the learning and practice of moral obligations, such as loving one's parents, respecting one's elders, and being trustworthy with one's friends. Theresa Kelleher's analysis of the structure and content of the *Elementary Learning* reveals that "clarifying human relationships" (*minglun* 明倫) dominated the content—there were 107 items devoted to this theme, in contrast to thirteen for education and forty-five for cultivation.[78] Of the five fundamental human relationships of parent-child, husband-wife, sovereign-subject, elder-younger, and friend-friend, the parent-child relationship receives the most treatment.[79] Kelleher explains that family reverence was considered the linchpin upon which the attitudes and skills of all other human relations depended upon in Confucian thought, and in family reverence Zhu Xi provided the justification for personal cultivation.[80] The text was considered part of the core curriculum in primary schools until even the Qing dynasty.[81]

Qing officials, intellectuals, and primary school teachers adhered to the Cheng-Zhu tradition in keeping with government policy, as evidenced by the educational discourse of the time. Indeed, Zhu's elementary primers and quotes were directly endorsed through inclusion in various primary education guidelines. For example, Zhang Boxing, director of the Board of Rites (*libu* 禮部) overseeing the imperial examinations during the high Qing period, wrote an annotated commentary of the *Elementary Learning*. His other contributions to Qing dynasty primary education include compiling related thoughts by the school of principle philosophers titled *Yang zheng lei pian* 養正類篇 (Writings on nurturing the correct nature of children) and his essay "Elementary learning" (*xiaoxue* 小學), which consisted of excerpts from Song dynasty educators. A notable follower of the Cheng-Zhu school and an educator with over a thousand students, Zhang in his writings echoed the centrality of respectfulness in Zhu Xi's teachings: "The teachings of a thousand sages can be summarized as respect. In learning, there is nothing more important than residing in respect" 千聖之學，括於一敬，故學莫先於主敬.[82]

Similarly, Chen Hongmou, provincial administration commissioner of Yunan, established over seven hundred charitable primary schools from the prefecture to county level during the Yongzheng reign.[83] His compilation *Yang zheng yi gui* 養正遺規 (Guidelines for proper upbringing) provided instructions on childhood education for family elders and teachers.[84] The first four essays in the volume are those of Zhu Xi, including the "Bai lu dong shuyuan tishi" 白鹿洞書院提示 (Regulations of the White Deer Grotto Academy), "Cangzhou jingshe yu xuezhe" 滄州精舍諭學者 (Instructions to the students of the Cang Province study center), "What Youngsters Should Know," and "Cheng dong xue ze" 程董學則 (Cheng and Dong's principles of learning). The second section also includes "Zhu's Methods of Reading." In the foreword, Chen references the *Meng* hexagram from the *Changes* and extends the meaning: "Water from the mouth of the spring in the mountains is pure, but water from the mountains is turbid, how is this the fault of the spring? 夫在山泉水清，出山泉水濁，緊豈泉之咎哉"[85] This echoes Zhu's idea of the purity of the child's innate nature that without education easily becomes tainted. Moreover, the structure of his book reflects Zhu's order of learning—beginning with ritual practice in daily life followed by learning from texts.

Other educators reinforced Zhu's concepts but embellished them with their original thoughts. School of principle philosopher Lu Shiyi, who was a lifelong educator, was praised in the *Complete Library of the Four Branches of Literature* as: "the most genuine scholar of contemporary times" 於近代講學諸家最為篤實.[86] The first chapter of his collected works, *Sibian lu ji yao* 思辨録輯要 (Essential collected records of thinking and distinguishing), is dedicated to primary education. He commends Zhu's annotation to the *Meng* hexagram that the most important principle in childhood education is "to eradicate external temptations and fully develop their true purity" 去其外誘，全其真純. Moreover, he echoes Zhu's learning theory that the young lack the intellectual or moral capacity to fully comprehend why they ought to behave according to certain behavioral standards, which Ridley argues is similar to cognitive development theory.[87] Lu elaborates that the child's memory capacity was most robust up to the age of fifteen, so teaching and learning strategies were directed toward memorization and behavioral ritual. With the development of intellectual capacities and greater exposure to the external world, the child would inevitably become contaminated by physical desires and their memory capacity would diminish.[88] Lu's association of externally mediated desires, intellectual capacity, and memory capacity had not been expressed by Zhu. He arguably draws from Han dynasty scholar Wang Chong 王充 (27–97), who was the first to propose that a person's habitual nature would be relatively fixed by the age of fifteen.[89] A corollary of this belief in the limited phase of childhood "nurture" is that education needed to start as early as possible—Lu advocated for children to start schooling at the age of six instead of eight. While Lu begins by admiring *Elementary Learning*, he later points to the limitations of the long sentences, difficult words, and irrelevant content for the student. Instead, he suggests that students read his compilation from the *Records on Ritual* titled *Jie yun you yi* 節韻幼儀 (Etiquette for children in rhyme).

In the period of the late nineteenth and early twentieth centuries in China, Jon Saari's historical study on childhood experiences documents the inherent sociopsychological tensions of a childhood dominated by Neo-Confucian thought facing reform.[90] He asserts that there remained the traditional assumption that the child's nature, being so vulnerable, needed to be protected from both the external environment and the child's internal desires. Moreover, the child's nature was to be fully developed through the education of parents and teachers, who would guide the child's thoughts and behavior in the pivotal period before the age of fourteen. Thus, the school of principle's concept of the child who required education for full development continued as the mainstay in the Qing dynasty.

The Cheng-Zhu school focused on the crucial role of primary education for the development of moral qualities. The purpose of primary education was to learn habits, knowledge, and attitudes. This would prepare students for investigating principle, refining inborn endowment, and eradicating selfish desire to become a sage, having recovered innate moral qualities. Such beliefs, values, and objectives remained significant in Qing dynasty educational thought.

1.2.2 Wang Yangming and the School of Heart-Mind

Studies on childhood in late imperial China indicate that the Southern Song and mid-Ming periods were viewed as turning points in thinking about the child.[91] Innovation in Neo-Confucian thought during the late Ming period was largely due to the work of Wang Yangming. Wang developed Song dynasty philosopher Lu Jiuyuan's 陸九淵 (1139–1192) theory on the heart-mind and brought the "school of heart-mind" into prominence. He not only established multiple academies in places including Longgang, Guiyang, and Lianxi but also community primary schools in provinces like Guangxi and Jiangxi.[92] Wang's theory of self-realization from within called for a child-oriented pedagogy rather than one imposed by rigid discipline. He challenged the restrictive nature of the Cheng-Zhu elementary program, and his influence on the development of Chinese primary educational thought is considered second only to Zhu Xi.[93]

The aim of education for Wang was also to restore our natural propensities. On these native propensities, both Zhu and Wang adhered to the Mencian theory of humanity's innate moral inclinations. Wang also accepted the school of principle founder Cheng Hao's 程顥 (1032–1085) description of the original nature being a universal oneness: "forming one body with Heaven, Earth, and all things" 天地萬物一體.[94] The fundamental difference was that Wang advocated an all-encompassing unity with the heart-mind, principle, knowledge and all external things. In other words, knowledge was also intrinsic. He argued that the original heart-mind would act with family reverence in the presence of parents and hence the principle of family reverence is not found in the parent or external objects but the heart-mind itself. As Feng Youlan clarifies: "For Zhu, the nature is Principle, whereas by Wang the heart-mind is Principle."[95] According to Wang, the heart-mind was one's will—an inner determination in the moment to accord with the principle or with desire. This was the key to his distinct program of self-cultivation.

How does imperfection arise despite these innate human propensities? Wang appears to adopt Cheng Yi's 程頤 (1033–1107) scheme of the unblemished "moral heart-mind" (*dao xin* 道心) and the "human heart-mind" (*ren xin* 人心) tainted by desire. However, Wang emphasizes that these are two states of the same heart-mind:

> 心一也。未雜於人謂之道心，雜以人偽謂之人心。人心之得其正者即道心。道心之失其正者即人心。初非有二心也。程子謂人心即人欲，道心即天理。語若分析，而意實得之。
>
> There is only one heart-mind. Before it is mixed with selfish human desires, it is called the moral heart-mind, and after it is mixed with human desires contrary to its natural state, it is called the human heart-mind. When the human heart-mind is rectified it is called the moral heart-mind and when the moral heart-mind loses its correctness, it is called the human heart-mind. There were not two heart-minds to start with. When Master Cheng Yi said that the human heart-mind is due to selfish desires while the moral heart-mind is due to the Principle of Nature, it sounds like dividing the heart-mind into two, but his idea is really correct.[96]

The original heart-mind ("moral heart-mind") has the ability to differentiate between right and wrong, termed the "innate knowledge of goodness" (*liang zhi* 良知). However, due to the interference of selfish desire, attachment to thoughts and even emotions,[97] the heart-mind becomes clouded (the "human heart-mind") and fails to realize our oneness with all people and things. Wang uses the analogy of a blocked nose: smelling a bad odor is akin to knowledge; however, a person with a blocked nose does not know of the odor and is not repelled, as would naturally occur.[98]

With desire, our innate knowledge cannot manifest, and we do not give rise to the humanity, care, and love for all others, as should be natural.

How does one realize our native human propensities? The elimination of selfish desires. Wang's method of moral self-cultivation was largely based on his interpretation of "investigation of things" (*gewu* 格物) in the *Great Learning*. The Cheng-Zhu school gloss of *gewu* was an objective investigation of the principle in external objects. In contrast, Wang interpreted *gewu* as "eliminating what is incorrect in the heart-mind to preserve the correctness of its original substance" 去其心之不正，以全其本體之正.[99] This is also expressed in his "Doctrine of Four Axioms":

> 無善無惡心之體，有善有惡意之動，知善知惡是良知，為善去惡是格物。
> In the original substance of the heart-mind there is no distinction of good and evil.
> When the will becomes active, however, such distinction exists.
> The faculty of innate knowledge is to know good and evil.
> *Gewu* is to do good and remove evil.[100]

A person's intention at any moment was the main tool in the restoration of the original mind. Thome Fang explains, "Intention is the motivation of mind. The pivotal point here is the intention which energizes the mind to get at the object of its own making."[101] The moral practice involved constantly harnessing the power of the will to preserve and sense one's innate knowledge of goodness, known as "extension of the innate knowledge of the good" (*zhi liangzhi* 致良知). Ivanhoe summarizes this cultivation as constant inner scrutiny of every thought and vigilance against selfish desire, thereby enabling our innate knowledge to function unhindered.[102] As Wang emphasized:

> 學者一念為善之志，如樹之種，但勿助勿忘，只管培植將去。自然日夜滋長。生氣日完，枝葉日茂。樹初生時，便抽繁枝，亦須刊落，然後根幹能大。初學時亦然。故立志貴專一。
> All depends on making up the mind. If the student makes up his heart-mind to have one thought to do good, his heart-mind will be like the seed of a tree. If only he neither forces it to grow nor neglects it, but keeps on

> cultivating and nourishing it, it will naturally grow larger every day and night. Its vitality will be increasingly great and its branches and leaves more luxuriant. When the tree first begins to grow, it shoots forth many branches. These must be cut before the roots and trunk may grow large. This is also true when one begins to learn. Therefore, in making up one's heart-mind single-mindedness is highly valued.[103]

As one's innate knowledge was the guide to the innate propensities, Wang diminished the role of the Confucian canonical texts, their commentaries, and the sages. This strictly diverged from the tradition that Zhu had established. For Wang, moral practice occurred in the activities of one's life rather than in book learning. He highlighted Confucius' contribution in simplifying the canonical works, Mencius' criticism of the *Shangshu* 尚書 (Documents), and breaches of ritual propriety by the sages to advocate the superiority of one's innate knowledge over intellectual learning.[104] He once wrote: "The thousand sages are all passing shadows. Innate knowledge alone is my teacher" 千聖皆過影，良知乃吾師.[105] Thus, authority lay in moral intuition. He emphasized that learned knowledge was personal experience, such as not knowing the taste of food until one eats it, as distinct from innate knowledge. In other words, concepts were not learned unless they were personally experienced through one's practice. For Wang, with regard to his doctrine of the unity of knowledge and action (*zhi xing heyi* 知行合一), true knowledge and action are supposedly identical.[106] Wang's visionary emphasis on knowledge through personal experience also found expression in his pedagogy for children.

Wang did not author any primary school textbooks, but his thoughts on elementary learning are captured in the letter "Instructions for Liu Bosong and Others on Fundamental Ideas on Elementary Education," which forms a chapter in his recorded teachings—*Instructions for Practical Living* (*Chuan xi lu* 傳習錄). The letter was issued to teachers and family elders in the community schools that Wang established in 1518.[107] In Ren Shixian's analysis of Qing dynasty educational theory, he identifies four key areas in Wang's letter relating to primary educational aims, values, teaching materials, and teaching methods.[108] Primary education aimed to restore the original nature as exemplified by Wang quoting the *Meng* hexagram: "Nourish the correct nature." The values to foster were family reverence, fraternity, loyalty, trustworthiness, ritual propriety, rightness, integrity, and shame. The teaching materials included poetry, ritual propriety, and books consistent with the ancients:

> 誘之歌詩，以發其志意；導之習禮，以肅其威儀；諷之讀書，以開其知覺。
>
> Lure them to singing so their will is roused, to direct them to practice ritual propriety so their demeanor will be dignified, and to urge them to read so their intellectual horizon will be widened.[109]

The teaching method must be child-oriented such that the students are stimulated to study, enjoy their learning, and feel unrestricted. The teacher nurtures the positive temperaments and addresses negative character traits through the imperceptible influence of the above activities. Another aspect of education that differed from the Cheng-Zhu school was Wang's attention to the physical development of the students. He writes:

> 導之習禮者，非但肅其威儀而已，亦所以周旋揖讓而動蕩其血脈，拜起屈伸而固束其筋骸也。
>
> To lead them to practice etiquette (*li* 禮) is not only to make their demeanor dignified. It is also to exhilarate their blood circulation through such activities as bowing and walking politely, and to strengthen their tendons and bones through kneeling, rising, and extending and contracting their limbs.[110]

Wang's elementary learning curriculum parallels the strategies and objectives in his moral self-cultivation. The first strategy is to develop the motivation of the child (the "will"), which occurs not by coercion but by stimulation. He justifies the activities of singing, ritual practice, and reading as educational, empowering, and entertaining:

> 凡此皆所以順導其志意，調理其性情，潛消其鄙吝，默化其麁頑，日使之漸於禮義而不苦其難，人於中和而不知其故。
>
> All this is smoothly to direct their will, adjust and regulate their nature and feelings, quietly to get rid of their meanness and stinginess, and silently to transform their crudeness and mischievousness, so that they

will gradually approach propriety and rightness without feeling that it is difficult to do so and will steep themselves in equilibrium and harmony without knowing why.[111]

Using the metaphor of sprouting plants, the child should "grow freely" rather than be "twisted or interfered with."[112] Wang uses this metaphor to express disapproval of the over-emphasis on restraint and discipline used by teachers. Instead, he advocated for the child's mental and physical health to be invigorated, with the resulting student being "happy and cheerful at heart." The child should remain in a relaxed and unrepressed state; for example, a child with the capacity to learn two hundred words should only be taught a hundred words so that they are not over-exerted. Enjoying their studies, the child would ultimately be self-motivated.

Another strategy of Wang's education is nurturing the student's sensitivity to detect selfish thoughts thus facilitating the "extension of innate knowledge." Wang outlined his ideas on a student's daily schedule with emphasis on heeding the innate knowledge programmed into the routine. He advocates that the first task in the morning is for teachers to ask each student to reflect on their words, acts, and thoughts from the previous day.

> 每日清晨，諸生參揖畢，教讀以次偏詢諸生：在家所以愛親敬畏之心，得無懈忽未能填切否？溫凊定省之儀，得無虧缺未能實踐否？往來街衢步趨禮節，得無放蕩未能謹飭否？一應言行心術，得無欺妄非僻未能忠信篤敬否？
>
> Every day, early in the morning, after the pupils have assembled and bowed, the teachers should ask all of them one by one whether at home they have been negligent and lacked sincerity and earnestness in their desire to love their parents and to respect their elders, whether they have overlooked or failed to carry out any details in caring for their parents in the summer or the winter, whether in walking along the streets their movements and etiquette have been disorderly or careless, and whether in all their words, acts, and thoughts they have been deceitful or depraved, and not loyal, faithful, sincere, and respectful.[113]

The third pedagogical approach is practicing the skill of "unity of knowledge and action" in daily activities. The focus on values including family reverence meant that cultivation was integrated into daily interactions and tasks. It was through action that the children would gradually develop their character. While his broader aim is similar to that of Zhu, Wang was one of the first proponents of the use of liberal learning methods in the history of primary education in China. Hence, he does admit that these unorthodox methods would not be widely accepted in his time. It must be noted that Wang's pedagogy is still considered traditional when compared to modern educational practices, particularly in his emphasis on book learning and ritual etiquette.[114]

Despite Qing intellectuals' rejection of the school of heart-mind generally, many of Wang's primary educational tenets were endorsed in the mainstream educational discourse. Child-oriented strategies seemed predominant in the Qing dynasty. For example, Chen Hongmou included Wang Yangming's letter on learning through ritual and poetry and himself selected poetry suitable for children from nineteen authors as a supplement to the section.[115] Lu Shiyi also argued for the importance of singing poetry and practicing rituals as an educational and enjoyable experience. He adds that this would "arouse the will and dignify the demeanor 發其志意，肅其威儀" of children and is aptly suited to the temperaments of children who delight in song and dance.[116] Indeed, parts of his essay read like a duplicate of Wang's letter. Moreover, Lu criticizes current primary school teachers for merely disciplining students on punctuating the texts without providing any encouragement that would help students become more self-motivated. Lu explained the idea of putting into practice one's learning as "knowledge and action occurring together" (*zhi xing bingxing* 知行並行), which resonates well with Wang's doctrine on the unity of knowledge and action. Qing philologist Wang Yun also explained that children must be given leisure time, as they have a limited attention span.[117] While remaining true to the central themes of the school of principle, educators adapted the pedagogy to suit the predominant thinking of the time.

Wang's propagation of the doctrine that all people and things are "one body" may have struck a chord with the scholar-officials and provided an impetus for the expansion of elementary schools in the southwest, where Wang had served.[118] Indeed, Bai explains how he made sagehood accessible for the common people, who may have been otherwise excluded by the elitism of book learning for moral cultivation championed by the Cheng-Zhu school.[119] Although the radicalism of Wang's followers led to a rejection of the school of heart-mind, Wang's ideas continued to have a lasting influence in primary education.

1.2.3 Gu Yanwu and Practical Learning

Practical learning (*shixue* 實學) was a new development in the intellectual thought of the Ming-Qing period. This movement was initiated by late Ming scholars who argued for a broader view of orthodoxy and civic engagement, hence the names it was given, "solid learning" and "practical statecraft." Practical learning later spawned the school of evidential learning (*kaoju xue* 考據學), also known as Han learning, which increasingly undermined the Cheng-Zhu school heritage starting in the mid-eighteenth century. Elman has provided a thorough historical critique of the political, institutional, and intellectual factors that led to the Qing academia's transition from philosophy to philology, which will not be further elaborated in this study.[120] As evidential research topics were included in the provincial and metropolitan examinations starting in the late eighteenth century,[121] primary education's role as exam preparation for the elite was inevitably affected. This is reflected in the educational theories of key Qing philologists such as Dai Zhen 戴震 (1723–1777) and Wang Yun. However, Zou Shengmai edited the *Treasury* in the early eighteenth century, so the incipient empiricist intellectual current of practical learning will be analyzed rather than the evidential research movement. I will begin by exploring the educational theory of Gu Yanwu 顧炎武 (1613–1682), who is generally considered the founding father of Qing evidential scholarship and the apotheosis of the statecraft interests of the conservative *fushe* 復社 (return to antiquity) literati societies.[122] Given that Gu did not outline an elementary program, the influence of practical learning principles will be gleaned from the writings of primary school educators in his time.

The educational aim of "learning to be a sage" was essentially unchanged from Zhu Xi and Wang Yangming's programs. The curriculum, which also remained knowledge-based, was couched in Neo-Confucian philosophical terms. However, a distinctive and pragmatic objective of bettering society was emphasized, which Gu Yanwu rearticulated as "understanding the Way and saving the world" (*ming dao jiushi* 明道救世). Although Neo-Confucianism had asserted the principle of "loving the people" to achieve order in the state and world peace, this dimension had received less attention compared to abstract philosophizing in the Ming period. William Theodore de Bary notes that there was already a detectable change in the Ming dynasty from "moral substantiality and metaphysical truth to the pursuit of objective, empirical investigation serving utilitarian ends."[123] John Henderson explains this as a shift from "inner cultivation or sagehood studies" to "world-ordering or kingship studies."[124] Gu Yanwu blamed the teachings of Wang Yangming for the intuitive and internally directed cognitive activity that neglected political-mindedness, leading to moral decline and the ultimate collapse of the Ming dynasty.[125] He criticized both the school of heart-mind and the school of principle for popularizing vacuous discourse—unsubstantiated subjective opinions without benefit to the empire. He wrote:

> 非好古而多聞，則為空虛之學。以無本之人，而講空虛之學，吾見其日從事於聖人而去之彌遠也。
> If one does not love the ancients and listen assiduously, then one's learning is empty and without substance. To be a man without a foundation and expound learning that is empty and without substance, I see as becoming more remote from the matters of the Sage every day.[126]

To counter the negative trends, Gu advocated for a learning program with different teaching methods and materials. Comprehending the Way would come about through the canonical readings of the Han period and historical texts—the "authentic" learning of principle (*lixue*).[127]

The curricular materials signaled a departure from the Four Books and Song dynasty interpretations that he believed were intermingled with Buddhist and Daoist influences. Instead, Gu felt that the content of the Five Classics was the Way and that the learning of principle was learning the canonical works. There was also an emphasis on studying the historical records to glean the lessons of the past in governance, while subjects of statecraft (*dangshi zhi wu* 當世之務), such as astronomy, geography, agriculture, hydrology, and geology, would instill practical knowledge to assist national development. There were many exponents of a revived interest in the canonical works starting in the early seventeenth century, such as the influential Donglin Academy restored in 1604 that required members to study the Five Classics.[128] The ideologies of the Donglin Academy and Restoration Society organizations were similar.[129] The restoration societies were popular in the mid-seventeenth century and were so named to revitalize ancient learning. Indeed, Yu Ying-shih has demonstrated that study of the canonical works was a logical development due to metaphysical debates between Neo-Confucians of different persuasions. This compelled scholars to cite the authority of the original texts as a means of validating their knowledge of the Way.[130] Such changes in the curricular objectives and materials had major implications for Qing pedagogy and learner attitudes.

The learning method was to verify the textual interpretation of the canonical works, thereby decoding the original meaning transmitted by the sages. It was believed that comprehension of the sage teachings of the texts would facilitate order in the world. Gu pioneered a rigorous empirical inquiry based on philological and phonological analysis:

> 故愚以為讀九經自考文始，考文自知音始。以至諸子百家之書，亦莫不然。
>
> I hold that reading the nine classics begins with examining the characters [with which the texts are written], and examining the characters begins with knowing the pronunciations [that the written characters represent]. This applies as well to the texts of all the writers and schools of thought [of the early period] without exception.[131]

First, accurate understanding of the characters necessitated the reconstruction of their ancient forms, sounds, and meanings. Interpretations were also corroborated with ancient artifacts and chronological and geographical evidence. Elman notes that explication of "names and their referents" (*mingwu* 名物) based on canonical and historical texts and pre–Song dynasty scholia was the first step in weakening Neo-Confucian metaphysical and cosmological systems of thought.[132] In effect, the restoration of the original definition of terms was to expose how Song scholars had imposed unverifiable philosophical interpretations on the texts. Questioning the sources of information and the conceptual framework was a focal concern. Gu's methods increasingly gained currency, becoming the primary scholarship techniques for the school of evidential learning: determining the authenticity of classical and historical texts, sourcing the etymologies of ancient classical terms, reconstructing ancient Chinese phonology, and clarifying the paleography of Chinese characters.[133] Through such an empirical approach, precise facts displaced Neo-Confucian abstract reasoning in importance.

Despite studies generally focusing on evidential learning as an intellectual and empirical movement,[134] morality in the high Qing remained a critical aspect of practical statecraft thinking. Ritual being the external norms of conduct came to prominence in moral cultivation. Kai-Wing Chow argues that ritual was the common ground in reconciling the teachings of Wang and Zhu regarding the interiority and exteriority of morality.[135] Chow provides evidence that Gu was influenced by Cheng-Zhu scholars on ritualism—Gu wrote, "Nothing was more important than ritual propriety; the Duke of Zhou had ruled the realm with ritual, and Confucius based his teachings on it" 周公之所以為治，孔子之所以為教，舍禮其何以焉.[136] Gu promoted education on ritual propriety (*lijiao* 禮教) as the linchpin to personal cultivation and social improvement, although Li Guojun believes that he merely reiterated school of principle arguments rather than providing new insight.[137]

"Solid learning" (*shixue*) ideas were an integral part of Qing primary education. The influence was manifest in two ways: the expansion of scholarship and the promotion of questioning. Despite being a Neo-Confucian, Lu Shiyi was also an adherent of practical statecraft and advocated for the inclusion of subjects such as agriculture and political institutions in his writings on advanced learning. As he states in "On Elementary Learning," "Not only the Four Books and Five Classics, but also astronomy, geography, history, and mathematics have their mnemonic verses and should be read to familiarity" 不但四書五經，即如天文、地理、史學、算學之類，皆有歌訣，皆須熟讀.[138] What is most revealing about his preference for solid learning is his inclusion of a paragraph almost identical to the *Explaining Simple Graphs and Analyzing Complex Graphs* postface on the importance of learning the etymology of characters and ancient scripts—the Later Han (25–220) lexicon being a core philological text. By the early nineteenth century, Wang Yun had pioneered an innovative character recognition pedagogy using the principles of paleography.[139] Arguing that the etymology of the characters was the first step in the child's learning, he compiled the primer *Character Learning for Young Children* based on *Explaining Simple Graphs and Analyzing Complex Graphs*. Tang Biao proposed reading a wide variety of texts not limited to the Song Neo-Confucian writings, such as the ancient writings of the pre-Qin and Qin-Han periods and their commentaries, gazetteers, decrees, and regulations.[140] Hence, broad learning in practical learning was interpreted as expanding the subject and knowledge base. This would prepare children for future textual analysis as part of the literati.

Another defining feature of Qing essays on primary education compared to early dynasties is the encouragement of student questioning. Having a questioning mind was considered a sign of the learner's diligent efforts to comprehend the text—the more questions the better, and such students were rewarded. Zhang Xingjian explains that teachers should not hinder a student from asking, because "knowing areas of uncertainties are opportunities for comprehension and asking questions helps students to realize their uncertainties. Hence students diligent in finding questions are assured of becoming accomplished" 疑者悟之機，問者疑之啟，故學徒勤問者，鮮不成材.[141] Qing dynasty elementary school teacher Li Xin'an 李新庵 (dates unknown) stated that teachers should stimulate students to ask questions.[142] Tang Biao echoed such sentiments. He elaborated on the importance of seeking knowledge from all people, taught how to approach renowned Confucian scholars, and urged teachers to question students when explicating the texts in order to gauge comprehension.[143]

The return to pre-Song texts and ancient writings, reinterpretation of the texts using a linguistics approach, and a renewed focus on the external aspects of self-cultivation as a pragmatic endeavor were vital changes in the Qing educational front. Gu Yanwu was considered a pioneer of practical statecraft thought but arguably had merely articulated an existing change in attitude toward intellectualism during the seventeenth century. The trend to extensive scholarship, philological techniques, and critical inquiry were important new elements in the elementary curriculum.

1.3 THE QING PRIMARY EDUCATIONAL PARADIGM

The general theories of education discussed above correlate in varying degrees with the primary education prescriptive discourse. Rather than starting fresh in formulating the aims of education and the human nature that was to be "educated," Qing educators reinterpreted and supplemented the existing traditions. As Richard Smith argues:

> One of the most prominent features of Chinese thought in late imperial times was its extraordinary eclecticism, its ability to tolerate diverse and sometimes seemingly incompatible notions with little sense of conflict or contradiction.[144]

Indeed, it is apparent that the integration of tradition and innovation defined Qing primary educational thought.

Learning also had practical aims that took into account the sociopolitical determinants of education.[145] Politically, elementary education was the means of transmitting the state orthodoxy and providing a training ground for officials. For the family, primary schooling led to literacy and socioeconomic advancement through the examination system. Thus, elementary education in the Ming and Qing was generally comprised of three broad components: moral education, knowledge education, and the written language.[146] Educators blended moral reasoning with academic pursuits and training for the examinations. The content and methods of the curriculum were grounded in the intellectual tradition.

First, the moral agenda in primary education can be summarized by a phrase from the *Changes,* "nourishing the correct." The traditional concept of humanity possessing native moral propensities was widely accepted by all schools of thought. Both Zhu and Wang asserted that innate moral propensities were clouded by selfish desire. The aim of education was to develop these natural dispositions. Primary education was a crucial stage in the establishment of moral character and habits to preserve and promote these moral propensities. Indeed, Qing primary school teacher Li Xin'an asserts that it is more important to have students of good character than those with simply intelligence or skill.[147] Zhang Xingjian also writes that moral education should be integrated into all parts of the curriculum and that the teacher should be a living exemplar of the morals.[148] However, the main points of contention lay in the methods of moral education. Van Norden outlines three models of moral cultivation:

> According to a discovery model, each human has innately and completely whatever cognitive and affective capacities are required for full virtue (be it knowledge, or certain dispositions, or some true nature). All that is necessary is for each of us to discover this source of virtue within ourselves and apply it. According to a re-formation model, in contrast, each of us must undergo some fundamental transformation to create in us whatever knowledge, dispositions, or nature is required for virtue. Finally, according to a development model, each person innately has incipient tendencies toward virtue that must develop in order for the person to achieve full virtue.[149]

At the elementary level, all schools advocated a reformation model in the adherence to ritual practice. Wang's methods in self-examination and Gu's critical thinking also adopted a development model, whereas for Zhu Xi this occurs at the advanced level. There were diverse teaching methods used such as verbal instruction, elementary textbooks, school rules, and personal demonstration of exemplary behavior by the teachers. Learning experiences permeated every aspect of the curriculum, both during and outside of class time, such as paying respect to the image of Confucius twice a month.[150] Moral knowledge included the learning of ethical vocabulary and concepts through texts and stories, such as family reverence and trustworthiness. At the same time, moral practice was fostered through school behavior, interpersonal interactions, and ritual propriety lessons.

Traditional Chinese education was based on an established written tradition. Knowledge acquisition through learning the literary canon, including the Four Books and the Five Classics and their commentaries and the historical works and other ancient writings, was an important aspect of primary education. While Zhu Xi stressed the Four Books, Gu Yanwu and the practical learning school emphasized the Five Classics. The canonical works were considered the authoritative knowledge base for moral values, and the overall literary tradition was considered the source of cultural values.

Language acquisition focused on the basic skills of reading and writing. Beyond basic character recognition, primers with rhymed sentences introducing learners to the ancient terms and concepts encountered in their subsequent textbooks were used to foster reading comprehension skills. This was a common practice in the Qing dynasty.[151] The Four Books were commonly recited at the same time as these primers. For students of the lower classes, these texts served to provide functional literacy. By the age of fifteen, students continuing to advanced education would have memorized the Four Books and the Five Classics and have started to learn the rudiments of the eight-legged essay for the state examinations.[152] Reading comprehension and writing were taught simultaneously from the age of ten.

Different elementary textbooks were used corresponding to the age of the child and their language abilities. Moreover, the content of the textbooks reflected the different intent of the authors in the development of specific abilities. Lacking in the current discussion are specific simple theories about educational practice, methods, and content and how these occurred through the textbooks. This will be discussed in the next chapters with a focus on how the three main schools of Qing dynasty educational thought influenced learning through textbooks as manifested in the *Treasury*.

CHAPTER TWO

STRUCTURE: APPROACHING PRACTICAL LEARNING

The *Treasury* was a popular primer during the Qing dynasty, a time of intellectual shift from the dominant framework of Neo-Confucianism to the emerging ideas of evidential scholarship. The question of "what knowledge is worth learning" was a point of contention. Despite divergent views, Zhu Xi and Wang Yangming both advocated the search for principle (*li* 理). This was encapsulated by the concept of "investigation of things and extension of knowledge" (*gewu zhizhi* 格物致知) in the *Great Learning*, which Zhu defined as an objective inquiry of the principle of all things and Wang as the rectification of the mind to accord with the principle. In contrast, evidential scholars argued for broader scholarship—moral, textual, and worldly. There was clearly a dichotomy between the educational agendas of the "extension of knowledge" for sagehood and "extensive knowledge" (*boxue* 博學) advocated in practical learning. A textbook produced in such an atmosphere necessarily reflected these diverse ideas.

The original author of the *Treasury*, Cheng Dengji, compiled the text based on his firsthand experience of student needs. However, it was Zou Shengmai who crafted the text resulting in its popularity in the Qing period. As a scholar-publisher, Zou recognized the broad intellectual audience and through his editing created a versatile textbook to meet multiple educational demands. His short foreword below offers a description of his intentions:

> 欣逢至治，擢取鴻才，時藝之外，兼命賦詩，使非典籍先悉於胸中，未有揮毫不窘於腕下者。然華子之《類賦》、姚氏之《類林》，卷帙浩繁，艱於記憶。惟程允升先生《幼學》一書，誠多士饋貧之糧， 而制科度津之筏也。但碎金積玉，原屬無多；則摘艷薰香，應增未備，庶幾文人，足供驅使。奈坊刻所補，殊不雅馴者，老成能知去取，固誚續貂；若初學未識從違，反亡全璧，一經習染，俗不可醫，即用針砭，難痊痼疾矣。爰采匯書，各增編末。文必絕佳，片箋片釋；經期可誦，一字一編。茲汰舊發之解離，易新詮之確當，詳所當詳而不厭其繁，略所當略而不嫌其簡，務歸明晰，一閱了然。如藍田之琬琰，玄圃之琳瑯，能令見者寶之，各欲私為枕秘，因顏之曰「瓊林」。覽是書者，其以余言為不謬否？時乾隆二十五年歲在庚辰仲春上浣，霧閣鄒聖脈梧岡氏書於寄傲山房。
>
> We are fortunate to have an excellent government that promotes and selects exceptional talent based on composing eight-legged essays and poetry. [However] wielding the brush for literary compositions is challenging without a comprehensive understanding of the authoritative texts within the breast. Hua Ximin's 華希閔 *Guang shilei fu* (Extended rhapsodies on categorized matters) and Yu Lizheng's 于立政 *Lei lin* (Forest of categories) being voluminous and prolix, are difficult to memorize. Only Cheng Yunsheng's *Youxue xuzhi* (Required knowledge for elementary learning) offers real assistance to examinees like food for the needy and a raft for crossing the river. Flowery expressions in poetry and prose are limited. Handpicking the splendid and infusing with fragrance to supplement deficiency makes a compelling reference for budding literati. But errors abound in the supplements [to the *Required Knowledge for Elementary Learning*] inscribed by workshops. The experienced who would discern the parts to discard or adopt attribute the errors to the supplements. However, novices ignorant of what is correct or contrary will inadvertently lose the entire treasure. Habits once established become irremediable customs. Even with the use of acupuncture, recovery from such chronic condition is difficult. Hence, a compilation of texts has been

> selected to provide supplements at the end of each chapter. The writing must be distinctively good, with annotation and explanation respectively. Each word and chapter can be recited in time. Here, the obsolete interpretations are eliminated, replaced with precise elucidations of new insights. Every detail is elaborated upon without tiring of its intricacies, while every summary is concise without disdain for its simplicity. The objective is to restore clarity, ensuring immediate comprehension at a glance. Like the jade tablets and pendants from Lantian and Xuanpu, this work will be treasured and collected by every reader. This book is therefore titled "Treasury" (literally, "Forest of jades"). May the reader be my judge. Written by Zou Shengmai (Wugang) at the Noble Mountain Residence in the first third of the second lunar month during the twenty-fifth year of the Qianlong reign (1760).[1]

In revising the original text, Zou Shengmai had students in mind as his readership. He identified their need for an accurate and accessible reference text. Zou was aware of the high level of literary skills required for examination success—candidates needed to draw on an extensive knowledge of ancient texts for composing poems and essays. The *Guang shilei fu* 廣事類賦 (Extended rhapsodies on categorized matters) and *Lei lin* 類林 (Forest of categories) were encyclopedic anthologies (*leishu* 類書) of poetic phrases,and his book would be a similar compendium of elegant terms and classical allusions. However, Zou focused on providing a text that could be recited and effectively assist in writing compositions. Zou's foreword specifically highlights his ideas of the educational needs in the Qing dynasty and his reworking of the form and content of the *Treasury* accordingly.

This chapter argues that the composition of the *Treasury* caters to the educational ideas of the school of principle and practical learning. The investigation surveys the concepts behind the macro-structure of the text: the categorization and ordering of content, the chapter structure, and the interlinear annotations. The approach will work backwards through the structure to extrapolate how the text may have particularly resonated with the broadened knowledge base and empirical inquiry advocated by practical learning educators.

2.1 CATEGORIZATION: THE BROADER WORLDVIEW

The *Treasury* was designed as a reference book of literary terms and allusions for composition. The *Treasury* is composed of 1329 sets of parallel sentences, also called "couplets," in a style of rhythmically balanced prose (*pianti* 駢體). The text is divided into four sections, with a total of thirty-three chapters, published as four volumes. When opening the book, the reader first encounters the table of contents (see Table 1). The organization of extensive material presents a classification system that would be both familiar and novel to the ten-year-old reader. Arranged in subject categories (*lei* 類), the text may be considered a type of encyclopedic anthology (*leishu*).[2] These categories not only served a practical function but also educated the reader in certain values and views of the world. As Xiaofei Tian explains:

> A *leishu* is thus much more than just a chest of drawers serving as a repository of knowledge and material aids to memory: it possesses in miniature the dimensions of the cosmos. Like the imperial garden, from which a *leishu* frequently takes its name, it is supposed to present an organized system of knowledge of the world, reflecting an orderly universe in its comprehensive, structured arrangement of ideas, concepts, and things.[3]

Being the first encyclopedia for the young student, the volume and scope of organized material in the *Treasury* would form a significant first impression of a worldview anchored in educational thought.

The *Treasury* unsurprisingly begins by introducing ancient cosmology derived from the exegetical tradition of the *Changes* through the triad between Heaven, the Earth, and humanity, known as the "three resources" (*sancai* 三才). "Heaven" (*tian* 天) in the Confucian context had several meanings: the universe, the sky, the lord of the spiritual and material worlds, the source of moral principles (the Way), and the ultimate reality.[4] However, it would be unjustified to say the first chapter, "Astronomy," provided an understanding of the origins of the world. Rather, the child is introduced to the significance of Heaven within the Confucian tradition and related ideas through the classical allusions. The following chapter, "Land and Environs," includes material about "Earth" (*di* 地), also a loaded concept connoting the co-creator of earthly life with Heaven and the physical terrain. This pivots into the "Years and Seasons"

Table 1. The table of contents of the *Treasury of Elementary Learning*—the chapters are divided into four sections.[90] The number of original and supplemented couplets for each chapter are provided in brackets on the left and right, respectively.

Section One	Section Two	Section Three	Section Four
1. 天文 Astronomy (32, 11) 2. 地輿 Land and Environs (37, 10) 3. 歲時 Years and Seasons (39, 10) 4. 朝廷 The Court (17, 10) 5. 文臣 Civil Officials (40, 13) 6. 武職 Military Officials (23, 12)	7. 祖孫父子 Grandparent, Grandchildren, Parent and Child (24, 12) 8. 兄弟 Elder and Younger Brothers (13, 11) 9. 夫婦 Husbands and Wives (19, 8) 10. 叔侄 Uncles and Nephews (6, 6) 11. 師生 Teachers and Pupils (9, 8) 12. 朋友賓主 Fellows, Friends, Guests and Hosts (22, 12) 13. 婚姻 Marriage (19, 7) 14. 女子 Women (22, 15) 15. 外戚 Relations by Marriage (11, 10) 16. 老壽幼誕 Birth and Birthdays (22, 12) 17. 身體 Human Body (61, 13) 18. 衣服 Attire and Apparel (24, 12)	19. 人事 Human Affairs (116, 12) 20. 飲食 Food and Drink (27, 11) 21. 宮室 Buildings and Rooms (24, 10) 22. 器用 Tools (35, 11) 23. 珍寶 Gems and Treasures (24, 10) 24. 貧富 Poverty and Wealth (20, 10) 25. 疾病死喪 Diseases and Death (40, 12)	26. 文事 Literary Matters (40, 13) 27. 科第 The Civil Examinations (16, 12) 28. 製作 Inventions (20, 7) 29. 藝術 Skilled Trades (14, 12) 30. 訟獄 Criminal Proceedings (18, 12) 31. 釋道鬼神 Buddhism, Daoism, Ghosts and Spirits (30, 12) 32. 鳥獸 Birds and Beasts (70, 13) 33. 花木 Flowers and Trees (35, 11)

chapter, covering festivals of the year, such as the solar terms.[5] A connection is made between the Way of Heaven and Earth giving rise to the natural phenomena governing human activity. The content then transitions to the human realm. Even the Qing dynasty's imperially commissioned encyclopedia, the *Collection of Books Past and Present* (completed 1706), placed human relations after Heaven and Earth—the 10,040 sections (*juan*) being divided into six categories of heavenly manifestations, earthly forms, normative human relationships, broad knowledge, texts and learning, and officialdom and statecraft.[6]

The worldview of humanity's innate nature arising from Heaven and leading to the unity between humanity and the universe was the backbone of the cosmology in the Cheng-Zhu school and the school of heart-mind.[7] In the Qing, harmony between Heaven, Earth, and humanity was the consensus. Although Qing scholars later developed variants on the exact relationship between principle, the Way, life, and the cosmos,[8] such subtleties were not the express concerns of elementary learning and certainly were not evidenced in the categories of this text. While Zhu Xi's *Elementary Learning* opens with reference to humanity and Heaven, this simply formed the premise for education and was not further elaborated.[9] The first sentences of other primers like the *Thousand Character Essay* and the *Three Character Classic* also merely touched on metaphysical concepts of nature and the universe as a taster for future learning.

Instead, humankind is the main theme in the *Treasury* and can be considered the staple of the elementary textbook genre. The categories related to human relationships in the *Treasury* are also consistent with the common format of morally educational primers. As Kelleher notes, the defining structure and content of the *Elementary Learning* were that of "clarifying human relations." The five relationships are known as the "all-pervading Way" (*da dao* 達道), as both the ancient and modern world were to practice such moral obligations to form a unity with Heaven and Earth, according to Zhu Xi's annotation to the *Doctrine of the Mean*.[10] Indeed, Rosemont Jr. and Ames propose that the early Confucian moral vision was a form of role ethics, as moral personhood was the sum of one's roles in life.[11] All three schools of thought covered in Chapter 1 viewed ethical conduct in interpersonal relationships (*lunli* 倫理) as the foundation of elementary education. Qing dynasty primary educators were also unanimous in prioritizing this subject, as Chen Hongmou states: "All in the world have human relationships, hence all education relates to our relationships" 天下無倫外之人，故自無倫外之學.[12] The structure of the first and second sections in the text is thus consistent with the Confucian framework of social relations.

What was unique to the *Treasury* was the order of the five relationships. As the opening line of the second section states: "What are the five fundamental relationships? Sovereign-subject, parent-child, elder sibling-younger sibling, husband-wife, and friend-friend" 何謂五倫，君臣、父子、兄弟、夫婦、朋友.[13] Prioritizing the sovereign-subject relationship differed from most primers that ranked the parent-child relationship first.[14] However, precedence for the ruler corresponded with the format of encyclopedias, such as the seventh-century *Yiwen leiju* 藝文類聚 (Classified extracts from literature), which began with chapters about the concepts of Heaven, Earth, and the imperial family.[15] These imperially commissioned encyclopedias not only espoused the established cosmological views but can also be interpreted as reinforcing the political legitimacy.[16] From the cosmological perspective, the sovereign was entitled the "Son of Heaven" and regarded as having been tasked by Heaven to govern the people and connect the three realms.[17] Politically, the ruler had been conferred the Mandate of Heaven (*tianming* 天命), a concept based on the Four Books and the *Documents*. Dynastic change and the authority of the ruler were dependent on their moral cultivation as a reflection of Heaven. The *Treasury* was written in the late Ming dynasty rather than following the Manchu conquest, but this concept would have been favored by the new rulers. Such a consideration was important for the editor and publisher in the period of the high Qing literary inquisitions. Thus, the *Treasury*'s fourth chapter focuses on the emperor—defined as the leader of all under Heaven.[18] Being an elementary text, the sovereign-subject relationship here also reflects a forward-looking emphasis on moral service beyond the family and a political consciousness that practical learning sought to instill. Underlining service to the state, the subsequent chapters devote much coverage to the role of officials, divided into the civil and military sectors. Officialdom thus concludes the first section, which comprises 20 percent of the text and is shorter than the other sections. This deliberate division caps off the concepts of Heaven, Earth, and the government.

The second section, which predominantly deals with the five relationships, is the longest of the four sections. The familial bonds of parent-child, siblings, and husband-wife are first addressed separately. This manifests the centrality of family reverence (*xiao* 孝) and fraternity (*ti* 悌)—the "root of humanity" (*ren* 仁), as it is explained in the *Analects*.[19] Although seemingly divergent, the "Uncles and Nephews" chapter is but an extension of the nuclear family. Outside the family, the child would encounter teachers and friends at school, which are the next two categories. Although not part of the five fundamental relationships, the teacher-student bond was crucial to understanding one's roles in life, as the *Records on Ritual* explains: "Teachers are not the same kind of thing as the five kinship groups, but these kinship groups could not be close and cordial without the lessons of the teacher" 師無當於五服，五服弗得不親.[20] The reader is then provided with further treatment of the husband-wife relationship in the chapters "Marriage" and "Women" and even "Relations by Marriage." This is explained by Chen Hongmou, who observed that many young men at the time were married before the age of twenty.[21] Believing that they would have lacked knowledge on managing a family due to their age, Chen felt compelled to provide such instruction in his compilation on primary education. The *Treasury* was likely preparing readers for their future roles and educating them on the moral significance of the roles. From the Confucian framework, the spousal relationship was considered the progenitor of all human relations.[22] The emphasis here on the significance of the family echoes the teachings in the *Great Learning*, which emphasizes that moral self-cultivation results in a harmonious order within the family, which in turn leads to national stability and ultimately world peace.[23]

Following the categories related to human relations, which outlines the "all-pervading Way" that enables humanity to be a co-creator with Heaven and Earth, the reader then begins the journey of life in the "Birth and Birthdays" chapter. There is a shift from the Way of Heaven to humanity in Section One, and here there is a transition from the moral life to daily life before the end of the second section. These are the practicalities of living. The later chapters, the "Human Body" and "Attire and Apparel," remain linked to the central notion of roles in this section. The body was perceived as a part of one's parents, thus care of the body was related to reverence for the family.[24] Clothing, too, was a key aspect of identity in society; for example, the capping ceremony at the age of twenty represented maturity for a young man.[25] However, the content in these chapters markedly differed from the rituals of behavior that characterized Zhu's textbooks and the moral internalization emphasized by Wang Yangming.

The categories in Sections Three and Four noticeably depart from the Cheng-Zhu school of thought, although the material remains humanistic. The theme in Section Three is the quotidian life, and the tone is decidedly practical. The first chapter in Section Three, which is also the longest chapter in the book, is "Human Affairs." The category reemphasizes the relational ethics of Section Two but covers the specifics of speech acts (ritual language will be covered in the next chapter) and prescribes attitudes to the daily matters of life that are based on Confucian values. The turn to mundane human considerations becomes even clearer in a quick survey of the rest of the section. Topics such as diet, buildings, and tools read like the Chinese idiom "*yishizhuxing* 衣食住行" (literally meaning "clothing, food, housing, and transport") referring to the basic needs of life. These point to a materialistic view of the world, particularly in "Gems and Treasures" and "Poverty and Wealth," possibly reflecting the economic revival of the late Ming dynasty and the resultant upward social mobility. Despite the promise of a manual for everyday life, the content remained consistent with previous sections—literary terms classical allusions and aphorisms. Rather than providing education on a healthy diet, "Food and Drink" relates to the names of common staples and customs surrounding eating, such as the etiquette in entertaining a guest. Similarly, "Gems and Treasures" covers names of prized treasures in history as well as stories and sayings of historical personages on riches and valuables. As expected, the Confucian values of frugality and ethics surpassing material desires are touted, which is further stressed in the following chapter "Poverty and Wealth." Beyond the moralistic platitudes, however, the realities of human desires are openly acknowledged. A Cheng-Zhu school purist may have omitted such content from elementary education, citing the *Analects*: "The exemplary person schemes for the Way, not for food . . . worries about the Way, not poverty. 君子謀道不謀食，君子憂道不憂貧"[26] However, an adherent of practical learning would likely concur with the importance of introducing young readers to the concerns of adult life and broadening their horizons. From the perspective of elementary education, such content challenges the Cheng-Zhu tradition of shielding the child from exposure to the negative aspects of life to "nurture the correct." This turn to the concrete and verifiable facts of life was characteristic of practical statecraft thought. Section Three then aptly ends with the grim reality of "Diseases and Death" and completes the life cycle.

The categories in Section Four relate to the predominant view on the order of learning. The *Three Character Classic* explicitly stated: "Learn to love parents and elders, then the rest; That is, master the numbers and read the texts" 首孝弟，次見聞。知某數，識某文.[27] Learning the five fundamental relationships and rituals is the priority in elementary education, followed by the literature, arts, and other hobbies. As Confucius taught: "With energy to spare, they should then study the literature and arts" 行有餘力則以學文.[28] The first chapter here, accordingly, is "Literary Matters" followed by the "Civil Examinations." Acknowledging that the audience may not necessarily be pursuing officialdom, the "Inventions" and "Skilled Trades" chapters point to a different career path. The categories of "Criminal Proceedings" and "Buddhism, Daoism, Ghosts, and Spirits" reveal popular attitudes and beliefs during the late Ming and Qing periods. However, the Confucian orientation of the *Treasury* is evidenced by the inclusion of such chapters in the final section—these topics not given priority. Such an attitude is expressed by Confucius, who once replied to a question on spirits by saying: "When you do not yet know how to serve human beings, how can you serve the spirits" 未能事人，焉能事鬼?[29] In other words, the understanding of human relations and the development of interpersonal skills prevail.

The text is brought to completion with a return to nature, but now through the "myriad things" (*wanwu* 萬物) in the chapters of "Birds and Beasts" and "Flowers and Trees." Far from being an introduction to zoology and botany, the material personifies animals and plants through an anthropomorphic perspective. This is rooted in moral thinking and earlier texts such as the *Shijing* 詩經 (Odes), which showcases the literary use of animals and plants to provide an analogy to the underlying message of the poem. Indeed, in the *Odes* Confucius had explained that the names of animals and plants were secondary to social learning.[30] Evidently, the ethical dimensions were prioritized, and the learning of flora and fauna helped to clarify Confucian values rather than merely focus on the natural sciences. In placing these chapters last, the *Treasury* has also been structured with such priorities in mind. Wang Yangming also discussed the human-centered way of relating to the outer world:

> 君臣也，夫婦也，朋友也，以至於山川鬼神鳥獸草木也，莫不實有以親之，以達吾一體之仁，然後吾之明德始無不明，而真能以天地萬物爲一體矣。
>
> Everything from ruler, minister, husband, wife, and friends to mountains, rivers, spiritual beings, birds, animals, and plants should be truly loved in order to realize my humanity that forms one body with them, and then my clear character will be completely manifested and I will really form one body with Heaven, Earth, and the myriad things.[31]

Also listed last in his description of the myriad things, Wang nonetheless considers creatures and plants as an integral part of realizing the innate nature. Ultimately, the reader returns to the greater moral life by the end of the text.

This overview of categories in the *Treasury* reveals an invigorating array of knowledge and the considerations at hand. The *Treasury* begins with the cosmos and then moving on to moral living through one's social roles and responsibilities, the necessities of life, and finally specialized knowledge or skills. In a nutshell, the pages of this elementary textbook unite the moral and the mundane, the philosophical and the practical. These polarizing undercurrents dominated the early-mid Qing intellectual scene and played out in the production and commentary of texts. A new practical-use encyclopedia that emerged during the late fifteenth to the sixteenth centuries was brought on by the Ming period economic revival, an expanded print culture, and restriction of examination quota leading to many Chinese serving as clerks without examination degrees. In documenting the phenomena in the Ming period compendia and encyclopedias, Elman observes that "investigating things and broad knowledge became regular bedfellows" in these texts.[32] The broader popular audience of such encyclopedias demanded a reorientation to literati customs, home rituals, and practical learning. These social factors were also relevant to the author and editor of the *Treasury*. Indeed, the *Treasury*'s thirty-three categories are within the range of the late imperial daily-use encyclopedias, which typically ranged from twenty to forty major categories.

A reading of the *Treasury*'s categories based on Zhu Xi's idea of the extension of knowledge would point to the holistic worldview. The chapters demonstrate the integration of transcendental and material to achieve the realization that the universal principle pervaded all things from Heaven and Earth to flora and fauna. However, one cannot ignore that the categories do diverge from the Neo-Confucian tradition and manifestly incorporate the concerns of practical learning. The *Treasury* was thus an encyclopedic work for children in the sense of structuring knowledge into distinctive categories. The contents of elementary textbooks were not often divided into knowledge categories. Of the standard literacy primer trilogy—the *Three Character Classic*, the *Hundred Surnames,* and the *Thousand Character Essay*—only the latter is sectioned based on the rhyme of the phrases. Primers for poetry training were generally structured by the various rhymes,[33] history textbooks were chronological, and instructions in moral education texts were arranged by topics such as interpersonal relations, moral qualities, or areas of daily practice.

The broad classification system of the *Treasury* resembles the macro-structure of ancient Chinese dictionaries—grouping by semantic relations.[34] A survey of representative Ming-Qing period dictionaries of lexical expressions intended for the composition of poetry and antithetical couplets also reveal similar categories, for example Heaven, geography, time sequence, grasses and trees, and birds and beasts.[35] These lexicons were becoming important tools employed by the literati to refute orthodox learning, highlighting the increasing link to the precise scholarship of evidential learning. This becomes more apparent in the micro-structure of the chapters, as discussed in the next section.

2.2 CHAPTER STRUCTURE: A LEARNER'S DICTIONARY

Wang Yun's *Character Learning for Young Children* that appeared in the early nineteenth century is arguably the epitome of the evidential scholarship approach to elementary learning. Wang Yun based his textbook content and structure mainly on the ancient character dictionary *Explaining Simple Graphs and Analyzing Complex Graphs*, combining the principles of philology and character learning for children. Although the annotated *Treasury* predates *Character Learning for Young Children* by almost a century, the design of the text was already reflecting and shaping learning in a new direction.

On the surface, the *Treasury* is a collection of classical allusions positioned as reference material for composition. However, the text was more than a reference book in the wider context of Qing educational thought, serving as a guide toward an expanded focus on the written tradition. Moreover, the emphasis on definitions and etymologies in the text resonates with a reorientation toward the analysis of terms in the broader worldview. The structure of the chapters corresponds with the strategy behind the categorization of knowledge—working within the Cheng-Zhu orthodoxy but simultaneously introducing new elements. Not only was knowledge broadened beyond moral principles, but there also was a noticeable shift in pedagogy in the elementary text. This was consistent with the growing emphasis on pre-Song textual learning and the revival of encyclopedias as a repository of things, events, and phenomena in ancient texts from the late Ming period.[36] This section argues that the *Treasury* also presented as a learner's dictionary. The *Treasury* reflects broader sources of knowledge through the content while simultaneously familiarizing students with the tools to read such ancient texts through the emphasis on definitions and etymologies.

The content is similar for each chapter: an introductory line is followed by terms, polite expressions, classical allusions, admonitions, and a concluding line based on the chapter topic. All content is arranged as couplets. Zou Shengmai's supplementary couplets were provided at the end of each chapter, and its internal order attempts to follow the same logic as the original couplets. The few Western studies on the *Treasury* to date have invariably mentioned the comprehensive nature of the material and the unique style of the couplets.[37] However, Lockhart's 1893 translation separates the parallel sentences and does not include the annotations. To provide an accurate impression of the structure of the *Treasury* and as a background to further discussion on the order of information and annotations, I have translated the couplets and annotations (indented) of one chapter in the text. The first two sections are seemingly more related to Neo-Confucian concepts, so the twenty-third chapter "Gems and Treasures" from the third section is used to illustrate the intertwining educational ideas in the text. Translation of the original couplets are below; a translation of Zou's supplementary couplets can be found in the Appendix.

Chapter 23. "Gems and Treasures" (*zhenbao* 珍寶)[38]

1 山川之精英，每洩為至寶；乾坤之瑞氣，恆結為奇珍。

The vital essence of the mountains and rivers often exudes the finest treasures. The propitious energy of Heaven and Earth perpetually condenses into wondrous gems.

精英，精粹之英。瑞氣，和祥之氣。至寶、奇珍，乃天地山川靈氣所鐘。

The "vital essence" refers to pure and excellent essence. The "propitious energy" refers to harmonious and auspicious energy. The "finest treasures" and "wondrous gems" are thus concentrations of the ethereal airs of Heaven, Earth, mountains, and rivers.

2 故玉足以庇（音秘）嘉穀，珠可以禦火災。

Therefore, jade can protect (pronunciation: *bi*) fine grains, and pearls can ward off fiery disasters.

《左》：王孫圉曰：「玉足以庇蔭嘉穀，使無水旱之災，則寶之。珠可以禦火災，則寶之。」

Zuo Tradition: Wang Sunyu states: "Jade is treasured for shielding fine grains, such that there are no floods or droughts. Pearls are treasured for warding off fiery disasters."

3 魚目豈可混珠，碔砆（音武夫）焉能亂玉。

How can fish eyes be confounded with pearls? How can the green stones (pronunciation: *wu fu*) be confused with jade?

《廣州記》：鯨魚目似明月珠。《埤雅》：龍珠在額，蛟珠在皮，蛇珠在口，鱉珠在足，蚌珠在腹。

Records on Guangzhou: Whale's eyes are like the "bright moon" pearl. *Supplemented Erya*: The dragon's pearl is at the forehead, the *jiao* dragon's pearl is in the skin, the snake's pearl is in the mouth, the turtle's pearl is at the foot, the clam's pearl is in the abdomen.

魏文候與西門豹論云：「夫物多相類而非也。白骨疑象，碔砆類玉，此皆似是而非者。」

Lord Wen of Wei discussed with Ximen Bao: "There are many objects that look similar. White bone can be mistaken for ivory and green stones for jade—all these seem the same but are not."

4 黃金生於麗水，白銀出自朱提（音殊時）。

Gold arises from the Li River. Silver comes from Shu shi (pronunciation: *shu shi*).

麗水在益州中，有金如糠，浮出水上。

The Li River in Yizhou province has gold that floats on the water like husks.

朱提，山名，在四川，多產白銀。

Shu shi is the name of a mountain in Sichuan province where much silver is produced.

5 曰孔方，曰家兄，俱為錢號；曰青蚨（音符），曰鵝眼，亦是錢名。

"Holey square" and "my elder brother" are both terms for money.[39] "Water beetles" (pronunciation: *fu*) and "goose eyes" are also names of currency.

魯褒《錢神論》：「錢之為體，有乾坤之象，親之如兄，字曰孔方。洛中朱衣，當途學士，見我家兄，不敢仰視。」

Lu Bao's *Discourse on the Spirit of Money*: "Money in its form, has its *yin* and *yang*, is intimate as one's elder brother, its name is "holey square." Influential officials in Luoyang and eminent scholars who meet my brother are humbled."

《搜神記》：南方有蟲，其形如蟬，取其子，母即飛來。以母血塗錢八十一文，以子血塗錢八十一文，或先用母錢，或先用子錢，皆復飛歸，輪環無已。故淮南子之術，以之還錢，名曰青蚨。《宋略》：沈慶之啟通私鑄，而錢大壞矣。每千長不滿三寸，謂之鵝眼錢。

In Search of the Supernatural: In the south, there is an insect that resembles a cicada. When one of the young insects is taken, the mother insect will immediately fly to her young. Daub the mother insect's blood on eight-one coins, and the young insect's blood on another set of eight-one coins. Regardless of whether the money with the mother's blood or the young blood is used first, they will all continue to return to one another. Thus, Master Huainan speaks of this as a way of recovering money, referring to cash as "water beetles."[40] The *Summary of Song Dynasty History*: Shen Qingzhi started minting coins privately but the coinage was of poor quality.

A thousand coins stacked no more than three inches high and were named "goose eye" coins.

6 可貴者明月夜光之珠，可珍者璠璵（音煩於）琬（淵上聲）琰（鹽上聲）之玉。

The "bright moon" and the "luminous night" refer to prized pearls. *Fanyu* (pronunciation: *fan yu*) and "rounded (*yuan*, rising tone) and pointed (*yan*, rising tone) tablets" of jade are precious.

《搜神記》：隋侯出行，見蛇被傷，救而治之，其後蛇銜明珠以報，其夜光可以照堂。

In Search of the Supernatural: While the ruler of Sui was traveling, he encountered a wounded snake, which he rescued and cured. Later, the snake returned with a bright pearl in its mouth in gratitude. The nocturnal luminescence of the pearl could illuminate a hall.

孔子曰：「美哉璠璵，遠而望之煥若也，近而視之瑟若也，一則理勝，一則孚勝。」《書》：「弘璧琬琰在西序。」

Confucius said: "Beautiful is the *fanyu* jade, seen as if shimmering from afar, as if pristine on closer inspection. On the one hand, the vein lines are superior; on the other hand, the external lustre is superior." The *Documents*: "The large round-and-convex jade and the rounded and pointed jade tablets, are in the western side-space."[41]

7 宋人以燕石為玉，什襲緹（音題）巾之中；楚王以璞玉為石，兩刖（音月）卞和之足。

A man from Song mistook a stone from Yan for jade and wrapped it in layers of orange-red (pronunciation: *ti*) silk. The rulers of Chu mistook rough jade for stone and twice maimed (pronunciation: *yue*) the feet of Bian He.

《說苑》：宋之愚人得燕石，以為至寶，以革櫃緹巾什襲藏之。有客聞而觀焉，主人齋戒七日，沐浴啟視，客笑曰：「石也。」宋人怒，藏之愈固。

Garden of Eloquence: An ignorant person from Song mistook a stone from Yan for the finest treasure. He wrapped it in layers of orange-red silk and stored it in a leather case. When a guest wished to view the gem, the owner fasted for seven days and bathed before opening the case. On inspection, the guest laughed, "This is just a stone." The man from Song was furious and stored it away even more securely.

楚人卞和遊荊山，得璞玉，獻之楚厲王。王使玉人相之，曰：「石也。」王怪其詐，刖其左足。有獻之武王，亦以為詐，刖其右足。

A man from Chu named Bian He was traveling through the Jing Mountains when he found rough jade. He presented this to King Li of Chu. The king ordered for an appraisal by the jade inspector, who said: "This is a stone." Blamed for such fraud, the king punished the man by amputating his left foot. Bian He later presented the same jade to King Wu of Chu who also considered it a fake and punished him by amputating the right foot.

8 惠王之珠，光能照乘；和氏之壁，價重連城。

King Wei of Hui's pearls could illuminate the length of carriages. The jade disc of Master He was worth cities.

《史記》：齊威王、魏惠王會田於郊。魏王曰：「齊有寶乎？」齊王曰：「無有。」魏王曰：「寡人國雖小，尚有徑寸之珠，照車前後各十二乘者十顆。豈齊大國而無寶乎？」

Records of the Historian: King Wei of Qi and King Hui of Wei were hunting together in the countryside. The king of Wei asked, "Does Qi have any treasures?" The king of Qi replied, "No." The king of Wei said, "My state is small and yet it has ten pearls, each measuring an inch in diameter, and able to illuminate a distance twelve carriages long. How can the large state of Qi be without treasures?"

《史記》：趙惠文王得楚和氏璧，秦昭王請以十五城易之。藺相如捧壁入秦，見秦王無償城意，欲以壁擊柱。王恐碎壁，不敢逼。因怒髮衝冠，完璧歸趙。

Records of the Historian: King Huiwen of Zhao attained the jade disc of Master He from Chu, which King Zhao of Qin requested in exchange for fifteen cities. Lin Xiangru entered Qin clasping the jade. When he observed that the king of Qin had no intention of fulfilling his promise, he threatened to smash the jade against a pillar. The king dared not coerce Lin in fear of damaging the jade. Due to Lin's burst of outrage, the jade disc returned to Zhao intact.

9 鮫（音交）人泣淚成珠，宋人削玉為楮。

The mermaid (pronunciation: *jiao*) wept tears that became pearls. The man from Song carved jade into a mulberry leaf.

《博物志》：「水國鮫人出寓人間賣綃，將去，從主人索一器，泣淚成珠滿盤，以謝主人。」

Treatise on Curiosities: The mermaid of the waterways came to dwell among the humans selling raw silk. About to depart, she asked the owner for a plate. She then wept tears that turned into pearls filling the plate in gratitude to the owner.

《列子》：宋人有為其君以玉為楮葉，三年而成，雜之楮葉中，不辨。

Master Lie: A person from Song made a mulberry leaf out of jade for his ruler. It took three years to complete and was indistinguishable when mixed with real mulberry leaves.[42]

10 賢乃國家之寶，儒為席上之珍。

Worthy ministers are the treasures of the state. Scholars are narrators of precious principles.

《漢詁纂疏》：秦欲伐楚，秦使觀楚之寶器。奚恤謂使者曰：「客欲觀楚之寶器乎？楚之所寶，即賢臣也，惟大國之所觀。」

Collected Commentaries of Han Dynasty Proclamations: The state of Qin wanted to attack the state of Chu and sent an envoy to view Chu's treasures. Xi Xu told the envoy: "Do you wish to view Chu's treasures? What Chu treasures are its worthy ministers, who your esteemed state now sees."

《家語》：魯哀公問儒行，孔子對曰：「儒有席上之珍，以待聘。」

School Sayings of Confucius: Duke Ai of Lu asked Confucius about the conduct of the scholar. Confucius replied, "The scholar has precious [principles] to narrate in anticipation of appointment."[43]

11 王者聘賢，束帛加璧；真儒抱道，懷瑾握瑜。

A king sends a roll of silk with a jade disc when appointing a worthy. A true scholar embraces the Way as they would keep the *jin* jade and hold to the *yu* jade.

《漢書》：武帝使使束帛加璧，以蒲裹車輪而迎申公。

History of the Former Han: Emperor Wu of Han sent an envoy with a roll of silk and a jade disc, and covered the carriage wheels with bulrushes to welcome Duke Shen.

《楚辭》：「懷瑾握瑜。」〔釋〕瑾、瑜，皆美玉。在衣為懷，在手為握。

Lyrics of Chu: "To keep the *jin* and hold the *yu*." Gloss: *Jin* and *yu* are brilliant jades. Keeping something in one's clothing is to "keep" (*huai*). Holding in one's hand is to "hold" (*wo*).

12 雍伯多緣，種玉於藍田而得美婦；太公奇遇，釣璜（音黃）於渭水而遇文王。

The fortunate Yong Bo planted jades in Lantian and married a fair wife. By a fortuitous coincidence, Tai Gong fished out a semicircular jade (pronunciation: *huang*) from the Wei River and met King Wen of Zhou.

雍伯，註詳《夫婦》。

Yong Bo, see annotation in the 'Husband and Wife' chapter.

《史記》：姜子牙年八十，釣於渭水。初下得鮒，次下得鯉，剖魚腹，中得璜玉，刻文曰：「周受命，呂佐之。」文王出獵於渭水，見老父釣，王問之曰：「叟樂此乎？」對曰：「君子樂行其志，小人樂供其事，吾非樂於漁也。」王謂左右曰：「得無是乎？」因載之後車以歸。與論政事，大悅之，曰：「吾先君太公嘗曰：『當有聖人適周，周賴以興。』子真是乎？太公望子久矣。」號太公望。

Records of the Historian: Jiang Ziya at the age of eighty was fishing in the Wei River. He initially caught a silver carp and then a common carp. Cutting open the abdomen of the fish, [he found] a semicircular jade engraved with the words: "Zhou receives Heaven's mandate, Lü assists Zhou." King Wen of Zhou was hunting at the Wei River. On seeing the old fisherman, he asked: "Old man, are you happy here?" Jiang replied: "The exemplary person is happy in working to achieve their aspiration, the petty person is happy in undertaking their tasks. I do not take joy in fishing." The King said to his attendants, "Is it possible that this is not so?" Consequently, the King drove Jiang back. When they discussed governing matters, he was most delighted, saying: "The late ruler, my grandfather, predicted: 'There will be a sage that comes to Zhou, Zhou will depend on them to prosper.' You must be the one? My grandfather has long waited for you." He was thus named the "grandfather's hope."

13 剖腹藏珠，愛財而不愛命；纏頭作錦，助舞而更助嬌。

Cutting open the abdomen to hide the pearl, cherishing possessions above life. Adorning the head with embroidery, enhancing the dancing and even more so the charm.

唐太宗曰：「吾聞西域賈胡得美珠，剖腹藏之，人皆笑彼之知愛珠，而不知愛其身也。」

Emperor Taizong of Tang said: "I have heard that when the Hu merchants in the Western regions obtain a beautiful pearl, they cut open their abdomens to hide it. People generally ridicule them—in their greed for gems, they do not care for their body."

杜贈妓詩：「笑時花近眼，舞罷錦纏頭。」唐明皇折千葉桃，插於妃子鬢曰：「此花亦能助嬌。」

Du Mu's poem to the courtesan: "When smiling, the flower approaches the eye. After dancing the embroidery adorns the head." Emperor Xuanzong of the Tang dynasty broke off a multi-petalled peach blossom and placed it in the imperial concubine's hair, saying: "This flower enhances your charm."

14 孟嘗廉潔，克俾合浦還珠；相如勇忠，能使秦廷歸璧。

Meng Chang's honesty and integrity caused the pearls to return to Hepu. Xiangru's courage and loyalty induced the court of Qin to return the jade disc.

漢合浦縣不產穀而出珠，民嘗采珠以易米。浦之太守貪污，珠漸徙去交趾。及孟嘗為合浦太守，除革前弊，未逾歲，去珠復還。

Hepu county during the Han dynasty produced pearls rather than crops. The people would exchange pearls for grain. The governor of Hepu was corrupt and the pearls were gradually transported to Jiaozhi. When Meng Chang became governor of Hepu, he eliminated fraudulent practices and the pearls were returned within a year.

相如，詳上「連城」。

On Lin Xiangru, see the above line: "The jade disc of He was worth cities."

15 玉釵作燕飛，漢宮之異事；金錢成蝶舞，唐庫之奇傳。

The jade hairpin becoming a flying swallow was the mystery of the Han palace. Gold coins turning into dancing butterflies was a strange story of the treasury in the Tang dynasty.

漢武帝起招雲閣，有二神女遺玉釵與帝，帝以賜趙婕妤。至元鳳中，宮人猶見此釵，謀欲碎之。明旦視匣中，惟見白燕飛天而去。

When Emperor Wu of the Han dynasty began recruiting for the Cloud Pavilion, two female spirits bequeathed him with jade hairpins, which he bestowed to Zhao Jieyu. By the Yuanfeng era, a palace maid saw the hairpin and planned to destroy it. The following morning, only a white swallow was found in the box, which flew away into the sky.

唐穆宗時，禁中千葉牡丹開，有黃白蝴蝶數萬，飛集花間。上令舉網張之，得數百，視之，乃庫中金錢也。

During the reign of Emperor Muzong of the Tang dynasty, the thousand-petalled peonies were blooming in the palace and some thousands of yellow-white butterflies settled amongst the flowers. The emperor ordered their capture. After several hundred were caught, they were found to be coins of the imperial treasury.

16 廣錢固可以通神，營利乃為鬼所笑。

Much money may even move the spirits. Striving for profit makes the spirits laugh.

唐張延賞將判獄，忽案上有一帖云：「奉錢十萬貫。」延賞曰：「錢至十萬貫，可通神矣。吾懼禍及，不得不止。」

Zhang Yanshang [a magistrate] of the Tang dynasty was about to settle a case when he suddenly found a note on his desk stating: "Offering a hundred thousand strings of cash." Zhang reasoned: "Money of a hundred-thousand strings of cash could move the spirits. I must stop proceedings for fear that trouble will arise."

宋劉伯龍歷官中外，貧窶尤甚。嘗在家時，營什一之利，一鬼在旁撫掌大笑，伯龍歎曰：「貧窮固有命，今日乃為鬼所笑也。」

Liu Bolong of the Former Song dynasty served an official in the capital and the provinces, and was extremely poor. One time at home, he was scheming for marginal profits. A spirit beside him patted his hand and laughed aloud. Liu sighed, "Poverty is certainly fated. Today I have been laughed at by a spirit."

17 以小致大，謂之拋（披交切）磚（音專）引玉；貪賤失貴，謂之買櫝還珠。

To gain much from less is expressed as "casting (*fanqie*: *pi jiao*) bricks (pronunciation: *zhuan*) to attract jade." Coveting the valueless and losing the valuable is expressed as "buying the coffer and returning the pearls."

趙嘏至吳，常建以其有詩名，必遊靈岩寺，建先題二句。及嘏遊寺，為續成之。人謂建乃拋磚引玉。

Zhao Gu came to the state of Wu. Chang Jian knew of Zhao's reputation as a poet and that he would travel to the Lingyan Temple. Chang visited the temple first and wrote two lines of a poem. Zhao subsequently completed the poem when he arrived. People refer to Chang's conduct as "casting bricks to attract jade."

《韓子》：楚人賣珠，為木蘭之櫝，熏以桂柏，綴以珠玉，緝以羽翠。鄭人買其櫝還其珠，只知櫝之美，不知珠之貴。〔釋〕櫝，櫃也。

Master Han Fei: A native from Chu sold pearls in magnolia wood coffers scented with cedar and laurel, decorated with pearls and jades, stitched with greenish-blue feathers. The people from Zheng bought the coffers and returned the pearl, only appreciating the beauty of the coffers without recognizing the worth of the pearl. Gloss: A coffer is a case.

18 賢否（音鄙）罹（音離）害，如玉石俱焚；貪吝無厭，雖錙銖（音支殊）必算。

Harming both (pronunciation: *li*) the good and otherwise (pronunciation: *bi*) are like burning both the jades and stones. Insatiable greed and miserliness take account of even the last trifle (pronunciation: *zhi shu*).

《書》：「火炎昆岡，玉石俱焚。」

Documents: "When the fire blazes over the ridge of Kun, both jades and stones are burned."[44]

《說文》：錙，六銖也。（按）黃鐘一龠，容二千百黍，重十二銖，二十四銖為兩。〔釋〕極言其細微。

Explaining Simple Graphs and Analyzing Complex Graphs: One *zi* is equivalent to six *zhu*. Comment: The *yue* unit of volume holds two-thousand one-hundred glutinous millet grains, which is as heavy as twelve *zhu*, twenty-four *zhu* is one tael. Gloss: Precise description of the miniscule.

19 崔烈以錢買官，人皆惡其銅臭；秦嫂不敢視叔，自言畏其多金。

Cui Lie bought an official position and all resented his "stench of copper." The sister-in-law of Su Qin dared not look at him, and she confessed to being awed by his vast wealth.

漢靈帝開鴻都門，鬻官爵。崔烈本冀州名士，因傅母入錢五百萬，得為司徒。烈問其子鈞曰：「吾居三公，外議何如？」鈞曰：「大人少有英稱，歷位卿守，但論者嫌棄銅臭耳。」〔釋〕傅母，教帝之母。

Emperor Ling of the Han dynasty introduced the practice of selling government positions. Cui Lie who was originally a renowned scholar of Jizhou, attained the rank of Minister of Education by paying the emperor's governess five million. Cui later asked his son Jun, "I am now one of the three most senior ministers, what do the people think of this?" Jun replied, "Father, you are rarely praised. Even as an important minister, they resent the 'stench of copper'." Gloss: Governess is the lady who educates the emperor.

《國策》：蘇秦字季子，初說秦不遇，歸，妻不下機，嫂不為炊。後說趙，趙王大悅，封為武安君，受相印。將說楚，路過洛陽，嫂蛇行匍伏，四拜自跪而謝。秦曰：「嫂何前倨而後恭乎？」嫂曰：「以季子位尊而多金也。」

Strategies of the Warring States: Su Qin, formal name of Jizi, initially persuaded the king of Qin without success. Returning home, his wife ignored him while weaving and his sister-in-law refused to cook for him. He later persuaded the king of Zhao who was greatly pleased—Su was enfeoffed as Prince Wu'an and appointed as chancellor. On his way to lobby Chu, he traveled past Luoyang and his sister-in-law crawled along the ground, bowed four times, kneeled and begged forgiveness. Su asked: "Why were you arrogant before and humble now?" She replied: "Because you are distinguished and wealthy."

20 熊衮父亡，天乃雨錢助葬；仲儒家窘，天乃雨金濟貧。

When Xiong Gun's father died, the heavens rained money to assist with the burial [expenses]. When Zhongru's family was destitute, the heavens rained gold to relieve their poverty.

唐熊衮為御史大夫，奉公守法，家無私積。父死不能葬，日夜號哭。一日天雨錢十萬，以襄葬事。

Xiong Gun of the Tang dynasty was an imperial censor who was conscientious and principled, without accumulating private funds. When his father died, he did not have enough money for the burial, and he sobbed day and night. One day, the heavens rained down money worth a hundred thousand to assist with the burial costs.

《述異記》：翁仲儒家極貧，一旦天雨金十斛於其家，由是與王侯爭富。

Tales of Strange Matters: Weng Zhongru was extremely poor, one morning the heavens rained down five *hu* (an ancient unit of weight) of gold upon their home. As a result, their family wealth became comparable to that of the aristocracy.

21 漢楊震畏四知而辭金，唐太宗因懲貪而賜絹。

Yang Zhen of the Han dynasty feared the four who knew and refused the gold. Emperor Taizong of the Tang dynasty bestowed silk to rebuke the greedy official.

漢楊震舉王密為邑令，密夜懷金以饋之。密曰：「暮夜無人知。」震曰：「天知地知，你知我知，何謂無知？」密慚而退。

Yang Zhen of the Han dynasty recommended Wang Mi to the position of county magistrate. During the night, Wang brought a gift of gold, insisting: "It is late in the evening, no one will know." Yang said, "Heaven knows, earth knows, you know, and I know, how can you say no one knows." Wang was ashamed and left.

唐長孫順德受人饋絹，事覺，太宗復賜絹十匹。胡演曰：「不致罪而復賜之，何也？」上曰：「彼有人性，得絹之辱，甚於受刑。」順德聞之羞慚。

Zhangsun Shunde of the Tang dynasty accepted a bribe of silk. When he was discovered, Emperor Taizong of the Tang dynasty granted him ten bolts of silk. Hu Yan asked: "Why did you not punish him but give him more silk?" Taizong replied: "He has a conscience, the shame of receiving the silk is worse than suffering the punishment." Shunde felt remorseful on hearing this.

22 晉魯褒作《錢神論》，嘗以錢為孔方兄；王夷甫口不言錢，乃謂錢為阿堵物。

Lu Bao of the Jin dynasty wrote the *Discourse on the Spirit of Money* in which he called money "holey square" and "my elder brother." Wang Yifu who would not mention the word "money," called it "this stuff."

《錢神論》，註詳上。

On the *Discourse on the Spirit of Money*, see the annotation above.

晉王夷甫妻郭氏，喜聚斂，夷甫不悅，口不言錢。妻欲試之，以錢繞床不得行。夷甫見之，命婢取阿堵物去。〔釋〕阿堵，猶言眼前物，謂錢也。

Wang Yifu of the Jin dynasty had a wife of the surname Guo who delighted in amassing wealth to his displeasure. He refused to mention the word "money." His wife wanted to test him and placed money around his bed such that it was inaccessible. When Wang saw this, he requested the maid to take away "this stuff." Gloss: "The stuff" refers to the objects in one's sight, meaning the money.

23 然而床頭金盡，壯士無顏；囊內錢空，阮郎羞澀（音森入聲）。
However, when the money at the head of the bed is exhausted, the hero loses face. When the purse was empty of money, Ruan was ashamed.

古詩：「床頭黃金盡，壯士無顏色。」

An ancient poem: "When the money at the head of the bed is exhausted, the hero loses face."

晉阮孚持一皂囊，遊會稽，客問其中何物，孚曰：「但有一錢守囊，恐其羞澀。」

Ruan Fu of the Jin dynasty kept a black purse. While traveling in Kuaiji, guests asked him about its contents. He replied: "There is only one coin guarding the purse, for fear that it feels ashamed."

24 但匹夫不可懷壁，人生孰不愛財。
Though a common person cannot keep the jade disc, who is not fond of money?

《左》：虞叔有玉，虞公求之，不獻。既而悔曰：「匹夫無罪，懷壁其罪。焉用此以買禍也。」遂獻之。

Zuo Tradition: Yu Shu had a jadestone, which he refused to present to the Duke of Yu. Yu Shu subsequently regretted his decision, saying: "A commoner is innocent, but keeping the jade disc makes them guilty. Why incur misfortune on account of this?" He then presented the jade.

The *Treasury* was compiled within the Cheng-Zhu school ideological parameters, and a traditional Neo-Confucian reading will first be discussed before evaluating its discrepancies. Like the order of the chapters, the chapter content and structure portrayed a similar logic and worldview. This is evident even in the topic of "gems and treasures," which seemingly encourages materialist rather than moralist tendencies. Why were certain things considered "treasures"? The first line invokes the cosmic unity of Heaven and Earth that produces the gemstone, rather than its aesthetic or financial value. Moreover, the gemstones are admired for practical functions, including protecting grains, preventing fiery disasters, and refracting light.[45] In other words, the vital essence of nature and the utility of the objects are to be valued. The text also undermines the desirability of the treasure by emphasizing the difficulties of distinguishing genuine gems—fish eyes can be mistaken for pearls, a stone from Yan for jade, and Bian He's rough jade twice assessed as a common stone.

Even before the halfway point of the chapter, the tone has changed. True value, the reader is told, is moral quality—as epitomized by the worthy minister and the scholar. What is to be treasured is not the gemstone but morality—a true scholar embraces the Way as if holding onto jade. Gems are merely used to express respect, as the minister of character cannot be bribed. The gemstone also appears secondary in the following classical allusions about Lin Xiangru 藺相如 (fl. third century BCE) and Meng Chang 孟嘗 (fl. 125–144), as their integrity and loyalty take precedence. Indeed, the transformation of the jade hairpin and gold coins points to the ephemeral nature of these material possessions, turning into the theme of guarding against greed. Those who seek fame and fortune are disdained by spirits ("Striving for profit makes the spirits laugh") and people (resenting the "stench of copper"). Even though Su Qin's 蘇秦 (d. 317 BCE) sister-in-law expresses respect, she is painted as a sycophant ("crawled along the ground, bowed four times, kneeled"). Multiple exemplars are cited as evidence of the importance of moral cultivation over wealth, such as Xiong Gun 熊袞 (853–922), Weng Zhongru 翁仲儒 (dates unknown), Yang Zhen 楊震 (d. 124), and Wang Yifu 王夷甫 (255–311). Zou Shengmai's supplemented couplets are arranged in the same way (see Appendix). He begins with the names of gems, then highlights the function of curios, before providing allusions on the virtuous, who are rewarded; the extravagant, who are deplored; and the worthies who did not care for such objects. Zou ends the chapter by quoting Confucius and the *Zuo Tradition*: "Able to do as I please, how can riches be attained by trying? Alive and well, one should treasure abstaining from greed" 從吾所好，豈曰富而可求；有命存焉，當以不貪為寶.[46] Citing the canonical works was a common device to prove the consistency of argument with the principles espoused in the Confucian canon. Hence, the exemplars and injunctions were carefully positioned and selected to embody an educational function based on Neo-Confucian ethics.

Practical learning in the high Qing remained embedded in Neo-Confucian norms, so the text leads the reader to similar moral conclusions, but the approach was different. The glosses of terms and classical allusions form most of the chapter—a clear priority. The opening sentence of the chapters in the *Treasury* demonstrates a twin approach: the instruction of traditional orthodox values and the glossing of terms. The above example takes the latter strategy, glossing the chapter title based on the individual characters *zhen* 珍 and *bao* 寶, which are often considered synonymous. The text, therefore, addresses the question "What are gems and treasures?" The answer stems from the cosmological concepts of *qian* 乾 (Heaven) and *kun* 坤 (Earth) but is fundamentally an elaborate definition. The "Attire and Apparel" chapter opens with a more explicit gloss of terms: "The cap is called the head dress. Clothes are called the body's shield" 冠稱元服，衣曰身章.[47] Even reference to historical personages function as a definition, for example: "The Three Sovereigns are termed *huang* 皇 [sovereign], the Five Emperors are termed *di* 帝 [emperor]. Those who esteem character are *wang* 王 [king], those who esteem force are *ba* 霸 [hegemon]" 三皇為皇，五帝為帝；尚德者王，尚力者霸.[48] Indeed, twenty out of the thirty-three chapters begin with a general statement of values espoused by the Confucian canon, while thirteen chapters start with definitions. Interestingly, the first chapter of Section Two, "Parents and Children," being most related to the Confucian human relations, commences by glossing the term "the five fundamental relationships." In contrast, Zhu Xi's chapter on 'Clarifying Human Relations' in *Elementary Learning* cites Mencius in explaining that human relations are the very purpose of education.[49] Although the school of principle did engage in philology and the elucidation of terms, this was merely for reading comprehension to fulfill the goal of self-cultivation and ultimately sagehood. In other words, glosses were secondary to instilling knowledge of the conceptual framework in *Elementary Learning* and normative behaviors in *What Youngsters Should Know*. However, the *Treasury*'s use of glosses in the opening sentence reveals that such knowledge was of equal importance to statements of moral value in primary education.

The text did not merely collate words and expressions related to the chapter topic, as in the character books genre of primary textbooks, but also provided explication. Key designative micro-structures are employed throughout the text: [X *wei zhi* 謂之 Y], [X *hao wei* 號為 Y], [X *yue* 曰 Y], [X *wei* 為 Y], and [X *ming wei* 名為 Y]—all these micro-structures generally mean "X is referred to as Y." In the case of two terms being provided, the micro-structures of [*yue* 曰 X, *yue* 曰 Y, *wei* 為 Z], [XY *jie* 皆 Z] and [X, Y *nai* 乃 Z] are used, meaning "Z is called X or Y." These are similar to the micro-structures in the oldest surviving Chinese dictionary, the *Erya*, and they demonstrate a conscious drawing out of signifiers (the terms) and the signified (the meaning).[50]

The *Erya* was a specialized dictionary, a dictionary for exegesis (*xungu* 訓詁) designed for clarifying word glosses in the commentaries to the canonical texts. Timothy Michael O'Neill has evaluated the structure of *Erya* and *Explaining Simple Graphs and Analyzing Complex Graphs* based on the Chinese language theory of "making words correct" (*zhengming* 正名)—the notion that the sages espoused "correct words" that are morally prescriptive definitions that encode the "signified."[51] He argues: "It is the practical use of words by humans according to proper social order that matters, not what the words 'mean' in some kind of abstract ideographic sense."[52] The correction of names was considered an important theory by pre-Qin thinkers and in Chinese hermeneutics. Additionally, this thinking led to lexicons such as *Explaining Simple Graphs and Analyzing Complex Graphs* to ensure that the reading of texts corresponded to the authentic thought of the sages. As Xu Shen 許慎 (30–124) explains, his main purpose was "to explicate errors and mistakes, enlighten scholars, and convey the fabulous meanings of words" 解謬誤, 曉學者, 達神恉.[53] That *Explaining Simple Graphs and Analyzing Complex Graphs* became a crucial tool in the philological movement beginning from the late Ming reflects a redefining of terms, as distinct from Song dynasty thought. Elman asserts that the Qing philologist was hoping to "eliminate linguistic confusion" and retrieve a "bedrock of timeless order" through the language of classical antiquity.[54] Similarly, Chow terms this a "hermeneutics of linguistic purism" in which the principles and methods of interpreting the canonical works were underpinned by a desire to expunge what was believed to be heterodox and uncanonical Song-Yuan elements, necessitating a return to Han exegeses.[55] Both have described a new emphasis on linguistic studies during the high Qing.

How does all of this relate to the *Treasury*? The textbook does not have an overt agenda of "correcting names," lacking the comprehensive framework for terms seen in the *Erya* and *Explaining Simple Graphs and Analyzing Complex Graphs,* and the term *zhengming* is also not mentioned.

Rather, the *Treasury* highlights that names as various as *sun* and *rooster* originate from an ancient written tradition. For example, the sun (*ri* 日 or *taiyang* 太陽) is considered the source of all *yang* 陽 energy and is symbolic of the sovereign according to the "Treatise on Astronomy" (*Tianwen zhi* 天文志),[56] and the rooster is known as the "virtuous bird" (*de qin* 德禽), originating from the *Han shi waizhuan* 韓詩外傳 (Han Ying's illustrations of the didactic application of the *Odes*).[57] Like the purpose of the *Erya*, the *Treasury* provided an entry to engagement with the ancient textual tradition. The texts would then furnish readers with the required conceptual understanding. Just like the analogy of the finger pointing to the moon, the *Treasury* points to the origin of the value system of the names—the ancient texts. For example, readers would learn that the "bright moon" and the "luminous night" are not simply nocturnal images but refer to specific prized pearls in history and allude to treasures generally; "water beetles" and "goose eyes" are not zoological terms but names for coinage. Hence, the text provided the cultural connotations and values imbued by the signifiers that would improve reading comprehension of advanced texts.

Since the Later Han, authority had been ascribed to the written word and state-sponsored texts considered the "canonical records" of sage teachings.[58] However, Qing dynasty practical learning extended the base of knowledge, which meant that ancient names, terms, and institutions needed explication to bridge the gap in comprehension. Zhang Zhigong highlights the quandaries confronted by the primary school teacher when teaching reading comprehension in premodern and early modern China.[59] First, the theoretical concepts and background knowledge, including terms and allusions, would be unknown to the child. Second, the literary language was in certain ways grammatically and syntactically different from the vernacular, spoken language. Textbooks like the *Treasury* were used to overcome these gaps in knowledge. These textbooks were to extend the child's vocabulary and familiarity with literary Chinese, functioning as stepping stones to the more abstruse canonical works (*jing* 經), historical works (*shi* 史), masters works (*zi* 子), and literary works (*ji* 集). The *Treasury*'s dictionary-like structure is particularly pronounced at the beginning of the chapters, such as the 'Land and Environs' chapter with a list of alternative names throughout history for Beijing, Nanjing, and thirteen provinces that the student would later encounter in the literature.[60] The text also defined allusions succinctly ("burning both the jades and stones" refers to "harming both the good and otherwise"). The annotation then provides the source of the idiom—the *Documents*. Hence, the rationale behind why "jades and stones" attained this connotation beyond their individual meanings is explained. The connection is made between learning and the greater context of the literary tradition, underscoring that knowledge originates from texts.

Although Neo-Confucian moral norms continued to be the primary emphasis, the *Treasury* guides the reader toward the wider scope of knowledge. Glosses and etymologies helped make ancient texts understandable. The text also starts to introduce the reader to the micro-structures and classifications used in the reference texts of evidential learning. The evidential school's agenda was to train scholars to verify such moral norms for themselves. The sentence structures in the text introduce the reader to the tools and principles of exegesis. Children were exposed to the Confucian culture, and some were embarking on the path to scholarship and officialdom from the moment they could read. As a publisher, Zou Shengmai was not merely responding to the student market but also the wider readership of clerks and merchant-scholars who aspired to high culture. Beyond the focus on glosses in the main text, the detailed annotations in the Qing dynasty edition of the *Treasury* manifests the accommodation of a shifting attitude to education to be explored next.

2.3 ANNOTATIONS: THE SCHOLARLY APPARATUS

Interlinear textual commentary had been a key feature of texts since the Han period.[61] In Cheng Duanli's 程端禮 (1271–1345) teaching schedule, children were to read the commentaries immediately after memorizing the original text of the Four Books.[62] Students were required to recite Zhu Xi's commentaries and explicate the texts accordingly, including explaining each word. For words not glossed by the commentary, the student was instructed to look up the relevant rhyme books and reference material. Annotations were not new to the primer genre. Several elementary textbooks, including the *Inquiries of the Young*, the *Thousand Character Essay*, and Zhu Xi's *Elementary Learning*, were read in their annotated versions. Wang Xiang's *Exegesis of the Three Character Classic* and *Summary of Evidential Research to the Hundred Surnames*, and Zhang Boxing's commentary of the *Elementary Learning* also emerged in the Qing dynasty. The late Ming dynasty Jianyang edition of the *Treasury* provided occasional annotations in the upper register, but Zou Shengmai's version of the *Treasury* that appeared in 1760 included expanded scholarly annotations for all sentences. Both the original and the supplemented text were interspersed with annotations. The *Treasury* was presented to the student in its annotated form, such that the main text was read together with the interlinear comments.[63] While such elements were not an innovation for an elementary textbook, annotations coupled with the lexicographic micro-structures and categorization of content would have resonated with an interpretive community reading for practical learning. The existence of such an interpretive community for the *Treasury* is corroborated by at least two editions of the text published in the nineteenth century in which the annotations become the focus—the annotations and the associated sources and quotations filling up most of the page.[64]

Both orthodoxy and practical learning considered education as derived and anchored in the ancient texts. However, the focus of the learning was becoming different, and the increasing interest in evidential research also affected the analysis of primary school texts.[65] For evidential research, students needed to be trained in the tools of knowledge production. The *Treasury*'s annotations worked to introduce students to the scholarly apparatus of linguistic and semantic glosses and functioned in teaching this interpretive strategy. The previous section discussed how the text and its annotations aided the transition to advanced learning material. This section will assess the significance of the scholarly apparatus for the young reader.

The nature and content of the annotations in the *Treasury* differed from the Neo-Confucian philosophical commentaries. Zhu Xi's commentary of the Four Books was dominated by metaphysical and ethical interpretations of the passage. The influence of the intellectual milieu is noted by Gardner when comparing He Yan 何宴 (195–249) and Zhu Xi's commentaries of the *Analects*.[66] Gardner argues that Zhu's more elaborate treatment was considered to actively shape the meaning of the text to defend the Confucian tradition and the *Analects* itself as a core text, while He Yan merely cited predecessors and provided glosses to preserve the received tradition. Philosophical explication in the annotations of the *Treasury* were manifestly limited compared to the commentary in other elementary primers like Wang Xiang's *Three Character Classic* and Zhang Boxing's *Elementary Learning*. The annotations in the *Treasury* were essentially quotes or paraphrases of the source text. Moreover, there are frequent glosses of terms that are brief and semantic. This is similar to annotations of pre–Song dynasty primers providing the source text, relevant quotes, and semantic glosses, such as the *Inquiries of the Young*,[67] the *Thousand Character Essay*,[68] *Yudui* 語對 (Parallel sayings),[69] and *Tuyuan cefu* 兔園冊府 (Repository of Rabbit Garden questions).[70]

During the Qianlong reign, intellectual inquiry through philological tools became the standard requirement in Qing Confucianism.[71] Scholarship was characterized by a need for verification through ancient sources. Analyzing the educational thought of Dai Zhen, who combined philology and philosophy in the Qing, Brokaw explains the necessity of textual verification: "The rules or principles of things could only be grasped through painstaking and arduous textual analysis and an accumulation of text-based truths and needed to be constantly verified against the evidence of the sacred texts."[72] Annotations in the *Treasury* quote the source text, indicating emphasis in textual study over metaphysical speculation. Engagement with the added layer of substantiation could train students in returning and verifying information with the source material. Moreover, the *Treasury*'s intratextuality provides an internal consistency that reflects this method of verification. Even within the single chapter of "Gems and Treasures", there are four intratextual references: the "bright moon" pearl, the jade disc of Master He, money referred to as "holey square" and "my elder brother," and Lin Xiangru's recovery of the jade disc. In relation to the account of the jade disc of Master He, Bian He's anecdote from *Han Fei zi* 韓非子 (Master Han Fei) is juxtaposed with the account of King Zhao of the state of Qin offering fifteen cities in exchange for the jade disc, as documented in the *Records of the Historian*.[73] Then, Lin Xiangru's courage is mentioned twice in this chapter and previously in the "Human Body" chapter.[74]

Through repetition of the literary allusions, the student becomes aware of the intertextuality of ancient texts but also that texts can correlate and corroborate, which occurs in the *Treasury* itself. Annotations bring the reader's attention to eighty-two intra-textual references that occur throughout the text. Students could thus be prepared for the interpretive method of "inter-explanation of the classics" advocated by Qing evidential scholars, whereby the content of the Confucian canonical texts was used to substantiate one another.[75]

The presence of annotation further exposes the reader to the established exegetical tradition and the activity of interpretation. The reader's simultaneous engagement with interlinear annotations indicates to the child that texts require commentary—text is necessarily accompanied by interpretation. Where annotations in the text are simply extracted from the sources, the main text in the *Treasury* itself becomes an interpretation of the source material. The historical anecdote or quote is distilled as a terse statement—crystallized in the literary tradition as an allusion. The subsequent explanation in the main text describes the connotation of the allusion. The received meaning of the allusion is often related to its original anecdote only in part and requires interpretation. For example:

> 紹箕裘，子承父業。
> Continuing the baskets and leather apron, the son carries on the father's enterprise.
>
> > 《禮》：「良冶之子，必學為裘。良弓之子，必學為箕。」
> > *Records on Ritual*: "The son of the master blacksmith must learn how to make the leather apron. The son of the master bow-maker must learn the craft of weaving baskets."[76]

This extract from "On Learning and Teaching" in the *Records on Ritual* refers to the training undertaken by the child who was likely an apprentice to their parent. Kong Yingda's sub-commentary explains this passage as referring to the correct order of learning and practice.[77] However, the main text in the *Treasury* provides the reader with a popular interpretation embodied in the idiom "to follow in one's father's footsteps" (*ke shao ji qiu* 克紹箕裘), literally meaning "able to continue the practice of training in the baskets and leather apron." As such, the baskets and leather apron in the idiom refer to the child carrying on the family enterprise and tradition. The teacher was likely to have provided a basic explication to the child who had not yet studied the *Records on Ritual* or its sub-commentary. The various layers of literal, textual, and popular connotations for terms throughout the text introduce the reader to exegesis. The text conveys information and provides examples of how to interact with texts, particularly engaging in the evidence of other reference materials such as lexicons, commentaries, and the wider literary tradition to formulate interpretations. Indeed, the child was to read at least fifteen different commentaries of the Four Books and clarify discrepancies in the later years of schooling.[78] The structure and content of the *Treasury* provide fertile ground for introduction to an exegetical outlook.

In the process of reading the *Treasury* and its interlinear annotations, the reader becomes aware of the extensive source material—all traditional branches of literature are included. The *Treasury* orients the reader toward philological bearings and a wide range of textual sources beyond the canonical works. The Four Books are cited forty-five times,[79] and the Five Classics are cited a total of 336 times. Table 2 below provides statistical data on the source titles cited in the *Treasury* based on the standard bibliographic classification system.

Table 2. Numbers of cited works in the *Treasury*.

	Canonical works	**Historical works**	**Masters works**	**Literary works**
Number of titles	26	52	111	85
Citations	442	460	355	206
Most cited text (number of citations)	*Odes* (102)	*History of the Former Han* (76)	*Zhuang zi* 莊子 (36)	*Zhaoming wen xuan* 昭明文選 (10)

These figures are based on titles mentioned within the annotations of the studied edition, which means that over half of the couplets had citations. It is noteworthy that contemporary commentaries such as Ma Ziyi's *Xin yi Youxue qionglin* 新譯幼學瓊林 (New interpretation of the *Treasury of Elementary Learning*) attempt to provide the source titles and original text for most of the terms and allusions.[80] However, many of the source titles cited are different from that of the studied edition. Wang Dan's analysis of the source text of allusions in a different edition of the *Treasury* yields similar results.[81] Wang notes that eighteen texts from the canonical work category were cited, with the Four Books and Five Classics being the most common citations; forty-four historical works, with the most commonly referenced being the *Records of the Historian,* compiled in 87 BCE; a hundred and thirty-one masters texts, with the *Shishuo xinyu* 世說新語 (A new account of tales of the world) compiled around the year 430 and the *Taiping guang ji* 太平廣記 (Extensive records of the Taiping reign) of 978 as the most popular; and the *Zhaoming wen xuan* 昭明文選 (Selections of refined literature) compiled around 526 being the most frequently cited of the literary collections.[82] Similar to her analysis, the largest proportion of source titles originated from the historical works and the smallest from the literary works.

An interesting phenomenon is the citation of texts beyond the canonical works in the annotation. For example:

> 餓死留君臣之義，伯夷叔齊。
>
> Bo Yi and Shu Qi starved to death preserving the rightness of the sovereign-subject relationship.
>
>> 《博物志》：伯夷、叔齊恥食周粟，采薇而食。有婦女曰：「子何食周之草木也。」兄弟於是餓死。
>>
>> *Treatise on Curiosities*: Boyi and Shuqi were ashamed to consume the grain of the Zhou state and picked ferns for food. A woman said: "Why are you eating the plants of the Zhou state?" The brothers consequently starved to death.[83]

Brothers Boyi 伯夷 (fl. 1046 BCE) and Shuqi 叔齊 (fl. 1046 BCE) were considered exemplars of the role of "subject." They were praised by Confucius as worthies who achieved humanity through their loyalty to the Shang dynasty (c. 1600–1046 BCE) and nonviolent dissent to King Wu of Zhou 周武王 (r. 1049/45–1043 BCE) overthrowing the regime.[84] The same evaluation is recorded almost verbatim in various texts, such as the *Analects*, the *Garden of Eloquence*, the *Han Ying's illustrations of the didactic application of the Odes*, and the *School Sayings of Confucius* of the pre-Qin and Han period. However, the source text referenced here is the *Treatise on Curiosities,* compiled in the third century. The *Treatise on Curiosities* was classified as a type of miscellaneous writing (*xiaoshuo* 小說),[85] combining assorted historical and mythical anecdotes, in the masters section of the *Complete Library of the Four Branches*.[86] As another example, the *Treasury* cites the "Biography of Lu Zhi" in the later historical work *Jiu Tangshu* 舊唐書 (Old history of the Tang dynasty) rather than the *Mencius*, which in the Qing dynasty was considered a canonical work:

> 以德行仁者王，以力假仁者霸。[87]
> One who practices humanity through one's character is a king. One who uses force on the pretense of humanity is a hegemon.
>
> > 《陸贄傳》：德合仁者謂之王。[88]
> > "Biography of Lu Zhi": One whose moral character adheres to humanity is known as a "king."

The *Treasury* thus demonstrates an extended knowledge base for intellectual thought beyond the Four Books and the Five Classics.

The form and content of annotations in the *Treasury* reflect the shifting intellectual paradigm in the high Qing. Interlinear commentary in the *Treasury* was likely to have two educational functions. First, the content helped expand the vocabulary and knowledge required for children to better understand the Four Books, the Five Classics, and other advanced texts. This is evident in the extensive source material presented through the annotations. Second, this element of the text introduced the reader to the tools of scholarly analysis they would be employing. The lack of philosophical explication is telling. By the time Zou had published the *Treasury*, the school of evidential learning scholars were producing annotations to challenge the foundations of the Cheng-Zhu orthodoxy.

Zou Shengmai's *Treasury* edition was an encyclopedic reference text for young students—its appearance in the high Qing, its structure and content, and its subsequent popularity show that the text resonated with underlying tensions in this period. Disenchantment with philosophical thinking based on the notion of the "investigation of principle and extension of knowledge" failing to solve personal and societal ills escalated with the collapse of the Ming. By this time, a rethinking of the sources of knowledge had already begun by redefining the ideal scholar as an engaged individual. This scholar was to be educated in a worldview encompassing both moral principle and the knowledge of life, the latter being the moral values of society and the former aiding in putting the values into practice. This was also the way to sagehood. Elman argues that late Ming encyclopedic works incorporated different intellectual outlooks:

> On the one hand, these new types of *leishu* covered a wider range of knowledge. On the other hand, they represented a form of classicism that approached things/events/phenomena textually, i.e., in a lexicographic and etymological way. Using the encyclopedic form, compilers increasingly applied the ideals for "investigating things and extending knowledge" (*gewu zhizhi*) beyond the classical corpus.[89]

The *Treasury* conveys such tension. The chapter topics and their order and internal structures touch upon various elements of educational thought—the shift from introspective moral speculation to the concrete aspects of the external world. The book pulls off a sophisticated balancing act that works within the orthodox Neo-Confucian mindset but incorporates philological ideas through the micro-structures and definitions of terms and allusions. Moreover, annotations provided the original text and citations to familiarize students with the commentarial tradition. Although book learning was central to traditional education, the *Treasury* extended the scope beyond the Four Books and the Five Classics. The encyclopedic content and source material reflected this broader outlook, although remaining limited to textual knowledge.

The cornerstone of the Confucian educational agenda was the full development of human potential, as espoused by all schools of thought in the high Qing. The perspective on the natural world, plants, and animals in the text was human-centered rather than scientific. Indeed, the person is placed squarely at the center of the worldview and allusions throughout the *Treasury*. Humans had innately moral dispositions, but there were two camps of thought on how moral qualities were to be nurtured through primary education. The early modern Chinese education of values through the *Treasury* will be the focus of the next chapter.

CHAPTER THREE

ALLUSIONS: ENGAGING WITH MORAL VALUES

The young Wang Yangming, being an adherent of the school of principle and the theory of the "investigation of things," once sat in front of bamboo trees for seven days to investigate their principle but became ill and abandoned the experiment.[1] This experience later motivated him to revise Song dynasty Neo-Confucian thought and further develop the school of heart-mind. For Wang, the highest good no longer rested in principle but in the heart-mind, and the key to learning was not in the external but the internal.[2] Wang emphasized the crucial element of reflection and personal commitment—that there was a need for a conscious evaluation of what was learned in relation to the innate moral qualities, which would lead one to realize moral sincerity. This process began as early as elementary education and was a lifelong task. In contrast, the Cheng-Zhu school provided a staged approach—primary education was characterized by the practice of everyday tasks and interactions, while advanced education provided an understanding of the meaning underlying such tasks. There was a clear divide between the emphasis on practice based on external (primary education) and internal comprehension (advanced education). Therein lay the difference in approach to primary education. While both schools agreed that a person's original nature was good, one adopted an approach based on inspiration (Wang Yangming) and the other used inculcation (Zhu Xi).

Based on the Cheng-Zhu school, the focus on learner comprehension and reflection of texts began from the age of fifteen.[3] This is evidenced by the curriculum of the school of principle educator Cheng Duanli, which was widely promoted in the early Ming dynasty.[4] However, educators from the late Ming dynasty started to rethink the sharp delineation between elementary and advanced learning. Lu Shiyi advocated three stages in education—recitation, comprehension, and extensive reading—and his essay was included in Chen Hongmou's anthology for teachers.[5] By the Qing dynasty, prescriptive educational discourses described the importance of explaining texts to students in primary education. Tang Biao considered that diligence in explicating the texts was the foremost responsibility of teachers, he wrote, "If texts are read without explication, the principles are not comprehended. [In this way] even if one were to read copiously, it would be no different to not reading at all" 若讀而不講，不明其理，雖所讀者盈笥，亦與不讀者無異矣.[6] This was reiterated by Wang Yun, who bluntly stated:

> 學生是人，不是豬狗。讀書而不講，是念藏經也，嚼木札也。...人皆尋樂，誰肯尋苦？讀書雖不如嬉戲樂，然書中得有樂趣，亦相從矣。
> Students are humans, not pigs or dogs. Reading without explanation is like reciting the Buddhist sutras or chewing wooden tablets. . . . All seek pleasure, who seeks pain? Although the joy of study is inferior to play, there is a delight to be found in books and learning should reflect this.[7]

These thoughts reveal the pivotal influence of Wang's ideas on child-oriented teaching—children needed to reflect on and comprehend their learning to derive internal motivation. The previous chapter explored the dichotomous emphasis on sources of knowledge between the school of practical learning and the school of principle evidenced by the structure of the text. This chapter argues that the *Treasury* extended the traditional Cheng-Zhu school approach by incorporating pedagogical strategies of the school of heart-mind, in particular by engaging readers with moral values through its literary allusions.

The *Treasury* was a collection of allusions, as the Chinese title makes clear. While Wang and Zhu criticized the isolated pursuit of poetry and essay composition and the use of language for these ends, they did not denounce allusions per se. Indeed, children's books that provided explanations and stories of allusions emerged as early as the Tang dynasty, which Limin Bai terms the "*gushi* 故事 genre."[8] She attributes the development of the genre to the flourishing of popular literature and the influence of Buddhism and Daoism in the Tang. However, prior to the Ming dynasty the educated elite devalued these primers as mere texts for the masses.[9] The teachings of Wang Yangming were significant in generating mainstream interest in and composition of this genre of primers during the late Ming and Qing period. The *Treasury* and *Longwen bian ying* 龍文鞭影 (The young horse and the shadow of a whip) are two examples of such primers.[10]

The *Treasury* delivered Song Neo-Confucian values through progressive literary devices reflective of Wang's ideas using the literary allusion. The Chinese "allusion" is also known as a "classical allusion," "historical allusion," or "historical anecdote" and in Chinese as *gushi* 故事, *yongshi* 用事, or *diangu* 典故. This is because the allusion refers to an ancient term, event, or story in preexisting writing.[11] A Western equivalent would be the current use of "sour grapes" as resentment toward the unattainable, which originated from Aesop's fable about the fox and his attitude toward the unreachable grapes. Allusions were literary devices, but also the origin of idioms and expressions, thus being an integral part of language acquisition for the child. Additionally, idioms provide a standard and condensed format of the allusion frequently expressed as a four-character phrase.

Allusions have been broadly classified as an "allusion of event" and an "allusion of concept" based on their substantive connotations.[12] An example of an allusion of event is the idiom "*tuo mian zi gan*" 唾面自乾, literally meaning "when spat on the face, let the spittle naturally dry."[13] This refers to an anecdote in the *New History of the Tang Dynasty*. The Tang dynasty chancellor Lou Shide 婁師德 (630–699), after foreseeing that his younger brother as provincial governor could be unfairly targeted, urged him to cultivate forbearance. His younger brother replied, "Even if another were to spit on my face, I would merely wipe it off without retaliating." Lou then advised, "That is not acceptable. Wiping it off would further infuriate the person. If you were to be spat on, let the spittle naturally dry." The idiom *tuo mian zi gan* was later used to mean forbearance but also connotes the upstanding character of Lou Shide. The allusion is primarily derived from a historical event, hence considered an allusion of event. An example of the allusion of concept would be "*ye mei su xing*" 夜寐夙興, literally "to sleep late and rise early," which implies diligence.[14] The phrase originated from the *Odes* and was also used in various other ancient texts like the *Zuo Tradition* and the *Xiaojing* 孝經 (Classic of family reverence). This allusion is employed for the concept of conscientiousness and does not refer to any historical account, so it can be considered an allusion of concept. The above two allusions are presented in the text as:

> 待人須當量大，師德貴於唾面自乾。
> One must be magnanimous in interacting with others, to be spat on the face and let the spittle dry naturally was Shide's character.
> 夜寐夙興，吾人之勤事。
> To sleep late and rise early, one's diligence in matters.

Instead of the reader having to decipher the contextualized message of allusions within the literature, the *Treasury* provided the allusion and the established message and frequently provided the literary source for ready reference. This chapter explores the three educational functions of the allusions in the text—as metaphors for thinking, providing ritual expressions, and showcasing exemplars from the literature.

3.1 METAPHORS: DISCOVERING NATURE

A popular anecdote from the *Three Character Classic*, also detailed in Liu Xiang's 劉向 (77–6 BCE) *Biographies of Exemplary Women*, concerns Mencius' mother. His mother wove cloth for a living, and when she discovered her son was engaging in truancy, she took up a knife and cut her half-woven cloth. She explained:

> 子之廢學，若吾斷斯織也。夫君子學以立名，問則廣知，是以居則安寧，動則遠害。今而廢之，是不免於廝役，而無以離於禍患也。何以異於織績而食？
> Your abandoning your study is like my cutting this weaving. A man of discernment studies in order to establish a name and inquires to become

> broadly knowledgeable. By this means, when he is at rest, he can maintain tranquility and when he is active, he can keep trouble at a distance. If now you abandon your studies, you will not escape a life of menial servitude and will lack the means to keep yourself from misfortune. How is this different from weaving and spinning to eat?[15]

It is said that through his mother's dramatic analogy, Mencius changed his attitude to learning and thereafter became the "second sage" to Confucius. Mencius' mother is lauded as a maternal exemplar through such anecdotes that demonstrate her skillfully drawing from everyday experiences and objects to relate the abstract notions of diligence and scholarship. This anecdote (*duan ji jiaozi* 斷機教子) became an allusion referring to commendable parental instruction.

Effective educational methods are thus those that used reason to instruct and persuade, rather than harsh punishment and rote learning. In the Qing dynasty commentary to the *Three Character Classic*, Wang Xiang's wording to describe young Mencius' moment of epiphany reveals the learning method.[16] He uses the term *ganwu* 感悟—*gan* 感is to "perceive," "feel," or "be moved by external stimuli," and *wu* 悟 means to "realize" or "understand." In other words, Mencius was able to internally process his mother's analogy—from the implications of uselessness for the cut cloth to his incompetence in neglecting his studies—and understand his faults. His subsequent conscientiousness was stimulated by external factors (his mother's action and explanation) but was ultimately caused by an inner change in attitude (his realization). Mencius did not blindly agree or repeat his mother's words but discovered the association. The need for comprehension was generally proposed by Qing educators, as Confucian scholar Shi Chengjin 石成金 (b. 1659) wrote: "It is vital that one applies one's learning. Those who can practice are adept at comprehending, to hear of this and associate with that, and understand through analogy" 讀書要能運用。運用者，善能解悟也，聞此知彼，觸類旁通.[17] This describes a process of comprehension or discovery from the imagery and metaphors in the text to the values to be learned. The process was not akin to the autonomous discovery advocated by Jean-Jacques Rousseau, but seemingly similar to the Platonian view of the child's freedom being subject to "the dictates of reason."[18] The child's discovery was guided by the Confucian principles prescribed in the textual tradition.

Wang Yangming's emphasis on reflection in elementary learning had the dual purpose of stimulating discovery of meaning and self-motivation. The literary allusions in the *Treasury* are a key linguistic trope in Chinese writing that invites the student to compare, associate, and conceptualize. The necessary task for students to unpack the historical context, original story, and meaning of the allusions challenges any assumptions of simple rote learning in reading the text. Moreover, as the allusions were to be later employed in prose and poetic compositions, the students required a sound grasp of the underlying content. Wang's instructions on reading are pertinent to the aim of seeking understanding:

> 諷誦之際，務令專心一志，口誦心維，字字句句紬繹反復，抑揚其音節，寬虛其心意，久則義禮浹洽，聰明日開矣。
>
> While reciting the pupils must be concentrated in mind and united in purpose. As they recite with their mouths, let them ponder with their minds. Every word and every phrase should be investigated and gone over again and again. The voice and rhythm should go up and down and their thoughts should be relaxed and empty. In time they will be in harmony with propriety and rightness and their intelligence will gradually unfold.[19]

It is apparent that the "investigation" Wang advocates goes beyond linguistic inquiry to a contemplation of values. Such contemplation would have been important to discover the content of the allusions in the *Treasury*.

Literary allusions engage the reader to create new meaning from seemingly disparate ideas—a form of metaphorical thinking. Imagery such as metaphors and allusions have been noted to have a similar function in poetic writing.[20] Yu-Kung Kao and Tsu-Lin Mei argue that literary allusion and metaphor are both composed of two terms that enter a relation of equivalence, in which their similarity and contrast create new dimensions of meaning.[21] In the case of the Chinese allusion, the two terms are a contemporary topic and a past event. They further describe the notion of words being related implicitly through similarities and differences (metaphoric relation) as opposed to relations among words being fully spelled out and constituted by grammar (analytic relation).[22] Both allusion and metaphor operate on the plane of "metaphoric relation." In this section, allusions will be discussed through the process of metaphoric thinking.

Metaphorical thinking was an important aspect in ancient Greek and Chinese discourse. Indeed, the two pioneering texts of literary criticism in the respective cultures both discussed metaphors. In the *Poetics*, Aristotle observed, "The greatest thing by far is to have a command of metaphor."[23] For his part, Liu Xie 劉勰 (465–522) in the *Wen xin diao long* 文心雕龍 (Literary mind and the carving of dragons) argued that metaphor was a central device in the verses of the *Odes*.[24] It has been argued that metaphors as a form of imagery in Chinese poetic writing differ from their Western counterpart due to the Chinese worldview. Pauline Yu writes that a fundamentally monistic view of the universe meant a oneness between humanity and the environment, and figurative language merely revealed the underlying connections. Yu states: "The connections between subject and object or among objects, which the West has by and large credited to the creative ingenuity of the poet, are viewed in the Chinese tradition as already pre-established."[25] In other words, metaphors were key to understanding abstract concepts about the universe beyond merely rhetoric embellishment. This was a common strategy in early Chinese philosophy; Sarah Allan argues that pre-Qin Confucian and Daoist canonical works show Chinese thinkers:

> . . . assumed that common principles informed the natural and human worlds. By studying nature, one could understand humankind. Thus, the natural world rather than religious mythology provided the root metaphors for the formulation of many of the earliest Chinese philosophical concepts.[26]

In exploring the metaphor of plants, Allan notes that the Chinese concept of "myriad living things" (*wanwu* 萬物) classifies plants, animals, and humans in a single category.[27] In this way, the principles of plant growth extend to an understanding of all living things, including humans. Neo-Confucian philosophy continued in the same vein in recognizing the unity of Heaven, Earth, and humanity. Zhu's educational aim was to realize the principle inherent in all things,[28] while Wang's goal was to attain oneness with the myriad things. However, for the Cheng-Zhu school this does not occur in primary education. In contrast, Wang advocated such training of the heart-mind from elementary education. Thus the use of natural phenomena in metaphor to conceptualize moral values was an established philosophical device dating from early Chinese writings but found particular educational application in elementary textbooks during the Ming-Qing period.

Conceptual metaphor theory will be employed here as a textual analytical tool to draw out the underlying educational knowledge, contextualized values, and conceptions embedded in the linguistic expressions and classification of the *Treasury*. Conceptual metaphor theory proposed by George Lakoff and Mark Johnson describes the role of metaphor in conceptualizing human experience.[29] They found that metaphors "structure how we perceive, how we think, and what we do."[30] The metaphor refers to a means of conceiving one thing in terms of another, with the primary function of creating understanding, while metonymy is the use of one entity to refer to another that is related to it, for example "new blood" used to refer to "new people."[31] Although metaphors and metonymies involve different kinds of processes, Lakoff and Johnson argue that both are grounded in the conceptual systems of cultures and in turn structure social and political reality. In metaphor, experiences from a "source domain" are used to describe a "target domain." For example, "time is money" is a cultural notion based on time being a limited resource and its association with work. In this metaphorical concept, "money" is the source domain used to conceptualize "time" as the target domain. This is evident in the expressions "you're *wasting* my time" and "borrowed time." Metaphorical linguistic expressions thus provide insight into the metaphorical concepts that structure thought processes.

The classical allusions in the *Treasury* can be considered metaphors, as the historical anecdote described in conventional wording connotes a new meaning, while literary terms can be viewed as metonyms. For example, *chun wang chi han* 唇亡齒寒 literally means "without the lips, the teeth feel the cold" connoting an interdependent relationship.[32] This classical allusion originates from the *Chunqiu zuoshi zhuan* 春秋左氏傳 (Zuo tradition of commentary to the *Spring and Autumn Annals*, abbreviated as "*Zuo Tradition*") when a senior minister used the phrase in advising his lord not to betray a neighboring state due to the mutually dependent nature of the interstate relationship. The physical body is a source domain to discuss human relations as the target domain. That relations with others are complementary and integral aspects of a single entity, like the human body, forms a significant concept in Confucian thought.

The following set of allusions from the *Treasury* examines the use of the tree as a metaphor. The "tree" is a key source domain for human roles (the target domain) in allusions throughout the text. Allusions related to trees (*shu* 樹 or *mu*木), including the parts of trees and different species of trees, appear in fourteen chapters. With each chapter considered a target domain in conceptual metaphor theory, the tree allusions cut across a broad spectrum of target domains, which makes their analysis particularly representative of the educational strategy of metaphor in the *Treasury* and represents the oneness of all things. Conceptual schemes related to the tree include: (1) the tree as a family; and (2) the tree as an individual.

The "tree as a family" conceptual scheme is consistent with the objective of educating children on interpersonal relations. The "tree as family" allusions are not only evident in the first two sections of the text that cover the five fundamental relationships but are also distributed throughout other chapters. The allusions are translated below in the order they appear in the text:

a) 用人如用木，毋以寸朽棄連抱之材。〈武職〉
Use officials as you would use wood, do not reject a thick piece of timber on account of one rotten inch.[33] ("Military officials")
b) 子孫發達，謂之蘭桂騰芳。〈祖孫父子〉
Successful children and grandchildren are referred to as "the ascending fragrance of the orchid and osmanthus."[34] ("Parents and Children")
c) 兄弟聯芳，謂之棠棣競秀。〈兄弟〉
Elder and younger brothers all enjoying an outstanding reputation are referred to as "the competing flowers of the cherry tree."[35] ("Elder and Younger Brothers")
d) 田氏分財，忽瘁庭前之荊樹。〈兄弟〉

When the Tian family divided their property, the black wattle in their courtyard suddenly withered.[36] ("Elder and Younger Brothers")

e) 暮雲春樹，想望豐儀。〈朋友賓主〉

When the evening mist shrouds the trees of spring, I think of and watch for your graceful presence.[37] ("Fellows, Friends, Guests, and Hosts")

f) 桃夭謂婚姻之及時。摽梅謂婚期之已過。〈婚姻〉

"The beautiful peach blossoms" expresses the proper time for marriage. "The fallen overripe plums" indicates that the time for marriage has passed.[38] ("Marriage")

g) 蒹葭依玉樹，自謙借戚屬之光；蔦蘿施喬松，自幸得依附之所。〈外戚〉

"The reed leans on the magnificent tree" is a modest expression for being supported by influential relations. "The cypress vine grows over the tall pine" is an expression for having fortunately secured a position through relatives.[39] ("Relations by Marriage")

h) 樹欲靜而風不息，子欲養而親不在，皋魚增感。〈疾病死喪〉

"The tree desires rest, yet the wind does not cease. The child wishes to care, yet their parents are no longer alive," said Gao Yu, who became more sorrowful.[40] ("Diseases and Death")

i) 故為人子者，當思木本水源，須重慎終追遠。〈疾病死喪〉

Thus a child is to be mindful of the root of the tree and the source of the stream, and place importance on the funeral rites and ancestral remembrance for the departed.[41] ("Diseases and Death")

j) 梁棟謂是大材。〈器用〉

"The pillars and beams of a house" refers to a person of extensive capability.[42] ("Tools")

k) 王祐知子必貴，手植三槐；竇鈞五子齊榮，人稱五桂。〈花木〉

Wang Hu, knowing that his sons would achieve honorable positions, personally planted three *huai* trees (Chinese scholar trees). Dou Yujun's five sons, being equally successful, were lauded as "the five branches of the orange osmanthus."[43] ("Plants and Trees")

Analyzed through conceptual metaphor theory, these expressions provide a framework to understand the five fundamental relationships. The target domain of the family, mapped in terms of the source domain of trees, employs a metaphorical entity. The nuclear family is seen as a grown tree with the parents as the roots. Just as the tree derives nourishment and grows from its roots, the family arises from and is nurtured by the parents. Offspring and descendants are the branches, flowers, and fruits of the tree, paralleling the English term of "scion" meaning both "a young shoot or twig of a plant" and "the descendant of a notable family." Children who mature and develop successfully are likened to the fragrance of flowers like the osmanthus and orchid. Young adults marrying at the appropriate time are compared to the peach tree in full bloom during the middle of spring. In contrast, those who have passed the optimal age for marriage are likened to overripe plums. Influential relatives are also portrayed as nearby trees that support one's career ("the magnificent tree" and "the tall pine").

Nonfamilial relations can also be described in terms of the personification of trees. Without blood ties, friends may be likened to other trees, such as Du Fu 杜甫 (712–770) likening the fond memories of his friend Li Bai 李白 (701–762) to the scene of spring trees.[44] In the sovereign-subject relationship, timber is likened to officials—the human resources of the state. Hence, the analogies of the child as branches of a tree and the minister being the "pillar of the nation" are not entirely unrelated. This imagery is further underscored by Zi Si's 子思 (492–431 BCE) remonstration to recognize talent ("do not reject a thick piece of timber on account of one rotten inch"). A summary of the ontological correspondences for the child reader is set out below:

a) Parents correspond to the roots.
b) Children correspond to the external growth from the roots, including branches, leaves, and fruits.
c) Successful children correspond to the beautiful blossoms and their fragrance.
d) Maturity and time for matrimony correspond to the spring flowering of the tree.
e) Those who have passed the optimal matrimonial age correspond to overripe fruit.
f) Relatives correspond to neighboring trees.
g) Friends correspond to other trees.
h) Children who become public officials correspond to quality timber.
i) The ruler corresponds to those that make use of the timber.

Behind the creative imagery are moral messages that are consistent with the Confucian values and obligations inherent in the five relationships. Parents as the "roots" explain the notion of family reverence—that parents and children are of the same entity. Children are urged to "be mindful of the root of the tree" as a metaphor for parents who give life and nurture. This was a remonstrance recorded in the *Zuo Tradition*.[45] Children are taught to cherish the common bond they share with their siblings through the imagery of inseparability as flowers of the same cherry tree—an allusion from the *Odes*. This is further highlighted in the story of the three Tian brothers who wished to divide the family property including the tree in their courtyard.[46] On witnessing that the tree had withered upon the eve of their planned division, they decided to continue living together, and the tree miraculously revived. The account unites the literal and figurative, with the branches and siblings remaining bonded. As part of the same family (the same tree), the *Treasury* positions the sibling relationship as an extension of family reverence. Siblings support each other to achieve the common goal of living in honor of parents and ancestors, becoming like the fragrant orange osmanthus. It was hoped that when the child matured, they would commence the sovereign-subject relationship in service to their community. As quality timber becomes the pillars holding up a tall building, the child must also become a pillar of the state. Moreover, marriage is depicted as a natural and delightful point in time during adulthood—like a tree in full blossom—in contrast to the unmarried state being compared to overripe plums. Evidently, the "tree as a family" concept features in expressions of the various human relations. Through the explanation and annotation, the expressions are ultimately imbued with Confucian values.

Another group of allusions employs the tree metaphor to represent the physical and psychological traits of an individual—the "tree as person" conceptual scheme. In terms of physique, the bareness of the trunk of the tree is related to an unadorned appearance in the idiom "*tu mu xinghai*" 土木形骸 (literally, "a body of clay and wood").[47] The slender appearance of the willow branch provides vivid imagery to describe a lithe figure ("a slender waist is termed willow waist" 腰細曰柳腰),[48] which also corresponds to the English term *willowy*. The deciduous nature of the willow tree is also highlighted: "The nature of the rush and willow is such that their leaves wither before the autumn comes" 蒲柳之姿，未秋先槁.[49] The phrase "nature of the rush and willow" (蒲柳之姿 *pu liu zhi zi*) was a modest expression of one's frail health. In contrast, the evergreen pine and cypress tree were praised as models of forbearance: "'The pine and cypress in the cold of the year' is a term of praise for integrity" 歲寒松柏，有節之稱.[50] By the quality of their wood, different trees connoted a person's capacity: "The ailanthus and oak are useless material; the Aralia and redwood provide excellent timber" 樗櫟乃無用之散材，楩楠勝大用之良木.[51] In caring for one's body, the text warns: "Indulging in wine and women is like felling a tree with two axes" 酒色是耽，如以雙斧伐孤樹.[52] Whether the tree represented the individual or the family, there is a connectedness that is evoked through the metaphor. These expressions being systematically linked to a conceptual metaphor work to further awareness of the world and moral ideas simultaneously.

The learning of metaphors occurs through the discovery of association. John R. Searle's seminal theory describes how metaphors are comprehended. As the metaphor would be nonsensical if interpreted literally, they are considered "false" or "defective" in the context of the sentence. The student therefore must search for possible meanings, as Searle states: "Where an utterance is defective if taken literally, look for an utterance meaning that differs from sentence meaning."[53] For example, in the sentence "Dou Yujun's five sons being equally successful were lauded as 'the five branches of the orange osmanthus,'" describing the sons as the branches of an orange osmanthus is semantically "defective." Recognizing this to be figurative language, the reader must search for the relevant meaning—how can the branches of the orange osmanthus be like boys? The annotation in the *Treasury* outlines the historical anecdote of Dou Yujun 竇禹鈞 (fl. 936–947). Dou's five sons all achieved success in their civil service examinations and official careers, and a poem was written praising them as "the five fragrant branches of the orange osmanthus 丹桂五枝芳." The aromatic orange osmanthus has culinary and medicinal applications, but food and medicine do not relate to the careers of the sons. Instead, the reader must discover through the teacher's explication and personal contemplation that it refers to its fragrance. The fragrance of the orange osmanthus that permeates and is appreciated by all is a metaphor for the widespread renown of the sons who bring honor to the family. This story, which is mentioned twice in the *Treasury,* would be familiar to the child reader from the *Three Character Classic*, with both texts exhorting the child to be a credit to their ancestors. The metaphor is similar to another idiom in the text:

> 為善則流芳百世，為惡則遺臭萬年
> One who does good will be esteemed (literally "leave fragrance") for a hundred generations; one who commits evil will be disgraced (literally "leave stench") for ten thousand years.[54]

The fragrance is a metaphor for being esteemed, while stench refers to humiliation. The search for the different meanings of the orange osmanthus relevant to Dou's sons is thus a cognitive process of discovery.

Metaphoric learning in education has been well described in ancient and modern literature, engaging the minds of philosophers, psychologists, educators, and cognitive linguists alike. As the earliest Chinese essay on education, "On Teaching and Learning," explains, "The ancient scholars gain insight into learning and teaching through association, connection, and comparison" 古之學者，比物醜類.[55] That metaphor furthers and establishes a novel relationship between different ideas was also described by Aristotle: "Metaphor most brings about learning."[56] That metaphor aids the progress of knowledge for the growing child was also recognized by Willard Van Orman Quine, who stated that metaphor "governs both the growth of language and our acquisition of it."[57] This is consistent with the work of cognitive linguists such as George Lakoff and Mark Johnson, who pioneered conceptual metaphor theory, which was extended by Gilles Fauconnier and Mark Turner in their theory of conceptual blending.[58] Modern educator Kieran Egan provides empirical evidence that the young child's ability to comprehend metaphor exceeds that of the older child and adult and that metaphor develops earlier and more easily than logic.[59] He concludes that metaphor is a potent cognitive tool for children's education because it helps students to view the world from multiple perspectives. Realizing a new association in concepts also causes delight in the reader. Understanding the metaphor is a creative and pleasurable act, resulting in a sense of achievement;[60] such joy thus serves as a driving force in learning. Learning though metaphor was one of a handful of child-oriented educational strategies employed by the *Treasury*.

The allusions in the text present metaphors to the student that engage them in a process of discovery. Multiple areas of understanding become associated; for example, the above allusions demonstrate how natural phenomena are linked with human qualities and behavior in interesting ways. These allusions helped to form a conceptual scheme, such as the "tree as a family" or "tree as a person," that the child could relate to in advanced texts. The child needed to understand the historical context of the allusion, gauge the different potential meanings of the new association, and realize the relevant meaning in the established use of the allusion. The reflection and delight involved in metaphoric thinking is consistent with Wang Yangming's educational ideas. On the other hand, Zhu Xi's curricular framework restricted conceptual contemplation in primary education. Being a collection of allusions, learning the *Treasury* required a pedagogy that differed from Zhu's educational ideas. This background to the theories of metaphoric learning and analysis of the allusions remains important in the following sections on the role of allusions in ritual expression and exemplar instruction.

3.2 RITUAL EXPRESSIONS: FROM POLITENESS TO RESPECT

The second function of allusions in the *Treasury* was to train the reader in ritual language. Ritual instruction in textbooks was to be applied in daily life with the aim of internalizing related moral attitudes. It was this internalization that enabled one to become a moral person rather than a follower of rules, but how internalization occurred in elementary education was an area of contention. The ritual content in the *Treasury* provides a glimpse into the educational theory. I begin by outlining ritual in traditional Chinese education and then follow by discussing the ritual content in the *Treasury* and associated learning mechanisms.

Ritual propriety (*li* 禮), variously translated as "rites," "rules of propriety," and "ritual," is a central and well-discussed concept in Confucianism. The scope of ritual propriety is extensive and does not equate to any single Western virtue. The term covers official ceremonies to rules of personal comportment and social etiquette—activities that are conceptualized differently by Westerners.[61] However, the underlying commonality of such human activities is that they are learned and both express and facilitate reverence.

Ritual was an important subject area in education—particularly as a recurrent theme in advanced education texts such as the *Analects* and the three ritual canons of the *Records on Ritual*, the *Ceremonial Rituals* (*Yili* 儀禮), and the *Rituals of Zhou* (*Zhouli* 周禮). Interestingly, the *Analects* records Confucius personally directing his son Boyu 伯魚 (532–483 BCE) to study the rituals: "If you don't study the rites, you won't have any basis to stand on" 不學禮，無以立.[62] The idea of ritual as the foundation of a person's conduct is echoed in other parts of the *Analects*, but here the reader is privy to the father-son interaction and the importance of being educated in the rites. Ritual was particularly emphasized in primary education as early as in the Western Zhou period. The *Rituals of Zhou* documented that the Guardian (*baoshi* 保氏) taught the "six Confucian arts" (*liuyi* 六藝), namely rites, music, archery, driving, literacy, and mathematics.[63] However, there is no further explanation of the curricular content. The *Records on Ritual* compiled in the Later Han was the first text to offer instructions on child behavior, as in this example: "A child should never be allowed to see an instance of deceit 幼子常視毋誑."[64] However, the *Records on Ritual* was studied by adults rather than children, and the wordbook primers of the Han period did not include such content. Zhu Xi later pioneered a type of children's textbook by extracting articles specifically on ritual conduct from the *Records on Ritual*, compiling the *Elementary Learning* and *What Youngsters Should Know*. For example:

> 凡對父母長上朋友，必稱名。凡稱呼長上，不可以字，必云某丈。
> When speaking to parents, elders or friends, one must refer to one's name. When addressing an elder, one should use their term of address and not their formal name.
> 凡出外及歸，必於長上前作揖，雖暫出亦然。
> When going out or returning home, one must pay respects to elders. One must do this even if going out for a short period.

> 凡飲食於長上之前，必輕嚼緩咽，不可聞飲食之聲。
> When eating or drinking in front of elders, one must chew carefully and swallow slowly, such that no eating or drinking sounds are heard.
> 凡飲食之物，勿爭較多少美惡。
> One should not argue or compare how much or how tasty the food is.[65]

A plethora of primers written in the Qing were based on Zhu's thoughts on primary education and modeled on his textbooks. These were generally structured by activities of daily life, such as rest, attire, and personal hygiene, with meticulously detailed guidelines for behavior. For example, the *You yi za zhen* 幼儀雜箴 (Etiquette and various admonitions for children) by Fang Xiaoru 方孝孺 (1357–1402), the *Tongzi li* 童子禮 (Ritual propriety for youngsters) by Tu Xishi 屠羲時 (fl. 1522–1566), and the *Dizi gui* 弟子規 (Guidelines for learners) by Li Yuxiu 李毓秀 (1647–1729) all provided instruction on ritual behavior. Other elementary textbooks that did not focus on ritual propriety still referred to the importance of such knowledge and practice for children. The *Three Character Classic* states: "A child must learn from teachers and peers, and practice etiquette from early years" 為人子，方少時，親師友，習禮儀.[66] Learning ritual propriety was therefore an established aspect of children's textbooks.

The *Treasury* contributed to the learning of ritual propriety for children. While other elementary textbooks focused on ritual conduct, behavioral norms were not a prominent feature of the text. For its part, the *Treasury* offered a handbook of ritual linguistics in the form of polite expressions. Through addressing others or making an apology, the child would be connected to moral values and obligations inherent in the various roles of the five fundamental relations that were central to elementary education.

The allusions used to provide ritual training in the *Treasury* markedly differ from the direct instructions for behavior and rules in Zhu's textbooks. The vivid metaphors associated with the honorifics stimulate cognitive processes beyond superficial acceptance of values. Terms of address at the beginning of the chapters appear easily comprehensible but are rich in meaning and metaphor. For example, the terms for the emperor are varied:

天子天下之主。

The Son of Heaven is the leader of all under Heaven.[67]

《曲禮》：「君天下曰天子。」《洪範》：「天者，君之父。地者，君之母。」

"*Summary of Rituals*": "One who governs all under the Heaven is the Son of Heaven." Commentary to the "Hong fan": "Heaven is the emperor's father, earth is the emperor's mother."

陛下，尊稱天子 。

"From the bottom of the steps" is an honorific for the Son of Heaven.[68]

應劭曰：「王者必有執兵陳於階陛之下，群臣與至尊言，不敢指斥，故呼在陛下者告之。」

Ying Shao said: "The king must have soldiers guarding the steps to the throne. All ministers speaking with utmost reverence would not dare to address the emperor directly. Thus, they address those at the bottom of the steps to convey their message."

天子尊崇，故稱元首。

The Son of Heaven is revered, hence referred to as the "principal chief."[69]

《書》：「元首明哉，股肱良哉。」

Documents: "The principal chief is wise, the arms and legs are competent."

If learning the text was purely through memorization of facts without the need for comprehension, the explanation of terms in the text and interlinear annotations would be superfluous. The text could instead have been written as: "The emperor is referred to as the Son of Heaven, from the bottom of the steps, and the principal chief." In the *Treasury*, the reader is introduced to the all-encompassing and significant role of the emperor, to whom all in the country are in service. This elaborates on the sovereign-subject relationship. How should one view the emperor? At first, the annotation seemingly provides two inconsistent glosses to the title "Son of Heaven." However, it becomes clear that the *Documents* provides the moral role, while the *Records on Ritual* explains the actual responsibility of governance. The title of the emperor reinforces the concept of the "Three Resources" and the oneness of humanity and nature. The emperor being the representative of humanity is thus aligned with Heaven and Earth, which are the co-creators of the universe. Being the "son" is not biological but symbolic of the moral task of the emperor, who must emulate the moral qualities of Heaven and Earth as a model for humanity. The emperor has distinct role descriptors to be deserving of the titles and respect; these are mentioned in the same chapter. For example, the difference between a "king" (*wang* 王) and a "hegemon" (*ba* 霸) is the use of moral power to govern by the former and military power by the latter.[70] The later annotation to "principal chief" also explains that the emperor must govern with understanding and insight to be considered the head of state, while his aides are the able "arms and legs."[71] The respect afforded the emperor is thus justified, rather than being blind subservience.[72] The reader is also subconsciously acquainted with conceptual metaphor schemes such as "high" being revered through the use of "Heaven" (instead of being titled the "Son of Earth") being the highest visible matter and "head" being the highest point on the body. In turn, the unity of all people is conveyed by the sovereign being the head, and by inference, all others are the rest of the body.

The *Treasury* also instructs on honorifics to be used when addressing family members. For example:

> 祖稱王父，父曰嚴君。
> The grandfather is referred to as the "royal father." The father is referred to as the "venerable lord."[73]
> 《易》：家人有嚴君焉，父母之謂也。
> *Changes*: "The household has the venerable lord, which is the term for the parent."

The title sets out the expectations of the parent-child relationship. The parents were the heads of the household, responsible for both managing the affairs and teaching the child, hence they were to be "venerated." Children were to respect and care for their parents as ministers were to serve the ruler. Using the terms *lord* and *royal* also suggests a transference of the attitude of respect within the family, as a child, to the emperor, at a later age. This is explained in the *Classic of Family Reverence*: "drawing upon their devotion to their fathers to serve their lord, the respect they feel for them is the same" 資於事父以事君，而敬同.[74] The terms of address for all social relations are treated in the same way. The child learns how to express not only respect but also the underlying rationale through explicit glosses and implicit connotations through the text. Analyzed using metaphor theory, the honorifics manifest the traditional Confucian hierarchy. Senior and powerful roles are described as precious, noble, larger, and higher. The converse is used for self-denigrating terms for the less powerful and junior positions. It has been noted that during the eighteenth century to early twentieth century several thousand terms of address in China existed.[75]

The use of jade in terms of address for respected and superior roles in Confucian society is a common metaphor. The conceptual scheme uses the physical appeal and value of the gemstone to afford the immaterial with the same merit and desirability. This is evident in terms related to the property of the ruler—as part of ritual propriety, reverence toward the sovereign also extended to their property. The emperor's seal was called "the jade signet" (*yuxi* 玉璽), and the imperial genealogical register was called "the jade records" (*yudie* 玉牒).[76] The source domain of the metonyms is jade. Why jade? Jade was considered the most valued gemstone since Chinese antiquity and had various qualities connotating moral character.[77] Moreover, Heaven is symbolized by jade and gold, according to the *Changes*.[78] Readers would have also seen frequent reference to jade in the "Gems and Treasures" chapter of the *Treasury*. Hence, jade is used linguistically to connote royalty, excellence, and purity. One learns from other parts of the *Treasury* that "capped with jade" (*guanyu* 冠玉) refers to a handsome appearance[79] and that "jade sticks" (*yuzhu* 玉箸) describe the tears of a beauty.[80] Moreover, requesting a reply to one's letter is expressed as "may you bestow your jade sound soon" (*zao ci yu yin* 早賜玉音),[81] and troubling another to visit is "hope your jade toes move" (*wang yi yu zhi* 望移玉趾).[82] The child is also acquainted with "part representing the whole" expressions as the addressee's letter is represented merely by a "sound" and the entire person by their "toes." Such indirectness is akin to addressing the emperor as "from the bottom of the steps," which is another linguistic technique to display veneration. The child is thus familiarized with a value system, social etiquette, and linguistic tropes simultaneously through the conceptual metaphors.

Another phenomenon that is not directly stated in the *Treasury* but implied throughout the ritual expressions is the concomitant need for humility. According to the *Records on Ritual*, "Regarding ritual—humble oneself and respect others" 夫禮者，自卑而尊人.[83] Ritual linguistics has been classified as a type of "politeness" phenomenon in the field of pragmatics. In Gu Yueguo's seminal paper, he notes four elements of historical Chinese politeness: respectfulness, modesty, attitudinal warmth, and refinement.

> "Respectfulness" is self's positive appreciation or admiration of other concerning the latter's face, social status, and so on. "Modesty" can be seen as another way of saying "self-denigration." "Attitudinal warmth" is self's demonstration of kindness, consideration, and hospitality to other. Finally, "refinement" refers to self's behavior to other which meets certain standards.[84]

Gu highlights that the core of ritual in language is deference to others and denigration of self. Yuling Pan and Dániel Z. Kádár have further corroborated that this twofold linguistic strategy of self-deprecation (*ziqian* 自謙) and elevation of the addressee (*zun ta* 尊他) was the "motor of politeness behavior" through their analysis of letters from eighteenth-century to early-twentieth-century China.[85] They argue that appropriate use of terms of address was necessary for all language users in society, regardless of their level of education.[86] Such learning likely occurred through family and primary education, provided universally during the Qing dynasty. Curricular materials such as the *Treasury* reflected this objective by elaborating on terms of address and speech acts.

While reading the texts, the student would have also engaged in ritual behavior, such as bowing to the statue of Confucius and the teacher when entering and leaving school.[87] This was learning the physical behavior required to express respect for those older and at the same time showing humility. In terms of language, honorifics frequently elevated the addressee or denigrated the speaker. Moreover, the concepts of "self" and "other" did not merely refer to the physical body or identity but also included property, values, actions, and relatives.[88] Hence, the wife of another was addressed as "your honorable lady" (*zunfuren* 尊夫人), while one's own partner was referred to as "the clumsy thorn" (*zhuojing* 拙荊).[89] The "clumsy thorn" is an allusion to Meng Guang 孟光 (fl. first century), who was known for her frugality in using a thorn as a hairpin and coarse material for clothing.[90] However, the later use of "clumsy thorn" by a husband was to denigrate his household as being poor. Similarly, the children of another are referred to with complimentary terms, such as "a vessel for the state" (*guoqi* 國器) or "a pearl in the palm" (*zhangzhu* 掌珠),[91] the former connoting competency to serve the state and the latter being a prized jewel. In contrast, one's child is humbly described as the "son of a pig or dog" (*tunquan zhi er* 豚犬之兒).[92] Although the reader would not have employed many of these terms in their youth, awareness of the different honorifics through the text exposed them to the politeness principle observable in life and in writings.

Introduction to the ritual lexicon was coupled with their application in different speech acts. The interaction between a host and their guest provides a form of ritual, in which the traditional conduct and dialogue are designed to evoke goodwill and respect.[93] The language used reflects the distinct roles that are played out when inviting the guest, exchanging greetings, giving gifts, sharing a meal, and parting. Each party engages in conscious self-denigration and social elevation of the other. This occurs through metonyms based on precious objects. Even when inviting close friends, the expression "[may I] presume to draw over your jade toes" (*gan pan yuzhi* 敢攀玉趾) is used, while "receive the orders of gold lotuses" (*feng ya jin lian* 奉迓金蓮) is for female guests.[94] In gift-giving, social convention dictated that one's gift must be denigrated regardless of its actual value.[95] Hence, expressions such as "offering the sun's heat" (*gan xiao xian pu zhi chen* 敢效獻曝之忱) and "offering celery" (*xianqin* 獻芹) are used.[96] The latter phrase is a classical allusion: a simple peasant, believing that others were unaware of the sun's warmth, wished to offer it to his prince. In the current usage, the sincerity of the peasant alludes to the attitude of the giver, while the lack of value of the warmth is a metaphor for the gift. "Offering celery" is an allusion regarding a rustic who told a rich man that celery was a delicacy, but the man was later nauseated by the taste. "Offering" is a term elevating the other, while "celery" denigrates oneself as giving something undesirable and even unworthy to be a present. According to ritual, the receiver of the gift must reciprocate by an appreciation of the gift through descriptions like the "handsome bestowal" (*houkuang* 厚貺).[97] "Handsome" raises the status of the gift and "bestowal" simultaneously elevates others and is self-deprecating; *bestow* is an honorific verb used to describe one of a higher social status giving something to one of a lower social status. Even a refusal of the gift, which can occur toward one of lower social status, is expressed as "returning the jade disc" (*fanbi* 反璧).[98]

In terms of hospitality, the host expresses modesty through such expressions as: "not setting out the sweet wine" (*lijiu bu she* 醴酒不設),[99] "giving unpolished rice" (*tuosu xiang liu* 脫粟相留),[100] or "an array of vegetables dishes" (*caoju zhi chen* 草具之陳).[101] Unpolished rice and simply vegetables being the humble fare of the impoverished. The guest is to reciprocate with gratitude for a meal "cooked with gold and gems" (*cui jin cuan yu* 炊金爨玉)—a metaphor for lavish delicacies.[102] In welcoming or sending off the guest, the host denigrates their own abode, such as saying "[your presence] has brought brightness to my straw hut" (*pengbi sheng hui* 蓬蓽生輝).[103] Although scripts of dialogue are not supplied in the *Treasury*, the host and guest utterances are juxtaposed within the same couplet or successive couplets such that the reader would need to understand the change in social role. The subtlety in changes to verbs and nouns challenges the child to read between the lines in realizing the essence of ritual—venerating the other and humbling oneself.

The same speech act is expressed in various ways and is distributed throughout different chapters, which requires judgment for their application. This goes beyond imitation and is not as straightforward as following ritual behavior instructions. For example, the *Treasury* provides expressions for the common emotion of gratitude in different iterations. There are degrees of appreciation based on the extent of kindness. To pay tribute to one's rescuer, there are the phrases "[being given] a new life" (*zaizao* 再造) and "[you are] the second heaven" (*ertian* 二天).[104] "Heaven" is a sacred and life-giving force in Chinese cosmology, of which there is only one, so referring to someone as "the second heaven" is literally to praise them to the skies. While being saved from a conundrum or crisis is generally appreciated among most cultures, there is broader significance considering the cultural view of the physical body. As stated in the *Classic of Family Reverence*, one's body has been bestowed by parents and must be vigilantly protected.[105] By extension, treasuring human life is part of one's duty to parents. Expressions of gratitude for significant service also had the physical body as a metaphorical source domain, for example: "engraved in the heart" (*mingxin* 銘心) and "imprinted on the bones" (*kegu* 刻骨) are for an indelible kindness.[106] This phrase is listed in the two chapters of the "Human Body" and "Human Affairs" representing the source and target domains, respectively. The origin of other allusions used for thankfulness interestingly also stemmed from stories of being saved, although they have come to be used for appreciation generally:

> 厚恩圖報，曰每飯不忘。
> Seeking to repay great kindness, say "remembering at every meal."[107]
> 結草銜環，知恩必報。
> "Knotting the grass" and "bringing a ring in the mouth," for being determined to return a favor.[108]

The annotation in the text explains that Emperor Wen of Han 漢文帝 (r. 180–157 BCE) was so grateful to a former military general for his meritorious service to the empire that he thought of him at every meal. "Knotting the grass" and "bringing a ring in the mouth" are classical allusions referring to stories in which the rescued party (or a relative) reciprocates the kindness of their rescuer. This promotes the concept that gratitude must be expressed through actions rather than merely words—kindness received is to be reciprocated. The importance of receiving feedback on one's character was also evident in the expressions. Saying "many thanks for your medicine" (*duo meng yaoshi* 多蒙藥石) is an acknowledgment of wise counsel.[109] Again, the physical body was often used as an analogy for the moral self with ailments representing moral deficiency. In recognition of the trouble of providing honest advice through direct face-to-face interactions, there is the expression "much obliged for instructing me to my ears and face" (*shen meng er ti mian ming* 深蒙耳提面命).[110] The text also teaches gratitude for specific favors, for example:

> 多蒙推轂，謝人引薦之辭。
> "Many thanks for pushing my wheel forward," for a recommendation.[111]
> 謝人寄書，曰辱承華翰。

> Thanks for another's letter, say "I have disgraced you by receiving your ornate letter."[112]
> 謝人許物，曰已蒙金諾。
> Thanks for a promise, say "I'm obliged for your golden promise."[113]

Those formal expressions were likely to be communicated by written correspondence. Evidently, appreciation was required for acts of kindness ranging from saving a life to sending a letter.

Given the variety of expressions, articulating gratitude must necessarily be a considered process. Employing allusions in written or verbal language requires an understanding of the extent of the kindness, one's position relative to the addressee, and the context of the allusion. Saying a simple "thanks" after being saved from fatal danger would be considered ungrateful. However, addressing another as "the second heaven" because they made a recommendation would be seen as obsequious. Moreover, saying "I'm obliged for your golden promise" to a servant would be inappropriate, given the addressee's station. *The Literary Mind and the Carving of Dragons* creatively describes a misused allusion "like using gold and jade to decorate one's legs or applying cosmetics to one's chest" 是綴金翠於足脛，靚粉黛於胸臆也.[114] The effect of an allusion used in the wrong context would be worse than not using the allusion at all.

The above discussion has provided a summary analysis of the types of ritual expressions in the *Treasury* and intimated multiple complexities in their comprehension. The question that remains to be answered is how ritual language transforms from merely polite words to an inner attitude of respect in the educational process. This is linked to the larger question of moral education—how does moral behavior translate into moral selfhood? The focus here will be on ritual. The Qing dynasty schools of thought inherited the beliefs that human nature was innately good and that this goodness was simultaneously tainted from birth and required education to restore. Ritual propriety was an innate moral quality but also an expression of this goodness. Hence, abiding by instructions of ritual propriety in texts was to speak and act according to one's innate goodness. Without the manifestations of goodness, goodness was not considered to have been learned or realized, which was the essence of Wang Yangming's unity of knowledge and action doctrine.

Ritual education was defined as a process of learning, but it was also a process of unlearning habits that were inconsistent with ritual propriety. As Herbert Fingarette explains:

> The (spiritually) noble man is one who has labored at the alchemy of fusing social forms (*li*) and raw personal existence in such a way that they transmuted into a way of being which realizes *de*, the distinctively human virtue or power.[115]

"Social forms" were the practices of ritual propriety. "Human virtue or power" refers to the moral qualities of the innate nature. "Raw personal existence" refers to selfish impulses that did not adhere to ritual, for example not using an honorific when addressing an elder.[116] It is aptly described as a labor because the process requires effort on an internal and cognitive level. Seemingly mechanical, the ritualized conduct was aimed at internalizing moral attitudes of respect and empathy. Moral attitudes were not immediately acquired but required constant conscious deliberation to infuse each ritual with the appropriate attitude at the beginner's level. This happened at the elementary level through practices like substituting neutral pronouns with respectful terms of address. Respect is not forced but must arise from understanding the rationale for admiration and gratitude. As seen in the glosses and annotations of the *Treasury*, implicit in the metaphors and metonyms of ritual language are reminders of the roles and responsibilities that each party must fulfill to be deserving of the terms of address. For example, expressions in the host-guest relationship demonstrate mutual esteem in the social interactions, whether in gift-giving or hospitality.

The *Treasury* shows a transition point between two extremes of learning—memorization and analysis. While Zhu did not prohibit explanations of practical tasks, he advocates reciting texts at the elementary level. However, Wang Yangming emphasized that learning was a continuum:

> 我這裏言格物，自童子以至聖人，皆是此等工夫；但聖人格物，便更熟得些子，不消費力。

> In this *gewu* that I am talking about here, from the boy to the sage, all require the same kind of effort, with the exception that the sage is more expert in investigating things and therefore does not need to spend any energy.[117]

Similarly, Karyn Lai argues that learning ritual occurs through stages of memorization and practice (first stage), then reflection and experimentation (second stage), and finally analysis and ease of expression (third stage).[118] The development of moral autonomy from novice to expert is associated with the respective learning methods. The initial phase is necessarily marked by simple instruction of moral norms, with memorization being the main mode of learning. Later stages involved explanation by the teacher and analysis or reasoning on the part of the student, leading to the "investigation of principle" in advanced learning. Indeed, Cui Xuegu (fl. 1697) states that teachers must explicate the texts and students should practice explication from the ages of eight or nine.[119] This approach was based on the belief that the child's memorization and comprehension skills are inversely related, and the ability to understand would gradually increase with age.[120] According to Ridley's research, the education of knowledge or beliefs, behavior, and skills all followed this learning continuum.[121] Hence there was a shifting reliance on the powers of memory to understanding the content and change from external dependency to self-autonomy for learning.

Ritual language in the *Treasury* stimulates the student to cognitively process the material. Beyond the first stage of memorizing the content, the diverse terms of address included in the text required a second stage of comprehension to delineate differences in their connotation. Moreover, the pervasive politeness principle is never explicitly articulated and therefore is to be conjectured. However, another phase of learning needed to occur for the student to ultimately apply the allusions in composition and daily writing or speech. The student must grasp not only the historical context and meaning but their current circumstances and appropriateness of the expressions. This contextual application was critical to perfecting the expression of "respect." With such knowledge, the learner was to engage in constant practice and refinement as part of the moral development espoused by all schools of educational thought at the time.

3.3 EXEMPLARS: HEROES OR VILLAINS

The *Thousand Character Essay* tells of pre-Qin philosopher Mo Zi 墨子 (c. 473–c. 390 BCE) observing silk being dyed and grieving over the loss of its true colors.[122] The silk represents the child, while the dye is a metaphor for the child's environment. Since pre-Qin philosophers, it was believed that children would emulate and establish habits, for better or worse, from those in close contact. Indeed, three main strands of early Chinese thought on children emerge from the secondary literature: the child's nature was considered malleable and required education for full development; the "nurture" phase was limited and a person's characteristics would be relatively fixed by the age of fifteen; and education needed to start as early as possible as what a child learned first would be most influential (*xian ru wei zhu* 先入為主).[123] Such views continued to the Qing dynasty, as Zhang Boxing quotes Cheng Yi:

> 古之人自能食能言而教之，是故小學之法，以豫為先。蓋人之幼也，智愚未有所主，則當以格言至論，日陳於前，盈耳充腹，久自安習，若固有之者，日復一日，雖有讒說搖惑，不能入也。
>
> The ancients would teach children as soon as they could eat and talk, hence prevention [of detrimental habits] was the approach to primary education. As the young have yet to become wise or foolish, they should be exposed to exemplary words and views every day, such that it fills their ears and their viscera. Over time, they will naturally be accustomed [to exemplary behavior]. By persevering in this approach, they will remain unaffected even by slander, gossip and temptation.[124]

Protection from immoral influences to prevent the development of poor habits in childhood formed an important principle in primary education. From the child's perspective, their parents, older siblings, and teachers were all to be models of proper behavior.[125] However, the texts they read daily were to also provide them with consistent ethical messages.

Emulation of exemplars was a central strategy in early Chinese thought. Through analysis of Western Zhou bronze inscriptions, Donald Munro claims that the concept of model emulation predates Confucius.[126] He observes that the early Confucians considered emulation "not just one way of learning; it was by far the most efficient way, and one could inculcate any virtuous behavior in people by presenting the right model."[127] Exemplars were integral to Confucius' pedagogy and self-cultivation program. Confucius instructs: "When you see a worthy person, think about how you can [follow] them. When you see an unworthy person, reflect on your conduct" 見賢思齊焉，見不賢而內自省也.[128] Moreover, Confucius believed that "exemplary persons depend on the presence of other exemplary persons for their development," according to May Sim.[129] Song dynasty Confucians also espoused such educational practices. In Zhu Xi's annotation of the first passage in the *Analects*, he explains that to learn means to emulate, some realize their original nature first and others must emulate them to achieve the same realization.[130] The Qing dynasty *Shuowen jiezi zhu* 說文解字注 (Annotated *Explaining Simple Graphs and Analyzing Complex Graphs*) also defined "teaching" (*jiao* 教) as "Superiors teach while juniors emulate" 上所施下所效.[131]

Recounting the words and deeds of exemplars was a common teaching method in Qing dynasty classrooms. Cui Xuegu wrote that stories of moral exemplars, historical accounts, and real-life examples should be used to teach good habits.[132] Li Xin'an further suggested that students recount one story a day, which would not only improve their character but also broaden their knowledge base.[133] Even Qing Emperor Yongzheng (r. 1722–1735) wrote that the young should hear virtuous words, observe virtuous conduct daily, and be instructed to emulate the upright.[134]

Use of exemplars was mainstream in elementary texts, for example, the *Three Character Classic* listed eighteen renowned diligent students in its final lines; the *Ershisi xiao* 二十四孝 (Twenty-four exemplars of family reverence) was expressly a selection of twenty-four role models; and the *Elementary Learning* devoted two sections to exemplars of the fundamental social roles, organized into those of the pre-Qin period and from the Han dynasty to the Song dynasty. In the *Treasury*, the reader encounters a rich assembly of figures from Chinese history through the allusions of events that evolve from stories in the literature. Providing exemplars is the third function of the literary allusions that will be explored here.

Lacking in the secondary literature is an analysis of the educational mechanism behind the phenomena. Cheng Yi asserts that exposing children to exemplars accustoms them to proper behavior but offers no further comment on how familiarization results in an actual behavioral shift. Zhu Xi's method of reading that required students to "experience the principles" bridges the gap between text and conduct, but this method was not generally used in elementary education in Zhu's curriculum. It is Wang Yangming's scheduled daily self-reflection that motivates the child to compare their conduct with behavioral norms and make the required adjustments. Reflection was also taught in the Ming dynasty primer *Xu Xiao'er yu* 續小兒語 (Further words of children): "At night, reflect on the deeds of the day; Rejoice in the good, let wrongs fade away" 白日所為，夜來省己，是惡當驚，是善當喜.[135] This section argues that the *Treasury* complements the process of self-reflection through its portrayal of exemplars.

The *Treasury* employed multiple strategies to ensure that students could draw the moral lessons from the exemplar. Exemplars were either depicted as virtuous and admirable (positive exemplars) or rendered immoral and contemptible (negative exemplars). There was limited moral ambiguity for young readers. How were the figures selected? Judgments of character were predicated on and derived their legitimacy from the textual tradition. For all schools, these were primarily the Five Classics, but for Zhu Xi the Four Books came first. The canonical works were afforded authoritative status as they were believed to contain the doctrines of the sages and worthies. As Munro clarifies, "The sages and worthies modeled on [the innate] nature and the reader models on the books containing their insights."[136] However, the canonical works covered only pre-Qin personages. From the Han dynasty onwards, it seems that the general principle was that positive exemplars provided an unequivocal embodiment of certain values and moral qualities that the educators aimed to inspire in children. Negative exemplars demonstrated the antithesis of the values serving to deter the readers from such behavior. There was a standard catalogue of moral values central to the Confucian tradition. Zhu Xi focused on models of the ten roles within the five relationships and their moral obligations.[137] Wang Yangming also highlighted the moral qualities of family reverence, fraternity, loyalty, trustworthiness, ritual propriety, rightness, integrity, and shame within the social framework.[138] Hence the exemplars selected were either sages or acknowledged for specific moral values.

Personages were portrayed in a mythic and simplistic manner to engage the child audience. For example, the sage-kings of high antiquity are well represented in the *Treasury*. The sage-kings were praised by Confucius in the *Analects*, featured prominently in the Four Books and the Five Classics, and were thus frequently alluded to in the elementary texts. They were considered to be "born knowing it" (*sheng er zhi zhi* 生而知之), that is, born with the realization of the original nature without the need for cultivation and represented exemplars in all moral qualities. Their references are repeatedly mentioned throughout the text rather than concentrated in the "The Court" chapter. For example, King Yao 堯帝 (trad. r. 2357–2255 BCE) and King Shun 舜帝 (trad. r. 2255–2205 BCE) are each referred to fourteen times and King Yu of Xia 夏禹王 (trad. r. 2205–2197 BCE) has ten mentions. The *Treasury* differs from the canonical works and other primers by highlighting the mythic elements of the figures. Their physical features are unique:

> 堯眉分八彩，舜目有重瞳。耳有三漏，大禹之奇形；臂有四肘，成湯之異體。文王龍顏而虎眉，漢高斗胸而隆準。孔子之頂若圩，文王之胸四乳。周公反握，作興周之相；重耳駢脅，為霸晉之君。此皆古聖之英姿，不凡之貴品。
>
> King Yao's eyebrows were of eight colors. King Shun's eyes had double pupils. Ears with three holes such was the extraordinary appearance of King Yu of Xia. Arms with double elbows, such was the unique body of King Cheng of Shang. King Wen of Zhou had a face like a dragon and eyebrows like a tiger. Emperor Gaozu of Han had a dipper-shaped thorax and a high nose. Confucius' cranium was like a dyke. King Wen's chest had four nipples. The Duke of Zhou had hyper extendable wrists and was the minister who made the Zhou dynasty flourish. Chong'er had fused ribs and was the ruler who led the state of Jin to hegemony. These are all the distinguished appearances of ancient sages—the noble characteristics of the extraordinary.[139]

The annotations in the *Treasury* provide textual sources of the information, but whether all the named were sages in the sense of "born knowing it" and the historical accuracy of their physical characteristics is beyond the scope of this discussion. From the educational perspective, the distinctive traits augment veneration of the "sage" and underline their extraordinary capabilities. Being positioned at the start of the "Human

Body" chapter further distinguishes these sages from the typical human being. This technique is also used for other exceptional rulers, such as Emperor Taizong of Tang 唐太宗 (r. 626–649) who was mentioned twenty-four times in the text. Apart from his various feats and qualities, Taizong was described as having "the elegance of a dragon and the beauty of a phoenix" (*long zhang feng zi* 龍章鳳姿) in his childhood.[140]

The reasons to emulate such figures become more persuasive considering their remarkable social impact. One reads of the peacefulness in King Yao's government characterized by people "singing and striking the soil" (*ji rang er ge* 擊壤而歌) in contentment as well as voluntarily yielding the boundary lands of their fields to each other under King Wen of Zhou 周文王 (r. 1099/56–1050 BCE).[141] The sages also evoked supernatural responses from Mother Nature. For example, King Shun's reign evoked the auspicious *jing* 景 star and five-colored clouds;[142] the heavens rained gold during the reign of King Yu of Xia;[143] and the sea was so calm that there were no waves during the time of King Cheng of Zhou 周成王 (r. 1042/35–1006 BCE) and the Duke of Zhou (r. 1042–35 BCE).[144]

The mythic element is also apparent in the stories of nonroyal exemplars. Attributed to their moral governance, locusts did not infest Zhongmu when Lu Gong 魯恭 (32–112) was the magistrate,[145] and the winds naturally extinguished a fire when magistrate Liu Kun 劉昆 (fl. 25–56) knelt before the blaze.[146] The stories of the virtuous being wrongfully punished are equally dramatic. When Song dynasty chancellor Kou Zhun 寇準 (961–1023) was demoted due to slander, he replanted a dead bamboo plant and vowed that the bamboo would be revived to show his innocence—the plant regenerated shortly after.[147] In another allusion, the unjust execution of the filial widow of the state of Qi led to three years of drought in the region.[148] The drought ended after the new governor held a memorial service at her grave after discovering the injustice. The transcendent feats of the exemplars and the dire consequences of harming such people draw attention to their model moral qualities.

There is markedly less detail on the negative exemplars compared to the positive exemplars. This is consistent throughout the text, which corresponds to the principle of "nourishing the correct." For example, rulers notorious for incompetence are featured. The epitome of tyrannical and incompetent rulership, King Jie of Xia 夏桀王 (trad. r. 1728–1675 BCE), has five mentions, while King Zhou of Shang 商紂王 (trad. r. 1075–1046 BCE) has four. The *Treasury* notes that "King Jie of Xia was inhumane, so the rivers Yi and Luo dried up" 夏桀無道而伊洛竭,[149] and due to Emperor Shihuang of Qin's 秦始皇 (r. 247–221 BCE) cruelty, there was no warm weather during the end of his reign.[150]

Such natural phenomena seem implausible from a modern perspective but were logically consistent with the belief in cosmic retribution, which was at the heart of all Chinese traditions of thought.[151] This was the notion that all human actions were recompensed rationally—good deeds resulted in reward and misdeeds led to punishment. Sixteenth-century Neo-Confucians reaffirmed and extended correlative cosmology.[152] The resonance and unity between humanity and Heaven meant that natural occurrences corresponded to personal deeds, particularly the conduct of the emperor who represented the state. This was the theoretical foundation of the ledgers of merit and demerit genre, which became popular starting in the late Ming. Indeed, a popular ledger titled the *Taishang ganying pian* 太上感應篇 (Exalted treatise on the response of the Dao) was employed in the moral education of children in the seventeenth and eighteenth centuries.[153] Cosmic retribution was also reflected in the literature through familiar narrative motifs as "the kind being rewarded" and "the unkind encountering misfortune." Moreover, moral retribution was integral to Confucian political philosophy, as evidenced by concepts like moral government (*dezhi* 德治), the Mandate of Heaven, and the importance of self-cultivation (*xiushen wei ben* 修身為本). These concepts were the basis of the depictions of sovereign and minister in the *Treasury*, but their explanation was left for advanced education when the canonical works would be analyzed.

It was more important for youngsters to distinguish good from bad and right from wrong at the elementary stage. Through the principle of retribution, the exemplars—their descriptions and impact—served to stress the distinction. Li Xin'an writes that teachers should recount stories of those who have demonstrated such moral qualities as family reverence and fraternity so that the students are motivated to emulate.[154] He also added that stories of those negative exemplars should also be told, including the misfortune they encountered, which helps students understand and be deterred by the consequences. Negative models provide a useful foil for positive traits. Linda Zagzebski argues that they may be equally important: "without the former, we might never have the thought that some traits and behaviors are worth imitating and others are not."[155] Wang Yangming explains the common goal of the canonical and historical works was to motivate readers to goodness. He states:

> 以事言謂之史，以道言謂之經。事即道，道即事……《五經》亦只是史。史以明善惡，示訓戒。
>
> A history deals with events while a classic deals with principles. However, events are really principles and principles are really events. . . . The Five Classics are also history, and no more. The principle of history is to distinguish good and evil and to give instructions to do good and warnings against evil.[156]

The nonduality of events and principles relates to Wang's doctrine that theory and practice are integrated. Theoretical knowledge is necessary to practice, while practice is a realization of one's knowledge. Therefore, principles (the theory) underlie the event (the practice), while the event illustrates the principle. Wang further interprets the canonical works as merely historical works, as they are a record of people and events in the past. He ultimately distills the textual tradition into one principle—to distinguish right and wrong, thereby educating one to do good. Indeed, the *Treasury* also does not attempt to delineate events and principles through its structure or content. In contrast to the *Elementary Learning,* which has sections dedicated to theory and practice (the exemplars), the *Treasury* instead assembles allusions based on source domain and target domain categories. The text being a collection of literary allusions rather than critical biographies meant that the narrative was limited and was rendered necessarily concise by the annotation format. Each allusion was a tightly packed story with an established message; hence the principle and event were to be learned at the same time.

Due to the nature of the allusion and the structuring of the text, there was undoubtedly intellectual work on the part of the reader to intuit the principle. The *Treasury* aided the evaluative process by direct value judgments of the figures. Where several references were made to the one person, the moral messages were consistent; for example, Zhuge Liang 諸葛亮 (181–234) is generally depicted as the skillful military strategist and loyal minister in the fifteen allusions.[157] The *Treasury* includes statements such as: "Kongming (Zhuge's formal name) was capable of being the emperor's aide" 孔明有王佐之才 and "Zhuge Liang supported the state of Shu Han like a dragon" 諸葛亮輔漢如龍. Moreover, the outcome was depicted as positive for the virtuous and negative for the unvirtuous. Yang Zhen was lauded for his integrity, specifically manifest in his refusal of a gift of gold and a proposal of business partnership.[158] Notably absent in the text is Yang's vilification by envious ministers as well as his demotion and subsequent suicide. Similarly, there is no mention of the loyal general Yue Fei's 岳飛 (1103–1141) execution at the age of thirty-eight due to false charges. Some characters with divergent evaluations of their moral standing in history, such as Feng Dao 馮道 (882–954), who was the chancellor for three dynasties during the Five Dynasties period, are not included in the textbook. Hence, the *Treasury* presents a relatively binary scheme of exemplars despite the abundance of characters and material.

The binary nature and mythical elements aided the young student in identifying positive exemplars for their fledgling moral conceptual schemes. As Zagzebski asserts, children and adults alike imitate without the prior notion of imitation nor the concept of good.[159] In other words, people can often identify exemplars in the absence of a moral theory, which creates the potential to formalize the features worthy of admiration in abstract and conceptual ethical frameworks. Indeed, Amy Olberding claims that given the piecemeal nature of the extracts in the *Analects*, exemplarism provides the most plausible moral theory—the traits of Confucius and his students represent a moral theory through the models.[160] In the same way, the child reader would develop ideas of moral qualities through the figures they encountered in the *Treasury*. The child may not have fully comprehended family reverence as an expression of the innate nature but would understand to cherish time with their parents through the exemplars, such as through the attitudes of Gao Yu 皋魚 (fl. fifth century BCE) and Zeng Zi 曾子 (b. 505 BCE) in the extract below:

> 樹欲靜而風不息，子欲養而親不在，皋魚增感；與其椎牛而祭墓，不如雞豚之逮存，曾子興思。
> "The tree desires rest yet the wind does not cease. The child wishes to care yet their parents are no longer alive," said Gao Yu who became more sorrowful. "Better to provide fowl and pigs for parents in their lifetime, than slaughtering an ox to sacrifice at their grave," was Zeng Zi's reflection.[161]
> 韓詩外傳：孔子適齊，中路聞哭聲甚哀，至則皋魚也，被褐捶胸，哭於道左。孔子下車而問故，對曰：「夫樹欲靜而風不息，子欲養而親不在。往而不可返者年也，逝而不可追者親也。吾於此辭矣。」泣哭而死。
> *Han Ying's Illustrations of the Didactic Application of the Odes*: En route to the state of Qi, Confucius heard the sound of sobbing and discovered Gao Yu, who was wearing mourning garments, pounding his chest, and crying on the side of the road. Confucius alighted from his carriage and inquired. Gao Yu replied: "The tree desires rest yet the wind does not cease. The child wishes to care yet their parents are no longer alive. That which progresses and cannot be turned back—the years, those who pass away and cannot be sought—our parents. These are my words." He wept and expired.
> 曾子讀《喪禮》，泣下沾襟，曰：「往而不可還者親也，子欲養而親不在。是故椎牛而祭，不如雞豚之逮親存也。」〔釋〕：椎，擊殺也。逮，及也。
> Zeng Zi read the "Rituals of Mourning" and with tears soaking his clothes, he said, "Those who depart and cannot return—our parents. The child wishes to care but their parents are no longer present. Therefore, it is better to provide fowl and pigs for parents in their lifetime, rather than slaughter an ox to sacrifice at their grave." Gloss: *zhui* means to slaughter, *dai* means to reach.

Such employment of exemplars corresponds to the traditional Chinese view of children developing reasoning and analytical abilities at a later age, hence moral theory was not elaborated on in elementary education.

Unlocking the *Treasury*

Contemporary moral education research also finds that the deliberative Piaget-Kohlberg reasoning is a fading paradigm; rather, it has now been shown that humans have two types of "minds."[162] The two minds are the conscious serial processing of the deliberative mind and the subconscious parallel processing of the intuitive mind. The intuitive mind develops sensibilities and responses from immersion in the environment, while the deliberative mind cultivates sophisticated moral reasoning. Lapsley and Narvaez argue that the two approaches to moral character education addressing each type of learning can be viewed as complementary.[163] Hence, it seems that Qing primary educational textbooks employed exemplars to engage the intuitive mind, while deliberative reasoning occurs in advanced education when the historical figure is later studied in the historical works.

The succinct portrayals, such as those of Gao Yu and Zeng Zi, also worked to provoke emotional reactions and help children gravitate toward the good. Confucius explained the desired attitude as: "Contemplating good, and pursuing it, as if they could not reach it; contemplating evil and shrinking from it, as they would from thrusting their hand into boiling water" 見善如不及，見不善如探湯.[164] In terms of emulating exemplars, the text aims to portray the good as beneficial to the self, while its opposite is detrimental. This concept is similar to Aristotle's emotion of emulation (*zēlos*)—distress at the absence in oneself of desired, honored goods, thus leading to striving for those things that are "appropriate attributes of the good."[165] Interestingly, Aristotle defines honored goods that are the objects of emulation as "the virtues" and "whatever is a source of advantage and benefit to others."[166] Exemplars demonstrate moral qualities in the *Treasury,* and the text was written with value judgments for exemplars, thus inspiring emulation of their associated qualities.

Key to the understanding of the mechanics of emulation in the Confucian setting is the belief that cognitive distinction and affective evaluation occur simultaneously. The duality between emotion and reason in Western thinking is less conspicuous in Chinese thinking, embodied in the translation of "*xin* 心" as the "heart-mind." Mencius asserted that the mind's sense of right and wrong (*shifei zhi xin* 是非之心) is the incipient innate quality of wisdom (*zhi* 智).[167] This ability to distinguish good and bad is also the basis of "sincerity" that Wang Yangming describes—sincerity being to accord with the innate knowledge of good, such that one naturally delights in the good and dislikes the bad. Kristján Kristjánsson has analyzed the Aristotelian concept of emulation in the context of moral education, describing the various elements as: affective (distress at lack of desired quality), conative (motivation to acquire the quality), cognitive (understanding why the quality is of moral worth and the self-transformation required to acquire it), and behavioral (actual striving for the quality).[168] A Neo-Confucian model would arguably subsume the "affective," "conative," and "cognitive" within a single category of "knowing." One must be taught how the good is desirable and beneficial, which then motivates learning and effort to attain the good.

Tailoring his pedagogy to young students, Wang Yangming developed this line of thought by making the instruction itself desirable. Recognizing that children would not have the capacity to reason in moral theory, Wang proposed strategies that would engage the child to be more receptive to learning the good. Elementary educational texts like the *Treasury* implemented this approach by packaging knowledge of moral qualities in creative ways, such as the compelling depictions of personages and highlighting the repercussions of their deeds.

The exemplar was a manifest educational mechanism in the *Treasury*, with the emulation of models being a key Qing educational theory and practice. The values espoused by the exemplars, based on Neo-Confucian social roles, were consistent across the primers of traditional Chinese elementary education. Through the rich variety of exemplars alluded to in the *Treasury*, there was a distinct difference in pedagogy compared to pre-Ming primers. Based on child-oriented strategies, students were to be guided in morality, and their innate knowledge, in turn, was supported to manifest. Instruction served to inspire and emulation was to stem from personal motivation.

Wang Yangming proposed that all things arise from the heart-mind, and the heart-mind is identical with principle. In other words, all phenomena were aids to moral understanding in life and learning. The first step in learning "*gewu*" as stated in the *Great Learning* was interpreted by

Wang as the rectification of the heart-mind to eradicate selfishness and restore principle. He explained:

> 先儒解『格物』為格天下之物，天下之物如何格得？且謂一草一木亦皆有理，今如何去格？縱格得草、木來，如何反來誠得自家意？我解『格』作『正』字義，『物』作『事』字義。...欲修身便是要：目，非禮勿視；耳，非禮勿聽；口，非禮勿言；四肢，非禮勿動。要修這個身，身上如何用得工夫？心者，身之主宰。
>
> Former scholars interpreted the investigation of things [*gewu*] as investigating all the things in the world. How can all things in the world be investigated? [Ch'eng I] even said "Every blade of grass and every tree possesses principle." How can we investigate? Even if we could succeed in investigating every blade of grass and every tree, how can we return to ourselves and make the will sincere? I interpret the word *ge* to mean rectifying and *wu* to mean affairs or events. . . . To cultivate the personal life means for the eyes not to see what is contrary to propriety, the ears not to hear what is contrary to propriety, the mouth not to say what is contrary to propriety, and the four limbs not to do what is contrary to propriety. But if we want to cultivate the personal life, how can we do so by applying the effort to the body? The mind is the master of the body.[169]

The perceptions of the senses would be relayed to the heart-mind, and the heart-mind was to select and "rectify" the input. For this to occur, the heart-mind needed to be motivated and guided by moral concepts through one's education. For primary education, Wang advocated that learning should be enjoyable such that children would be stimulated to learn.

That teachers must explain and stimulate the interest of students formed an important argument in early Confucian texts related to education, which Wang Yangming further evolved into a child-oriented educational strategy in the Ming dynasty. Indeed, in the "On Teaching and Learning" chapter in the *Records on Ritual*, it is difficult to deny the constant criticism leveled at ineffective teachers who simply read the texts.[170] In contrast, excellent teachers are those who enlighten and inspire: "to lead students forward through reasoning and inspiration rather than to drag them, to offer them encouragement rather than to hold them back, to open their minds rather than to provide them with fixed answers" 道而弗牽，強而弗抑，開而弗達.[171] Granted, this is a description of the practices of the Han dynasty Imperial Academy, which is advanced education, but the chapter being canonized in the *Five Classics* manifests the importance of such a pedagogy in general. Many of the complaints could be mistaken for those of Ming-Qing dynasty primary educators. By the late Ming dynasty, the tide was turning against the rigid discipline that had developed from Zhu Xi's elementary educational thought. Wang's call for change was unequivocally echoed by later writings from educators such as Tang Biao, Lu Shiyi, and Chen Hongmou, who often quoted Wang's letter on primary education verbatim.

Such renewed attitudes toward making education tailored to the young influenced the composition of teaching materials, such as the *gushi* genre. The *Treasury* employs literary allusions in various ways that distinguish the textbook from other normative, prescriptive books in pre-Ming times. First, the rich metaphoric language in the text unites the literal and figurative, enhancing both knowledge and language. Second, ritual language aided familiarity of moral obligations in different social roles, but its application required further reflection on metaphoric content and context. Third, the allusions served as concise stories centered on exemplars who furthered moral meaning. Education occurred through understanding, which led to inspiration and emulation.

CHAPTER FOUR

BETWEEN THE LINES: TRAINING FOR THE EXAMINATIONS

Discourse on education in late imperial China inevitably addresses the pervasive influence of the civil service examinations. The examination system was an institution that traversed socioeconomic and ethnic groups and was integral to the sociopolitical fabric of the state. Since the Song emperors made the imperial examinations the central means of talent recruitment,[1] prescriptive and descriptive statements on pedagogy in late imperial China addressed the issue of examination preparation. There were generally two opposing camps—those who maintained that learning was undertaken to become a sage and urged students not merely to seek to pass examinations and those who readily capitalized on learning for self-advancement. This is an important debate that relates to the historically tenuous relationship between literary training and moral cultivation in education. Just as ritual acts and expressions did not necessarily equate to genuine respect, the composition of elegant poetry and essays did not directly reflect the writer's actual character. Even in Confucius' time, he lamented: "Formerly people studied to improve themselves; now they do so to impress others" 古之學者為己，今之學者為人.[2] Zhu Xi later used this quote to criticize the learning of literary skills as a deviation and detriment to learning for sagehood.[3] By the Qing dynasty, educators continued to excoriate the distortion of education into examination training.

In particular, they criticized the deliberate study of model eight-legged essays for the civil service examinations, advocating that a thorough learning and healthy appreciation of the ancient texts would naturally result in high-caliber compositions.[4] Despite the universal rejection of studying examination essays for the improvement of writing skills, many scholars provided instruction on the art of writing. Writing remained the primary avenue to public office, a crucial instrument to effect political influence, and a key means of formal expression.

Notwithstanding the noble aspiration toward sagehood espoused by the three Qing schools of thought outlined in Chapter 1, the reality for families was often markedly different. Examination preparation was a significant practical consideration for families seeking social reward and recognition. For these children, studying was a means to an end, that end being success in the civil service examinations to join the ranks of officialdom or to undertake social and business activities. The practical purposes were not entirely stripped of the motivation to verify sources of information or even develop moral character—these aims were merely subsumed within and secondary to material considerations. Tutors catering to these groups of students would inevitably create a different reading of the primers. Interpretive strategies would highlight the literary content and textual structures that would need to be memorized or familiarized to achieve sufficient literacy.

In the case of the *Treasury*, the reader's motive to prepare for the examinations and the author's intent seemingly correlate. The foreword reveals that Zou Shengmai sought an aid for the examinations and a compilation to improve writing skills. This chapter focuses on the role of the *Treasury* as a tool for examination preparation by familiarizing students with the literary Chinese language and cultural knowledge. The learning and teaching of examination composition styles, such as the specifications of the essay or rules of poetic verse, will not be addressed as writing was a skill that was developed at a later stage of the child's education. Instead, the textual features of the *Treasury* are analyzed through two major techniques—mnemonic tools and cultural literacy. These techniques, arguably common to the primer genre, are grounded in the traditional Chinese pedagogy and educational beliefs. Thus, the first section addresses how the structure of the *Treasury* aided in the memorization of classical Chinese literacy for civil service examination preparation. The second section focuses on how the content of the text is aligned with the literary tradition.

4.1 MNEMONICS: THE LITERARY LANGUAGE

During the early Qing, provincial and metropolitan civil service examinations consisted of three sessions.[5] The first session, which carried the most weight, required candidates to compose three essays on the Four Books and four essays on one of the Five Classics. Essays were to be written in the eight-legged format with a maximum length of 550 Chinese characters, later increased to 650 characters in 1681 and to 700 in 1778.[6] Responses were to reflect the Cheng-Zhu school interpretations. The second and third sessions required a discourse essay, documentary-style answers, identification of five judicial terms, and answers to five public policy questions. Having embarked on the path of preparation for the civil service examination, the young learner faced a long list of material to be learned and remembered beyond the rudiments of character recognition as the first step in developing literacy. This included the text of the Four Books and at least one of the Five Classics verbatim (a minimum of 75,000 characters depending on the canonical work chosen); Zhu Xi's commentaries on the Four Books and his moral philosophy; and the grammar of literary Chinese and stylistics of the eight-legged essay.[7] The requirement to compose poetry was added in 1756, and essay questions for all the Five Classics were compulsory starting in 1787. This meant the additional memorization of Tang regulated verses (*lüshi* 律詩) and a total of about 470,000 characters in the canonical works.[8] Utilizing the observable and physiological rapid synaptic connections of the young brain, literary training started from an early age. Indeed, one had to have memorized the Four Books by the age of fifteen.[9]

Memorization through repeated vocalized reading was the first step in the late imperial Chinese learning process. By the Qing dynasty, educators also increasingly advocated for teachers to explicate the text in tandem with this preliminary step. The learning method of memorization has been criticized by modern Chinese and Western scholars.[10] However, it is interesting that the literature on traditional Chinese literacy education has refuted claims that such a method is ungrounded. Memorization was based on linguistic concerns, philosophical thought, and ideas on cognitive development in childhood. Zhang Zhigong and Rawski believed that the nature of the Chinese language inevitably meant that committing characters and syntax to memory was the most efficient learning method.[11] If reading required simultaneously mastering the pronunciation (reading), orthography (writing), and semantics (comprehension) of each character, the process would be extremely slow and would hinder the development of other intellectual skills. Hence the use of a nonalphabetic script was what obliged the students to learn elementary texts in an order that shifted the focus from character recognition to reading comprehension and then writing. Moreover, this learning method was likely necessitated by the classical language itself. The texts to be studied in advanced learning were written in literary Chinese, which was also the writing style for the civil service examinations. However, the lexicon and grammatical patterns of classical Chinese differed from vernacular Chinese—a situation that has been described as a form of diglossia.[12] Literary Chinese, learned through rigorous training, was used by the educated elite in formal, sophisticated writing, while vernacular Chinese referred to the informal, colloquial expression of the population generally. The literary language was largely incomprehensible to the uneducated, so much so that modern scholars have considered it a different language.[13] Based on the characteristics of the written language, Ridley asserts that through memorization, "the traditional Chinese may have chosen the simplest and wisest approach to language teaching."[14] In the emphasis of memory for language development, there are interesting parallels with medieval European culture.[15] Even into the seventeenth century, the schoolboy's skills in Latin composition also required memorization and explication of Roman authors.[16]

The importance of committing textual information to memory in the educational process was also considered from a philosophical and physiological basis. In her thesis on reading, Li Yu cites Song dynasty philosophers, among them Zhang Zai 張載 (1020–1077), who stated, "As long as [the classics] were memorized, they could be stated; as long as they could be stated, they could be practiced" 故記得便說得，說得便行得.[17] Remembering the text meant familiarity with not only the syntax and semantics of literary Chinese but also the moral instructions and exemplars. Similarly, in medieval European scholarship, Mary Carruthers writes:

> The process [of memorization] familiarizes a text to a medieval scholar, in a way like that by which human beings may be said to familiarize their food. It is both physiological and psychological, and it changes both the food and its consumer.[18]

In other words, memorization was believed to aid in implementing education and self-development. From a physiological perspective, Lu Shiyi wrote that the child's memory capacity was most robust up to the age of fifteen, and this early period should ideally be dedicated to memorization. Memorization was thus an established educational practice and a key consideration in the production of primers.

Primers played an integral role in developing the requisite skills and knowledge of the classical language through aiding memory retention. The three dimensions of language—semantics, phonetics, and syntax—provide a basic framework in the following discussion of how the *Treasury* aided elementary readers in mastering the classical language. An overview of each linguistic dimension exhibited in the *Treasury* will serve as a background to its mnemonic techniques. It will be argued here that the *Treasury* facilitated the development of literary Chinese skills and cultural literacy, which was vital to both reading comprehension and composition.[19]

4.1.1 Semantics and Pronunciation

In terms of semantics, the *Treasury* collects and presents the reader with lists of literary Chinese vocabulary. As discussed previously, designative micro-structures draw out literary terms and their meaning, thus decoding unfamiliar characters for the student. Notwithstanding the debates surrounding the definition of the "word" and the "morpheme" in Chinese, the semantic unit for new vocabulary introduced in the text ranges from the monosyllabic word, the multisyllabic word, and the phrase. In the following examples, novel vocabulary is bolded:

上服曰衣，下服曰裳；衣前曰襟，衣後曰裾。[20]

The upper garment is called ***yi***, the lower garment is called ***chang***. The front of the garment is called the ***jin*** (lapel), the back of the garment is called ***ju*** (train of the robe).

敝衣曰襤褸，美服曰華裾。[21]

Shabby clothes are called ***lanlu*** (ragged and tattered), beautiful attire is called ***huaju*** (splendid garment).

大掾史，推美吏員；大柱石，尊稱鄉宦。[22]

"**Great secretarial administrator**" is a commendation for the minor official. "**Great stone pillar**" is an honorific for the county official.

蜀犬吠日，比人所見甚稀；吳牛喘月，笑人畏懼過甚。[23]

"**The dog from Shu barking at the sun**" is a metaphor for a person with limited knowledge. "**The cow from Wu gasping at the moon**" is used to ridicule those who are overly anxious.

The *Treasury,* being a lengthy volume, considerably adds to the reader's vocabulary. The main text of the *Treasury*, excluding Zou's annotations, was composed of 24,723 characters in total. In comparison, the primers for character recognition were much shorter: the *Three Character Classic* with 1,128 characters, the *Hundred Surnames* with 568 characters, and the *Thousand Character Essay* with 1,000 characters.

Pronunciations are also sporadically provided for characters in the original and supplemented text of the *Treasury*. Pronunciations were indicated using two methods—a homophone (*zhiyin* 直音) and the *fanqie* 反切 formula. The homophone, a character with the same sound and tone, was the most common method and was expressed in texts as "X *yin* 音 Y," meaning "X sounds like Y." For example: "Guizhou Province is near the south and known as Qian (pronunciation: *qian*) since ancient times" 貴州省近蠻方，自古名為黔（音鉗）地.[24] The *fanqie* formula indicated the pronunciation using two other characters: the first character denoted the initial, the second character denoted the final and the tone, followed by either the character *fan* 反or *qie* 切.[25] For example, "Ji An (*fanqie*: *yi han*) was Emperor Wu of Han's chancellor, a minister who is truly faithful to the state" 汲黯（乙漢切）相漢武，真是社稷臣.[26] Occasionally, the tonal information is provided alone or in combination with a homophone, as in this example: "To cross swords is to confront an adversary (pronunciation: *lei*, rising tone)" 交鋒為對壘（音雷上聲）.[27] Pronunciation and tonal indicators occur after the relevant character in the main text, which manifestly aids sequential reading. In contrast, reference books like *Explaining Simple Graphs and Analyzing Complex Graphs* or *Guangyun* 廣韻 (Extended rhymes) provided such information in the annotation for consultative reading. Therefore, the *Treasury* presented the meaning and pronunciation of novel vocabulary for the expedience of the young reader.

Analyzing the structures of the *Treasury* based on findings from modern memory research highlights the ways the material enhances the retention of linguistic information. Psychological studies have outlined three requirements to achieving superior memory ability: information should be processed meaningfully in relation to preexisting knowledge (encoding), cues should be stored with the information to aid subsequent recall (retrieval), and encoding and retrieval processes should be practiced for efficient function (speed-up).[28] Fergus Craik and Robert Lockhart first postulated that the level by which new information is processed directly correlates with its retention, a theory now widely accepted in psychology.[29] They write:

> Preliminary stages [of perception] are concerned with the analysis of such physical or sensory features as lines, angles, brightness, pitch, and loudness, while later stages are more concerned with matching the input against stored abstractions from past learning. . . . This conception of a series or hierarchy of processing stages is often referred to as "depth of processing" where greater "depth" implies a greater degree of semantic or cognitive analysis.[30]

The processing of information for storage in long-term memory is known as "encoding." Deeper levels of encoding by ascribing meaning or relevance (elaborative encoding) improves memory. Indeed, Craik and Lockhart observe that processing sentences semantically was significantly superior to the recall of words compared to non-semantic processing.[31] This is a key strategy in the *Treasury*. Vocabulary, including terms, names, allusions, and idioms, is glossed within the main text. Semantic information is provided without the child needing to consult a dictionary, which aids in processing the relevance and meaning of the new word or phrase. Although the entire text is read, it is merely the literary terms and allusions that require memorizing and utilizing in composition. Therefore, the additional words serve in the elaborative encoding of the literary knowledge. In the following examples, the bolded text is the literary information, while the rest of the sentence is the explication.

> 御食曰珍饈，白米曰玉粒。[32]
> Imperial food is called "**precious delicacy**." White rice is called "**jade grain**."
> 慈母望子，倚門倚閭；游子思親，陟岵陟屺。[33]
> "**Leaning against the house door and the village gate**" is said of a mother waiting for the return of her child. "**Ascending the bare and wooded heights**" is said of the traveling child thinking of their parents.

Moreover, the semantic information presented is multilayered, which contributes to deeper processing. First, a gloss is provided within the sentence, for instance the reader is told that "precious delicacy" is a term for imperial food. Second, synonyms or related terms are juxtaposed within the parallel lines. In the first example, "precious delicacy" and "jade grain" both refer to fine food. In the second set of sentences, "leaning against the house door and the village gate" describe the feelings of the mother and "ascending the bare and wooded heights" those of the child. Both phrases relate to affection within the parent-child relationship. Third, the sentence is read as part of an entire chapter of literary information within the same subject category—the "Food and Drink" chapter has a total of thirty-eight couplets, while "Grandparent, Grandchildren, Parent, and Child" has thirty-six couplets. Therefore, the reader can potentially encode the terms through a hierarchy of different semantic fields. For example, "precious delicacy" relates to imperial food, fine food, and food generally; "ascending the bare and wooded heights" may be associated with the traveling child, the duties of a child, the parent-child relationship, and the moral quality of family reverence.

Whether the child engaged in elaborative encoding or superficially read the words without consciously making semantic associations would largely have depended on the instructions of the teacher. In analyzing primers of the pre-Tang and Tang periods, Nugent argues that the use of the primers strongly implied that "meaningful instruction in texts began quite early in the educational process and well before students would tackle the classics themselves."[34] Instruction in primers is logical given the content provided a foundation to further study. This is evident in the elementary school pedagogy of the Ming-Qing period, in which the practice of explicating texts for children was emphasized in the writings of educators such as Zhang Boxing, Cui Xuegu, and Tang Biao.[35] Texts were to be explicated via a gradual process of explaining each word, then each phrase, then each sentence, and finally the entire section. This resonates well with encoding and suggests deep-level processing of information.

In addition to the teacher's explication, an understanding was aided by the text itself. The textual explanation in practically every sentence in the *Treasury* is unparalleled in the primer genre. Although the first third of the *Three Character Classic* lists philosophical and cultural terms, the explanations are limited by the strict adherence to three-character phrases. Moreover, the terms are not semantically linked, as they adhere to numerical order. Other elementary texts teaching allusions, such as the *Thousand Character Essay* and the *Inquiries of the Young*, were written in four-character sentences and merely list the allusions without further elaboration, such as annotation, word, or pronunciation glosses.

In terms of memory retrieval, the thirty-three chapters of the text function as semantic categories in which the literary vocabulary and allusions are classified. Classification based on either the source or target domain of the allusions provide cues for retrieval. Memories stored in long-term memory are grouped as networks of associated memories that are semantically related.[36] The networks are organized at three levels—superordinate categories at the top (e.g., human relations), basic-level categories in the intermediate level (e.g., parent-child relation), and subordinate categories at the bottom (e.g., mother-child bond). When recovering a particular memory, cues activate associations with various networks. By classifying information into semantically related groups, the *Treasury* helps the reader subconsciously develop or integrate information into long-term memory categories, which leads to easy retrieval. This potentially explains why most categories are concrete nouns, which means that the person (e.g., civil officials, brothers) or things (e.g., tools, birds, animals) can be visualized in the child's mind. This is known as the dual coding theory—words that can be encoded visually and semantically provide two routes of recovery, thus allowing faster retrieval.[37] In contrast, abstract nouns do not offer retrieval-efficient categories and thus were not used as chapter headings in the *Treasury*. This is evident in phrases related to such values as "frugality" and "cherishing time" being distributed across various chapters in the text.

Additionally, there is evidence that an increased number of cues has super-additive benefits for retrieving the required memory in comparison to a single cue.[38] Distinct from other primers that have limited repetition of text, multiple allusions recur in the *Treasury* according to the semantic categories of both their source and target domains. For example, the text notes twice that Li Linfu 李林甫 (d. 752), who flattered Emperor Xuanzong of Tang while ruthlessly eliminating personal opponents, was resented by contemporaries for being "honey-mouthed and dagger-hearted口蜜腹劍."[39] The references are found in two chapters—"The Human Body" (relating to "mouth" and "mind") and "Human Affairs" (relating to Li Linfu's interpersonal relations). Another example is the expression for parents and children united in purpose, "willing to lay foundations and erect halls 肯構肯堂," which is noted in both "Grandparent, Grandchildren, Parent, and Child" and "Buildings and Rooms."[40]

This section has briefly discussed how the *Treasury* facilitates learning of extensive novel vocabulary through in-text explanation and pronunciation cues. Moreover, memory retention is enhanced by the deliberate arrangement of information to engage deeper levels of encoding. This includes semantic association within the sentence, between juxtaposed sentences, and the chapter. Multiple cues for memory retrieval are integrated by use of chapter headings that are concrete nouns and reiteration of literary allusions based on the target domain and source domain. Next, I explore the *Treasury*'s parallel sentence structures in the development of writing skills.

4.1.2 Syntax and Parallelism

The *Treasury* familiarizes the reader with the syntax of literary Chinese primarily through its parallel sentence structure.[41] Parallelism was a central aesthetic phenomenon in classical Chinese poetry and prose.

Parallelism was integral to the eight-legged essay form, as Andrew Plaks writes: "Without a doubt, the culmination of this stylistic tendency is the [eight-legged] essay form since here the chains of parallel lines are extended to unprecedented length and complexity."[42] While learning reading comprehension, the students would start to write by composing parallel word pairs (*shudui*屬對). Instruction progressed from composing pairs of antithetical characters, then parallel couplets of two, three, and five characters.[43]

The five rules for parallel constructions are that the two lines should have an equal number of characters, related meaning, the same lexical categories of corresponding characters (also known as "character pairs"), the same grammatical function of corresponding characters, and inverse tones.[44] However, parallel sentences without strict adherence to the rules may allow for repetition of characters, tonal variation, and dissimilar lexical categories. Liu Xie was the first to describe linguistic parallelism noting four types of couplets,[45] but it is Kūkai 空海 (774–835) who exhaustively categorized twenty-nine types of parallelism.[46] Later scholars have criticized the unsystematic nature of Kūkai's classification, as many of the categories were not mutually exclusive.[47] James Robert Hightower proposed three general types of parallelism: metrical, phonic, and grammatical, which will be used here to analyze the *Treasury*.[48]

Metrical parallelism refers to the use of metrical units of three, four, five, six, or seven beats in the couplet. This produces the characteristic rhythm of parallelism. The *Treasury* employs seventy-three sentence structures. The versatile use of sentence composition in the *Treasury* has been commended for its originality and readability,[49] which enabled diverse literary material and explanation to be incorporated. In contrast, the majority of textbooks incorporating rhyme had sentences of a fixed length. The *Three Character Classic* and the *Guidelines for Learners* were written in three-character phrases. The four-character sentence structure was the most common, as employed by primers such as the *Cang Jie Primer*, *Thousand Character Essay*, the *Kaimeng yaoxun* 開蒙要訓 (Essential instructions for educating the young), the *Inquiries of the Young*, the *Hundred Surnames*, the *Young Horse and the Shadow of a Whip*, and the *Si zi jian lue* 四字鑒略 (Summary of history in four-character phrases). Both *Xiao'er yu* 小兒語 (In the words of children) and the follow-up,

Further Words of Children, of the Ming period included four-character and six-character sentences. Evidently, prosodic considerations were important in the composition of elementary texts to improve readability.

The basic and most prevalent structure in the *Treasury* is the undivided sentence, of which the four-character sentences dominate. Parallel sentences in the text are also found to be divided into two, three, and four parts with a diverse range of phrasal lengths, which correspond to the metric pattern. Although modern punctuation was absent in the Qing dynasty edition,[50] the division of the sentences into phrases would have naturally occurred based on function words (*xuci* 虛詞). For example, the comma before the word "hence" (*gu* 故) in the following sentence leads to a caesura in reading the six-four phrasal pattern:

> 二戴曾刪《禮記》，故曰《戴禮》；二毛曾注《詩經》，故曰《毛詩》。
>
> The two [editors] with the surname Dai had deleted parts of the *Records on Ritual*, hence titled *Dai Li* [the Dai edition of the rituals]. The two [scholars] with the surname Mao annotated the *Odes*, hence titled *Mao Shi* [the Mao edition of the *Odes*].[51]

Indeed, the teacher reading the text to the students would have ensured that the pauses at the end of the phrases were correctly recited.[52] Although the exact metric pattern used to read the text cannot be verified, the grammar of the sentences is such that the caesura would be akin to the punctuation in the current editions of the text. Variations in content across editions of the *Treasury* have yielded different results in the analysis of parallel constructions; for example, Ye Yulin's 葉玉麟 *Youxue baihua ju jie* 幼學白話句解 (Explanation of the *Treasury* in vernacular Chinese) was found to have forty-seven types of parallel sentences.[53] However, the common finding remains that the *Treasury* innovated in incorporating diverse sentence patterns.

The category of phonic parallelism refers to the arrangement of sounds in a similar fashion between pairs of lines. While alliteration, repetition, and rhyming binomes are employed within the context of the idioms and allusions, the irregular occurrence of these devices in the text indicates that phonic parallelism was not a key concern in the *Treasury*. The main phonic element of note is the tone of the last character in the parallel lines. The four tones of Middle Chinese are divided into two types for rhyme: level (*ping* 平) and oblique (*ze* 仄) tones. The sequence of tones in parallel lines can either be matched or inverted. In the *Treasury*, the tones of the last character in the parallel sentences are strictly inverted. This occurs throughout the text in both original and supplementary couplets. In the following examples, the tones are indicated, with "—" being "level" and "｜" being "oblique."

> 冠稱元服，
> — — — ｜
> 衣曰身章。[54]
> — ｜ — —

Although the interlinear tonal pattern is inconsistent, the tone of the last character in the parallel lines is generally inverted. This also occurs regularly for the last character of the phrases. For example:

> 卜子夏甚貧，鶉衣百結；
> ｜ ｜ ｜ ｜ — — — ｜ ｜
> 公孫弘甚儉，布被十年。[55]
> — — — ｜ ｜ ｜ ｜ ｜ —

As mentioned, this pattern is notable, but does not suggest that phonic parallelism was important in the compilation of the *Treasury*.

In terms of grammar, the *Treasury* employs six types of simple grammatical parallelism in words consisting of one or more graphs:

(1) Repetition of a word or words, e.g., the word *extremely* (*shen* 甚) is repeated in "Zi Xia was extremely poor, his shabby clothes had a hundred patches; Gongsun Hong was extremely frugal, he [used the same] cloth quilt for ten years" 卜子夏甚貧，鶉衣百結；公孫弘甚儉，布被十年.[56]
(2) Synonyms, e.g., the adjectives *distinguished* (*zuizhu* 最著) and *extraordinary* (*duoqi* 多奇) are similar in meaning: "Han, Liu, Ou, and Su are distinguished scholar-officials; Qi, Jian, Po, and Mu are

extraordinary military generals" 韓柳歐蘇，固文人之最著；起翦頗牧，乃武將之多奇.[57]

(3) Antonyms, e.g., the word pairs of virtuous (*shan* 善)/non-virtuous (*e* 惡) and fragrance (*xiang* 香)/odor (*chou* 臭): "Friendship with the virtuous is like entering a room of angelica and orchids, the fragrance becomes undetectable after some time. Friendship with the non-virtuous is like entering a fish shop, the odor becomes imperceptible after some time" 與善人交，如入芝蘭之室，久而不聞其香；與惡人交，如入鮑魚之肆，久而不聞其臭.[58]

(4) Words belonging to the same category, e.g., numerals: "The livelihoods of people [come from] three, teachers have four crafts" 民生有三，師術有四.[59]

(5) Words belonging to different lexical categories (in combination with obvious parallel types), e.g., "Cai Yong wore shoes backwards to receive guests, the Duke of Zhou gathered up his hair to welcome worthies" 蔡邕倒屣以迎賓，周公握髮而待士.[60] The words *shoes* (*xi* 屣) and *hair* (*fa* 髮) have the same grammatical function as nouns but are semantically different, only associated as things neglected by the two personages in their haste to welcome guests.

(6) When ostensibly parallel words are not grammatically similar (embedded with other types of parallelism), e.g., "Sweet, crispy, greasy, and flavorful foods are called poison that ruins the intestines. Those who consume weed soup and dry rations, difficult to speak to about the taste of the oxen" 甘脆肥膿，命曰腐腸之藥；羹藜含糗，難語太牢之滋.[61] The words *call* (*ming* 命) and *difficult* (*nan* 難) are grammatically and semantically different within the other grammatically parallel word pairs.

Additionally, parallelism between lexical units of more than one character can occur in two types.

(1) Complex parallelism occurs when a pair of words is parallel in more than one way, both semantically and structurally. For example, "Superior wine is known as Qingzhou's retainer. Inferior wine is named Pingyuan's local inspector." 好酒曰青州從事，次酒曰平原督

郵.[62] The words *Qingzhou* 青州/*Pingyuan* 平原 refer to place names, and *retainer* (*congshi* 從事)/*local inspector* (*duyou* 督郵) refer to official positions; however, combined they allude to the quality of the wine.

(2) Double parallelism occurs when a word has its first parallel in the same line. For example, "'To wear the stars and don the moon' refers to rushing from dawn to dusk. 'To be washed by the rain and combed by the wind' refers to toilsome travel" 披星戴月，謂早夜之奔馳；沐雨櫛風，謂風塵之勞苦.[63] In the first sentence, the parallel word pair *wear* (*pi* 披)/*don* (*dai* 戴)" are verbs related to the wearing of clothes, while *stars* (*xing* 星)/*moon* (*yue* 月) are nouns related to celestial objects. These are then matched by *washed* (*mu* 沐)/*combed* (*jie* 櫛) (verbs relating to grooming of the body) and *rain* (*yu* 雨)/*wind* (*feng* 風) (nouns relating to weather) in the second sentence.

The prosodic features of the *Treasury* work in concert with semantic relatedness in improving the memory of both literary Chinese vocabulary and syntax. That the metric units of sentences in primers correspond to working memory capacity has been noted by Nugent.[64] George Miller observed that working memory is limited to "the magical seven plus or minus two" items of information,[65] which is consistent with the phrase lengths of the *Treasury*. Although the maximum sentence length in the text is eleven characters, vocalized reading would have sectioned the sentence into shorter phrases. For example, the following sentence could be read with a caesura (indicated by the slash), thereby sectioning it into three characters and eight characters: "宋真宗 / 以美珠箝諫臣之口 *Song zhenzong / yi mei zhu qian jian chen zhi kou*."[66] Presenting information in graspable units for working memory would result in efficient processing for long-term memory retention.

Rhythm in the text, as outlined above in the discussion on metric parallelism, creates temporal predictability. Aural devices such as rhyme and rhythm create expectancy for upcoming words and draw attention to subsequent information. Predictability thus enhances attention. Attention in turn keeps information in the working memory for encoding into long-term memory.[67] This has been confirmed by studies in cognitive psychology that show that rhyme and word placement improves the learning of novel difficult words in children aged two to five years.[68] Novel words and phrases in the *Treasury* are also frequently situated at the end of the sentences, for example: "Beauty and ugliness ill-suited is expressed by 'joining a dog's tail fur on to sable fur.' Unsatiated desire is expressed by the 'snake desiring to swallow the elephant'" 美惡不稱，謂之狗尾續貂；貪圖不足，謂之蛇欲吞象.[69] The two idioms are found at the end of the parallel sentences after the caesura, enhancing attention to the new information.

The parallel constructions further draw attention to the syntax of literary Chinese. The distinction between the two main word classes was one of the first lessons in composition. The two main word classes are: the content words (*shizi* 實字), which had an intrinsic nominal, verbal, or adjectival meaning; and function words (*xuci*), also known as "empty words" or "particles," which indicated grammatical relationships. Cui Xuegu writes: "When students learn composition, they must first understand subject and predicate, function and content words, comparison and contrast, elaboration and summation" 弟子學文，第一要曉得賓主、虛實、正反、開合.[70] Formulaic basic sentence structures with the word classes in the first line being reflected in the second line are repeated throughout the text. In the examples below, content words are denoted as "C" (monosyllabic words) or "C—" (disyllabic words) and function words as "F."

(1) 麟為毛蟲之長，虎乃獸中之王。[71]
C F CC FC   C FCCFC
The unicorn is the chief of furry creatures. The tiger is the king of beasts.[72]

(2) 伯牙絕弦失子期，更無知音之輩；
C — CCC C —   F F   C— F C
Boya broke the strings [of his zither] after the passing of Ziqi and [as] there were no longer any soul mates.
管寧割席拒華歆，謂非同志之人。[73]
C —CCCC —   F F C — FC
"Guan Ning cut the mat refusing to associate with Hua Xin" refers to those without similar goals.[74]

Mirroring of word classes in the parallel constructions meant that students could learn related words, including synonyms and antonyms. In the above examples, word pairs with overlapping meanings include: *is* (*wei* 為) and *to be* (*nai* 乃); *chief* (*zhang* 長) and *king* (*wang* 王); *soul mate* (*zhiyin* 知音) and *similar goals* (*tongzhi* 同志) both meaning a close friend; and *a kind of person* (*bei* 輩) and *person(s)* (*ren* 人). Although each word could have various definitions, the word pairs across the parallel lines revealed that they were related.

Parallelism as a mnemonic technique for learning poetry and encyclopedia works in medieval China has been previously analyzed.[75] Memory is facilitated as the requirements of parallelism limit the semantic context—the word pairs are often similar in topic and/or semantic fields. Such structures assisted students to recognize and better memorize such words for later application. Indeed, using synonyms was a critical skill in composition. For the eight-legged essay, the opening line required a restatement of the essay topic, and the parallel sentences within the essay required the second line to reiterate the first line.[76] In both poetry and prose, the repetition of words would indicate limited vocabulary or lack of consideration and hence was to be avoided.

Through grammatical parallelism, the reader not only identified the word class of novel vocabulary but also the underlying sentence structure. The position of the function words particularly highlights the syntax. In the first example, both lines are framed as "X is Y of Z." In the second example, the sentences are roughly structured as "X did Y as Z." These sentence forms could be initially imitated and later elaborated upon with instruction and experience. Indeed, it was widely acknowledged in late imperial China that memorizing Tang and Song poetry was the way to learn the composition of regulated verse.[77] The child may not have immediately comprehended the terse phrases but by committing the verses to memory, the experience was that the patterns were subconsciously assimilated. Contemporary memory research shows that the repetition of foreign language utterances enables the consolidation of long-term representations of words and word sequences, which leads to superior explicit, metacognitive knowledge about the underlying grammatical rules.[78] Reciting the texts was thus a process of familiarizing oneself with the forms and terms of literary Chinese.

The importance of prosody in Chinese elementary texts is highlighted on further consideration of the learning strategy. Vocalized reading was the principal mode of committing texts to memory, which meant that the readability of the primers would directly affect knowledge transmission. Psychological studies confirm personal experience that enjoyment and motivation enhance memory—this is also through added attention to the learning material.[79] Compilers of traditional primers seemed to implicitly understand the relationship between children enjoying and retaining the material. For example, the *Cang Jie Primer*, one of the earliest primers compiled in the Han dynasty, is composed of four-character sentences that rhyme every other sentence.[80] Additionally, the lack of a standardized primary education curriculum, compared to the Four Books and the Five Classics for advanced education, meant that the readability of the textbook would undoubtedly also improve its marketability.

The above analysis has explored how the stylistic devices in the *Treasury* aided memory. However, the question remains: how does remembering information lead to reading ability and, ultimately, language use? According to the cognitive theory of reading known as the "Simple View of Reading," reading comprehension is the product of language decoding and comprehension.[81] Decoding and comprehension are cumulative skills that improve with prior knowledge of vocabulary and grammar. Nick C. Ellis and Susan G. Sinclair explain this aptly in their study of working memory:

> Short-term representation and rehearsal allows the eventual establishment of long-term sequence information for language. There are, in turn, reciprocal interactions between long-term sequence representations and short-term storage whereby long-term sequence information allows the chunking of working memory contents that accord with these consolidated patterns, thus extending the span of short-term storage for chunkable materials. The more the long-term storage of frequent language sequences, the more easily can they serve as labels for meaning reference. The more automatic their access, the more fluent is the resultant language use, concomitantly freeing attentional resources for analysis of

the meaning of the message, either for comprehension or for production planning.[82]

Memorized semantic, phonological, and syntactical information facilitates the easier encoding of new and related information. Contemporary research on literary Chinese comprehension also confirms that so-called "lower-level language skills" (decoding, vocabulary, and grammar) that are essential for understanding the words and sentences in a text support "higher-level language skills" (inferencing, comprehension monitoring, and prior knowledge) that enable readers to comprehend the text's meaning beyond the sentence level.[83] The higher-level language skills, in turn, enhance word recognition, vocabulary, and grammar.

The relationship between memorization and comprehension has also been corroborated by modern qualitative educational studies. Theoretical positions to learning are traditionally divided into surface and deep, with the latter involving comprehension of the learning material. However, David Kember reviewed evidence of Asian learners as demonstrating a learning approach characterized by the intention to both understand and memorize—the third approach.[84] Bo Dahlin and David Watkins's study of German and Hong Kong Chinese secondary students further corroborated this third approach. While both cultural groups recognized the importance of repetition in reading, the Chinese students described repeated reading as useful for creating a deep impression (memorizing) and discovering new meaning (understanding).[85] Beyond the literature on basic reading skills forming a foundation for higher-order comprehension, another mechanism for comprehension of the material is that the learning technique of repeated reading simultaneously incorporates directing attention to the material read, which enables new meaning to be discovered and in turn deepens and develops understanding—surface and deep learning occurring together.

This section has explored how the *Treasury* may develop "lower-level language skills" for literary Chinese, which prepares the reader for advanced learning texts and composition. Improved memory of literary Chinese terms and allusions occurs through semantic relatedness.

Indeed, the chapters are a conscious authorial decision to provide a scaffold upon which learners can anchor their memory of disparate allusions. Moreover, the *Treasury* is defined by its parallel sentences and their metric and grammatical parallelism, which additionally serve to facilitate memory of the literary Chinese syntax. The next section turns to the higher-level language skill of prior knowledge or knowledge schemas, exploring the content of the *Treasury* within the context of the potential examinee's required reading.

4.2 CULTURAL LITERACY: LITERARY KNOWLEDGE

Beyond mastering the stylistics of the literary language, particularly the complexities of the eight-legged essay format and the Tang regulated verse, the candidate had to be equipped with the information that would help with reading comprehension and ultimately form the content of their composition. The student needed to learn "how" and "what" to write. Examinees learned a circumscribed body of knowledge that related to the aims of the imperial government and literati. The early modern Chinese elementary curriculum for examination preparation can be considered a knowledge-centered curriculum. This is akin to E. D. Hirsch Jr.'s cultural literacy curriculum, which advocates that children learn intergenerational and shared information that is grounded in the national culture to become competent readers.[86] Hirsch explains:

> Cultural literacy lies above the everyday levels of knowledge that everyone possesses and below the expert level known only to specialists. It is that middle ground of cultural knowledge possessed by the "common reader."[87]

Beyond simple facts and vocabulary lists, cultural literacy to Hirsch also included the attitudes and assumptions that the literate group (in his case, literate Americans) share. In this way, cultural literacy was the prerequisite knowledge for the comprehension of texts and general communication—"the oxygen of social intercourse."[88] Similarly,

Elman notes that the elite educated in China shared a common cultural mindset:

> Reproduction of classical values and historical mind-sets among candidates for public office meant that gentry, military and merchant families from all over the empire had more in common culturally and linguistically with each other than did lower social groups in their native areas, who remained tied to local traditions, temples, and dialects that did not transcend local life. . . . Preparation for the civil service thus entailed mental mastery of orthodox and regionalized schemes of classical language, thought, perception, appreciation, and action.[89]

Central to this description is that a common body of information needed to be absorbed in order to be considered "literate."

Hirsch's theory of cultural literacy developed in response to deteriorating national literacy levels in America during the 1980s. He incorporated burgeoning psychological research on the importance of background knowledge in reading to justify a knowledge-intensive curriculum for children. Hirsch's theory has not been without criticism. Axiological arguments point to the difficulty of delimiting the scope of "culture" and identifying the "shared" knowledge possessed by literate Americans. The main concern relates to biased selection of curricular content failing to include multicultural and pluralistic values. There are also questions of pedagogy, such as the depth to which extensive facts are delivered to primary schoolchildren. The issues surrounding cultural literacy theory in modern American education are less relevant when examining the Qing dynasty elementary school curriculum. Cultural literacy in the Qing dynasty was predominantly based on the Han Chinese textual tradition, ratified by the imperial government, and specified by the requirements of the examination system. Although Qing dynasty educational thought was not static or monolithic, it can be said that a predetermined scope of cultural literacy existed in the Qing. The debate on the merits of this scope and issues of cultural memory for the collective will not be covered here. Instead, the following analysis examines how the *Treasury* aided the educational endeavor of examination preparation for the individual through concepts of cultural literacy curricular theory.

The required knowledge and reading material for Qing dynasty examinees as part of their educational journey will be explored first, which serves to map out potential sources of Qing dynasty cultural literacy and provide context to the material in the *Treasury*. Although the principal essay questions were extracted quotes from the Four Books and the Five Classics, sole knowledge of these texts would have been inadequate. Not only the orthodox Cheng-Zhu school commentaries but also the historical writings, the masters works, and selected writings of literary masters were prerequisite knowledge for interpreting and answering examination questions. As early as the Song dynasty, the *Three Character Classic* taught children: "Read the masters after the classics . . . Read history after the classics and masters" 經既明，方讀子 . . . 經子通，讀諸史.[90] Extensive reading in an ordered sequence remained established practice in the Qing dynasty as reflected by the prescriptive educational discourse, albeit with a modified order and an increased number of texts. Cheng Duanli's curriculum in the *Guidelines for Proper Upbringing* has a substantial reading list of texts—from the Four Books, the Five Classics, and various commentaries of the canonical works, to historical works and literary works.[91] Tang Biao's *Jiashu jiaoxue fa* 家塾教學法 (Family school teaching methods) further corroborates extensive reading, listing canonical works, historical works, and prose masters of the Tang and Song dynasties from the perspective of learning composition techniques.[92] This continued throughout the imperial dynasty, with late Qing scholar-official Zhang Zhidong 張之洞 (1826–1909) compiling a formidable reading list of over 2,200 texts for youngsters.[93] Liang Qichao also produced a voluminous reading list for Chinese students drawn from each of the four bibliographical divisions of the imperial library. Following the bibliography, he named twenty-six titles as the minimum book list to be mastered for one to be considered a Chinese scholar.[94] It should be noted that these educational prescriptions were distillations of the vast Chinese literary tradition and involved only the seminal and essential titles. Yet this casual survey of Qing educators highlights the substantial amount of reading expected of the student. Despite the consensus of a knowledge base, it is surprising that there was not a dictionary of terms (e.g., personages, places, events) required for the examinations. This was ultimately the role of the elementary textbooks.

As children made the transition from word-recognition primers like the "*san bai qian*" to the advanced texts in the reading lists, elementary textbooks served to bridge the gap in cultural knowledge and classical literacy. This would also lay the foundations for later composition. Educator and statesman Cai Yuanpei wrote:

> The goal of traditional Chinese education was to achieve scholarly honor and [thereby] become an official. To this end, one had to undertake the imperial examinations. For the examinations, one was required to write poetry and prose. To compose, one had to learn ancient words, study ancient texts and remember ancient particulars. As such, one started with texts such as the *Thousand Character Essay*, the *Shentong shi* 神童詩 [Verses of child prodigies], the *Young Horse and the Shadow of a Whip*, and the *Treasury*. Next would be the Four Books and Five Classics, followed by learning the eight-legged essay and the verses of five-character phrases and eight rhyming words.[95]

Cai directly states the reality of education for officialdom and explains the stepwise progression from the primers to advanced texts to written composition. Texts like the *Treasury* assisted learners not only with the literary language but also to "learn ancient words, study ancient texts and remember ancient particulars." Feng Youlan's biography mentions the *Treasury* in the same light—as reading material for literary allusions and other tropes in preparation for exam compositions.[96] In other words, the elementary textbooks provided the necessary cultural literacy. In terms of American cultural literacy, Hirsch's seminal work boldly proposed a list of "what literate Americans know."[97] This list developed into a dictionary of terms covering the Bible; mythology and folklore; proverbs; idioms; literature; philosophy and religion; conventions of written English; fine arts; history; politics; geography; anthropology, psychology, and sociology; business and economics;

mathematics and the physical sciences; earth sciences; life sciences; medicine and health; and technology.[98] Similarly, one could ask: What did the Qing dynasty literate know? What would a Qing cultural literacy dictionary include? The answer would involve extracting and classifying concrete units of information from all the titles in the aforementioned reading lists. While this is beyond the scope of this study, an analysis of the personages and literature cited in the *Treasury* does offer preliminary insights into the nature and content of cultural literacy in the Qing dynasty.

4.2.1 Personages

The imperial Chinese education was decidedly literary in focus, underpinned by a moral philosophy based on ancient writings. The type of assessment used for an official appointment was also a major factor in education. Exam composition required strict adherence to the philosophical discourse of the Cheng-Zhu school and reproduction of related texts and commentaries in the tradition. Cai Yuanpei remarked: "Despite children earnestly wanting to understand such knowledge as the natural sciences and social sciences, these subjects were not taught as they did not pertain to the examinations."[99] The restriction to literary knowledge due to the Confucian humanistic tradition has also been linked to the requirements of writing stylized essays and poetry, along with the cultural, historical, geographical, and sociopolitical considerations in Ridley's analysis.[100] The knowledge requirements for the examination are reflected in part by the contents of elementary primers. The *Treasury* was a collection of allusions, but the main text and annotations also proffered a voluminous array of cultural elements—from people and places to events and texts. This section will touch upon the personages in the text.

There are 1,488 personages named in the *Treasury* throughout the main text and annotations, including historical, mythical, and fictional characters. Although the text is not ordered chronologically, the period covered spans from high antiquity, beginning from the creation myth of Pan Gu 盤古, to the Ming dynasty, represented by the poet Yang Shen

楊慎 (1488–1559). As a comparison, there are six thousand persons in the *Biographical Dictionary of the Qin, Han, and Xin Periods (221 BC–AD 24),* which is largely drawn from the standard histories (*zhengshi* 正史), while there are over eight thousand entries for the Later Han period.[101] This amounts to a total of over fourteen thousand personages from the Qin, Xin, and Han dynasties alone, which the students would later encounter in their study of the historical works. Students were introduced to key figures in history and literature in the elementary primers and reacquainted with them in advanced texts. This repetition of information served to improve the strength of the association in the child's memory. The same figures featured even across the primers. As expected, there is considerable overlap between the personages mentioned in the *Treasury* and the other primers—for example, forty-three out of the forty-eight individuals in the *Three Character Classic* and thirty-six out of the forty-eight persons in the *Thousand Character Essay*. In terms of the 289 personages in the Four Books, the *Treasury* mentions nine out of the twelve persons in the *Great Learning*, all eleven persons in the *Doctrine of the Mean*, 38 out of 140 in the *Analects*, and 45 out of 175 in the *Mencius*. The limited coverage from the *Analects* and the *Mencius* was arguably due to the characters being students or contemporaries of the respective philosophers who may not have achieved historical eminence themselves.

Beyond merely providing repeated exposure to the same cultural information, the *Treasury* elaborates on prior knowledge through different anecdotes and forms of address. Personages are frequently known by various names, including their personal name, style name, titles, and posthumous title. For example, poet Su Shi 蘇軾 (1036–1101) is mentioned sixteen times, inclusive of references to his literature, and is variously addressed by his personal name, style name "Su Zizhan" 蘇子瞻, and his art name "Su Dongpo" 蘇東坡; calligrapher Wang Xizhi 王羲之 (321–379) is also known by his military position "You jun" 右軍. Rulers could also be known by their personal name, posthumous name, or temple names. As the different names were used interchangeably in the literature, the *Treasury* provided readers with this understanding through the annotations.

The most popular figure is, unsurprisingly, Confucius who is mentioned forty-nine times, followed by Emperor Gaozu and Emperor Wu of the Han dynasty, who appear thirty-five times and thirty-three times, respectively. Although categorizing the personages could shed light on the cultural and philosophical thought in the text, it is technically difficult to do so. This is because many of the personages have various professional roles—as scholar, philosopher, official, historian, essayist, even poet. Moreover, they are ascribed multiple social roles, such as parent, child, leader, or minister. The chapters of the *Treasury* are grouped as semantic categories, and one significant cultural framework that is embodied by the categorization is the five fundamental human relations. There are two roles in each relationship, and each role is stereotyped in the primers with moral significance as part of the tradition of elementary learning. But this was also necessitated by the examinations requiring interpretation through the lens of the Cheng-Zhu orthodoxy. As such, the stereotypes were presented as positive or negative exemplars of the roles based on various characteristics. In contrast to shorter primers, the *Treasury* allows multidimensional portrayals of personages. Simultaneously, connections to diverse schemas in the child's mind can be formed as the following analysis of the Duke of Zhou demonstrates.

A central figure in the development of Confucian thinking is the Duke of Zhou (hereafter referred to as "the duke"), who was prominently represented in the primers and canonical works. The duke is first encountered in the *Three Character Classic*, which states that he composed the *Rituals of Zhou*, while the *Thousand Character Essay* instead addresses the duke by his style name "Dan" 旦 in association with his fiefdom the state of Lu: "Then, to make a livable residence of Qufu, if not Dan, who could have managed it?" 奄宅曲阜，微旦孰營.[102] The duke is mentioned fifteen times in the *Treasury* in either the main text or annotation. As the child reads sequentially through the text, different anecdotes of the duke are slowly revealed in fourteen chapters (from the second chapter to the final chapter) and across all four sections. The development of knowledge is cumulative and builds on earlier reading. The fourteen references to the duke in order of presentation are translated below.

Chapter	Main Text	Annotation
“Land and environs”	海不揚波，知中國有聖人。[103] The sea has no waves, one knows that there is a sage in the kingdom of the Central Plains.	周成王時，交趾越裳氏重三譯來獻白雉，周公曰：「德澤不加，君子不享其質；政令不施，君子不臣其人。」譯曰：「吾受命吾國之黃耇，曰『天無烈風淫雨，海不揚波三年矣，意者中國有聖人乎，蓋往朝之。』」使者還，迷歸途，周公賜以指南車，常為先導。 During the reign of King Cheng of Zhou, an envoy from the state of Yuechang in Jiaozhi came to pay tribute with a white pheasant and required several interpreters. The duke said: “The ruler does not enjoy gifts from areas in which their virtue is not conferred. The ruler does not consider as subjects those who do not receive his commands.” The interpreter replied: “I am ordered by the elders of my state. They said: ‘There have not been storms and waves for three years. This means there is a sage in the kingdom of the Central Plains—we ought to pay tribute.’” The envoy was uncertain of the path for his return journey and the Duke of Zhou presented him with a south-pointing chariot to lead the way.

Chapter	Main Text	Annotation
"Years and Seasons"	日月其除，志士正宜待旦。[104] As time flies, the noble scholar waits for the sunrise.	除，去也。言日月舍我而去，當效周公坐以待旦而急於行也。 *Chu* means passing. This means that the days and months pass before us. One should emulate the Duke of Zhou in sitting to wait for the sunrise before urgently attending to tasks.
"Grandparent, Grandchild, Parent, and Child"	橋木高而仰，似父之道；梓木低而俯，如子之卑。[105] A *qiao* tree is tall and rising like the way of the father. The *zi* tree is low and drooping like the humility of the son.	《世說》：伯禽與康叔見周公，三見三笞之。伯禽莫知其故，問於商子。商子曰：「南山之陽，有木名橋，南山之陰，有木名梓，何不往觀？」二子往，見橋木高而仰，梓木低而俯，還告商子。商子曰：「橋者，父道也。梓者，子道也。」 *Shishuo*:[106] Boqin and Kangshu visited the Duke of Zhou. They visited three times and were whipped each time. Boqin did not know why and consulted Master Shang, who said: "On the south side of the South Mountain, there is a tree called *qiao*. On the north side of the South Mountain there is a tree called *zi*. Why don't you go and have a look?" The two went and saw that the *qiao* tree was tall and rising, while the *zi* tree was low and drooping. They returned to report to Master Shang, who said: "The *qiao* represents the way of the father, the *zi* the way of the son."

Chapter	Main Text	Annotation
“Elder and Younger Brothers”	東征破斧，周公大義滅親。[107] Marching eastward and breaking axes, the Duke of Zhou put an end to his relatives for the greater good.	《詩》：「既破我斧，又缺我斨，周公東征，四國是皇。」（按）武王克商，使弟管叔鮮、蔡叔度監紂子武庚之國，而二叔以武庚叛。故周公東征，三年乃得二叔而誅之。 *Odes*: “We have broken our axes, we have splintered our hatchets; but the Duke of Zhou marched eastward, the states of the four quarters, them he corrected.”[108] Comment: King Wu of the state of Zhou overthrew the Shang dynasty and had his younger brothers Guanshu and Caishu oversee Wu Geng (fl. 1043)—the son of the deposed King Zhou of the Shang dynasty. However, they later allied with Wu Geng in attempting a coup. Thus the Duke of Zhou conducted a punitive expedition in the east and after three years, his two brothers were captured and put to death.

(*Continued*)

Chapter	Main Text	Annotation
"Fellows, Friends, Guests, and Hosts"	周公握髮而待士。[109] The Duke of Zhou gathered up his hair to welcome worthies.	成王封周公之子伯禽於魯，周公戒之曰：「子毋以魯國驕士，吾嘗一飯三吐哺，一沐三握髮，以延天下之賢士。」 King Cheng of the Zhou dynasty conferred the state of Lu on the Duke of Zhou's son Boqin. The duke instructed him: "Do not on account of the state of Lu become arrogant toward scholars. I receive worthy scholars from across the kingdom with such urgency that I once interrupted my bathing and my meals three times."
"Human Body"	周公反握，作興周之相。[110] The Duke of Zhou had hyper-extendable wrists—he was the chancellor who brought the Zhou dynasty to prominence.	《相法》：周公兩手如綿，可以反握。 *Principles of Appearances*: The Duke of Zhou's hands were like cotton; they could extend backwards.

Chapter	Main Text	Annotation
"Attire and Apparel"	襁褓乃小兒之衣。[111] Swaddling clothes are clothes for the infant.	史：武王崩，成王少，在襁褓之中，周公踐阼攝政，代成王當國，負扆以朝諸侯。 Historical records: When King Wu of Zhou passed away, the young King Cheng was still in swaddling clothes and the Duke of Zhou acted as regent. Acting on behalf of the king, he would hold assemblies with the feudal lords.
"Buildings and Rooms"	白屋是布衣之家。[112] The humble abode is the common person's home.	《家語》：周公居冢宰之尊，而猶下白屋之士。 *School Sayings of Confucius*: The Duke of Zhou had the respected position of chief minister of the state yet he would visit humble scholars personally.

(*Continued*)

Chapter	Main Text	Annotation
"Literary Matters"	《易經》乃姬周文王、周公所繫，故曰《周易》。[113] Both King Wen of Zhou and the Duke of Zhou provided commentary on the *Changes*, thus entitled the *Zhouyi*.	《易》，卦象之書，有交易、變易之義，故曰《易》。《易》卦伏羲所畫，《彖》乃周文所繫，《象》、《爻》乃周公所繫。《繫辭》、《文言》、《序卦》、《雜卦》，乃孔子釋經之詞也。凡二萬九千一百零七字。 The *Changes* is a book of hexagrams; it has the meaning of interaction and transformation, hence it is entitled *Changes*. The trigrams of the *Changes* were drawn by Fuxi, the commentary "On the Hexagram Statements" was appended by King Wen of Zhou; the commentary "On the Images" and "Line Statements" appended by the Duke of Zhou; the commentaries "On the Appended Phrases," "Sayings on Pattern," "On the Trigrams," "Sequenced Hexagrams," and "Interposed Hexagrams" were Confucius' explanations of the main text. There is a total of 29,107 characters.

Chapter	Main Text	Annotation
"Literary Matters"	不學無術，漢霍光之為人。[114] One is unskilled without learning—this describes Huo Guang of the Han dynasty.	班固讚霍光云：「擁昭立宣，光為師保。雖周公阿衡，何以加此。然光不學無術，闇於大理。」 Ban Gu praised Huo Guang: "Supporting Emperor Zhao of the Han dynasty and installing Emperor Xuan of the Han dynasty, Huo was the preceptor and guardian. Even the Duke of Zhou and Yi Yin could not surpass this. However, without learning from the ancients and without strategy, Huo would be in the dark about important principles."
"Inventions"	周公作指南車，羅盤是其遺制。[115] The Duke of Zhou invented the south-pointing chariot, the compass is a legacy of this.	越裳氏獻白雉，迷其歸路，周公作指南車，以為先導。 The Yuechang envoy presented a white pheasant. As he could not find his way home, the Duke of Zhou designed the south-pointing compass to lead the way.

(*Continued*)

Chapter	Main Text	Annotation
"Inventions"	周公獨制禮樂。[116] The Duke of Zhou alone created the system of rites and music.	周成王幼，周公攝政，朝諸侯於明堂，制禮作樂，頒度量，而天下大服。 King Cheng of the Zhou dynasty was young, and the Duke of Zhou became regent. The duke held assemblies with the feudal lords at the Hall of Brightness, established the system of ritual and music, promulgated standards for measures and weights, and achieved the allegiance of the kingdom.
"Birds and Beasts"	愛屋及烏，謂因此而惜彼。[117] "Fondness of the house extends to the nesting crows" means cherishing one thing on account of another.	周武王登夏台以臨殷民，周公曰：「愛其人者，愛其屋上烏。憎其人者，憎其餘胥。」〔釋〕烏巢近屋，恐毀巢而傷其屋。 King Wu of Zhou ascended the Xia dynasty tower to look over the Shang population. The Duke of Zhou said: "Loving their people, one loves the crows above their home. Despising their people, one despises the village walls." Gloss: The crow's nest is near the house, and one fears harming the home when destroying the nest.

Chapter	Main Text	Annotation
"Flowers and Trees"	成王剪桐封弟，因無戲言。[118] Duke Cheng of Zhou cut the leaf of the *tong* tree and conferred [territory] to his younger brother because he could not talk flippantly.	史：周成王與弟叔虞削桐葉為珪，戲曰：「吾以此封汝。」周公請擇日，王曰：「無特戲之耳。」周公曰：「天子無戲言。」遂封叔虞與堯之故墟，曰唐侯。 Historical records: King Cheng of Zhou gave his younger brother Shu Yu the leaf of the *tong* tree cut in the shape of a jade tablet, and jokingly said: "With this, I give you a bestowal." The duke then asked the king to set a date [to confer a fiefdom]. The king replied: "I did not confer a specific fiefdom." The Duke of Zhou responded: "The Son of Heaven does not talk flippantly." Shuyu was subsequently conferred the former areas of King Yao and titled "Prince of Tang."

(*Continued*)

Within the *Treasury*, the persona of the "Duke of Zhou" is elaborated upon and associated with various cultural concepts. Despite the superficial snippets of information, the duke lies within a web of related knowledge, including persons, events, geographical names, sayings, texts, and items. The cognitive schema of stereotypes is activated as the reader deepens their understanding of the duke. The following analysis is of information solely found in the *Treasury* without reference to other works.

In the first encounter with the duke, the reader learns that the duke has the role of "ruler." He is described as a sage ruler whose moral qualities result in incredible natural phenomena like the sea being without waves for three years. His sagely character is characterized in the various entries as reluctance to receive undeserved tribute from a non-vassal state, gifting a south-pointing chariot for their safe return journey, diligence in cherishing time, putting public interest over kinship bonds, expressing the utmost respect for worthies, and enacting the system of rites and music. At the same time, the duke embodies the exemplary "minister" to the young King Cheng of Zhou. Beyond the above traits, his dedication to the task of minister is also seen in admonishing King Cheng. As a father, he teaches Boqin (fl. eleventh century BCE) through both his words and his example. As a brother, he offers advice to King Wu of Zhou and can discipline his brothers when they rebel. Hence the reader is offered ways of interpreting various roles based on the practice of a "sage." In terms of personages, the duke is also associated with names such as King Cheng of Zhou (nephew), King Wu of Zhou (brother), Guanshu (fl. 1043; brother), Caishu (fl. 1043; brother), Kangshu (fl. 1043; brother), King Zhou of Shang (c. 1105–1046 BCE; previous ruler), Wu Geng (son of King Zhou of Shang), and Boqin (son), who are contemporaries, as well as the Han dynasty regent Huo Guang (d. 68 BCE). In terms of historical events, the duke is linked to the overthrow of the Shang dynasty and the "Rebellion of the Three Guards." Geographical terms related to the duke include the state of Lu. Moreover, he is first associated with the south-pointing chariot, but in a later chapter he is named as its inventor. Thus, the depiction of the duke in the *Treasury* enables a rich network of semantic meanings to be created.

The information is consolidated with texts in the child's reading journey, where the portrayals are further imbued with cultural values in the canonical works. In the Four Books, the duke's name is mentioned in all but the *Great Learning*. However, the duke's voice and authority are evident in the *Great Learning* as his instruction to Kangshu—the "Announcement to Kang" (*Kang gao* 康誥) from the *Documents*—is quoted multiple times.[119] As for the duke's status as a sage, this is explicitly stated in the *Mencius,* which describes him as a "sage of antiquity" (*gu shengren* 古聖人) and mentions the duke in the same breath as Confucius ("delighting in the Way of the Duke of Zhou and Confucius" 悅周公、仲尼之道).[120] His sagehood is also implied in the *Analects,* as Confucius reveres the duke—he considers not dreaming of the duke as a decline in his character.[121] In terms of his regency, the *Doctrine of the Mean* and the *Mencius* state that the duke realized the benevolent government envisaged by Kings Wen and Wu of Zhou.[122] In other words, rulership based on benevolent government is exemplary. His leadership strategy is further described in the *Analects*, which is consistent with his perspicacious management of personnel that the reader is acquainted with in the *Treasury*.[123] The passage in the *Analects* is framed as an instruction to his son titled the "Duke of Lu," which resonates with the depictions of the duke as a father in the *Treasury*. Moreover, the duke achieving the humane vision of his forefathers is labeled as being of the utmost family reverence in the *Doctrine of the Mean*, offering new light on the duke in the role of a "son" and the practice of family reverence.[124] His role as a sibling is further supplemented as Mencius explains that he appointed and trusted his older brother Guanshu without knowing he would later rebel.[125] The occurrence of characters in the primer may seem irregular but finds coherence when evaluated in the broader framework of human relations. The five fundamental relations are a key concept in elementary education. Although several familial, historical, and philosophical associations can also be drawn from extracts of the duke in the *Treasury*, these schemas may not be as established in the young reader's mind. While the Four Books help the reader's understanding of the duke, it is in the Five Classics and historical works that detailed narratives of the duke's life and leadership are to be found. The canonical works and their commentaries also involve Confucian political philosophy and the idea of "inner sageliness and outer kingliness" that the duke epitomized.[126] By this time, the cognitive schemas of the duke in his various roles would easily accommodate the learning of additional details.

There is an unequivocal connection and continuity of the classical knowledge between the *Treasury* and the canonical works. Even though elementary primers tended to eschew theoretical analysis of ethical and political topics, the stock of personages were integral elements in the arguments of such topics in advanced learning. How does this work at the cognitive level? Semantic memory is stored as schemas, of which there are two types—scripts for events and frames that are cognitive structures referring to aspects of the world.[127] For example, the flow of events during a restaurant meal is a "script," whereas one's concept of a "building" having floors and walls would be a "frame." The influence of these schemas, which can be considered as prior knowledge, on memory encoding and retrieval is well established in the psychological and educational literature. A famous experiment was conducted in which children outperformed adults in memorizing the positions of chess pieces on a chessboard.[128] This was because the chess pieces were arranged as actual moves during a game and the children were skilled chess players while the adults were not. Better memory was solely the result of background knowledge of chess moves (a preexisting schema) by which the children could readily interpret and encode new information. Richard C. Anderson later tailored the schema theory to explain reading comprehension, noting that schemas had six functions in terms of the reading process: (1) providing scaffolding for assimilating information in the text; (2) facilitating selective allocation of attention; (3) enabling inferences that elaborate on the information; (4) allowing orderly searches of memory; (5) facilitating editing and summarizing of new information; and (6) permitting the construction of information where there are gaps in memory through inference.[129] Although there is debate on the configuration of semantic memory based on various sensory inputs, there is a general consensus that existing knowledge in the act of memory-making is significant. This is particularly so for children, as Catherine A. Haden explains:

> Indeed, what an individual already knows may be the most important determinant of what gets into memory. When children can make sense of what they are experiencing, they are able to attend more fully, and thus, encode information more completely than would otherwise be the case.[130]

New information activates existing knowledge and is more readily assimilated and encoded into memory if a preexisting scaffold of understanding is in place. Writing about the developing child's brain, Torkel Klingberg explains, "One of the most critical factors of memory storage is the ability to associate new memories with earlier ones."[131] It has also been shown that children's contextual background knowledge improves the readability of the material, even in the presence of syntactically complex sentences.[132]

The importance of prior knowledge was crucial in the sequence of Chinese education that children experienced. It was believed that earlier understanding would guide future thought and behavior; thus, what a child learned first would be most influential (*xian ru wei zhu* 先入為主). This was the rationale for the focus on moral knowledge from an early age, as previously discussed, which can be considered as establishing related schemas—frames for moral values and scripts for ritual behavior. However, Qing dynasty scholar Zhang Xuecheng 章學成 (1738–1801) interestingly uses the same phrase (*xian ru wei zhu*) when referring to developing writing ability.[133] In other words, cognitive and moral development were comparable in the educational approach and utilization of memory. The reiterative content of Chinese elementary textbooks reflects the understanding that the strength of an association in memory increases with repetition. For example, the concept of respecting talented scholars can be considered a cognitive "frame" with associated historical personages and reverential acts (e.g., the ruler personally visiting their abode, conferring handsome emolument, and so on). This frame is not only repeatedly activated in extracts related to the duke but generally within the *Treasury* and in prior and future reading material. In Zhang Zhigong's seminal analysis of premodern and early modern primers, he classifies the *Treasury* as a type of "transitional" textbook that furthers the child's knowledge of allusions, idioms, and cultural knowledge generally.[134] Zhang observes that ancient educators, recognizing that such knowledge needed to be memorized as the basis for future reading comprehension, compiled this type of textbook for the young reader, who at this stage in life has peak memory capacity and abundant time for reading.[135] Mindful of cognitive growth, Lu Shiyi emphasized the need for children to be acquainted with the knowledge base for adulthood prior to the age of fifteen.[136] Indeed, Hirsch also writes:

> At an early age when their memories are most retentive, children have an almost instinctive urge to learn specific tribal traditions. At that age, they seem to be fascinated by catalogues of information and are eager to master the materials that authenticate their membership in adult society.[137]

The rapidly growing synaptic connections in the child's mind were poised for cultural literacy—the foundation of their reading and writing. Persons, places, and events were important aspects of knowledge; however, from the perspective of Chinese early modern education, familiarization with the literary tradition was also important. Next, I turn to the presentation of literature for cultural literacy in the *Treasury*.

4.2.2 Literature

The diversity of material in the text can be gleaned from the citations of source titles alone. The extensive coverage of all branches of traditional literature in the *Treasury* has been previously outlined in the discussion on practical learning. Here the focus is not on the extension of reading material for textual verification of the sages' meaning but on the pragmatic purpose of mining the ancient texts for content relevant to examination writing and compositions. The ten-year-old reader, being the target audience for the *Treasury*, would not have been able to read, understand, and extract relevant material for composition from all 277 titles referenced in the *Treasury*. Hence, true to its name, the text was a "treasury" of literary information. As titles are cited for just over half the couplets, establishing the original texts of all the material was not a strong priority. Additionally, it can be argued that the allusions were selected for inclusion rather than the source texts themselves. On the other hand, that the source text was essential for examination or widely read would also correlate with the number of allusions it contributed to literary consciousness. Thus, firm conclusions cannot be drawn on the literary texts for cultural literacy by their inclusion in the *Treasury* but can hint at a set of popular texts.

Twenty-seven canonical works are cited, with the most popular references being the Five Classics (336 citations), far exceeding the forty-five citations for the Four Books. The Five Classics together are greater in volume, and it was only from the year 1787 that examination questions for all Five Classics were decreed compulsory. Indeed, the full "Thirteen Classics" comprise some 396 citations—the Five Classics with the addition of the *Rituals of Zhou*, the *Ceremonial Rituals*, the three commentaries on the *Spring and Autumn Annals*, the *Erya*, the *Mencius*, the *Analects,* and the *Classic of Family Reverence*. The other major category of canonical works is the philological works (thirty-three citations), including the *Extended Rhymes*, the *Guangya* 廣雅 (Extended *Erya*), the *Shiming*, the *Jiyun* 集韻 (Collected rhymes), and the *Piya*, with the most frequently cited work being *Explaining Simple Graphs and Analyzing Complex Graphs* (fourteen citations). The historical works comprise the largest number of citations (460), likely due to historical anecdotes later becoming allusions. As expected, the standard histories are highly referenced (289 citations). There are also a number of geographical records, annals, miscellaneous histories, biographical works that are each mentioned only once. The masters works boast the highest number of titles (111), with the largest category being miscellaneous writings (*xiaoshuo*), including anecdotes, essays, and records. Indeed, titles and citations from Daoist works and syncretic (*zajia* 雜家) and encyclopedic anthologies exceed those coming from the Confucian writers. These works also span the pre-Qin period to the Ming dynasty, as seen in the inclusion of the Ming dynasty elementary primer the *Extended Collection of Wise Words*. In terms of the literary collections, the *Treasury* names the prose writer or poet, but whether the composition was sourced from a literary anthology or collected works of the individual is unknown. There are a total of eighty-five titles and names mentioned—the most referenced being the anthology *Zhaoming wen xuan* and Han Yu's 韓愈 (768–825) writings. Evidently, an immense scope of literature is included in the *Treasury*.

The myriad of titles was introduced by way of the allusion, even if the actual texts were not read or studied until a much later age. Citing the source titles in the *Treasury* creates an association of information to the named text, thus consolidating understanding of the textual content before the text was read. Qing dynasty elementary school teacher Chen Fangsheng 陳芳生 (fl. 1662–1722) advised fellow teachers to write a short description of each book in the school library and then briefly explain the function and content of each text and where one could find certain information.[138] Chen provides that familiarity with even the title of the books would pique interest in reading them and inspire the children to develop erudition at a later stage.

There are also several nonspecific citations, for example, some ninety annotations merely stating "historical record" (*shi* 史), "Han dynasty historical record" (*Han shi* 漢史), "Tang dynasty historical record" (*Tang shi* 唐史), or the "History of the Tang dynasty" (*Tang shu* 唐書).[139] In relation to literary works, annotations noted "an ancient poem" (*gushi* 古詩), "a poem of the Tang dynasty" (*Tangshi* 唐詩), "a poem of the Song dynasty" (*Song ren shi* 宋人詩), or "an ancient music bureau poem" (*gu yuefu* 古樂府). This may seem surprising to the modern reader who has access to great information at their fingertips. However, physical library collections in early modern China could only be assembled by private book collectors, private book printers, or members of the imperial court. It is likely that the original material could not be sourced. Merely labeling the annotation as related to one of the four bibliographic divisions or a further subdivision in history would suffice to aid the curious young mind. Moreover, this association would still create and activate knowledge schemas, linking to prior and future reading.

To contextualize the material in the child's learning trajectory and gauge how the *Treasury* further adds to prior knowledge, I now turn to some reading from an earlier stage. The *Three Character Classic* was one of the first primers read by the Qing dynasty child and is similarly comprised of cultural knowledge on literature. The *Three Character Classic* deliberately offers laconic descriptions of key texts in the order of the student's learning. The reading list begins with the Four Books and details the traditionally acknowledged author, the structure, or the main content. This is followed by the *Classic of Family Reverence* and then the Five Classics. Each of the Five Classics is given the same treatment in a pair of rhymed sentences as extracted below:

> 有連山 有歸藏 有周易 三易詳
> 有典謨 有訓誥 有誓命 書之奧
> 我周公 作周禮 著六官 存治體

大小戴 註禮記 述聖言 禮樂備
曰國風 曰雅頌 號四詩 當諷詠
詩既亡 春秋作 寓褒貶 別善惡
三傳者 有公羊 有左氏 有穀梁[140]

Detailing the Changes are the *Zhouyi*
The *Lianshan* and the *Guicang*, all three
In the *Documents* are canons, oaths, instructions
counsels, decrees, proclamations, and injunctions.
The Duke of Zhou set the *Rituals* grand;
Only six offices to govern the land
Of the *Records on Ritual* the two Dais wrote;
Of teachings on propriety and music, they note.
State songs, odes, and hymns;
Four-verse forms rhythm.
As collecting odes ceased, the *Annals* were compiled;
Ascribing praise and blame, judgements reconciled.
Its commentaries are three, the *Zuo zhuan*,
The *Gongyang zhuan* and the *Guliang zhuan*.

The *Treasury* mirrors the *Three Character Classic* in providing such textual information on the Five Classics at the beginning of "Literary Matters":

《書經》載上古唐虞三代之事，故曰《尚書》；《易經》乃姬周文王、周公所繫，故曰《周易》。二戴曾刪《禮記》，故曰《戴禮》；二毛曾注《詩經》，故曰《毛詩》。孔子作《春秋》，因獲麟而絕筆，故曰《麟經》。榮於華袞，乃《春秋》一字之褒；嚴於斧鉞，乃《春秋》一字之貶。（〈文事〉）

The *Documents* records the accounts of Emperor Yao, Emperor Shun, and the Three Dynasties of high antiquity, hence titled the *Shangshu* [records of high antiquity]. The *Changes* was supplemented by King Wen of Zhou and the Duke of Zhou, hence titled the *Zhouyi* [the Zhou *Changes*]. The two [editors] with the surname Dai had removed parts of the *Records on Ritual*, hence titled *Dai Li* [the Dai edition of the rituals]. The two [scholars] with the surname Mao annotated the *Odes*, hence titled *Mao Shi* [the Mao edition of the *Odes*]. Confucius wrote the *Spring and*

> *Autumn Annals* but stopped after a unicorn was caught, hence titled the *Lin jing* [Unicorn classic]. One word of praise in the *Spring and Autumn Annals* is as glorious as magnificent imperial robes. One word of censure in the *Spring and Autumn Annals* is as severe as the [punishment of the] hatchet or battle-axe.[141]

There is limited duplication of information when comparing the *Three Character Classic* with the *Treasury*. In the *Treasury*, the Five Classics are described through their titles. Alternative titles of the Five Classics that the children would encounter in other texts are explained by reference to content, author, editor, or the circumstances surrounding the writing of the canonical work. The annotations detail the traditional textual history and provide further background on the structure, even including the total number of words in the text. New information builds upon preexisting knowledge of the text. For example, the *Three Character Classic* names the *Zhouyi*, while here the reason for "Zhou" in its name is related to the commentaries that are traditionally thought to be compiled by King Wen of Zhou and the Duke of Zhou; the two ritual texts in the earlier primer are explained in the *Treasury*'s annotation as being part of three ritual texts; the significance of "praise and blame" in the *Spring and Autumn Annals* is further elaborated by a quote in the annotation from the *Guliang Commentary*, which readers would recognize as being one of the three commentaries, although this is not specifically stated.

The *Three Character Classic* continues by addressing notable masters works through the names of the philosophers: "The five philosophers are Xunzi, Yang Xiong; Wen Zhongzi, Laozi, and Zhuangzi" 五子者，有荀揚，文中子，及老莊.[142] All these works are cited, and anecdotes related to the philosopher are included in the *Treasury*. The historical works before the Song dynasty, when the *Three Character Classic* was written, are simply described as the "seventeen histories," and the literary collections are not addressed at all.[143] Based on the sheer volume of the *Treasury*, the material consolidates and develops prior knowledge, while also increasing the child's literary repertoire.

Like many other elementary primers, the *Treasury* was a pastiche of quotes or appropriations of quotes from the texts arranged in mnemonically effective ways to connect to later learning. The *Elementary*

Learning anthologizes material from pre-Song and Song dynasty texts, and the sentences are copied verbatim. Kelleher's analysis shows a predominance of canonical works in the "Inner chapters," while the "Outer Chapters" has a majority of historical and masters works—dynastic histories and works of the Confucian masters.[144] Indeed, Nugent argues that the lines in the *Thousand Character Essay* primarily served as cues to a wider and deeper body of cultural knowledge for the child. He writes:

> . . . its true value was in serving as a series of mnemonic pegs on which to hang more important elements, namely the classical writings (ranging from poetry to historical anecdotes) and explanations found in the paratext (in the form of annotations). Additionally, new paratextual expansions were created that themselves aided in setting to memory not the text of the *Qianzi wen* itself, but the information to which its lines point and which is made explicit in the paratextual annotations.[145]

Most of the lines of the *Thousand Character Essay* have this function, and such dense intertextuality sows the seeds for later knowledge consolidation.

Intertextuality was a prominent feature of Chinese writing throughout history and particularly the eight-legged essays. Wendy Swartz argues that the ability to appropriate from textual sources and cultural meanings was a condition of writing in early medieval China. She explains: "Referencing certain texts, topics or notions could signal not only cultural literacy but also membership in the cultural elite, which was formed to a great extent by shared interests, values and education."[146] The cultural elite referred to those educated in literary Chinese forms and broadly read in the literary traditions. In the fifth century, Liu Xie poetically described the utilization of past literature in writing:

> 經籍深富，辭理遐亙。皓如江海，鬱若崑鄧。文梓共采，瓊珠交贈。用人若己，古來無懵。
>
> Profound and rich are the Classics and ancient texts,
> Their language is exquisite and their ideas have far-reaching implications,

> Their realm is vast as rivers and seas,
> And fruitful as Mount K'un and Forest Teng;
> They are [filled with literary allusions and timber] for a literary carpenter to choose and take,
> And jade and pearls in abundance as gifts.
> To be able to use the words of others as if they were one's own creation
> Is to have perfect understanding of the past.[147]

Indeed, one's skills in writing were not so much based on creative imagination but the creative appropriation of the textual tradition. In discussing the literary style of the Tang dynasty, Charles Hartman also wrote: "Originality does not consist of devising new formulations but rather of displaying virtuosity at juxtaposing old formulas."[148] Such notions of writing remained ingrained in the culture such that it became the very standard for examination until the end of the Qing dynasty. The body of cultural and philosophical knowledge for the civil service examinations was standardized by the imperial government, and the candidate was to reproduce this in their writing. In Gong Duqing's study of Qing eight-legged essays, he argues that the essays were based on one's ability to reproduce the lines, structure, and values of ancient texts. As a result, the essays were highly reproducible to the extent that "if the examination topic was the same, the eight-legged essay answer and its line of reasoning based on the commentaries (i.e., the content and structure) would be similar regardless of where, when, or who wrote it."[149] However, composition was not a blind transcription of choice phrases but entailed interpreting and adapting the raw material for the new context. Reading and memorizing texts for this purpose was an essential part of exam preparation.

In the *Treasury*, each parallel construction pertains to a literary allusion, and several allusions are frequently included in the same couplet. The annotations thus contain citations from the source titles that are lengthier than the main text. The condensed main text is the received interpretation of the allusion and the consensus appropriation of the original text, which is packaged in parallelism to aid memory. Moreover, intertextual references were openly cited for the reader's convenience. These references further existing knowledge of the texts themselves from earlier primers but broaden their literary horizons to hundreds of titles across the bibliographic spectrum.

Scholarly achievement in the imperial examinations was a key concern in Qing education. In the introduction to his essay on education, Wang Yun remarks:

> 不敢望子弟為聖賢，亦當望子弟為鼎甲。
> Even if you cannot dare to expect that your child will become a sage or worthy, you should expect him to place among the three highest grades in the palace examination.[150]

His comment humorously throws light on the dichotomous aims of the educational process. That becoming a sage could even be commensurate with a rank in the palace examination would be absurd for Cheng-Zhu school loyalists, but that the comment is made casually indicates this was a common view at the time. Indeed, Kai-wing Chow notes that many writers, compilers, and editors of books on the canonical works, history, prose, and poems were in fact preparing for their own examinations.[151] What little is known of Cheng Dengji and Zou Shengmai is that both were erudite but did not achieve examination success nor an official career. However, Cheng as a primary school teacher and Zou as a publisher compiled the *Treasury* for a specific audience—readers who were preparing for the examinations. A vital outcome of the late imperial educational process was exam readiness. Such education began with training in the ability to read and write in the literary language and culminated in mastering the eight-legged essays and regulated verse. Elementary textbooks were vital tools in this training, as Brokaw notes of the Sibao publishing trade: children learned various skills through the reading of the primers, including learning characters, absorbing behavioral precepts, acquiring familiarization with vocabulary and concepts of canonical texts, and understanding the parallelism and rhythms of classical Chinese.[152]

This section has analyzed how the *Treasury* served as an aid for examination preparation. The structure and content of the primer helped the budding scholar become familiar with the form and knowledge of advanced texts. From the chapter framework to each line and annotation, the text offered semantic, phonologic, and syntactic cues to the literary language. The text was akin to a bridge in knowledge and skills, as the child progressed from accumulating vocabulary (lower-level language skills) to understanding sentences and cultural connotations (higher-level language skills). The cognitive journey can be seen as an accumulation of semantic memory and establishing the relevant schemas.

The presentation of information in the *Treasury* is consistent with the theory of cultural literacy. The terms and allusions are extensive and seemingly superficial, but the disparate fragments of material had a cumulative effect. On one level, the text itself was to be read sequentially, with the reader expected to assimilate knowledge in the reading process. This is evident through the first mention of a person, in which the reader is given background information (e.g., personal name, style name, dynasty) in the annotation, while subsequent mentions of the same character refer to prior annotations. On another level, the intertextuality gives cues for future reading. That is, the allusions themselves in the main text are mnemonic tools, the prior knowledge for advanced texts. The text was highly cognizant of the child's developing mind—ready to encode facts and knowledge. Engaging the memory was the first step in learning, but cultural literacy required understanding and nuanced appropriation of the knowledge for composition. Essay writing was undoubtedly the culmination of one's classical literacy learning. It was also hoped that the concepts and values were internalized and practiced in daily life. In this way, articulation in essays would not be mere regurgitation or rhetoric.

CONCLUSION

> *Many very successful species, such as ants, crocodiles, viruses and butterflies, come into the world preprogrammed with the equipment to survive. Humans, however, are a species that can only survive by learning. Without it, we would have no language, no complex tools, no transport systems, and little in the way of society.*
>
> —Alan Baddeley, Michael W. Eysenck, and Michael C. Anderson, *Memory*

Learning is a necessary human endeavor, and education is a universal project. Teaching and learning have thus occupied minds throughout human history. Qing China also offered a variety of theories, practices, and resources for the educational endeavor. My findings on Qing dynasty primary education as reflected in the elementary primer *Treasury* demonstrate a sophisticated and complex educational agenda. This concluding chapter turns to the wider implications of the research findings for contemporary educational discourse and cross-cultural dialogue.

I begin by discussing some issues that may hinder cross-cultural engagement in this area before offering potential solutions through my research. Misconceptions of education in late imperial China broadly relate to two stereotypical notions: the "East" and the "traditional." First, the assumption of a fundamentally distinct culture such that Eastern and Western educational ideas are incommensurable. Admittedly, there are difficulties for the education scholar who is a non-Sinologist due to the seemingly impenetrable nature of the specialist Chinese knowledge. Despite translations of the seminal texts of premodern Chinese education, there are also foreign names, dynastic periods, and cultural details to grasp. After this hurdle, the educational concepts are shrouded in philosophical jargon that must be elaborated upon using modern educational terms to gauge their scope of meaning, such as the notions of "family reverence" and "self-cultivation." In this regard, much can be learned from the area of comparative philosophy. The history of dialogue between Eastern and Western philosophy is described as undergoing three stages of appropriation, critical engagement, and comparison.[1] In the stage of comparison, Shun has also drawn attention to an asymmetrical analytical tendency with scholars using Western philosophical frameworks to discuss Chinese thought.[2] Arguably, the first steps toward dialogue are inevitably asymmetric, as one party reaches out to engage the other. This is manifest in the current cross-cultural educational discourse, which is largely dominated by specialists of Chinese studies—academics in philosophy or education.

The last decade has seen comparative research on educational practices across the analytic and continental traditions, and Chinese traditions become increasingly popular.[3] These studies have explored resonances between individual philosophers, contemplative practices, educational concepts, and ethical self-cultivation, among other themes, to stimulate mutual learning between cultures. However, the studies have analyzed within the scope of advanced learning in the Confucian perspective, and there is less literature on primary education and associated texts. Despite this, the comparative studies provide definitive evidence that there are educational goals and processes shared across cultures that are worthy of further dialogue.

Any comparative study should begin with "an initial assertion of commonality."[4] For example, education scholar Jin Li has been criticized for her premise that European-American learning is defined cognitively, while the Chinese take a moral outlook to education, and hence the educational traditions of the two cultures "did not and are still not likely to intersect."[5] Granted, there is a certain degree of incommensurability between a modern Western curriculum framework and that of late imperial China. However, many researchers engaged in cross-cultural educational discourse would disagree with the total absence of areas of intersection. Beyond an initial assumption of commonality, the comparative methodology is significant to prevent dichotomies and generalizations without an understanding of the underlying intellectual history and philosophy.[6] In their volume on cross-cultural perspectives on Confucian learning, Roland Reichenbach and Duck-Joo Kwak begin by highlighting unproductive East-West dualisms, including "formality versus free-thinking, conformity versus independence or obedience versus autonomy."[7] Such dichotomies easily fall apart upon examination of the rich history of ideas in "Eastern" and "Western" education. Mindful of the pitfalls, I will elaborate on a potential framework for discussion later.

Dialogue on Chinese education must overcome not only cultural dichotomy but also the tradition-modernity polarity. "Tradition," seen as a condition ultimately transformed by modernization,[8] inevitably paints historical values and practices in an unfavorable light. Within China, the education that occurred in early and imperial China was previously disregarded as "feudalist" by scholars before the New Confucianism movement but has since become increasingly researched.[9] Labeling these past educational theories and practices as "traditional" is further compounded by both reductionist and misguided views of the premodern and early modern Chinese curriculum as solely "philosophical," "moral education," or "rote learning." Indeed, my study of the nuanced pedagogy in the high Qing hopes to facilitate comparison with contemporary educational strategies.

While this study was not comparative in intent or design, the research furthers future cross-cultural dialogue at various levels—educational philosophy, pedagogic strategies, and the cognitive development of students. First, the analysis of primary educational thought is grounded in the intellectual history of the period, rather than using a modern hermeneutic of current educational ideas. My research having evaluated the underpinning educational philosophies of the high Qing, a future approach may be to compare such theories of human nature and educational aims in a similar period of another culture. We have seen that Qing dynasty elementary education was shaped by myriad sociopolitical circumstances and philosophical trends that interacted in creative ways. The eclectic nature of Qing education also lends itself to possible comparison with

Western curriculums that may have emerged through the ideas of different models and educators.

Indeed, the evolution of elementary education in the Qing presents an interesting parallel to the traditional liberal education adapting to progressive education and pragmatist progressivism.[10] Zhu Xi's reemphasis on a distinct stage of elementary learning influenced late imperial Chinese education, not least as it was endorsed as state orthodoxy after the Yuan dynasty. Zhu's approach to the learner becoming a sage began through a primary education that promoted ritual conduct ("the learning of tasks") and recitation of classical texts. However, teachers who implemented the curriculum were criticized for their limited concern toward student interest, and this element became increasingly challenged by the Ming dynasty. Wang Yangming, who was disillusioned by Zhu's program, advocated that principle was not external but inherent in the heart-mind. His new beliefs, which were considered progressive at the time, modified elementary schooling ideas, thereby redirecting emphasis to the attitude of the student. He asserted that students should be stimulated to learn and reflect on their thoughts, ultimately putting knowledge into practice. By the late Ming and increasingly in the Qing dynasty, evidential scholars considered that philosophers of the Song and Ming dynasties had imposed "subjective" interpretations onto the canonical works, leading to vacuous discourse. Gu Yanwu advocated for education to have practical endpoints and critical inquiry. Such influence on elementary learning manifested in the early training of philological and textual research skills. Moreover, the sources of information broadened to facilitate evaluation and verification of the authentic meaning of ancient texts. Established in the mid- to late eighteenth century, the Tongcheng school (*Tongcheng pai* 桐城派) attempted to reconcile escalating tensions in Qing scholarship within a threefold scheme of learning: moral principle (*yili* 義理), evidential inquiry (*kaoju* 考據), and classical prose composition (*cizhang* 辭章). Although the school's degree of influence in the contemporary discourse has been questioned,[11] its learning structure undeniably delineates the three most highly contested educational positions of the time. These concerns were brought to bear on the elementary curriculum and accordingly underpin the three core chapters focusing on practical learning, moral learning, and examination learning, respectively. The debates on educational aims, human development, and teaching that were occurring in late imperial China remain topical in the philosophy of education today.

Second, I provide a close reading of the *Treasury* identifying textual features that correspond to the educational ideas and then explore how learning may have occurred. Without an imperially standardized curriculum, the picture of primary education in Qing China is expectedly complicated. This study has employed the theoretical model of interpretive communities to group teaching approaches in acknowledgment of the different intellectual schools in existence. Although the currents of scholarship may be difficult to define as discrete entities, their educational ideas can be identified as broadly stemming from three schools of thought—the school of principle, the school of heart-mind, and statecraft learning, which are associated with the philosophy of three main thinkers: Zhu Xi, Wang Yangming, and Gu Yanwu, respectively. This preliminary framework enables a comparison of the works of Ming-Qing educators. Educators such as Lu Shiyi, Zhang Xingjian, Tang Biao, Zhang Boxing, Cui Xuegu, Chen Hongmou, and Wang Yun were either primary school teachers, preeminent scholars, or officials, and they influenced children's education through their respective work and writings. Despite being associated with certain philosophical positions, their educational ideas reveal disparate pedagogies, curricular content, values, and skills. How they reconciled competing educational emphases is pertinent to educational philosophers today who must also balance the interests of various stakeholders—government, schools, primary caregivers, teachers, and the child. By establishing that Qing elementary education was dynamic, this study challenges the misconception of homogeneity in early modern Chinese education.

Third, I have attempted to analyze traditional educational premises and practices through the findings of modern psychological research. The identification of mnemonic strategies highlights a potential for understanding how educational texts develop memory. Indeed, the intratextual and intertextual organization of material for the child learner in the *Treasury* to a large extent finds support in our scientific understanding of memory. With modern scientific research being increasingly brought to bear on the understanding of Western pedagogies, considering these in the context of Chinese pedagogical discourse enables early modern Chinese thinking to be scrutinized within similar frameworks. Such an approach to finding points of intersection on philosophical, intellectual, and scientific fronts may help to bridge gaps in cross-cultural and interdisciplinary dialogue.

What has been lacking in the current cross-cultural educational literature is a feasible framework to guide the conversation. As Tim Murphy and Ralph Weber observe in the comparative study of issues in philosophy, "Fertile ground for such analysis is provided when thinkers from both traditions address the same or similar questions."[12] For education, cross-cultural discourse may be facilitated through curricular questions and vocabularies that speak to both cultures today. The analysis in the preceding chapters has been contextualized and rooted in the terminology of the Ming-Qing period. Where possible, I have substantiated claims with Western educational and philosophical discourse but remaining within the prism of Qing dynasty schools of thought to draw similarities. However, many of the pedagogical debates and issues from the discussion may find resonance with curricular discourse beyond China and offer fruitful insights for contemporary educational theorists and professionals. Below I will attempt to decontextualize the findings of learning from the *Treasury* and summarily reframe them in terms of curricular concerns that may serve to stimulate cross-cultural dialogue.

There are many ways of understanding the primary education curriculum. For example, from the philosophy of education, different stages of cognitive development, the standpoint of the teacher, the learner's perspective, the knowledge to be covered, or the skills to be taught. Key questions in the Western curriculum theory literature provide a useful starting point in structuring thoughts about education that are cross-cultural in nature.[13] Some of these are: What are the goals of the curriculum? What knowledge is of the most worth? What values should be taught? What essential skills are at stake? What do we believe about students? I have isolated four elements for discussion: curricular content, skills training, learning approaches, and teaching strategies as evidenced through the textbook. This section does not attempt to comparatively evaluate Chinese and Western elementary educational thought; rather, my intent is to offer an important preliminary step toward framing educational discourse in the future.

CURRICULAR CONTENT

Confucius highlighted the contrasting goals of "learning for self-development" and "learning for self-advancement," which remained an ongoing problematic for educators throughout Chinese history.[14] Early Song dynasty philosophers were to reorient education for self-cultivation from the acquisition of classical knowledge.[15] However, the divergent goals of learning for self-cultivation, academic knowledge, or career opportunity, using modern terms, were nevertheless present throughout late imperial China. The cornerstone of the late imperial Chinese educational agenda was to fully develop one's human potential, termed "becoming a sage," and then help others achieve this state. In *Guidelines for Proper Upbringing*, Chen Hongmou emphatically stated, "Learning is about learning to become human" 學也者所以學為人也.[16] Such development of the human was multidimensional, including intellectual, social, aesthetic, and ethical themes in the curriculum. The *Treasury*'s content reflects the different themes, which will be addressed separately below.

Acquisition of knowledge in this educational agenda was not the same as seeking knowledge for its own sake. Notions of knowledge have existed since early China but cannot be easily compared to the propositional knowledge of Western philosophy defined as "true justified belief."[17] Knowledge for the Neo-Confucians meant the recognition of principle—an objective truth of the universe. The three schools had different means of obtaining such knowledge: through predominantly external investigation (school of principle), introspection (school of heart-mind), and empirical textual inquiry (practical learning). In other words, the sources of knowledge differed. At the level of elementary education, book learning was generally advocated. Knowledge, values, attitudes, and behavior were not based on contemporary thought or the author's personal opinion but were distilled from a long-established written tradition. Despite not explicitly referring to the concept of "principle," the canonical works and historical works are the most cited in the *Treasury*. Most of the sentences in the *Treasury* contain references to classical writings,[18] and such knowledge acted as a scaffold onto which the content of advanced texts could be better comprehended at a later stage. Due to the requirements of the civil service examinations, which were linked with the philosophical traditions, intellectual aims were largely restricted to the mastery of literary knowledge rather than scientific knowledge.

Practical learning (*shixue*) remained committed to the aim of sagehood in its formative years. However, scholarly pursuits became increasingly academic and were removed from the philosophical concerns of human improvement.[19] This was characterized by an accumulation of textual facts from diverse sources through meticulous methodologies. The *Treasury* brings together literary allusions sourced from all four traditional branches of literature. Zhu Xi had prescribed that the Four Books be studied first; however, source material for the *Treasury* extended beyond those canonical works. Citing a total of 274 source titles and organizing its information into thirty-three categories, the *Treasury* has been aptly described as a "children's encyclopedia." Such emphasis on a broader range of knowledge in late Ming and Qing dynasty education has been attributed to the rise of evidential scholarship. Elman argues that natural and historical phenomena were approached textually through glosses and etymologies, culminating "in the creation of encyclopedias and collectanea that served as textual repositories simulating 'textual museums.'"[20] The requirement for broad book knowledge was further reflected in the Qing dynasty educational discourse with formidable reading lists for youngsters. The content of the *Treasury*, therefore, reflects an increasingly academic outlook.

The realization of one's potential was through living out the learning in daily tasks and interactions. Social areas of learning relate to developing the self through relations with family, community, and the state. Students were taught to think beyond the self to "love the people" (Zhu Xi), to "form one body with Heaven, Earth, and the myriad things" (Wang Yangming), and to have active civic engagement (Gu Yanwu). From the classification of knowledge and order of the chapters in the *Treasury*, there is clearly a preoccupation with the human as a social being. The first section aligns the government with the notions of Heaven and Earth, underscoring political service as the epitome of social contribution. The second section, comprised of familial and social relations, is the longest of the four sections. Viewing oneself within a network of relationships was a fundamental cognitive schema in primary education. The anthropomorphic view of the world is apparent even in the seemingly scientific categories of geography, the birds and the beasts, flowers, and trees. The natural world is personified and used as metaphors for human interactions and qualities. Through the textbooks, the child was learning about the various roles they would undertake and how to function within the community. Social learning was imbued with normative values and hence integrated with moral development.

Based on Neo-Confucian thought, moral nurturance was a major objective of primary education in the Qing dynasty. Primers reflected this moral component. Thus, the *Treasury* does include material related to character education, although the textbook was not specifically used for this purpose. Ethical thinking was fostered through historical exemplars and ritual expressions in the text. This was achieved predominantly through the framework of the five relationships as compared to metaphysical or moral qualities at the advanced learning level. Stereotypes of these social roles were portrayed through their moral qualities and distinguished as positive or negative exemplars. For example, in the sovereign-subject relationship, the *Treasury* underlines the minister's dedication rather than their political or economic achievements. Moreover, polite expressions were taught to help internalize a general principle of respect for others. Even terms of address in the text aided familiarity with one's moral obligations. Many features of the *Treasury* serve to advance the aims of fulfilling one's innate moral potential.

Aesthetic learning content is embedded in the literary allusions and how they are arranged. The six elements of aesthetic learning as described by John Dewey, including active engagement, sensory experience, connections, imagination, perceptivity, and risk-taking, have relevance to metaphoric learning.[21] The *Treasury*'s literary allusions act as metaphors for the child to discover its connotations. For example, the conceptual scheme of the "tree as a family" with "parents as the roots" encourages the student to make connections between the environment (knowledge of parts of a tree) with the imaginative (the idea of the roots as parents). The literal is combined with the figurative and the practical with the philosophical. As advocated by Wang Yangming, the reader must actively engage in a process of discovery with the material—being open to new possibilities is related to the idea of "risk-taking." The child's senses are also stimulated by reading aloud the parallel sentences with their prosodic features.

A consistent debate throughout the ages was learning for sagehood versus for examination success and officialdom. Vocational goals are apparent through the very intent of the *Treasury*—the foreword declares the text as a reference book for examinees ("like food to the needy and a raft to cross the river"). Learning literary Chinese was essential not only for the civil service examinations but also for the daily document writing and procedural reporting of bureaucratic work. The *Treasury* increases the child's vocabulary at the level of the monosyllabic word and multisyllabic terms and phrases. Significantly, the *Treasury* can be considered a text for cultural literacy by familiarizing students with the personages, historical events, literature, geography, idioms, and other information needed to comprehend the ancient texts. Topically organized, the *Treasury* was a ready reference for literary terms and allusions for writing. Hence, knowledge of the examination writing style and substance was implicit in the composition of the textbook.

Unfortunately, the examination culture in the late imperial period spurred students to be oriented solely toward scholarly success. In efforts to stem the malignant effects of glibness related to the eight-legged essays, the Tongcheng school advocated that the exam essays should also serve the moral purpose of ancient prose.[22] Additionally, it should be noted that learning for a vocation was not necessarily incompatible with self-development. Effective written communication was one of the many tools required for the Confucian project of helping others realize their moral potential ("loving the people").

Even from the limited perspective of a language development textbook such as the *Treasury*, there is a multifaceted and comprehensive approach to primary education in the Qing dynasty. It is worth noting that although the textbook predominantly deals with classical literacy and cultural knowledge, the content also reflected other goals in primary education. Different types of primers would contribute more than others to certain goals. These findings may help educators today consider how different goals may be realized within the same teaching material. For example, how knowledge acquisition through book learning can also facilitate social engagement and character development while furthering vocational aims. Moreover, the content of the *Treasury* incorporates a broad variety of texts—to what extent is it feasible in modern schools to include content from various ancient texts across cultures and in which subjects? These are some preliminary questions that can be derived from the above discussion. Indeed, the *Treasury* reveals diverse and interlinked content areas that may have relevance to the goals advanced by modern educators.

SKILLS TRAINING

A skill can be described as "the capacity to do something well and perform certain tasks competently," which is the result of one's learning and experience.[23] While physical skills such as bike riding correspond directly to this definition, cognitive skills often also involve knowledge acquisition. It has been argued that the word *skill* is used broadly and ambiguously in the educational literature due to the interrelation between "knowing that" (having knowledge about the activity) and "knowing how" (being able to perform an activity).[24] Given the nature of this study as a textual investigation, skill here refers to nonphysical competencies. Moreover, an understanding of skills in the context of a single elementary primer that was not a manual for practical activities must be extrapolated to skills developed in concert with other teaching activities rather than the book itself. As such, the *Treasury* does hone skills to the extent of providing the student with the mental tools and knowledge of certain tasks. The text incorporates both knowledge of facts and knowledge of practices. All Qing dynasty schools of thought were knowledge-centered in the sense of focusing on book learning. However, each school also emphasized different practical aspects to be gained—Wang Yangming even espoused the doctrine of unity between knowledge and action.

From the perspective of evidential scholarship, cognitive skills to evaluate knowledge were vital for rigorous textual inquiry. This was related to the value of critical autonomy—scholars were to validate the textual interpretations themselves. The *Treasury* presented information like an exegetical dictionary—the main text with its micro-structures highlighting the connotations of the words and phrases. The annotations would also provide the source text from which the literary terms and allusions originated and glossed various key vocabulary in the allusions. Moreover, the annotations cited philological reference texts such as *Explaining Simple Graphs and Analyzing Complex Graphs* and *Extended Rhymes*. Consequently, the annotations were lengthier than the main text, but the philosophical interpretations or metaphysical concepts characteristic of the Cheng-Zhu school exegeses were notably absent. In other words, the reader was provided with the requisite background information and the quoted source text was left open to different readings. How did this develop their skills in textual analysis? The elementary primer introduced the methods and tools by which they could critically evaluate the information, including glosses, reference texts, and source texts. In time, they would employ such means to attest to the truth of the knowledge themselves.

Skills in the form of ritual living relate to the social and ethical content of learning. All schools of thought prescribed ritual training in elementary education as a means to self-development. Training in ritual etiquette was deemed an important skill of moral living and formed the content of multiple children's textbooks. Compared to etiquette-based primers that proliferated after the Song dynasty, the *Treasury* did not overtly specify behavioral norms. However, the text provided the common lexicon and performative utterances for instruction in the ritual language. Speech acts included requests, apologies, greetings, expressions of gratitude, and compliments. The exact phrasing of expressions, the specific situation for their application, the literary origin and meaning were provided by the text to aid practice. The subtleties of such interactions were also manifest through different ways of expressing the same intention in the book. However, the expressions were straightforward such that children could comprehend and apply them, and the language learned could be readily observable in daily life.

Aside from their practical use, the "formalities of polite conversation and good manners" (*yingdui jintui* 應對進退) that Zhu Xi proposed as the basis of elementary education were deemed to be expressions that had an important ethical dimension with regard to education. Verbal and body language were the manifestations of Confucian values. Key attitudes that are reiterated throughout all the speech acts are those of humility and respect. Deference toward others and denigration of the self was the core principle in ritual linguistics. Knowledge of the complex written or spoken pronouns, set phrases, and allusions in the *Treasury* were the first step. The actual practice of such self-deprecation and deference was a skill. The ritual vocabulary was to be adopted based on one's role relative to the addressee, which is apparent in the very structure of the chapters familiarizing students with various adult roles. Respecting others through language involved complimentary terms not only for the addressee's physical and mental traits but also for their partner, family members, and personal property. The skill of addressing others was to conjure up the polite phrase appropriate to the situation, hence both target and source domain categorization of the expressions in the *Treasury* assists the novice. For example, ritual language related to dining with others features in the "Fellows, Friends, Guests, and Hosts" and "Food and Drink" chapters. Other pragmatically focused chapters deal with certain occasions. For example, "Birth and Birthdays" concerns the celebration of anniversaries, "Human Affairs" relates to work and interpersonal relations, and "Diseases and Death" helps to understand the rites of mourning and how to express condolences. Interestingly, a significant amount of the ritual language in the *Treasury* remains in use today, not least in the context of formal writing (*yingyongwen* 應用文) handbooks. These social skills not only facilitated cooperative interactions, but having mutual respect for others also helped to foster character development. For example, the text instructs: "One's feelings after a long period of separation are expressed as 'long away from your manner and example'" 敘契闊曰久違顏範.[25] By stating that one admires another's positive example also implies that one should focus on the strengths of others.

To understand how the *Treasury* aided vocational skills, one must understand the career that students were generally training for and the selection criteria. The primary career pursuit was a position in public service. To this end, one needed to pass the civil service examinations, which involved writing eight-legged essays and verses. Writing skills in the prescribed genres was the bane of the budding examinee's existence. Such composition was acknowledged by Qing educators to be the culmination of one's formal language training. This began with the lower-level reading skills of decoding, vocabulary, and grammar. Subsequent higher-level reading skills, such as the use of prior knowledge, built upon this foundation. Composition began with the physical skills of using the writing brush, followed by writing parallel word pairs, and then verses and different parts of the essay. The *Treasury* provides accumulated semantic, phonetic, and syntactic knowledge for the reader. The mnemonic strategies through parallelism, semantic association, and cultural literacy laid the foundations for proficiency in reading skills and, ultimately, written expression.

Skills were also transferrable between domains of learning. Reading skills not only aided writing but would also help develop critical inquiry skills. Textual research competency would uncover the principle, which would foster moral understanding and practice. Interpersonal skills such as empathy and respect were also fundamental to workplace relations. As the next section explains, all skills were grounded in foundational training that emphasized practice. Constant practice would require the ability to remain focused and disciplined, which would, in turn, realize the intellectual, ethical, and vocational goals. The correlation was well established; for example, the *Literary Mind and the Carving of Dragons* states: "One wins their mastery of literature through the excellence of their character, and their character is manifested in their literary excellence" 文以行立，行以文傳.[26]

Such content in the *Treasury* demonstrates the twin emphases of knowledge-based and process-based learning, and this is consistent with Hirsch's argument that facts and skills are inseparable in the curriculum.[27] Since the times of ancient China, philosophers and educators have been cognizant of the difficulties of ensuring that knowledge was practiced and lived out. The findings of the study are not sufficient to answer the question of the transfer of knowledge into action within the curriculum. This is because a single text is investigated as a brief period within the learner's lifelong journey and may not cover all aspects of student assessment. However, the text does develop knowledge of values and skills echoing process curriculum models that view learning as perpetual refinement. Where skills such as the interpretation of texts, interpersonal ability, moral practice, and Chinese language literacy are valued in modern subjects, the methods by which these skills were developed in the past may be drawn upon to enrich class activities today.

LEARNING APPROACHES

Learning relates to the actual absorption of the information in the student's mind as distinct from the process of teaching.[28] As evidenced in the above section on skills, there was a learning continuum in Qing dynasty primary education. The *Treasury*'s readers were likely aged between nine and eleven years and were transitioning to more mature modes of learning.[29] The academic and self-developmental content in the text provides a view of the child's study process.

Engaging the powers of memory was the main learning strategy at the beginning of the child's formal schooling. Underpinning this practice was the recognition that the child's ability to encode information was strongest prior to the age of fifteen. There were two approaches to the use of memory: repeatedly reciting texts in an ordered sequence for literacy and rehearsing ritual etiquette for personal development. Unlike the method of loci first described by Cicero and popularly used in medieval Europe,[30] the Chinese memorized by iteration of the texts aided by prosodic and semantic cues. Research shows that mnemonic techniques were a characteristic feature of primers. There was a conscious organization of the *Treasury*'s content to mediate memory of the information reflecting this first stage in learning. The semantic, phonological, and syntactical knowledge is creatively transmitted through parallel sentences. Moreover, different types of metric parallelism involving rhythm create temporal predictability enhancing attention, which is crucial for long-term memory encoding. Novel vocabulary in the text was also frequently situated at the end of the sentences for attention. The sentences involve grammatical parallelism, and repetition of such sentences would help consolidate long-term representations of parallel prose structures.

There are two elements worth elaborating on in this initial stage of learning. First, the recurrent encounter with the learning material—either a specific skill or knowledge. From the observer's perspective, it may seem monotonous and mechanical. Indeed, a common misconception is that traditional Chinese memorization equates with "rote learning," which is a surface approach. Studies in the educational literature have shown that memorization is integrated with understanding, and repeated reading enables the discovery of new ideas and perspectives in the same material.[31] In terms of cognitive skills, nuances of the text are noted with each reading, and familiarity increases. Each reading consolidates prior knowledge and simultaneously assimilates new information.

The content of the *Treasury* reflects an inherent understanding that prior knowledge was needed. This is evidenced by comparisons made to the content of "*san bai qian*" primers the child had read. Learning was considered a gradual cumulative process—establishing cognitive schemas (e.g., historical figures) and incorporating new information into these. External patterns in learning, such as the rhythms of parallel sentences, the wording of allusions, or the timing of ritual acts were to become internalized as if second nature. Based on the psychological literature, internalization may relate to well-developed schemas for knowledge and action.

This learning process was also extrapolated to the continuous rehearsal of ritual acts. In describing the development of moral competence through ritual, Karyn Lai draws an analogy with performing music—familiarization with techniques of sound production in the early stages—while improvisation and considering contextual appropriateness occurs at a later stage.[32] In the performance of ritual, continuous and rigorous practice comes first. The astute learner can detect subtleties of the act and make further improvements based on their preexisting and growing competency. The understanding of the meaning and context of the ritual act gradually occurs through this process.

The second element of learning was to reflect upon and understand the learning material for application and appropriation. As Wang Yangming explains: "As they recite with their mouths, let them ponder with their minds" 口誦心維.[33] The allusions in the *Treasury* act as metaphors inviting the reader to associate new and old meanings in a "discovery" process. Using conceptual metaphor theory, each literary allusion can be seen to have a source domain (the literal meaning) and a target domain (the connotation). The original context of the allusion as the literary meaning would have to be understood through the annotation and the teacher's explanation. Then the contemporary consensus and use of the allusion provided by the explanation in the main text would need to be identified. Similarly, there is evident scope for reflection in the ritual expressions, as neither the moral quality of ritual propriety nor the politeness principle were explicitly explained. Moreover, different verbal expressions were provided for the same speech act across various chapters and required judgment for usage. In other words, students were required to reflect upon the text to suitably use the allusions in their written and spoken language.

A point pertinent to transcultural dialogue on learning that will be briefly addressed here is the degree to which students could express themselves creatively. In the context of the Qing dynasty civil service examinations, students were required to adhere to a strict word count as well as style requirements in the eight-legged essay and regulated verse in the examinations. The content and argument of their responses also needed to accord with the Cheng-Zhu schools' moral philosophy. Although there was an element of reinterpreting ancient texts to resolve present issues, these stultifying writing patterns were ultimately not designed to promote literary creativity.[34] The examination essay was undoubtedly a means to an end, a necessary evil equivalent to the standardized essays in present-day university admission assessments used in many parts of the world. However, the essay was but one genre of writing. Having mastered the basics of prose and cultural literacy and passed the examinations, scholars would often write in other genres. Chen Shouyi writes that Qing writers by the eighteenth century had already surpassed previous ages in the styles of ancient prose (*guwen* 古文) and rhythmically balanced prose through innovation:

> Practically all the classical masters had been outgrown and imitation was made only to serve a transitory apprenticeship. Thus Chao Ch'i-t'ao (1718–1769) insisted that good balanced prose should be "clear, new, elegant, and attractive."[35]

Originality was evidently possible beyond the examinations, and Qing scholars both excelled at and valued it. As imitating and adapting tradition was a stepping stone to developing one's distinctive style, it may be thought of as a "transitory apprenticeship." Such creativity occurred by working within and then innovating upon conventional forms.

In summary, whether in language, behavior, or attitude, the child's learning material was reinforced by recurrent encounters with the learning material, reflection, and understanding. Angle's analysis of Zhu's primary education explains a natural progression in learning:

> As one first begins to learn the proper way to perform rituals, to engage in polite conversation, to clean and sweep, one follows explicit instructions. Often one is awkward and rigid, only knowing to follow the precise instructions one has been given and unsure how to proceed if one finds oneself in a slightly novel situation. . . . Gradually, one develops a "direct understanding" [*zhi lihui* 直理會] of the activities so that one can begin to perform them more flexibly.[36]

The child's "direct understanding" relates to their roles and tasks, to the extent they can competently interact with others and perform specific activities. Reasoning and abstract analysis of philosophical theory would occur at the level of advanced education. The common approach to many areas of learning, both knowledge and skill, is aptly encapsulated by the notion of "practice" in the etymology of the Chinese character (*xi* 習). *Explaining Simple Graphs and Analyzing Complex Graphs* states that "practice" means the repetitive efforts of young birds who are learning to fly.[37] Learning for the beginner student was a matter of encoding memory—knowledge and skills—through repeated exposure to learning material with deepening levels of familiarity and recall. This parallels the notion of prior knowledge that modern psychological research has confirmed as important in the memory-making process as previously discussed. Encoded memories were the prior knowledge—the cognitive scaffold—that could then accommodate further information. In this way, new concepts could readily be associated with preexisting knowledge, which led to later stages of abstract reasoning. Through practice, one could reach mastery and competency, such as manifesting literary flair and moral autonomy, like the young bird that finally takes flight.

TEACHING STRATEGIES

Teaching paralleled the learning continuum. Zhu Xi delineated two stages of education—elementary and advanced. The first stage was dominated by external prescriptive cues by texts and teachers rather than focusing on student motivation and enjoyment. Child-oriented practice was the point of divergence in the elementary thought of Zhu Xi and Wang Yangming. Wang argued for a liberal attitude toward elementary education and asked educators to adopt methods encouraging children to learn, such as songs and ritual activities. Book learning was to stimulate the child's innate knowledge that could differentiate between right and wrong, which would arouse their interest to help them become self-motivated learners. Educators in the Qing dynasty tended toward this more progressive position; for example, the Cheng-Zhu school adherent Lu Shiyi criticized Zhu Xi's primer, the *Elementary Learning*, which is also absent and was presumably excluded from Chen Hongmou's anthology. Although the content knowledge was similar, Wang proposed a broader tool kit of pedagogical approaches to engage with the reader.

Children's textbooks with literary allusions proliferated in the Ming dynasty, and the *Treasury* was part of the trend. This is implicit in Zou Shengmai retitling the *Treasury* to include the word *gushi* 故事 (literary allusion). Allusions being intertextual references to an anecdote or concept often involved stories of historical personages. The allusions in the *Treasury* could be used to practice polite expressions but also learn through storytelling. Importantly, they were enjoyable as well as intellectually stimulating. Wang Yun particularly writes that students should be taught allusions during their leisure: "Children have a limited attention span and must have time away from study. During this free time, they should be taught classical allusions . . ." 小兒無長精神，必須使有空閑，空閑即告以典故.[38] His statement exemplifies the attitude that instruction was to be tailored to the student's state of mind as well as their developmental needs.

Unlike primers that provided more complete narratives on specific role models, e.g., the *Twenty-four Exemplars of Family Reverence*, the characters in the *Treasury* are revisited throughout the text with varying degrees of detail and association with other personages. Linking to prior and future reading, this was a graduated introduction to the myriad cultural figures that constructed and consolidated a picture of the world of the past. The children were learning the allusions as part of their literacy training but simultaneously and subconsciously exposed to history, mythology, literature, and moral ideas. The lack of strict subject demarcation meant different students could be engaged in different ways with the text. In terms of student interests, some might enjoy the aesthetics of parallel lines absorbing the syntactical pattern, while others might focus on the historical figures and their stories. From the perspective of their cognitive development, students more advanced in reading could interpret for themselves how the allusion evolved from its original text in the annotations, while those still enlarging their vocabulary could be satisfied by the main text explanations (e.g., X refers to Y).

The anecdotes were part of the cultural lore, literary tradition, and instilled ethical behavior and thus were common to all themes of the curriculum. Within the anecdotes, the portrayal of personages was to inspire children, particularly their motivation to behave in an ethical manner. In recognition of the child's limited reasoning ability and difficulty with moral ambiguity, the *Treasury* provides a largely binary scheme of exemplars—the righteous and the reprehensible. For example, the rulers of high antiquity were portrayed as mythical through their unique physical features and their impact on the people and natural phenomena. The allusions themselves acted as metaphors that served to underscore character traits through imagery, for example:

> 與善人交，如入芝蘭之室，久而不聞其香；與惡人交，如入鮑魚之肆，久而不聞其臭。
>
> Friendship with the virtuous is like entering a room of angelica and orchids, the fragrance becomes undetectable after some time. Friendship with the nonvirtuous is like entering a fish shop, the odor becomes imperceptible after a time.[39]

A young reader may be incapable of recognizing the impact of nonvirtuous associations but would likely have experienced the repulsive smell of a fish shop. Linking the two would thus have helped the student to identify what was to be emulated and avoided. Moreover, a moral quality was further shown to be desirable by presenting multiple figures throughout the text who exemplified the same quality. Moral instruction was therefore not explicit but was to be intuited.

The *Treasury* was consistently structured as parallel sentences in both the original and supplemented text. Awareness of the learning approach of recitation the rhythms of the writing enabled the act of reading aloud to be more enjoyable. As previously mentioned, such textual features served a mnemonic function to help the child encode information into long-term memory. Teaching through the *Treasury* enabled the engagement of a diverse readership. Compilers were cognizant of the child's development and learning styles, thereby encapsulating the knowledge in creative and versatile ways. The presentation of information related to the learning and teaching continuum may be relevant for modern learning beyond elementary schooling—the progression from beginner to expert occurs in any subject area, as does the engagement of memory. For example, metaphoric learning for deep approaches to learning and the revisiting of information with varying levels of detail across texts were key strategies for memory.

Zou Shengmai ends his foreword thus: "This book is therefore titled 'Treasury.' May the reader be my judge." The analysis in this study attests to how aptly the *Treasury* is titled. The primer serves not only as a collection of allusions for the examinee but also as an integration of the diverse educational thoughts in the Qing dynasty. Like its parallel sentences, the *Treasury* effectively balances the various demands of the wide readership through its contents and structures. The success of such features is corroborated by the text's enduring popularity, which lasted through to the end of imperial China and even to this day.

Analysis of the structure and content of this popular children's primer during the Qing period provides evidence of diverse and multifaceted educational theories and practices. This reflects the eclectic nature of Qing dynasty primary educational thought, drawing from the school of principle, the school of heart-mind, and the school of practical learning.

Although the *Treasury* offers a snapshot in time of the child's learning journey and is not representative of the entire genre of elementary texts, the lengthy textbook presents as a worthwhile consideration as it encompasses various curricular themes. Learning goals ranged from self-cultivation and intellectual advancement to vocational concerns. Skills fostered involved literacy, writing, critical evaluation, interpersonal interactions, respect, and humility. The approach to learning started with employing the powers of memory to achieve familiarity with knowledge and skills—but this was merely establishing the foundations. Without developing essential skills to reflect and comprehend the material, how could the child later appropriate texts in writing or apply judgment in real-life situations? Reflection and understanding were thus imperative for such learning to be applied in one's scholarship and living. Teaching practices accordingly recognized and corresponded to this learning continuum. Textbooks like the *Treasury* presented complex material in the form of allusions that required higher-order reading skills. Moreover, a child-oriented outlook was pervasive in Ming-Qing primers that attempted to edify and entertain. The early modern Chinese pedagogy thus has the potential to provide fruitful insights for contemporary educational discourse.

Although primers are a growing area of Sinological research, this study recommends that such educational literature also presents an important area for transcultural educational dialogue. Comparative philosophy has a long history, but recent years have seen advocacy to bring Chinese thinking into philosophy departments that have traditionally taught and researched Anglo-European thought, thereby empowering students with a multicultural outlook.[40] Besides the field of philosophy in tertiary education, this transcultural and transnational perspective may also be rewarding in other disciplines. As early as the fifth century BCE, the ancient Greek historian Herodotus examined the customs of Egypt and Persia to better inform practices in his society.[41] As the world is increasingly connected, the next generation must cope with the challenges of navigating issues of cultural diversity with sensitivity and understanding. Such tools may not necessarily be achieved by introducing a multicultural curriculum in schools.[42] However, educational theorists and educators, having an appreciation of the goals, knowledge, skills, pedagogy, and literature of another culture, may find inspiration for richer ideas for practice. As Ronnie Littlejohn and Qingjun Li aptly articulate in the field of comparative philosophy:

> What is being created as a result of the dialogue between Chinese and Western philosophy is just the sort of thing that education is meant to produce. This current dialogue does not result in some new theory that unlocks all the riddles or solves all the quandaries arising in philosophy. Instead, the outcome is the emergence of a different sort of philosopher. These new philosophers bend language and culture. They do not so much inhabit one or both of the standpoints represented by the traditions from which they draw, as they give birth to an emerging standpoint different from them and which is thereby creatively a new way of seeing the human condition.[43]

This study has concluded by presenting a cognitive scaffold in preparation for future discussion, a foundation to facilitate constructive engagement with current educational scholarship. As such, not only will the significance of the research on the *Treasury* be considered from a new perspective, but it is my hope that intercultural dialogue in education may be enhanced. May the reader be my judge.

APPENDIX

TRANSLATION OF "GEMS AND TREASURES" SUPPLEMENTARY COUPLETS

1. 斑斑美玉，瑟瑟靈珠。

Ban ban is a beautiful jade. *Se se* is an auspicious pearl.

《事文類聚》：斑斑，玉名。瑟瑟，珠名。

Classified Collection on Historical Facts and Literature: *Ban ban* is the name of a jade. *Se se* is the name of a pearl.

2. 琉璃瓶最宜卜相，琥珀盞尤可酌賓。

The glass bottle is most suited to divination for a chancellor. The small amber cup is especially for drinking with guests.

《廣州志》：琉璃出大秦、高麗、日南諸國，其性堅，刀割不動。白色，厚半寸許，此自然之物，彩澤光潤。

Records on Guangzhou: Glass originates from the states of the Roman empire, Koguryô, and Rinan. It is strong, impenetrable by blade, white in color, and approximately half an inch thick. This naturally occurring substance is bright and shiny.

《五代史》：廢帝欲擇相，左右言盧文紀及姚顯有人望。帝因書姓名，納之琉璃瓶中，焚香祝天，以箸挾之，得文紀，遂以為相。

History of the Five Dynasties: Emperor Fei of the Later Tang wished to select a chancellor. His attendants said both Lu Wenji and Yao

Xian were reputable. The emperor wrote their names and placed them in a glass bottle. After burning incense and praying to the heavens, he used chopsticks to pick out a name, it was Lu Wenji. Consequently, Lu became the chancellor.

《博物志》：松脂淪入地中，千年化為茯苓。再千年化為琥珀，又名珠光。

Treatise on Curiosities: When the resin of a pine tree seeps into the ground, it will become root fungus after a thousand years. After another thousand years it will turn into amber, which is also named "pearl light."

3. 嗣續將盛，鳴鳩化金帶之鉤；爵祿彌高，飛鵲幻（音宦）玉紋之印。

When descendants are about to prosper, a turtledove transforms into a golden belt hook. When rank and emolument further increase, the flying magpie becomes (pronunciation: *huan*) a patterned jade seal.

《韻府群玉》：山西張氏，世有陰德。忽有鳩入室，祝之曰：「爾為禍耶，飛上承塵。為福耶，飛入我懷。」鳩飛入懷，以手探之，得一金帶鉤，遂寶焉，自是子孫日富盛。

Archive of Rhymes from the Imperial Library: The Zhang family of Shanxi had accumulated quiet merits over many generations. [One time] a turtledove suddenly flew into the house. He said to the bird, "If you signify misfortune, fly up to the canopy. If you signify good fortune, fly into my arms." The turtledove flew into his arms, and he attained a golden belt hook upon touching it. It became a treasure and thereafter his descendants became more prosperous with each day.

唐張璟見飛鵲忽墜於地，化而為石，剖之得玉印，文曰：「忠孝侯之印」。

Zhang Jing of the Tang dynasty saw a flying magpie unexpectedly drop to the ground and turn into stone. After breaking the stone open, he attained a jade seal that was inscribed with the words: "Seal of the loyal and filial prince."

4. 魏博鐵鑄錯，猶惜不成；張說記事珠，忽然頓悟。

Casting an error with the iron of Wei and Bo is to begrudge one's failure. Zhang Yue had a memory pearl—one touch would lead to recollection.

《五代史》：羅紹威以魏博牙兵驕甚，盡殺之，後遂為朱溫所制。乃謂親吏曰：「聚六州四十三縣鐵，鑄一個錯不成。」〔釋〕六州，魏、博、貝、相、澶、衛也。鑄錯不成，蓋歎氣誤殺牙兵也。

History of the Five Dynasties: Luo Shaowei killed all the Weibo headquarter troops due to their arrogance and subsequently became reliant on Zhu Wen. He confided to an associate, "The iron from the six prefectures and forty-three counties could not cast such a failure." Gloss: The six prefectures are Wei, Bo, Bei, Xiang, Chan, and Wei. "Casting such a failure" refers to his regret over the misguided killing of the headquarter troops.

唐張說為相，有記事珠，事之遺忘者，弄其珠則恍然悟。

Zhang Yue, who was a chancellor during the Tang dynasty, had a pearl that could trigger memories. Those who had forgotten something could suddenly remember by touching the pearl.

5. 夏桀乃昏庸主，國有瑤台；郭況是貴戚卿，家多金穴。

King Jie of the Xia dynasty was a benighted, mediocre ruler—his state had a platform made of chalcedony. Guo Kuang was a noble relative and a high official—his home had many caves of gold.

《通鑒》：夏桀無道，為肉山酒池，瓊宮瑤台。

Comprehensive Mirror in Aid of Governance: King Jie of Xia did not accord with the proper way, he constructed a hill of meat, a pond of wine, a palace of jade, and a platform made of chalcedony.

郭況，漢光武郭后之弟也。帝數幸其第，賞賜黃金甚多，時謂之金穴。

Guo Kuang was the younger brother of the Empress Guo to Emperor Guangwu of the Han dynasty. As the emperor frequently visited his home and bestowed him with much gold, his home became known as the "caves of gold."

6. 韓嫣（音煙）一出，兒童覓綠野之金丸；漢祖既還，亞父撞鴻門之玉斗。

When Han Yan (pronunciation: *yan*) went out, the children would look for gold pellets in the green fields. When Emperor Gaozu of the Han dynasty returned, the "second father" smashed the jade wine dippers from the Hongmen feast.

韓嫣性奢侈，以金為彈丸，一日所失者十餘。長安為之語曰：「若饑寒，逐彈丸。」京師兒童每伺嫣出輒隨往，望彈丸所落而拾之。

Han Yan was extravagant by nature. He made pellets from gold and would lose over ten of these each day. Those in Chang'an would say: "If you are hungry and poor, follow the pellets." Children in the capital would follow Yan whenever he went out and watch for where his pellets dropped to collect them.

《史記》：漢祖鴻門之宴，起如廁。樊噲曰：「大行不顧細謹，大禮不辭小讓。如今人方為刀俎，我為魚肉，何辭焉！」遂逃歸灞上，留張良以白璧謝羽，以玉斗謝范增。增置之地，拔劍撞破之，曰：「唉！豎子不足與謀！奪項王天下者，必沛公也。」

Records of the Historian: During the Hongmen feast, Liu Bang left as if going to the washroom. Fan Kuai said: "One undertaking great deeds minds not the cautionary details. One observing major protocols minds not the minor concessions. We are about to become the meat on their chopping board, why say goodbye?" They escaped and returned to Bashang. Zhang Liang was left with gifts of white jade discs for Xiang Yu and jade wine dippers for Fan Zeng. Fan Zeng put the dippers on the ground, drew his sword and smashed them to pieces, saying, "Ah! It does not do to lay plans with an idiot! The governor of Pei is bound to take the empire from you."[1]

7. 刻岷姬之形以玉，好色惟然；鑄范蠡之像以金，尊賢乃爾。

Only the lascivious would engrave the names of the Mount Min concubines onto jade. One venerating the worthy made a gold sculpture of Fan Li.

《敦煌紀年》：桀伐岷山，岷山之君獻桀以二女，曰琬曰琰。桀受二女，刻其名於苕華之玉。

Dunhuang Chronicles: When King Jie of Xia attacked Mount Min, the ruler of Mount Min offered his two daughters—Wan and Yan to the king. King Jie accepted them and engraved their names on the *Tiaohua* jade.

《吳越春秋》：越既破吳，范蠡遂泛舟於五湖，莫知所終。勾踐思之，以黃金鑄像而朝禮之。

Spring and Autumn Annals of Wu and Yue: After the state of Yue defeated the state of Wu, Fan Li became a recluse, and no one knew where he went. King Goujian of Yue thought of him and cast a gold statue to pay homage to Fan Li.

8. 珊瑚樹，塞滿齊奴之室；瑪瑙盤，捧來行儉之家。

The coral trees filled Qi Nu's rooms. The agnate tray was brought to Xingjian's home.

石崇小名齊奴。王愷與崇鬥富，不勝，武帝出珊瑚樹，高三尺，助愷。崇擊破之。帝欲其賠，崇以高六七尺者賠之。四五尺者，殆不勝數。

Shi Chong's childhood name was Qi Nu. Wang Kai and Shi Chong would try to outdo each other in displays of wealth and Wang was unsuccessful. Emperor Wu of the Jin dynasty helped Wang by giving him a coral tree that was three *chi* tall.[2] When Shi smashed it, the emperor requested compensation. Shi recompensed with a coral tree that was six to seven *chi* tall. He had countless coral trees that were four to five *chi* tall.

唐裴行儉有瑪瑙盤，廣二尺，文采粲然。軍吏趨跌，盤碎，惶愧叩頭。行儉曰：「汝非故也。」色不少變，君子服其量。

Pei Xingjian of the Tang dynasty had an agnate tray measuring two *chi* wide with lustrous patterns and colors. A minor military official who was in a rush, tripped and broke the plate. He then kowtowed in fear and shame. Without the slightest change in countenance, Pei responded, "It was not your fault." Those of character were convinced of his magnanimity.

9. 燕昭王之涼珠，炎蒸無暑；扶餘國之火玉．冽沍無寒。

King Zhao of Yan's cooling pearl keeps away the feverish heat. The kingdom of Fuyu's fiery jade keeps away the bitter cold.

《拾遺記》：燕昭王時，外國獻黑蚌珠，暑月懷之極清涼，號招涼珠。

Notes on Neglected Matters: During the reign of King Zhao of the state of Yan, a foreign state presented a black clam pearl. As holding this pearl during the summer months would be extremely cooling, it was named the "cooling pearl."

唐武宗時，扶餘國進火玉，可以燃鼎，置室中，不必挾纊。

During the reign of Emperor Wuzong of the Tang dynasty, the kingdom of Fuyu presented a fiery jade, which could ignite a cauldron and if placed within a room, one would not need to wear clothes with cotton wadding.

10. 錦帆錦帳，炫人耳目；金埒（音劣）金塢（烏上聲），駭我見聞。

The brocaded sails and canopies attract a person's attention. The golden enclosure (pronunciation: *lie*) and golden trowel (*wu*, rising tone) are, to me, startling facts.

錦帆，註詳《貧富》。錦帳，註詳《衣服》。

For "brocaded sails," see the annotation in the "Poverty and Wealth" chapter; for "brocaded canopies," see the annotation in the "Attire and Apparel" chapter.

晉王武子養馬，編錢布地，號金埒。金塢，註詳《貧富》。

Wang Wuzi of the Jin dynasty bred horses on a floor of woven cash, which was known as the "golden enclosure." For "golden trowel," see the annotation in the "Poverty and Wealth" chapter.

11. 從吾所好，豈曰富而可求；有命存焉，當以不貪為寶。

Able to do as I please, how can riches be attained by trying? Alive and well, one should treasure abstaining from greed.

《論語》：子曰：「富而可求也，雖執鞭之士，吾亦為之。如不可求，從吾所好。」

Analects: The Master said: "If one could get rich just by trying, then although it meant being a herald with whip in hand, I would go along with that. But if one can't get rich just by trying, I prefer to follow my own desires."[3]

《左傳》：宋人或得玉，獻諸子罕。子罕曰：「我以不貪為寶，爾以玉為寶，若以與我，皆喪寶焉，不若人有其寶。」卒弗受。〔釋〕喪寶，謂一喪廉，一喪寶。

Zuo Tradition: There was a man from the state of Song who obtained a piece of jade and presented it to Zihan. Zihan said: "I consider abstaining from greed to be a treasure, while you consider the jade a treasure. If you give it to me, then we both lose what we treasure. It is better for each of us to keep his own treasure." He ultimately refused to accept it.[4] Gloss: "Lose what we treasure" refers to one losing integrity and the other losing the gem.

Notes

INTRODUCTION

1. In discussing the importance of early education, Jia Yi 賈誼 (200–168 BCE) was the first to assert the importance of prenatal and early education as crucial distinct phases of education through philosophical discourse. Thus, Anne Kinney claims that the "discovery of childhood" and child developmental concerns occurred in the Han dynasty (206 BCE–220 CE). Anne Behnke Kinney, "Dyed Silk: Han Notions of the Moral Development of Children," in *Chinese Views of Childhood*, ed. Anne Behnke Kinney (Honolulu: University of Hawai'i Press, 1995), 19–20.
2. "On Teaching and Learning" [*Xueji* 學記], trans. Xu Di, Yang Liuxin, Hunter McEwan, and Roger T. Ames, in *Chinese Philosophy on Teaching and Learning: Xueji in the Twenty-First Century*, ed. Xu Di and Hunter McEwan (Albany: State University of New York Press, 2016), 16. Exact dating of the chapter is unknown, but it is generally acknowledged that the *Liji* 禮記 (Records on ritual) emerged from the complicated manuscript culture of the preimperial and early imperial era. See Liu Yucai and Luke Habberstad, "The Life of a Text: A Brief History of the *Liji* 禮記 [Rites Records] and Its Transmission," *Journal of Chinese Literature and Culture* 1, no. 1–2 (2014): 291–296.
3. The line from the *Three Character Classic* states: "A piece of jade that remains uncut will never become a sacred vessel, and a person that does not learn will never realize their duty. 玉不琢，不成器；人不學，不知義" The last character in the sentence was modified for rhyming effect. Huang Peirong 黃沛榮, *Xin yi Sanzi jing* 新譯三字經 (A new interpretation of the *Three Character Classic*) (Taipei: San min shuju, 2003), 21–22.

4. Described as "the most recited book for at least 600 years in the most populous country on earth." James T. C. Liu, "The Classical Chinese Primer: Its Three-Character Style and Authorship," *Journal of the American Oriental Society* 105 no. 2 (1985): 191.
5. Daniel K. Gardner, *Learning to Be a Sage: Selections from the Conversations of Master Chu, Arranged Topically* (Berkeley: University of California Press, 1990), 93. (With modifications.)
6. Michael Nylan, "Calligraphy: The Sacred Text and Test of Culture," in *Character and Context in Chinese Calligraphy*, ed. Cary Y. Liu, Dora C. Y. Ching, and Judith G. Smith (Princeton: Princeton University, 1999), 39–40.
7. In this study, I generally refer to the bibliographic classification used in the Qing dynasty encyclopedia *Siku quanshu* 四庫全書 (Complete library of the four branches of literature): the canonical works (*jing* 經), historical works (*shi* 史), masters works (*zi* 子), and literary works (*ji* 集).
8. Ban Gu 班固, *Hanshu* 漢書 (History of the Former Han) in *Wenyuange Siku quanshu* 文淵閣四庫全書 (Wenyuange edition of the Complete Library of the Four Branches of Literature), vol. 249 (Taipei: Taiwan shangwu yinshuguan, 2013), 807.
9. Thomas H. C. Lee, *Education in Traditional China: A History* (Boston: Brill, 2000), 434.
10. Xu Zi 徐梓, *Mengxue duwu de lishi toushi* 蒙學讀物的歷史透視 (Perspectives on the history of reading materials for elementary studies) (Wuhan: Hubei jiaoyu chubanshe, 1997), 4.
11. Peter Hunt, *Children's Literature* (Oxford: Blackwell Publishers, 2001), 2.
12. Zhang Zhigong 張志公, *Chuantong yuwen jiaoyu jiaocai lun: ji mengxue shumu he shu ying* 傳統語文教育教材論：暨蒙學書目和書影 (Discussion of teaching materials for language learning in traditional Chinese education including bibliography and images of the elementary education texts) (Beijing: Zhonghua shuju, 2017), 7.
13. Cai Dongfan 蔡東藩, *Huitu xinzeng Youxue gushi qionglin* 繪圖新增幼學故事瓊林 (Supplemented *Treasury of Elementary Learning* with drawings) (Shanghai: Hui wen tang shuju, 1924), 1.
14. The "Four Books" refer to the four texts selected by Zhu Xi as the authoritative, foundational texts in the Confucian tradition: *Daxue* 大學 (Great learning), *Zhongyong* 中庸 (Doctrine of the mean), *Lunyu* 論語 (Analects), and *Mengzi* 孟子 (Mencius).
15. Zhang He 張河 and Mu Zhi 牧之, *Zhongguo gudai mengshu jijin* 中國古代蒙書集錦 (Anthology of premodern Chinese elementary education texts) (Jinan: Shandong youyi shushe, 1989), 72.

16. Zou Shengmai 鄒聖脈 and Hu Xiazhi 胡遐之, *Youxue qionglin* 幼學瓊林 (Treasury of elementary learning) (Changsha: Yueli shushe, 1986), 8.
17. Kecheng jiaocai yanjiusuo 課程教材研究所, *Yuwen juan* 語文卷 (Volume on language learning), Ershi shiji zhongguo zhong xiaoxue kecheng biaozhun jiaoxue dagang huibian 二十世紀中國中小學課程標準教學大綱彙編 (Collection of curriculum standards and teaching guidelines of primary and secondary schools in the twentieth century) (Beijing: Renmin jiaoyu chubanshe, 2001), 1; Li Yu, "Character Recognition: A New Method of Learning to Read in Late Imperial China," *Late Imperial China* 33, no. 2 (2012): 10.
18. Zhang and Mu, *Zhongguo gudai mengshu jijin*, 65; Zou and Hu, *Youxue qionglin,* 7; Ye Guangda 葉光大, *Youxue gushi qionglin yizhu* 幼學故事瓊林譯注 (Annotated translation of the *Youxue gushi qionglin*) (Guiyang: Guiyang renmin chubanshe, 1991), 1.
19. Inō Kanori, *Taiwan bunkashi* (A history of Taiwanese culture), trans. Jiang Qinglin 江慶林 et al. (Taipei: Taiwan Shufang chuban youxian gongsi, 2011), 37; Dongfang Xiaoyi 東方孝義, *Taiwan sisu* 台灣習俗 (Taiwan customs) (Taipei: Nantian shuju, 1997), 107.
20. Ping-Ti Ho notes the extension of the frontier of rice culture, the commercialization of farming, the nationwide rise of the cotton textiles industry, the growth of industries and crafts, the development of domestic and international trade, the influx of silver from Europeans and Japanese, and increasing commutation of labor services during the Ming period. Ping-Ti Ho, *The Ladder of Success in Imperial China: Aspects of Social Mobility, 1368–1911* (New York: Columbia University Press, 1964), 220.
21. Ibid., 219.
22. Susan Naquin and Evelyn Sakakida Rawski, *Chinese Society in the Eighteenth Century* (New Haven: Yale University Press, 1987), 106.
23. Joseph McDermott, "The Ascendance of the Imprint in China," in *Printing and Book Culture in Late Imperial China*, ed. Cynthia J. Brokaw and Kai-Wing Chow (Berkeley: University of California Press, 2006), 78–80.
24. Cynthia J. Brokaw, "On the History of the Book in China," in *Printing and Book Culture in Late Imperial China*, ed. Cynthia J. Brokaw and Kai-Wing Chow (Berkeley: University of California Press, 2006), 30.
25. Benjamin A. Elman, *A Cultural History of Civil Examinations in Late Imperial China* (Berkeley: University of California Press, 2000), 56.
26. The eight-legged essay was so named because the writing was composed of eight parts, which Elman translates as: "(1) breaking open the topic (*poti* 破題), (2) receiving the topic (*chengti* 承題), (3) beginning discussion (*qijiang* 起講), (4) initial leg (*qigu* 起股), (5) transition leg (*xugu* 續股), (6) middle leg

(*zhonggu* 中股), (7) later leg (*hougu* 後股), and (8) conclusion (*dajie* 大結)." However, there are variations in naming and sectioning with up to thirteen parts of the essay being outlined, depending on the level of detail described. Elman, *A Cultural History of Civil Examinations in Late Imperial China*, 389–390; Zhao Jiyao 趙基耀 and Li Xu 李旭, *Qingdai baguwen yi zhu* 清代八股文譯註 (Modern Chinese translations and annotations of Qing dynasty eight-legged essays) (Shanghai: Shanghai guji chubanshe, 2011), 16 and 23–29.

27. McDermott notes that the printing of examination essays in Hangzhou in around 1480 initiated the growth of examination aids generally. Joseph McDermott, "The Ascendance of the Imprint in China," 81; Wang Kaifu 王凱符, *Baguwen gaishuo* 八股文概說 (An overview of the eight-legged essay) (Beijing: Zhongguo heping chubanshe, 1991), 45.
28. The Ming dynasty phenomena of popular encyclopedias has been well discussed by Tadao Sakai and Benjamin Elman. See Tadao Sakai, "Confucianism and Popular Educational Works," in *Self and Society in Ming Thought*, ed. William Theodore de Bary (New York: Columbia University Press, 1972), 331–366; Benjamin A. Elman, "Collecting and Classifying: Ming Dynasty Compendia and Encyclopedias (Leishu)," *Extrême-Orient, Extrême-Occident* 1, no. 1 (2007): 131–157.
29. Zou and Hu, *Youxue qionglin,* 7.
30. For example, Qiu Jun 邱浚, *Jiaozheng Youxue xuzhi chengyu kao* 較正幼學須知成語考 (Corrected edition of the *Required Knowledge for Elementary Learning* with verification of the idioms) (Guangdong: Wei jing tang, 1872), HathiTrust Digital Library, https://babel.hathitrust.org/cgi/pt?id=keio.10811605590&view=1up&seq=3.
31. Roland Altenburger, "Appropriating Genius: Jin Shengtan's Construction of Textual Authority and Authorship in his Commented Edition of *Shuihu Zhuan* (The Water Margin Saga)," in *That Wonderful Composite Called Author: Authorship in East Asian Literatures from the Beginnings to the Seventeenth Century*, ed. Christian Schwermann and Raji C. Steineck (Leiden: Brill, 2014), 196.
32. Wang Zichen 王咨臣, "Cheng Dengji shengping jiqi zhuzhuo *Youxue qionglin*" 程登吉生平及其著作幼學瓊林 (Life of Cheng Dengji and the *Treasury of Elementary Learning*) in *Jiangxi lishi mingren yanjiu* 江西歷史名人研究 (Research on eminent people in Jiangxi history), ed. Chen Wenhua 陳文華 (Beijing: Zhongguo renshi chubanshe, 1995), 135–137.
33. Cheng Dengji 程登吉, *Jiantang chongding Youxue xuzhi biandu gushi* 簡堂重訂幼學須知便讀故事 (A concise reader of allusions in the *Required Knowledge for Elementary Learning*, revised by the Bamboo Slip Studio) (Jianyang: Yang

Xiaomin Shulin, publication date unknown), HathiTrust Digital Library, https://babel.hathitrust.org/cgi/pt?id=keio.10811743594&view=1up&seq=16&skin=2021.

34. Li Ren-yuan, "*Necessary Knowledge for Young Students* and the Commercial Publishing in 17th to Early 20th Century China," *Asia Major* 35, no. 2 (2022): 7.
35. Lucille Chia, *Printing for Profit: The Commercial Publishers of Jianyang, Fujian (11th–17th Centuries)* (Cambridge: Harvard Asia Center, 2002), 297.
36. Li, "*Necessary Knowledge for Young Students* and the Commercial Publishing in 17th to Early 20th Century China," 1–56.
37. Cheng Dengji 程登吉, annotated by Huang Wangruo 黃汪若, and corrected by Qian Yuanlong 錢元龍, *Ziwen ge chongding Youxue xuzhi ju jie* 紫文閣重訂幼學須知句解 (*Required Knowledge for Elementary Learning* Explained Phrase by Phrase revised by Ziwen ge) (Jingjiang: published by Qian Yuanlong, 1881), 1, Chinese University of Hong Kong Library's Chinese Rare Book Digital Collection: https://repository.lib.cuhk.edu.hk/en/item/cuhk-702758#page/2/mode/2up.
38. Li, "*Necessary Knowledge for Young Students* and the Commercial Publishing in 17th to Early 20th Century China," 19.
39. Ibid.
40. Xu, *Mengxue duwu de lishi toushi*, 101; Zhang and Mu, *Zhongguo gudai mengxue jijin*, 72.
41. Cynthia J. Brokaw, *Commerce in Culture: The Sibao Book Trade in the Qing and Republican Periods* (Cambridge: Harvard University Press, 2007), 82–83.
42. Xie Shuishun 謝水順 and Li Ting 李珽, *Fujian gudai keshu* 福建古代刻書 (Premodern publishing in Fujian) (Fuzhou: Fujian renmin chubanshe, 1997), 469.
43. Cynthia J. Brokaw, "Commercial Publishing in Late Imperial China: The Zou and Ma Family Businesses of Sibao, Fujian," *Late Imperial China* 17, no. 1 (1996): 61.
44. Li Fengrui 李逢蕊, *Kejia zongheng* 客家縱橫 (Research on Hakka culture) (Fujian: Minxi kejiaxue yanjiuhui, 1992), 131.
45. The literary inquisition (*wenzi yu* 文字獄) in premodern China refers to the political persecution of intellectuals for their writings. Lianchengxian difang zhi bianzuan weiyuanhui 連城縣地方志編纂委員會, *Lianchengxian zhi* 連城縣志 (Liancheng gazetteer) (Beijing: Qunzhong chubanshe, 1993), 902–903; Liu Decheng 劉德城 and Zhou Xianying 周羨穎, *Fujian mingren cidian* 福建名人詞典 (Dictionary of eminent people from Fujian) (Fuzhou: Fujian renmin chubanshe, 1995), 148.
46. Ibid.

47. Xie and Li, *Fujian gudai keshu*, 469.
48. The capping ceremony (*guanli* 冠禮) was a coming-of-age ritual for boys at the age of twenty.
49. Brokaw, *Commerce in Culture*, 411–421.
50. Kanori, *Taiwan bunkashi*, 37; Dongfang, *Taiwan sisu*, 107.
51. Lu Xun 魯迅, *Lu Xun quanji* 魯迅全集 (Complete works of Lu Xun) (Beijing: Renmin wenxue chubanshe, 1973), 300.
52. Hu Shih 胡適, *Sishi zishu* 四十自述 (An autobiographical account at forty) (Beijing: Zhongguo wenlian chuban gongsi, 1992), 21.
53. Feng Youlan 馮友蘭, *San song tang zixu*三松堂自序 (Self-preface by the master of the House of Three Pines) (Beijing: San lian shudian, 1984), 3; Lin Desheng 藺德生, *Bagu fengguang wubai nian* 八股風光五百年 (Five-hundred-year history of the eight-legged essay) (Beijing: Yuwen chubanshe, 2011), 55.
54. He Jiuying 何九盈 et al., eds., *Ciyuan* 辭源 [Origins of words] (Beijing: The Commercial Press, 2017), 1337–1338.
55. Ibid.
56. Ibid., 1761–1762.
57. Duan Yucai 段玉裁, *Shuowen jiezi zhu* 說文解字注 (Annotated *Explaining Simple Graphs and Analysing Complex Graphs*) (Taipei: Yee Wen Publishing Company, 2007), 10.
58. He, *Ciyuan*, 2766.
59. Ibid., 2768.
60. The term *literati* in late imperial China refers to a nonaristocratic elite status group achieved by means of success in the civil service examinations. For further explanation of social and intellectual identity of the literati, see Benjamin A. Elman, "Social Roles of Literati in Early to Mid-Ch'ing," in *The Cambridge History of China: Volume 9, Part 1, The Ch'ing Dynasty to 1800,* ed. Williard J. Peterson (Cambridge: Cambridge University Press, 1998), 365.
61. William T. Rowe, *China's Last Empire: The Great Qing* (Cambridge: Harvard University Press, 2009), 112.
62. Angela Ki Che Leung, "Elementary Education in the Lower Yangtze Region in the Seventeenth and Eighteenth Centuries," in *Education and Society in Late Imperial China, 1600–1900*, eds. Benjamin A. Elman and Alexander Woodside (Berkeley: University of California Press, 1994), 132.
63. Evelyn Sakakida Rawski, *Education and Popular Literacy in Ch'ing China* (Ann Arbor: University of Michigan Press, 1979), 4.
64. Ibid., 140.
65. Brokaw, *Commerce in Culture,* 404.

66. See Richard Lufrano's study on mid-level merchant culture of self-cultivation. In particular, he highlights how merchants valued elementary education for Neo-Confucian moral ideas, which were also incorporated into the apprentice's education. Richard John Lufrano, *Honorable Merchants Commerce and Self-Cultivation in Late Imperial China* (Honolulu: University of Hawai'i Press, 1997), 72–75.
67. Wang Jinmin 王錦民, "Education in Schools and in Society," in *The History of Chinese Civilization* (volume 4), ed. Yuan Xingpei 袁行霈, Yan Wenming 嚴文明, Zhang Chuanxi 張傳璽, and Lou Yulie 樓宇烈 (Cambridge: Cambridge University Press, 2012), 501.
68. Brokaw, *Commerce in Culture,* 323.
69. Rawski, *Education and Popular Literacy in Ch'ing China*, 33; Liu Zhaobin 劉兆璸, *Qingdai keju* 清代科舉 (Qing dynasty civil service examinations) (Taipei: Dongda chubanshe, 1979), 110.
70. The empire's schools were estimated to reach no more than 3 percent of the people in the first half of the 1700s. Benjamin A. Elman and Alexander Woodside, "The Expansion of Education in Ch'ing China," in *Education and Society in Late Imperial China, 1600–1900*, ed. Benjamin A. Elman and Alexander Woodside (Berkeley: University of California Press, 1994), 529.
71. Brokaw, *Commerce in Culture,* 149.
72. Naquin and Rawski, *Chinese Society in the Eighteenth Century*, 115.
73. Sakai, "Confucianism and Popular Educational Works," 334–335.
74. Cheng Dengji 程登吉, supplemented and annotated by Zou Shengmai 鄒聖脈, collated by Zou Tingyou 廷猷 and Xie Meilin 謝梅林, *Xinzeng Youxue gushi qionglin* 新增幼學故事瓊林 (Newly expanded *Treasury of Literary Allusions for Elementary Learning*), n.d., cover.
75. Li, "*Necessary Knowledge for Young Students* and the Commercial Publishing in 17th to Early 20th Century China," 24. (With modifications.)
76. For a sustained discussion on book printing and the rise of evidential scholarship, see Benjamin A. Elman, *From Philosophy to Philology: Intellectual and Social Aspects of Change in Late Imperial China* (Cambridge: Harvard University Press, 1984), 140–169.
77. Brokaw, *Commerce in Culture,* 210.
78. Cynthia J. Brokaw, "Reading the Best-Sellers of the Nineteenth Century: Commercial Publishing in Sibao," in *Printing and Book Culture in Late Imperial China*, ed. Cynthia J. Brokaw and Kai-Wing Chow (University of California Press, 2006), 185.
79. Brokaw outlines a similar textual history for the popular poetry primer *Qianjia shi* 千家詩 (Myriad poems). Brokaw, *Commerce in Culture,* 368.

80. Yang notes 74 editions in total: 20 woodblock imprints, 29 lithographic imprints, and 25 editions published after the Second Sino-Japanese War (1937–1945). Yang Yung-chih 楊永智, " *Youxue qionglin* liuchuan Taiwan kao" 《幼學瓊林》流傳臺灣考 (Research on the transmission of the *Youxue qionglin* in Taiwan), *Donghai daxue wenxueyuan xuebao* 47, no. 7 (2006): 83–116.
81. Li, "*Necessary Knowledge for Young Students* and the Commercial Publishing in 17th to Early 20th Century China," 34–36.
82. Li, "*Necessary Knowledge for Young Students* and the Commercial Publishing in 17th to Early 20th Century China," 35; Benjamin A. Elman, "Ch'ing Dynasty "Schools" of Scholarship," *Qing shi wen ti* 4, no. 6 (1981): 3–5.
83. James Haldane Stewart Lockhart, *A Manual of Chinese Quotations* (Hong Kong: Kelly and Walsh, 1893), ii.
84. Li, "*Necessary Knowledge for Young Students* and the Commercial Publishing in 17th to Early 20th Century China," 33–34.
85. Cai, *Huitu xinzeng Youxue gushi qionglin*; Dong Jianzhi 董堅志, *Huitu Youxue gushi qionglin* 繪圖幼學故事瓊林 (The *Treasury of Elementary Learning* with drawings) (Shanghai: Shanghai jin zhang tu shuju, 1928).
86. Ma Ziyi 馬自毅, *Xin yi Youxue qionglin* 新譯幼學瓊林 (New interpretation of the *Treasury of Elementary Learning*) (Taipei: San min shuju, 2010), 5.
87. Li, "*Necessary Knowledge for Young Students* and the Commercial Publishing in 17th to Early 20th Century China," 46.
88. A survey of the writings of important scholars of the period before 1890 showed little concern with the West: "It is not that they rejected the West, they simply ignored it." Hao Chang, "The Intellectual Context of Reform," in *Reform in Nineteenth-Century China*, ed. Paul A. Cohen and John E. Schrecker (Cambridge: East Asian Research Center Harvard University, 1976), 148.
89. William Ayers, *Chang Chih-tung and Educational Reform in China* (Cambridge: Harvard University Press, 1971), 3.
90. Ibid., 227–228.
91. Cai, *Huitu xinzeng Youxue gushi qionglin*, 5:3.
92. Elman documents the New Governance policies and reformed curriculum in 1902. Science was subdivided into astronomy, geology, arithmetic, chemistry, physics, and zoology-botany. See Benjamin A. Elman, *On Their Own Terms: Science in China, 1550–1900* (Cambridge: Harvard University Press, 2005), 404.
93. Even at the beginning of the 1930s, around 66.5 percent of educated males in the countryside had been educated at a traditional school (*sishu* 私塾). Sébastien Billioud and Joël Thoraval, *The Sage and the People: The Confucian Revival in China* (New York: Oxford University Press, 2015), 18–19.

94. Zou and Hu, *Youxue qionglin*, 1986; Zou Gang 鄒剛 and Zou Zhiyuan 鄒志瑗, *Youxue qiongling yizhu* 幼學瓊林譯注 (Annotated translation of the *Treasury of Elementary Learning*) (Nanchang: Jiangxi remin chubanshe, 1990); Hu Yunfu 胡云富, Li Chunmei 李春梅, and Fu Delin 傅德林, *Youxue qionglin xinzhu* 幼學瓊林新注 (Newly annotated *Treasury of Elementary Learning*) (Beijing: Beijing shifan daxue chubanshe, 1992); Jiang Ming 蔣明 and Zhang Daqing 張大慶, *Youxue qionglin zhu du: jian fan duizhao ben* 幼學瓊林助讀: 簡繁對照本 (*Treasury of Elementary Learning* reader with simplified and traditional Chinese) (Beijing: Zhongguo guoji guangbo chubanshe, 1998).
95. Wang Longlin 汪龍麟 and Zong Yanfu 踪岩夫, *Youxue qionglin* 幼學瓊林 (Treasury of elementary learning) (Beijing: Beijing shaonian ertong chubanshe, 1995); Zhang Mei 張梅and Chang Guojie 暢國傑, *Tales from the Children's Knowledge Treasury* (Beijng: China Intercontinental Press, 2013); Zhang Mei 張梅, *Tales from the Children's Knowledge Treasury (Chinese Japanese edition)* (Beijng: Sinolingua, 2010); Woniu fangzi 蝸牛房子, ed., *Youxue qionglin zao zao du* 幼學瓊林早早讀 (Reading the *Treasury of Elementary Learning* in the early years) (Fuzhou: Fujian shaonian ertong chubanshe, 2015).
96. For an analysis of the official discourse, see Sébastien Billioud, "Confucianism, 'Cultural Tradition,' and Official Discourses in China at the Start of the New Century," *China Perspectives* 2007, no. 3 (2007): 50–65. For an exploration of Confucian revival at the popular level, see Billioud and Thoraval, *Sage and the People*.
97. The Chinese Ministry of Education has issued several directives on the compulsory inclusion of traditional Chinese culture in primary school and middle school teaching materials. Ministry of Education of the People's Republic of China, "Wanshan Zhonghua youxiu chuantong wenhua jiaoyu zhidao gangyao" 完善中華優秀傳統文化教育指導綱要 (Essential guidance on refining education of the excellent traditional Chinese culture), 26 March 2014, accessed 23 March 2022, http://www.moe.gov.cn/srcsite/A13/s7061/201403/t20140328_166543.html; Ministry of Education of the People's Republic of China, "Zhonghua youxiu chuantong wenhua jin zhong xiaoxue kecheng jiaocai zhinan" 中華優秀傳統文化進中小學課程教材指南 (A guide on incorporating the excellent traditional Chinese culture in primary and middle school curricular materials), 8 January 2022, accessed 18 March 2022, http://www.gov.cn/zhengce/zhengceku/2021-02/05/content_5585136.htm.
98. Cheng Dengji 程登吉and Zou Shengmai 鄒聖脈, *Youxue gushi qionglin* 幼學故事瓊林 (Treasury of literary allusions for elementary learning) (Shanghai: Shanghai guji chubanshe, 2018).

99. The United Nations Terminology Database (UNTERM), "Definition of Primary Education,' adopted 13 June 2013, https://dcp.unesco.org/UNTERM/Display/Record/UNHQ/NA?OriginalId=7220a2a02d079913852569fd00038002.

100. *Zhouyi zheng yi* 周易正義 (Orthodox exegesis of the *Changes*), commentary by Wang Bi 王弼, sub-commentary by Kong Yingda 孔穎達, (Beijing: Peking University Press, 2000).

101. Wang and Kong, *Zhouyi zheng yi*, 45.

102. Zhu Xi 朱熹, *Zhouyi benyi* 周易本義 (The original interpretation of the *Changes*) (Beijing: Renmin chubanshe, 2009), 17.

103. Wang and Kong, *Zhouyi zheng yi*, 45. Translation from *The I Ching*, trans. James Legge (New York: Dover, 1963), 217. It is notable that James Legge used the 1715 imperial edition for his English translation.

104. Wang and Kong, *Zhouyi zheng yi*, 46.

105. Duan, *Shuowen jiezi zhu*, 357.

106. Qiao Weiping 喬衛平 and Cheng Peijie 程培傑, *Zhongguo gudai you'er jiaoyu shi* 中國古代幼兒教育史 (History of premodern Chinese early childhood education) (Hefei: Anhui jiaoyu chubanshe, 1989), 157.

107. Chen Hancai 陳漢才, *Zhongguo gudai you'er jiaoyu shi* 中國古代幼兒教育史 (History of premodern Chinese early childhood education) (Guangzhou: Guangdong gaodeng jiaoyu chubanshe, 1996); Clara Wing-chung Ho, *Zhongguo gudai yu'er* 中國古代育兒 (Premodern Chinese children's education) (Taipei: Taiwan shangwu yinshuguan, 1998).

108. Chinese thinkers were deliberating on issues of life, but whether this can be considered "philosophy," "moral theory," or "moral philosophy" from the perspective of modern Western philosophy has been debated. For an overview of the discussion on the moral philosophy of the *Analects,* see Stephen C. Angle, "The *Analects* and Moral Theory," in *Dao Companion to the Analects*, ed. Amy Olberding (Dordrecht: Springer Netherlands, 2014), 225–258.

109. Philip J. Ivanhoe, *Confucian Moral Self Cultivation* (Indianapolis: Hackett Publishing Company, 2000), ix.

110. JeeLoo Liu, *An Introduction to Chinese Philosophy: From Ancient Philosophy to Chinese Buddhism* (Oxford: Blackwell Publishing, 2006), 5–6.

111. Thome H. Fang, *The Chinese View of Life: The Philosophy of Comprehensive Harmony* (Taipei: Linking Publishing Company, 1980), 11–17; Tu Wei-ming, "The Sung Confucian Idea of Education: A Background Understanding," in *Neo-Confucian Education: The Formative Stage,* ed. William Theodore de Bary and John W. Chaffee (Berkeley: University of California Press, 1989), 141–142; Ivanhoe, *Confucian Moral Self Cultivation*, 1.

112. David L. Hall and Roger T. Ames, *Thinking Through Confucius* (Albany: State University of New York Press, 1987), 237–238.
113. Liu, *An Introduction to Chinese Philosophy,* 6.
114. Lee, *Education in Traditional China,* 433–435.
115. Ban, *Hanshu*, 249:807.
116. Ban Gu 班固, *Food and Money in Ancient China: The Earliest Economic History of China to A.D. 25, Han Shu 24, with Related Texts, Han Shu 91 and Shih-Chi 129*, trans. Nancy Lee Swann (Princeton: Princeton University Press, 1950), 130. (With modifications.)
117. Kinney, "Dyed Silk," 20–21.
118. Ban Gu 班固, *Bai hu tong* 白虎通 (The comprehensive discussions in the White Tiger Hall) in *Wenyuange Siku quanshu* 文淵閣四庫全書 (Wenyuange edition of the Complete Library of the Four Branches of Literature), vol. 850 (Taipei: Taiwan shangwu yinshuguan, 2013), 33.
119. The bibliographic treatise catalogues twelve works as *xiaoxue* (literacy textbook). Ban, *Hanshu*, 249:807.
120. Gardner, *Learning to Be a Sage,* 89.
121. The *Complete Library of the Four Branches of Literature* categorizes exegetical reference works as part of the canonical works.
122. Li Guojun 李國鈞, "Ming Qing mengxue jiaoyu shuping" 明清蒙學教育述評 (Review of elementary education in the Ming and Qing dynasties), in *Lidai jiaoyu zhidu kao* 歷代教育制度考 (Educational systems in Chinese history), ed. Gu Mingyuan 顧明遠 (Wuhan: Hubei jiaoyu chubanshe, 2004), 1536.
123. Rawski, *Education and Popular Literacy in Ch'ing China*, 37.
124. On the difference between *xiaoxue* and *mengxue*, Chi Xiaofang claims that *xiaoxue* specifically refers to the learning received in elementary schooling, while *mengxue* has a broader definition including instruction received in primary school, at home, through society and through educational materials for the young. Chi Xiaofang 池小芳, *Zhongguo gudai xiaoxue jiaoyu yanjiu* 中國古代小學教育研究 (A study on elementary education in premodern China) (Shanghai: Shanghai jiaoyu chubanshe, 1998), 2.
125. Qiao and Cheng, *Zhongguo gudai you'er jiaoyu shi*, 157.
126. Chi, *Zhongguo gudai xiaoxue jiaoyu yanjiu*, 324–328.
127. Jacques Gernet, "L'éducation des Premières Années (du XIe au XVIIe siècles)," in *Education et Instruction en Chine. 1. L'éducation élémentaire*, ed. Catherine Despeux and Christine Tri Nguyen (Paris-Louvain: Peeters, 2003), 7–60; Giulia Falato, *Alfonso Vagnone's Tongyou Jiaoyu (On the Education of Children, c. 1632)* (Leiden: Brill, 2020), 23–49.

128. Tian Zhengping 田正平, ed., *Zhongguo xiaoxue changshi jiaoxue shi* 中國小學常識教學史 (History of general knowledge teaching in Chinese primary schools), *Zhongguo xiaoxue geke jiaoxue shi congshu* 中國小學各科教學史叢書 (Series on the history of Chinese primary school subjects) (Jinan: Shandong jiaoyu chubanshe, 1996); Gao Qianmin 高謙民, *Zhongguo xiaoxue sixiang pinde jiaoxue shi* 中國小學思想品德教學史 (History of moral education in Chinese primary schools), *Zhongguo xiaoxue geke jiaoxue shi congshu* 中國小學各科教學史叢書 (Series on the history of Chinese primary school subjects) (Jinan: Shandong jiaoyu chubanshe, 1995); Lin Zhijin 林治金 and Ma Zhaoming 馬兆銘, *Zhongguo xiaoxue yuwen jiaoxue shi* 中國小學語文教學史 (History of language learning in Chinese primary schools), *Zhongguo xiaoxue geke jiaoxue shi congshu* 中國小學各科教學史叢書 (Series on the history of Chinese primary school subjects) (Jinan: Shandong jiaoyu chubanshe, 1996).
129. Leung, "Elementary Education in the Lower Yangtze Region in the Seventeenth and Eighteenth Centuries," 393 and 396.
130. Rawski, *Education and Popular Literacy in Ch'ing China*.
131. Charles Ridley, "Educational Theory and Practice in Late Imperial China: The Teaching of Writing as a Specific Case," (PhD thesis, Stanford University, 1973).
132. Xu, *Mengxue duwu de lishi toushi*, 5.
133. Weng Yanzhen 翁衍楨, "Gudai ertong duwu gaiguan" 古代兒童讀物概觀 (An overview of premodern children's books), *Tushuguan xueji kan* 10, no. 1 (1936): 91–146; Chang Jinghai 常鏡海, "Zhongguo sishu mengtong suo yong keben zhi yanjiu" 中國私塾蒙童所用課本之研究 (Study of Chinese private school children's textbooks), *Xin Dongfang* 1, no. 8 (1940): 103–114. Hu Huaichen 胡懷琛 wrote *Mengshu kao* 蒙書考 (A study of beginners' books) dated 1941, which listed approximately one hundred extant elementary texts. Referenced in Zhang, *Chuantong yuwen jiaoyu jiaocai lun: ji mengxue shumu he shu ying*, 7.
134. Ju Junong 瞿菊農, "Zhongguo gudai mengyang jiaocai" 中國古代蒙養教材 (Premodern Chinese elementary education teaching materials), *Beijing shifan daxue xuebao* 4 (1961): 45–56.
135. Chi examines the pre-Qin to Six Dynasties period, Sui and Tang dynasties, Song and Yuan dynasties, Ming dynasty, and Qing dynasty. Lin Wenbao, contrariwise, divides the historical development into the Han to Tang period, Song and Yuan dynasties, and Ming-Qing period. Chi, *Zhongguo gudai xiaoxue jiaoyu yanjiu*, 203–253; Lin Wenbao 林文寶, *Lidai qimeng jiaocai chutan* 歷代啓蒙教材初探 (Preliminary study on elementary education

teaching materials throughout Chinese history) (Taipei: Wan juan lou tushu youxian gongsi, 1996).

136. Thomas Lee classifies the elementary texts into those for learning about day-to-day life, vocabulary, proverbs, Neo-Confucian moral norms, and anthologies of famous poems. Lee, *Education in Traditional China,* 431–468.

137. Zhang, *Chuantong yuwen jiaoyu jiaocai lun.*

138. Limin Bai, *Shaping the Ideal Child: Children and Their Primers in Late Imperial China* (Hong Kong: The Chinese University of Hong Kong, 2005).

139. Mnemonic techniques in a variety of educational texts in premodern China were discussed in a session of the 2021 Association for Asian Studies Annual Conference. Texts analyzed included the *Erya* 爾雅 (Approaching standard), the *Cang Jie Primer*, the *Lienü zhuan* 列女傳 (Biographies of exemplary women), and the Dunhuang pedagogical manuscript *Yu dui* 語對 (Parallel sayings). Association for Asian Studies, "G001: 'A Rhyme for a Reason': Conceptualizing Euphony and Other Mnemonic Strategies in Pre-Modern Chinese Didactic Texts," accessed 6 July 2021, www.eventscribe.net/2021/AASVirtual/SearchByPresentation.asp?pfp=BrowsebyTitle.

140. Theresa Kelleher, "Back to Basics: Chu Hsi's Elementary Learning (Hsiao-hsueh)," in *Neo-Confucian Education: The Formative Stage*, ed. William Theodore de Bary and John W. Chaffee, 219–251 (Berkeley: University of California Press, 1989).

141. Christopher M. B. Nugent, *Manifest in Words, Written on Paper: Producing and Circulating Poetry in Tang Dynasty China* (Cambridge: Harvard University Asia Center, 2010); Christopher M. B. Nugent, "Structured Gaps: The *Qianzi wen* and Its Paratexts as Mnemotechnics," in *Memory in Medieval China: Text, Ritual, and Community*, ed. Wendy Swartz and Robert Ford Campany (Leiden: Brill, 2018), 158–192; Christopher M. B. Nugent, "Medieval Encyclopedias," in *Literary Information in China: A History*, ed. Jack W. Chen et al. (New York: Columbia University Press, 2021), 295–305; Christopher M. B. Nugent, *Textual Practices of Literary Training in Medieval China: Evidence from Dunhuang Manuscripts* (Leiden: Brill, 2023).

142. The five primers are the *Kaimeng yaoxun* 開蒙要訓 (Essential instructions for educating the young), *Thousand Character Essay*, *Yudui* 語對 (Parallel sayings), *Zachao* 雜抄 (Miscellaneous excerpts) and *Tuyuan cefu* 兔園冊府 (Repository of Rabbit Garden questions). See Nugent, *Textual Practices of Literary Training in Medieval China.*

143. Wang Xiaoping, "On *Qianzi wen* in the Sinological Literary History of Asia," *Frontiers of Literary Studies in China* 3, no. 3 (2009): 348–364.

144. Peter Francis Kornicki, *Languages, Scripts, and Chinese Texts in East Asia* (Oxford: Oxford University Press, 2018), 274–279.
145. Imre Galambos, *Translating Chinese Tradition and Teaching Tangut Culture: Manuscripts and Printed Books from Khara-Khoto* (Berlin: De Gruyter, 2015), 135–176.
146. Zhang Youheng 張有恆, *Shijiao sanzijing baihua jieshi* 釋教三字經白話解釋 (Three character classic of Buddhism) (Tainan: Zhang Youheng, 2020), 13; Roberta Tontini, *Muslim Sanzijing: Shifts and Continuities in the Definition of Islam in China* (Leiden: Brill, 2016), 62; Anthony E. Clark, *A Chinese Jesuit Catechism: Giulio Aleni's Four Character Classic* (Singapore: Palgrave Macmillan, 2021).
147. Limin Bai, *Fusion of East and West: Children, Education, and a New China, 1902–1915* (Leiden: Brill, 2019); Shih-Wen Sue Chen, *Children's Literature and Transnational Knowledge in Modern China: Education, Religion, and Childhood* (Singapore: Palgrave Macmillan, 2019); Clark, *A Chinese Jesuit Catechism*.
148. Curriculum theory can be prescriptive, descriptive, or a combination of both. Prescriptive theories provide intended programs or offer expert opinions on questions of value and priorities for study. They outline what "ought to happen" and have a future orientation. Arthur K. Ellis, *Exemplars of Curriculum Theory* (New York: Routledge, 2013), 5–7.
149. Fish's development of the theoretical basis of interpretive communities is best outlined in *Is There a Text in This Class?* Stanley Fish, *Is There a Text in This Class?* (Cambridge: Harvard University Press, 1980).
150. Ibid., 322–326.
151. Elizabeth Freund, *The Return of the Reader: Reader-Response Criticism* (London: Methuen and Co., 1987), 107.
152. The concept of "interpretive communities" has been applied across Confucian and Daoist canonical works. See On-Cho Ng, "Religious Hermeneutics: Text and Truth in Neo-Confucian Readings of the *Yijing*," *Journal of Chinese Philosophy* 34, no. 1 (2021): 6; Thomas Michael, "The Original Text of the *Daodejing*: Disentangling Versions and Recensions," *Religions* 13, no. 4 (2022): 325, https://doi.org/10.3390/rel13040325.
153. Ng, "Religious Hermeneutics," 6.
154. Daniel K. Gardner, *Zhu Xi's Reading of the Analects: Canon, Commentary, and the Classical Tradition* (New York: Columbia University Press, 2003), 5.
155. Contemporary education studies provide evidence that the reading practices of teachers were aligned with the pedagogical goals and reading instruction provided to their students. Emily C. Rainey and Scott Storm, "English Teacher Interpretive Communities: An Exploratory Case Study of Teachers' Literacy

Practices and Pedagogical Reasoning," *Literacy Research and Instruction* 60, no. 4 (2021): 352–371; Virginia Richardson et al., "The Relationship between Teachers' Beliefs and Practices in Reading Comprehension Instruction," *American Educational Research Journal* 28, no. 3 (1991): 559–586.

156. Although mindful of the complexities surrounding the term *modernity* in describing Chinese history, this study employs the term *early modern* to describe the sixteenth to eighteenth centuries in China. "Premodern" China in this study thus refers to the period before the sixteenth century.
157. Dorothy Ko, "Pursuing Talent and Virtue: Education and Women's Culture in Seventeenth- and Eighteenth-Century China," *Late Imperial China*, 13, no. 1 (1992): 23–25; Wang, "Education in Schools and in Society," 514.
158. "Neo-Confucianism" in this book is used as an umbrella term for the philosophical discourse associated with particular figures from the Song to Qing dynasties rather than particular schools of thought. See John Makeham, ed., *Dao Companion to Neo-Confucian Philosophy* (Dordrecht: Springer Science + Business Media B.V, 2010), xi–xiii.
159. Here *xin* 心 has been translated as "heart-mind" to avoid an unreflective dualism between body and mind.

CHAPTER ONE

1. Robin Barrow, *Giving Teaching Back to Teachers: A Critical Introduction to Curriculum Theory* (New York: Routledge, 2015), 40–42.
2. Willard J. Peterson, "Dominating Learning from Above During the K'ang-Hsi Period," in *The Cambridge History of China: Volume 9, Part 1, The Ch'ing Dynasty to 1800,* ed. Willard J. Peterson (Cambridge: Cambridge University Press, 1998), 571.
3. For more detailed discussion on the history of Cheng-Zhu learning in the Ming Dynasty, see Willard J. Peterson, "Confucian Learning in Late Ming Thought," in *The Cambridge History of China: Volume 8, Part 2, The Ming Dynasty, 1368–1644,* ed. Denis C. Twitchett and Frederick W. Mote (Cambridge: Cambridge University Press, 1998), 708–788.
4. Robert Kent Guy, *The Emperor's Four Treasuries: Scholars and the State in the Late Ch'ien-lung Era* (Cambridge: Harvard University Press, 1987), 18–19.
5. It is recorded that Kangxi's daily tutoring program began with the *Xiaojing* 孝經 (Classic of family reverence) and the Four Books. Lawrence D. Kessler, *K'ang-Hsi and the Consolidation of Ch'ing Rule, 1661–1684* (Chicago: University of Chicago Press, 1976), 143.

6. These publications were imperially stamped, titled as "by imperial order" (*qinding* 欽定) or even accompanied with a preface written by Emperor Kangxi. Wing-tsit Chan, "The *Hsing-li* and *ching-i* and the Ch'eng-Chu School of the Seventeenth Century," in *The Unfolding of Neo-Confucianism*, ed. William Theodore de Bary (New York: Columbia University Press, 1975), 544.
7. Kessler, *K'ang-Hsi and the Consolidation of Ch'ing Rule, 1661–1684*, 143.
8. Mao Lirui 毛禮銳 and Shen Guanqun 沈灌群, eds., *Zhongguo jiaoyu tongshi* 中國教育通史 (Comprehensive history of Chinese education) (Jinan: Shandong jiaoyu chubanshe, 1987), 397.
9. Luther Carrington Goodrich, *The Literary Inquisition of Ch'ien-lung* (New York: Paragon Book Reprint, 1966), 30–36.
10. Mao and Shen, *Zhongguo jiaoyu tongshi*, 396.
11. Goodrich, *Literary Inquisition of Ch'ien-lung*, 19.
12. Xiao Yishan 蕭一山, *Qingdai tongshi* 清代通史 (Comprehensive history of the Qing dynasty) (Taipei: Shangwu yinshu guan, 1963), 939–940.
13. Peterson, "Dominating Learning from Above During the K'ang-Hsi Period," 600.
14. Rowe, *China's Last Empire,* 81; Chi, *Zhongguo gudai xiaoxue jiaoyu yanjiu*, 135.
15. Benjamin A. Elman, "Changes in Confucian Civil Service Examinations from the Ming to the Ch'ing Dynasty," in *Education and Society in Late Imperial China 1600–1900*, ed. Benjamin A. Elman and Alexander Woodside (Berkeley: University of California Press, 1994), 111.
16. Chan, "The *Hsing-li* and *ching-i* and the Ch'eng-Chu School of the Seventeenth Century," 543–579.
17. Peterson, "Dominating Learning from Above During the K'ang-Hsi Period," 599.
18. Liu Xiusheng and Yang Yuqing, *Zhongguo Qingdai jiaoyu shi* 中國清代教育史 (History of Qing dynasty education) (Beijing: Renmin chubanshe, 1994), 3–4.
19. Elman, "Social Roles of Literati in Early to Mid-Ch'ing," 365.
20. Liu and Yang, *Zhongguo Qingdai jiaoyu shi*, 29.
21. Kai-wing Chow, *Publishing, Culture, and Power in Early Modern China* (Stanford: Stanford University Press, 2004), 150.
22. Ridley, "Educational Theory and Practice in Late Imperial China," 209.
23. Elman, "Social Roles of Literati in Early to Mid-Ch'ing," 360.
24. Ibid., 465–468.
25. Chi, *Zhongguo gudai xiaoxue jiaoyu yanjiu*, 135.
26. The "Five Classics" are the five Confucian canonical works designated as the core curriculum for civil servants since the Han dynasty, including the

Shijing 詩經 (Odes), the *Shujing* 書經 (Documents), the *Liji* 禮記 (Records on ritual), the *Yijing* 易經 (Changes), and the *Chunqiu* 春秋 (Spring and Autumn annals).

27. In the Shandong provincial examinations in 1873, there were more than 12,900 candidates competing for only 69 positions. Chang Chung-li, *The Chinese Gentry: Studies on Their Role in Nineteenth-Century Chinese Society* (Seattle: University of Washington Press, 1970), 170.
28. Hsiung Ping-chen, *A Tender Voyage: Children and Childhood in Late Imperial China* (Stanford: Stanford University Press, 2005), 110.
29. Liang Qichao 梁启超, *Qingdai xueshu gailun* 清代學術概論 (Intellectual trends in the Qing period) (Shanghai: Shanghai guji chubanshe, 1998), 7.
30. Qian Mu 錢穆, *Zhongguo jin sanbai nian xueshu shi* 中國近三百年學術史 (Chinese intellectual history of the recent three hundred years) (Taipei: Shangwu yinshu guan, 1967), 1.
31. Yu Ying-shih, "Some Preliminary Observations on the Rise of Qing Confucian Intellectualism," in *Chinese History and Culture Volume 2, Seventeenth Century through Twentieth Century*, ed. Yu Ying-shih, Josephine Chiu-Duke, and Michael S. Duke (New York: Columbia University Press, 2016), 1–39.
32. Elman, "Ch'ing Dynasty 'Schools' of Scholarship," 3–5.
33. See Stephen C. Angle, *Sagehood: The Contemporary Significance of Neo-Confucian Philosophy* (New York: Oxford University Press, 2010); Erin Cline, *Families of Virtue: Confucian and Western Views on Childhood Development* (New York: Columbia University Press, 2015).
34. Chi, *Zhongguo gudai xiaoxue jiaoyu yanjiu*, 95 and 200; Elman, *A Cultural History of Civil Examinations in Late Imperial China*, 261.
35. Gardner, *Learning to Be a Sage,* 3.
36. Xiao, *Qingdai tongshi*, 994.
37. Tang Jian 唐鑑, *Qing xue'an xiaozhi* 清學案小識 (Small records of the cases of learning in the Qing) (Taipei: Shangwu yinshu guan, 1968), 1.
38. Lin Guobiao 林國標, *Qing chu Zhuzi xue yanjiu* 清初朱子學研究 (Early Qing period research on Master Zhu scholarship) (Changsha: Hunan renmin chubanshe, 2004), 74–78.
39. Feng Youlan 馮友蘭, *A History of Chinese Philosophy, Volume II, The Period of Classical Learning*, trans. Derk Bodde (Princeton: Princeton University Press, 1983), 631. (With modifications.)
40. Tu, "The Sung Confucian Idea of Education," 149.
41. Gardner, *Learning to Be a Sage,* 97. (With modifications.) On the translation of *xing* 性 as "human propensities" rather than "human nature," which assumes an essentialist, abstract, *a priori* conception of human nature,

see Roger T. Ames, *A Conceptual Lexicon for Classical Confucian Philosophy* (Albany: SUNY Press, 2022), 201–208.

42. Wing-tsit Chan, *A Source Book in Chinese Philosophy* (Princeton: Princeton University Press, 1963), 86. (With modifications.)
43. Zhu Xi 朱熹, *Sishu zhangju jizhu* 四書章句集註 (The Four Books in chapter and verse with collected commentaries) (Beijing: Zhonghua shuju, 2012), 3.
44. Li Jingde 黎靖德, *Zhuzi yu lei* 朱子語類 (Classified sayings of Master Zhu), vol. 1 (Taipei: Shi hua chubanshe, 1987), 63.
45. Li, *Zhuzi yu lei*, 7:2895.
46. Ibid.
47. Daniel K. Gardner, *The Four Books: The Basic Teachings of the Later Confucian Tradition* (Indianapolis: Hackett Publishing, 2007), 3.
48. Li, *Zhuzi yulei*, 1:58.
49. Zhu Xi 朱熹, *Jin si lu* 近思錄 (Record of reflections on things at hand), commentary by Zhang Boxing 張伯行 (Taipei: Shangwu yinshuguan, 1996), 31.
50. Li, *Zhuzi yu lei*, 1:68.
51. You Zhuran, A. G. Rud, and Yingzi Hu, *The Philosophy of Chinese Moral Education: A History* (New York: Palgrave Macmillan, 2018), 183.
52. Chi, *Zhongguo gudai xiaoxue jiaoyu yanjiu*, 136.
53. Chan, *A Source Book in Chinese Philosophy*, 86–87. (With modifications.)
54. Han Zhongwen 韓鐘文, *Zhuxi jiaoyu sixiang yanjiu* 朱熹教育思想研究 (Research on Zhu Xi's educational thought) (Jiangxi: Jiangxi jiaoyu chubanshe, 1989), 84.
55. In Zhu Xi's vocabulary, sincerity (*cheng* 誠) means to accord with one's innate nature. Gardner, *Learning to Be a Sage,* 89.
56. Chan, *Source Book in Chinese Philosophy*, 107–108.
57. Zhu, *Sishu zhangju jizhu*, 32–33.
58. Tu Wei-ming, *Centrality and Commonality: An Essay on Confucian Religiousness* (Albany: State University of New York Press, 1989), 83.
59. Ibid., 84.
60. Michael Nylan, *The Five "Confucian" Classics* (New Haven: Yale University Press, 2001), 2.
61. Chen Junmin 陳俊民, ed., *Zhuzi wenji* 朱子文集 (Collected works of Master Zhu) (Taipei: De fu wenjiao jijinhui, 2000), 2860–2861.
62. Ibid.
63. Peter Bol, "Chu Hsi's Redefinition of Literati Learning," in *Neo-Confucian Education: The Formative Stage*, ed. William Theodore de Bary and John W. Chaffee (Berkeley: University of California Press, 1989), 159–160.

64. Zhang Hong 張洪 and Qi Bi 齊燹, *Zhuzi dushu fa* 朱子讀書法 (Master Zhu's method of reading), *Wenjinge Siku quanshu* 文津閣四庫全書 [Wenjinge edition of the Complete Library of the Four Branches of Literature], vol. 235 (Beijing: Shangwu yinshuguan, 2005), 757–780.
65. Qian Mu 錢穆, *Zhuzi xin xue an* 朱子新學案 (New compendium to Master Zhu), vol. 3 (Taipei: San min shuju, 1971), 613.
66. Mao and Shen, *Zhongguo jiaoyu tongshi*, 208.
67. Gardner, *Learning to Be a Sage,* 92. (With modifications.)
68. Ibid., 93. (With modifications.)
69. Zhu Xi 朱熹, "Tongmeng xuzhi" 童蒙須知 (What youngsters should know), in *Yang zheng yi gui* 養正遺規 (Guidelines for proper upbringing) compiled by Chen Hongmou 陳宏謀 (1696–1771), in *Xu xiu Siku quanshu* 續修四庫全書 (Supplement to the Complete Library of the Four Branches of Literature), vol. 951 (Shanghai: Shanghai guji chubanshe, 2002), 5–7.
70. Zhang Boxing 張伯行, *Xiaoxue ji jie* 小學集解 (Collected commentaries on *Elementary Learning*), vol. 981 (Beijing: Zhonghua shuju, 1985), 7.
71. Ibid., 14.
72. Zhu, "Tongmeng xuzhi," 14.
73. Ibid., 19.
74. Bai, *Shaping the Ideal Child,* 105.
75. Ban, *Hanshu*, 250:222.
76. Zhu, *Sishu zhangju jizhu*, 47–48.
77. Zhang, *Xiaoxue ji jie*, 1.
78. Kelleher, "Back to Basics," 227.
79. Ibid.
80. Ibid.
81. Alexander Woodside, "Some Mid-Qing Theorists of Popular Schools: Their Innovations, Inhibitions, and Attitudes toward the Poor," *Modern China* 9, no. 1 (1983): 19.
82. Zhao Erxun 趙爾巽, *Qing shi gao* 清史稿 (Draft history of the Qing), vol. 33 (Beijing: Zhonghua shuju, 1999), 9939–9940.
83. Wang, "Education in Schools and in Society," 502.
84. *Yang zheng yi gui* 養正遺規 (Guidelines for proper upbringing), comp. Chen Hongmou 陳宏謀, in *Xu xiu Siku quanshu* 續修四庫全書 (Supplement to the Complete Library of the Four Branches of Literature), vol. 951 (Shanghai: Shanghai guji chubanshe, 2002), 1–2.
85. Ibid., 2.
86. Lu Shiyi 陸世儀, *Sibian lu ji yao* 思辨録輯要 (Essential collected records of thinking and distinguishing) in *Wenyuange Siku quanshu* 文淵閣四庫全

書 (Wenyuange edition of the Complete Library of the Four Branches of Literature), vol. 724 (Taipei: Taiwan shangwu yinshuguan, 2013), 1.

87. Ridley, "Educational Theory and Practice in Late Imperial China," 295–297.
88. Lu, *Sibian lu ji yao*, 724:5.
89. Wang Chong 王充, *Xin bian Lun heng* 新編論衡 (Newly compiled *Lun heng*) (Taipei: Taiwan guji, 1990), 19.
90. Jon L. Saari, *Legacies of Childhood: Growing up Chinese in a Time of Crisis, 1890–1920* (Cambridge: Harvard University Press, 1990).
91. John W. Dardess, "Childhood in Premodern China," in *Children in Historical and Comparative Perspective*, ed. Joseph M. Hawes and N. Ray Hiner, 71–94 (New York: Greenwood Press, 1991); Hsiung, *A Tender Voyage*, 9–10.
92. Gao, *Zhongguo xiaoxue sixiang pinde jiaoxue shi*, 138.
93. Lin, *Lidai qimeng jiaocai chutan*, 127; Bai, *Shaping the Ideal Child*, 50–51.
94. Wing-tsit Chan, *Instructions for Practical Living and Other Neo-Confucian Writings by Wang Yangming* (New York: Columbia University Press, 1963), 56.
95. Feng, *A History of Chinese Philosophy, Volume II, The Period of Classical Learning*, 609.
96. Chan, *Instructions for Practical Living and Other Neo-Confucian Writings by Wang Yangming*, 16–17. (With modifications.)
97. "When the seven feelings follow their natural courses of operation, they are all functions of innate knowledge, and cannot be distinguished as good or evil. However, we should not have any selfish attachment to them. When there is such an attachment, they become selfish desires and obscurations to innate knowledge." Ibid., 229.
98. Ibid., 10.
99. Ibid., 15.
100. Ibid., 243. (With modifications.)
101. Thome H. Fang, *Chinese Philosophy, Its Spirit and Its Development* (Taipei: Linking Publishing Company, 1981), 453.
102. Ivanhoe, *Confucian Moral Self Cultivation*, 65.
103. Chan, *Instructions for Practical Living and Other Neo-Confucian Writings by Wang Yangming*, 73. (With modifications.)
104. Phillip J. Ivanhoe, *Ethics in the Confucian Tradition: The Thought of Mencius and Wang Yang-ming* (Atlanta: Scholars Press, 1990), 122–125.
105. Wang Shouren 王守仁, *Wang wen cheng gong quanshu* 王文成公全書 (Collected works of Wang Yangming) (Taipei: Shangwu yin shu guan, 1979), 631.
106. "Knowledge is the beginning of action and action the completion of knowledge." Chan, *Instructions for Practical Living and Other Neo-Confucian Writings by Wang Yangming*, 11.

107. Ibid., 182.
108. Ren Shixian 任時先, *Zhongguo jiaoyu sixiang shi* 中國教育思想史 (History of Chinese philosophy of education), vol. 44 (Shanghai: Shanghai shudian, 1992), 232–233.
109. Chan, *Instructions for Practical Living and Other Neo-Confucian Writings by Wang Yangming*, 182–183. (With modifications.)
110. Ibid.
111. Ibid., 183. (With modifications.)
112. Ibid.
113. Ibid., 184.
114. Ren, *Zhongguo jiaoyu sixiang shi*, 233.
115. Chen, *Yang zheng yi gui*, 951:42–50.
116. Lu, *Sibian lu ji yao*, 724:6.
117. Wang Yun 王筠, "Jiao tongzi fa" 教童子法 (Methods for teaching children), in *Guoxue jiaoyu ji yao jiaofa juan* 國學教育輯要教法卷 (Essentials of traditional Chinese education: Volume on teaching methods), ed. Jun Yihao 君藝豪 and Jiao Yuhua 焦玉華 (Beijing: Minzhu yu jianshe chubanshe, 2015), 166.
118. Elman and Woodside, "The Expansion of Education in Ch'ing China," 528.
119. Bai, *Shaping the Ideal Child,* 120.
120. Elman, *From Philosophy to Philology,* 1–36.
121. Elman, "Changes in Confucian Civil Service Examinations from the Ming to the Ch'ing Dynasty," 143.
122. Yu Ying-shih, "Qing Confucianism" in *Chinese History and Culture Volume 2, Seventeenth Century through Twentieth Century*, ed. Yu Ying-shih, Josephine Chiu-Duke, and Michael S. Duke (New York: Columbia University Press, 2016), 115; Elman, *From Philosophy to Philology: Intellectual and Social Aspects of Change in Late Imperial China*, 113.
123. William Theodore de Bary and Irene Bloom, eds., *Principle and Practicality: Essays in Neo-Confucianism and Practical Learning* (New York: Columbia University Press, 1979), 25.
124. Ibid., 55.
125. Willard J. Petersen, "Advancement of Learning in Early Ch'ing: Three Cases," in *The Cambridge History of China: Volume 9, Part 2, The Ch'ing Dynasty to 1800,* ed. Willard J. Petersen (Cambridge: Cambridge University Press, 2016), 539–540.
126. Gu Yanwu 顧炎武, *Record of Daily Knowledge and Collected Poems and Essays*, trans. Ian Johnston (New York: Columbia University Press, 2017), 204.
127. Petersen, "Advancement of Learning in Early Ch'ing," 534–535.

128. Kai-Wing Chow, *The Rise of Confucian Ritualism in Late Imperial China: Ethics, Classics, and Lineage Discourse* (Stanford: Stanford University Press, 1994), 41; Harry Miller, *State Versus Gentry in Late Ming Dynasty China, 1572–1644* (New York: Palgrave Macmillan, 2009), 142.
129. Miller, *State Versus Gentry in Late Ming Dynasty China, 1572–1644*, 142.
130. Yu, "Qing Confucianism," 115.
131. Peterson, "Advancement of Learning in Ch'ing in Early Ch'ing: Three Cases," 543.
132. Elman, *From Philosophy to Philology,* 46.
133. Elman, *A Cultural History of Civil Examinations in Late Imperial China*, 38–54.
134. Yu, "Some Preliminary Observations on the Rise of Qing Confucian Intellectualism," 6; Elman, *From Philosophy to Philology,* 54–55.
135. Chow, *Rise of Confucian Ritualism in Late Imperial China,* 40.
136. Ibid., 45. (With modifications.)
137. Li Guojun 李國鈞, *Zhongguo jiaoyu sixiang tongshi* 中國教育思想通史 (Comprehensive history of Chinese educational thought) (Changsha: Hunan jiaoyu chubanshe, 1994), 201–202.
138. Lu, *Sibian lu ji yao*, 724:5.
139. Yu, "Character Recognition: A New Method of Learning to Read in Late Imperial China," 12–18.
140. Tang Biao 唐彪, *Jiashu jiaoxue fa* 家塾教學法 (Teaching methods for the family school) (Shanghai: Hua dong shifan daxue chubanshe, 1992), 57–58.
141. Zhang Xingjian 張行間, "Shu zhong suo yan" 塾中瑣言 (Common remarks in the private school), in *Mengxue yaoyi* 蒙學要義 (Essential ideas in primary education), ed. Xu Zi 徐梓 and Wang Xuemei 王雪梅 (Taiyuan: Shanxi jiaoyu chubanshe, 1991), 106.
142. Li Xin'an 李新庵, "Chong ding xun xue liang gui" 重訂訓學良規 (Revised useful guidelines for moral education), in *Mengxue yaoyi* 蒙學要義 (Essential ideas in primary education), ed. Xu Zi 徐梓 and Wang Xuemei 王雪梅 (Taiyuan: Shanxi jiaoyu chubanshe, 1991), 124.
143. Tang, *Jiashu jiaoxue fa*, 69–70 and 76–79.
144. Richard J. Smith, *The Qing Dynasty and Traditional Chinese Culture* (Lanham: Rowman & Littlefield, 2015), 207.
145. Here the term *utilitarian* is avoided, as *utilitarianism* is a separate concept in Western philosophical theory.
146. Wang, "Education in Schools and in Society," 504.
147. Li, "Chong ding xun xue liang gui," 119.
148. Zhang, "Shu zhong suo yan," 103.

149. Van Norden, *Virtue Ethics and Consequentialism in Early Chinese Philosophy* (New York: Cambridge University Press, 2007), 43–44.
150. Ibid.
151. Lin and Ma, *Zhongguo xiaoxue yuwen jiaoyu shi*, 162.
152. Ridley, "Educational Theory and Practice in Late Imperial China," 369–378.

CHAPTER TWO

1. Cheng and Zou, *Youxue gushi qionglin*, foreword; Ma, *Xin yi Youxue qionglin*, 1.
2. Huang Zifang 黄子房, "Leishu he *Youxue qionglin*" 類書和幼學瓊林 (Encyclopedic anthologies and the *Treasury of Elementary Learning*), *Journal of Hainan Normal University (Social Sciences)* 4 (2006): 132–135.
3. Xiaofei Tian, "Literary Learning: Encyclopedias and Epitomes," in *The Oxford Handbook of Classical Chinese Literature (1000 BCE–900 CE)*, ed. Wiebke Denecke, Wai-yee Li, and Xiaofei Tian (New York: Oxford University Press, 2017), 136.
4. Xinzhong Yao, *An Introduction to Confucianism* (Cambridge: Cambridge University Press, 2000), 142.
5. The solar terms (*jieqi* 節氣) refers the ancient Chinese division of the sun's annual motion into twenty-four periods, also based on seasonal changes, astronomical and other natural phenomena. The solar terms guided agricultural activity and were celebrated through festivities.
6. Wai-Yee Li, "Textual Transmission of Earlier Literature during the Yuan, Ming, and Qing Dynasties," in *The Oxford Handbook of Classical Chinese Literature (1000 BCE–900 CE)*, ed. Wiebke Denecke, Wai-yee Li, and Xiaofei Tian (New York: Oxford University Press, 2017), 327–328.
7. Wang Yangming stated, "Our nature is the substance of the mind and Heaven is the source of our nature." Chan, *Instructions for Practical Living and Other Neo-Confucian Writings by Wang Yangming*, 13. Zhu stated, "The mind of Heaven and Earth is to produce things, and in the birth of man and things, each receives this mind of Heaven and Earth to be his mind." Wing-tsit Chan, ed., *Chu Hsi and Neo-Confucianism* (Honolulu: University of Hawai'i Press, 1986), 11.
8. Fang, *The Chinese View of Life,* 89.
9. The first line of the *Elementary Learning* quotes the first line of the *Doctrine of the Mean*.
10. Ian Johnston and Ping Wang, *Daxue and Zhongyong: A Bilingual Edition* (Hong Kong: Chinese University Press, 2012), 449.

11. See Henry Rosemont Jr. and Roger T. Ames, *Confucian Role Ethics: A Moral Vision for the 21st Century?* (Gottingen: Vandenhoeck & Ruprecht, 2016).
12. Chen, *Yang zheng yi gui*, 951:3.
13. Cheng and Zou, *Youxue gushi qionglin*, 63.
14. The parent-child relationship is ranked first in Qing primers such as the *Three Character Classic*, the *Dizi gui* 弟子規 (Guidelines for learners), *Elementary Learning*, and the *Classic of Family Reverence*.
15. Xiaofei Tian, "Literary Learning," 137.
16. Ibid., 136.
17. *Mencius* 1B.3. Yang Bojun 楊伯峻, *Mengzi yizhu* 孟子譯註 (Annotated translation of the *Mencius*) (Beijing: Zhonghua shuju, 2015), 28–29.
18. Cheng and Zou, *Youxue gushi qionglin*, 35.
19. *The Analects of Confucius*, trans. Burton Watson (New York: Columbia University Press, 2007), 16.
20. "On Teaching and Learning," 16.
21. Chen, *Yang zheng yi gui*, 951:19.
22. Cheng and Zou, *Youxue gushi qionglin*, 102.
23. Chan, *A Source Book in Chinese Philosophy*, 86–87.
24. Rosemont Jr. and Ames, *Confucian Role Ethics,* 92.
25. Ma, *Xin yi Youxue qionglin*, 185.
26. *The Analects of Confucius*, 110. (With modifications.)
27. Huang, *Xin yi Sanzi jing*, 27.
28. *Analects of Confucius*, 16.
29. Ibid., 73.
30. Ibid., 122.
31. Chan, *Instructions for Practical Living and Other Neo-Confucian Writings by Wang Yangming*, 273.
32. Elman, "Collecting and Classifying," 135.
33. Zhang Jian and Chen Dandan, "Primers and Poetry in Ancient China: Shenglü Fameng and Beyond," *Journal of Chinese Literature and Culture* 1, no. 1–2 (2014): 194–195.
34. Comparisons have been made between the categories in the *Treasury* and the pre-Qin *Erya* and Han dynasty *Shiming* 釋名 (Explanation of terms) lexicons. Wang Dan 王丹, "*Youxue qionglin* yanjiu" 幼學瓊林研究 (A study on the *Treasury of Elementary Learning*) (Master's thesis, Northeast Normal University, 2018), 27–30.
35. Heming Yong and Jing Peng, *Chinese Lexicography: A History from 1046 BC to AD 1911* (Oxford: Oxford University Press, 2008), 330–335.

36. Elman, "Collecting and Classifying," 133.
37. Christian Soffel, "Lesebücher aus dem späten kaiserlichen China am Beispiel des *Youxue gushi qionglin*," in *Aspekte des Lesens in China in Vergangenheit und Gegenwart: Referate der Jahrestagung 2001 der Deutschen Vereinigung fur Chinastudien* (Aspects of reading in China, past and present: Collected papers of the 2001 annual meeting of the German Association for Chinese Studies), ed. Bernhard Führer (Bochum: Projekt Verlag, 2005), 220–225; Li, "*Necessary Knowledge for Young Students* and the Commercial Publishing in 17th to Early 20th Century China," 22.
38. Cheng and Zou, *Youxue gushi qionglin*, 209–214.
39. Ancient Chinese coins were minted with a square-shaped hole in the middle, hence the name "holey square."
40. *In Search of the Supernatural: The Written Record*, trans. Kenneth J. DeWoskin and James I. Crump Jr. (Stanford: Stanford University Press, 1996), 157. (With modifications.)
41. *Shu Ching Book of History—A Modernized Edition of the Translations of James Legge*, trans. Clae Waltham (London: George Allen and Unwin Ltd., 1971), 213. (With modifications.)
42. *The Book of Lieh-tzu: A Classic of the Tao*, trans. A. C. Graham (New York: Columbia University Press, 1990), 161.
43. While the idiom "*xi shang zhi zhen* 席上之珍" literally means "a gem atop a sitting mat," the commentaries explain that "mat" means to unfold or explain, and the "gem" refers to the benevolent principles of the ancient sage kings. *Liji zheng yi* 禮記正義 (Orthodox exegesis of the *Records on Ritual*), commentary by Zheng Xuan 鄭玄, sub-commentary by Kong Yingda 孔穎達 (Beijing: Peking University Press, 2000), 1842, 1845.
44. *Shu Ching Book of History*, 61.
45. The commentary to the *Documents* explains that jade is used as ritual vessels when making sacrifices to the spirits. One's moral character in conducting the sacrifices results in the spirits responding through timely weather conditions. Hence, one's character ultimately protects crops and prevents natural disasters. *Shangshu zheng yi* 尚書正義 (Orthodox exegesis of the *Documents*), commentary by Kong Anguo 孔安國, sub-commentary by Kong Yingda 孔穎達 (Beijing: Peking University Press, 2000), 232.
46. Cheng and Zou, *Youxue gushi qionglin*, 216–217.
47. Ibid., 143.
48. Ibid., 87.
49. Chen Xuan 陳選, *Xiaoxue jizhu* 小學集註 (Collected annotations of the *Elementary Learning*), in *Wenyuange Siku quanshu* 文淵閣四庫全

書 (Wenyuange edition of the Complete Library of the Four Branches of Literature), vol. 699 (Taipei: Shangwu yinshuguan, 2013), 528.

50. Timothy Michael O'Neill, *Ideography and Chinese Language Theory* (Boston: Walter De Gruyter, 2016), 202–205.
51. Ibid., 191–192.
52. Ibid., 235.
53. Ibid., 267.
54. Elman, *From Philosophy to Philology,* 3.
55. Chow, *Rise of Confucian Ritualism in Late Imperial China,* 161.
56. Cheng and Zou, *Youxue gushi qionglin*, 2.
57. The five qualities akin to virtues of humans are: culture (the rooster's comb resembles the scholar's cap), military prowess (the rooster has feet with spurs), courage (the rooster is daring in battle), humanity (the rooster alerts others to food), and trustworthiness (the rooster keeps watch of time and announces dawn without fail). Ibid., 287.
58. Nylan, "Calligraphy," 39–40.
59. Zhang, *Chuantong yuwen jiaoyu jiaocai lun*, 70–73.
60. Cheng and Zou, *Youxue gushi qionglin*, 12–14.
61. Gardner, *Zhu Xi's Reading of the Analects,* 4.
62. Cheng Duanli 程端禮, "*Dushu fen nian richeng*" 讀書分年日程 (A yearly program of study at the Cheng family school), in *Guoxue jiaoyu ji yao jiaofa juan* 國學教育輯要教法卷 (Essentials of traditional Chinese education: Volume on teaching methods), ed. Jun Yihao 君藝豪 and Jiao Yuhua 焦玉華 (Beijing: Minzhu yu jianshe chubanshe, 2015), vol. 1, 5.
63. Hu, *Sishi zishu*, 22.
64. Li, "*Necessary Knowledge for Young Students* and the Commercial Publishing in 17th to Early 20th Century China," 34–36.
65. Xie Qikun's 謝啓昆 textual study published in 1889 investigated linguistic texts, although literacy texts such as the *Thousand Character Essay* were also included. Xie Qikun 謝啓昆, *Xiaoxue kao* 小學考 (A study on primary education) (Hefei: Anhui jiaoyu chubanshe, 2002).
66. Gardner, *Zhu Xi's Reading of the Analects,* 164–167.
67. Imre Galambos, "Confucian Education in a Buddhist Environment: Medieval Manuscripts and Imprints of the *Mengqiu*," *Studies in Chinese Religions* 1, no. 3 (2015): 272.
68. Nugent, *Textual Practices of Literary Training in Medieval China,* 91–107.
69. Ibid., 133–137.
70. Ibid., 281–282.

71. Yu, "Qing Confucianism," 118.
72. Cynthia J. Brokaw, "Tai Chen and Learning in the Confucian Tradition," in *Education and Society in Late Imperial China, 1600–1900*, ed. Benjamin A. Elman and Alexander Woodside (Berkeley: University of California Press, 1994), 278.
73. Cheng and Zou, *Youxue gushi qionglin*, 210.
74. Ibid., 129, 210, and 212.
75. Dennis Chi-hsiung Cheng, "Inter-Explanation of the Classics: Qing Scholars' Methods for Interpreting the Five Classics," in *Interpretation and Intellectual Change: Chinese Hermeneutics in Historical Perspective*, ed. Ching-I Tu (New Brunswick: Transaction Publishers, 2005), 203.
76. Cheng and Zou, *Youxue gushi qionglin*, 65. Translation from "On Teaching and Learning," 16.
77. Repairing the leather and creating baskets uses similar skills and provides essential training for the trades of blacksmithing and bow-making, respectively. Zheng and Kong, *Liji zheng yi*, 1246.
78. Cheng, "*Dushu fen nian richeng*," 6.
79. The *Great Learning* is cited two times, the *Doctrine of the Mean* once, the *Analects* twenty-one times, and the *Mencius* twenty-one times.
80. Ma, *Xin yi Youxue qionglin*.
81. The recension of the *Youxue qionglin* that Wang Dan analyses is not specified in the dissertation.
82. Wang, "*Youxue qionglin* yanjiu," 54–60.
83. Cheng and Zou, *Youxue gushi qionglin*, 219.
84. *Analects of Confucius*, 49. Bo Yi and Shu Qi are also noted in the "Elder and Younger Brothers" chapter of the *Treasury* as model siblings who ceded the throne to each other and eventually renounced the kingdom of Guzhu. Cheng and Zou, *Youxue gushi qionglin*, 74.
85. The cataloguing term *xiaoshuo* 小說 in traditional Chinese bibliography refers to writings incongruous with other categories of masters works, rather than referring to "fiction" in the modern sense. Xiaohuan Zhao, "Xiaoshuo as a Cataloguing Term in Traditional Chinese Bibliography," *Sungkyun Journal of East Asian Studies* 5, no. 2 (2005): 160–161.
86. Zhang Hua 張華, *Bowu zhi* 博物志 (Treatise on curiosities) in *Wenyuange Siku quanshu* 文淵閣四庫全書 (Wenyuange edition of the Complete Library of the Four Branches of Literature), vol. 1047 (Taipei: Taiwan shangwu yinshuguan, 2013), 573.
87. The quote originates from the *Mencius* 2A.3. Yang, *Mengzi yizhu*, 67.
88. Cheng and Zou, *Youxue gushi qionglin*, 35.

89. Elman, "Collecting and Classifying," 131.
90. Translation from Brokaw, "Reading the Best-Sellers of the Nineteenth Century," 210. (With modifications.)

CHAPTER THREE

1. Chan, *Instructions for Practical Living and Other Neo-Confucian Writings by Wang Yangming*, xxii.
2. Ibid., 275.
3. This is described in *Zhu's Method of Reading* as "attain familiarity and apprehension" and "experience the principles."
4. Cheng, "*Dushu fen nian richeng*," 9.
5. Lu Shiyi 陸世儀, "Lun dushu" 論讀書 (On learning), in *Yang zheng yi gui* 養正遺規 (Guidelines for proper upbringing), compiled by Chen Hongmou 陳宏謀 in *Xu xiu Siku quanshu* 續修四庫全書 (Supplement to the Complete Library of the Four Branches of Literature), vol. 951 (Shanghai: Shanghai guji chubanshe, 2002), 30.
6. Tang, *Jiashu jiaoxue fa*, 10.
7. Wang, "Jiao tongzi fa," 165.
8. Bai, *Shaping the Ideal Child*, 55–56.
9. Ibid., 47.
10. The title of *Longwen bianying* 龍文鞭影 (The young horse and the shadow of a whip) is a metaphor itself. The fine young horse that bolts upon seeing even the shadow of a whip—the child is likened to the horse, while the book is the shadow of the whip that is considered an excellent aid for the child's learning. Xiao Liangyou 蕭良有, *Longwen bianying* 龍文鞭影 (The young horse and the shadow of a whip) (Shanghai: Shanghai guji chubanshe, 2014).
11. Ben ju *Da cidian* bianzuan weiyuanhui 本局大辭典編纂委員會, *Da cidian* 大辭典 (Comprehensive Chinese dictionary) (Taipei: San min shuju, 1985), 409.
12. Enhua Edward Peng, "The Role of Allusion in Classical Chinese Poetry" (PhD thesis, University of California, 1994), 137.
13. Cheng and Zou, *Youxue gushi qionglin*, 128.
14. Ibid., 32.
15. Liu Xiang 劉向, *Exemplary Women of Early China: The Lienü Zhuan of Liu Xiang*, trans. Anne Behnke Kinney (New York: Columbia University Press, 2014), 18.

16. Wang Xiang 王相, *Sanzi jing xungu* 三字經訓詁 (Exegesis of the *Three Character Classic*) (Beijing: Zhongguo shudian, 1991), 5.
17. Shi Chengjin 石成金, "Dushu xinfa" 讀書心法 (Attitudes for reading), in *Guoxue jiaoyu ji yao jiaofa juan* 國學教育輯要教法卷 (Essentials of traditional Chinese education: Volume on teaching methods), ed. Jun Yihao 君藝豪 and Jiao Yuhua 焦玉華 (Beijing: Minzhu yu jianshe chubanshe, 2015), 580.
18. Robin Barrow, *Plato and Education* (New York: Routledge, 2012), 41.
19. Chan, *Instructions for Practical Living and Other Neo-Confucian Writings by Wang Yangming*, 185. (With modifications.)
20. James J. Y. Liu, *The Art of Chinese Poetry* (Chicago: University of Chicago Press, 1966), 136.
21. Yu-Kung Kao and Tsu-Lin Mei, "Meaning, Metaphor, and Allusion in T'ang Poetry," *Harvard Journal of Asiatic Studies* 38, no. 2 (1978): 288–289.
22. Ibid., 288.
23. Aristotle, *The Poetics of Aristotle*, trans. Samuel Henry Butcher (London: Macmillan and Co, 1907), 87.
24. Liu Hsieh 劉勰, *The Literary Mind and the Carving of Dragons*, trans. Vincent Yu-chung Shih (Hong Kong: The Chinese University Press, 2015), 257.
25. Pauline Yu, *The Reading of Imagery in the Chinese Poetic Tradition* (Princeton: Princeton University Press, 1987), 33.
26. Sarah Allan, *The Way of Water and Sprouts of Virtue* (Albany: State University of New York Press, 1997), 4.
27. Ibid., 95.
28. Donald Munro evaluates Zhu Xi's use of imagery, including water and plants. His discussion on the "plant" image highlights how nurturing others was conveyed through the different stages of plant development. Donald J. Munro, *Images of Human Nature: A Sung Portrait* (Princeton: Princeton University Press, 1988), 138–142.
29. George Lakoff and Mark Johnson, *Metaphors We Live By* (Chicago: University of Chicago Press, 1980).
30. Ibid., 4.
31. Ibid., 35-37.
32. Cheng and Zou, *Youxue gushi qionglin*, 135.
33. Cheng and Zou, *Youxue gushi qionglin*, 58–59.
34. Ibid., 64.
35. Ibid., 72.
36. Ibid., 74.
37. Ibid., 93.

38. Ibid., 101.
39. Ibid., 116.
40. Ibid., 232; Lockhart, *Manual of Chinese Quotations*, 424.
41. Ibid.
42. Ibid., 201.
43. Ibid., 311.
44. Lockhart, *Manual of Chinese Quotations*, 116.
45. Cheng and Zou, *Youxue gushi qionglin*, 232.
46. Ibid., 74.
47. Ibid., 132.
48. Ibid., 135.
49. Lockhart, *Manual of Chinese Quotations*, 218.
50. Ibid., 212.
51. Cheng and Zou, *Youxue gushi qionglin*, 308.
52. Ibid., 167.
53. John R. Searle, "Metaphor," in *Metaphor and Thought*, ed. Andrew Ortony (New York: Cambridge University Press, 1993), 114.
54. Cheng and Zou, *Youxue gushi qionglin*, 174; Lockhart, *Manual of Chinese Quotations*, 397. (With modifications.)
55. "On Teaching and Learning," 16.
56. George A. Kennedy, *On Rhetoric: A Theory of Civic Discourse* (Oxford: Oxford University Press, 2007), 218.
57. Willard Van Orman Quine, "A Postscript on Metaphor," in *On Metaphor*, ed. Sheldon Sacks (Chicago: University of Chicago Press, 1979), 160.
58. See Lakoff and Johnson, *Metaphors We Live By*; Mark Turner and Gilles Fauconnier, *The Way We Think: Conceptual Blending and the Mind's Hidden Complexities* (New York: Basic Books, 2002).
59. Kieran Egan, *The Educated Mind: How Cognitive Tools Shape Our Understanding* (Chicago: University of Chicago, 1997), 56.
60. Don R. Swanson, "Toward a Psychology of Metaphor," in *On Metaphor*, ed. Sheldon Sacks (Chicago: University of Chicago Press, 1979), 162.
61. Lee H. Yearley, *Mencius and Aquinas: Theories of Virtue and Conceptions of Courage* (New York: State University of New York Press, 1990), 36.
62. *Analects of Confucius*, 118.
63. *Zhouli zhushu* 周禮注疏 (Commentary and sub-commentary on the *Rituals of Zhou*), commentary by Zheng Xuan 鄭玄, sub-commentary by Jia Gongyan 賈公彥, in *Wenyuange Siku quanshu* 文淵閣四庫全書 (Wenyuange edition of the Complete Library of the Four Branches of Literature), vol. 90 (Taipei: Taiwan shangwu yinshuguan, 2013), 253.

64. *The Sacred Books of China: The Texts of Confucianism, Part III: The Li Ki I–X*, trans. James Legge (Delhi: Motilal Banarsidass, 1968), 69–70.
65. Zhu, "Tongmeng xuzhi," 19.
66. Huang, *Xin yi Sanzi jing*, 23.
67. Cheng and Zou, *Youxue gushi qionglin*, 35.
68. Ibid.
69. Ibid., 36.
70. Ibid., 35.
71. Akin to being the "right-hand man" or "wingman" in English usage.
72. Indeed, the respect is mutual. The competent minister must constantly scrutinize and keep the emperor to task as seen in the remonstrances recorded.
73. Ibid., 63.
74. Henry Rosemont Jr. and Roger T. Ames, *The Chinese Classic of Family Reverence: A Philosophical Translation of the Xiaojing* (Honolulu: University of Hawai'i Press, 2009), 107.
75. Yuling Pan and Dániel Z. Kádár, *Politeness in Historical and Contemporary Chinese* (London: Continuum, 2011), 44.
76. Lockhart, *Manual of Chinese Quotations*, 45.
77. Charles A. S. Williams, *Chinese Symbolism and Art Motifs: A Comprehensive Handbook on Symbolism in Chinese Art through the Ages* (North Clarendon: Tuttle Publishing, 2006), 237–240.
78. *The I Ching*, trans. James Legge, 430.
79. Cheng and Zou, *Youxue gushi qionglin*, 133–134.
80. Ibid., 131.
81. Ibid., 156.
82. Ibid., 158.
83. Zheng and Kong, *Liji zheng yi*, 20.
84. Gu Yueguo, "Politeness Phenomena in Modern Chinese," *Journal of Pragmatics* 14, no. 2 (1990): 239.
85. Pan and Kádár, *Politeness in Historical and Contemporary Chinese*, 40–43.
86. Ibid., 63.
87. Shi Chengjin 石成金, "Tong li zhi yao" 童禮知要 (Essential knowledge for childhood etiquette), in *Guoxue jiaoyu ji yao jiaofa juan* 國學教育輯要教法卷 (Essentials of traditional Chinese education: Volume on teaching methods), ed. Jun Yihao 君藝豪 and Jiao Yuhua 焦玉華 (Beijing: Minzhu yu jianshe chubanshe, 2015), 278.
88. Gu Yueguo, "Politeness Phenomena in Modern Chinese," 246–247.
89. Cheng and Zou, *Youxue gushi qionglin*, 78.

90. Ma, *Xin yi youxue qionglin*, 103.
91. Lockhart, *Manual of Chinese Quotations*, 78.
92. Ibid., 251.
93. Yearley, *Mencius and Aquinas,* 37.
94. Ibid., 133.
95. Li Yan 李艷, "Chang li ju yao" 常禮舉要 (Essentials of daily etiquette), in *Guoxue jiaoyu ji yao jiaofa juan* 國學教育輯要教法卷 (Essentials of traditional Chinese education: Volume on teaching methods), ed. Jun Yihao 君藝豪 and Jiao Yuhua 焦玉華 (Beijing: Minzhu yu jianshe chubanshe, 2015), vol. 2, 311.
96. Both these expressions originate from classical allusions of the *Liezi* 列子. Cheng and Zou, *Youxue gushi qionglin*, 7, 155, and 313; Yang Bojun 楊伯峻, *Liezi ji shi* 列子集釋 (Collected explanations of the *Liezi*) (Beijing: Zhonghua shuju, 1985), 237–238.
97. Cheng and Zou, *Youxue gushi qionglin*, 155.
98. Ibid.
99. Ibid., 184.
100. Ibid.
101. Ibid., 187.
102. Lockhart, *Manual of Chinese Quotations*, 274.
103. Cheng and Zou, *Youxue gushi qionglin*, 193.
104. Ibid., 6.
105. Rosemont Jr. and Ames, *Chinese Classic of Family Reverence,* 105.
106. Cheng and Zou, *Youxue gushi qionglin*, 133, 163.
107. Ibid., 187.
108. Ibid., 163.
109. Ibid., 371.
110. Ibid., 366. (With modifications.)
111. Ibid., 368.
112. Lockhart, *Manual of Chinese Quotations*, 362.
113. Ibid., 363. (With modifications.)
114. Liu, *Literary Mind and the Carving of Dragons*, 270.
115. Herbert Fingarette, *Confucius: The Secular as Sacred* (New York: Harper and Row, 1972), 7.
116. Zhu, "Tongmeng xuzhi," 19.
117. Chan, *Instructions for Practical Living and Other Neo-Confucian Writings by Wang Yangming*, 250.
118. Karyn Lai, "Li in the *Analects*: Training in Moral Competence and the Question of Flexibility," *Philosophy East and West* 56, no. 1 (2006): 71.

119. Cui Xuegu 崔學古, "You xun" 幼訓 (Instructions for children), in *Mengxue yaoyi* 蒙學要義 (Essential ideas in primary education), ed. Xu Zi 徐梓 and Wang Xuemei 王雪梅 (Taiyuan: Shanxi jiaoyu chubanshe, 1991), 79; Li, "Ming Qing mengxue jiaoyu shuping," 81–82.
120. Lu, *Sibian lu ji yao*, 724:5.
121. Ridley, "Educational Theory and Practice in Late Imperial China," 333.
122. "Mo grieved when silk was dyed" 墨悲絲染. Francis W. Paar, ed., *Ch'ien Tzu Wen* 千字文 *The Thousand Character Classic: A Chinese Primer* (New York: Frederick Ungar Publishing Company, 1963), 12.
123. Kinney, *Chinese Views of Childhood*, 31.
124. Zhang, "Xiaoxue," 14.
125. Tang, *Jiashu jiaoxue fa*, 3.
126. Donald J. Munro, *Concept of Man in Early China* (Stanford: Stanford University Press, 1969), 99.
127. Ibid., 96.
128. *Analects of Confucius*, 34.
129. May Sim, *Remastering Morals with Aristotle and Confucius* (New York: Cambridge University Press, 2007), 139.
130. Zhu, *Sishu zhangju jizhu*, 47.
131. Duan, *Shuowen jiezi zhu*, 128.
132. Cui, "You xun," 83–84.
133. Li, "Chong ding xun xue liang gui," 122.
134. Shengzu Xuanye 聖祖玄燁, *Sacred Edict Containing Sixteen Maxims of the Emperor Kang-Hi, Amplified by his Son the Emperor Yoong-Ching*, trans. William Milne, commentary by Shizong Yinzhen 世宗胤禛 (Shanghai: American Presbyterian Mission Press, 1870), 137.
135. Lü Xinwu 呂新吾, "Xu xiao'er yu" 續小兒語 (Further words of children), in *Yang zheng yi gui* 養正遺規 (Guidelines for proper upbringing), compiled by Chen Hongmou 陳宏謀 in *Xu xiu Siku quanshu* 續修四庫全書 (Supplement to the Complete Library of the Four Branches of Literature), vol. 951 (Shanghai: Shanghai guji chubanshe, 2002), 22–27.
136. Munro, *Images of Human Nature*, 163.
137. Zhu Xi 朱熹, "Bai lu dong shuyuan tishi" 白鹿洞書院提示 (Regulations of the white deer grotto academy) in *Guoxue jiaoyu ji yao jiaofa juan* 國學教育輯要教法卷 (Essentials of traditional Chinese education: Volume on teaching methods), ed. Jun Yihao 君藝豪 and Jiao Yuhua 焦玉華 (Beijing: Minzhu yu jianshe chubanshe, 2015), vol. 2, 379.
138. Chan, *Instructions for Practical Living and Other Neo-Confucian Writings by Wang Yang-Ming*, 195.

139. Lockhart, *Manual of Chinese Quotations*, 159–160. (With modifications.)
140. Cheng and Zou, *Youxue gushi qionglin*, 133.
141. Ibid., 20 and 23.
142. Ibid., 7–8.
143. Ibid., 8.
144. Ibid., 21; Lockhart, *Manual of Chinese Quotations*, 25. (With modifications.)
145. Cheng and Zou, *Youxue gushi qionglin*, 49.
146. Ibid., 50.
147. Ibid., 314.
148. Ibid., 7.
149. Ibid., 24; Lockhart, *Manual of Chinese Quotations*, 24. (With modifications.)
150. Cheng and Zou, *Youxue gushi qionglin*, 31.
151. Cynthia J. Brokaw, *The Ledgers of Merit and Demerit: Social Change and Moral Order in Late Imperial China* (Princeton: Princeton University Press, 2014), 31.
152. John B. Henderson, *The Development and Decline of Chinese Cosmology* (New York: Columbia University Press, 1984), 132–136.
153. Brokaw, *Ledgers of Merit and Demerit*, 221–222.
154. Li, "Chong ding xun xue liang gui," 116.
155. Linda Tinkaus Zagzebski, *Divine Motivation Theory* (Cambridge: Cambridge University Press, 2004), 52
156. Chan, *Instructions for Practical Living and Other Neo-Confucian Writings by Wang Yang-Ming*, 23.
157. Cheng and Zou, *Youxue gushi qionglin*, 47–48, 263–264, 291, and 298.
158. Ibid., 88, 171, and 213.
159. Zagzebski, *Divine Motivation Theory*, 52.
160. See Amy Olberding, *Moral Exemplars in the Analects: The Good Person is That* (New York: Routledge, 2012).
161. Cheng and Zou, *Youxue gushi qionglin*, 232.
162. Larry Nucci, Darcia Narvaez and Tobias Krettenauer, eds., *Handbook of Moral and Character Education* (New York: Routledge, 2014), 141.
163. Ibid., 142.
164. *The Chinese Classics: Translated into English, with Preliminary Essays and Explanatory Notes*, trans. James Legge (London: N. Trubner and Co, 1869), 236.
165. Kennedy, *On Rhetoric,* 146–147.
166. Ibid., 147.
167. *Mencius*, trans. Irene Bloom (New York: Columbia University Press, 2009), 35.
168. Kristján Kristjánsson, "Emulation and the Use of Role Models in Moral Education," *Journal of Moral Education* 35, no. 1 (2006): 45.

169. Chan, *Instructions for Practical Living and Other Neo-Confucian Writings by Wang Yang-Ming*, 247.
170. "On Teaching and Learning," 12–15.
171. Ibid., 13.

CHAPTER FOUR

1. Although the civil service examinations had been established in the sixth century during the Sui dynasty (581–618), it did not become the primary determinant of talent recruitment for the government until the Song dynasty. See Benjamin A. Elman, "Political, Social, and Cultural Reproduction via Civil Service Examinations in Late Imperial China," *Journal of Asian Studies* 50 (1991): 9.
2. *Analects of Confucius*, 100.
3. Bol, "Chu Hsi's Redefinition of Literati Learning," 156–157.
4. Cui Xuegu 崔學古, "Shaoxue" 少學 (Education for youth), in *Mengxue yaoyi* 蒙學要義 (Essential ideas in primary education), ed. Xu Zi 徐梓 and Wang Xuemei 王雪梅 (Taiyuan: Shanxi jiaoyu chubanshe, 1991), 87; Li, "Chong ding xun xue liang gui," 175; Lu, *Sibian lu ji yao*, 724:6; Wang, "Jiao tongzi fa," 167.
5. Elman, "Changes in Confucian Civil Service Examinations from the Ming to the Ch'ing Dynasty," 118–121.
6. The eight-legged essay was so named because the writing was composed of eight parts, which Elman translates as: (1) breaking open the topic (*poti* 破題), (2) receiving the topic (*chengti* 承題), (3) beginning discussion (*qijiang* 起講), (4) initial leg (*qigu* 起股), (5) transition leg (*xugu* 續股), (6) middle leg (*zhonggu* 中股), (7) later leg (*hougu* 後股), and (8) conclusion (*dajie* 大結). However, there are variations in naming and sectioning with up to thirteen parts of the essay being outlined, depending on the level of detail described. Elman, *A Cultural History of Civil Examinations in Late Imperial China*, 389–390; Zhao Jiyao 趙基耀 and Li Xu 李旭, *Qingdai baguwen yi zhu* 清代八股文譯註 (Modern Chinese translations and annotations of Qing dynasty eight-legged essays) (Shanghai: Shanghai guji chubanshe, 2011), 16 and 23–29.
7. Elman, "Changes in Civil Service Examinations from the Ming to the Ch'ing Dynasty," 267.
8. Ibid.
9. Cheng, "*Dushu fen nian richeng*," 8.

10. Xu Di, "The Teaching and Learning Principles of Xueji in the Educational Practice of the World Today," in *Chinese Philosophy on Teaching and Learning: Xueji in the Twenty-First Century*, ed. Xu Di and Hunter McEwan (Albany: State University of New York Press, 2016), 39-60.
11. Zhang, *Chuantong yuwen jiaoyu jiaocai lun*, 35; Rawski, *Education and Popular Literacy in Ch'ing China*, 49.
12. Chris Wen-chao Li, "Classical Chinese," in *The Routledge Encyclopedia of the Chinese Language*, ed. Chan Sin-wai (New York: Routledge, 2016), 414. Christoph Harbsmeier argues that there not a "strict dichotomy" between classical and colloquial Chinese prior to the May Fourth Movement, but this relates to the spoken language rather than literary language, which he notes used the "authoritative *wenyanwen*." Harbsmeier, "May Fourth Linguistic Orthodoxy and Rhetoric: Some Informal Comparative Notes," in *New Terms for New Ideas: Western Knowledge and Lexical Change in Late Imperial China*, ed. Michael Lackner, Joachim Kurtz, and Iwo Amelung (Leiden: Brill, 2001), 377 and 397.
13. Ridley, "Educational Theory and Practice in Late Imperial China," 390; Elman, *A Cultural History of Civil Examinations in Late Imperial China*, 373.
14. Ridley, "Educational Theory and Practice in Late Imperial China," 351.
15. For a comparison of the role of memorization in medieval Europe and Chinese literary culture, see Nugent, *Manifest in Words, Written on Paper*, 72–117.
16. Charles Hartman, *Han Yu and the T'ang Search for Unity* (Princeton: Princeton University Press, 1986), 235–236.
17. Yu Li, "A History of Reading in Late Imperial China, 1000–1800" (PhD thesis, Ohio State University, 2003), 49–51.
18. Mary J. Carruthers, *The Book of Memory: A Study of Memory in Medieval Culture* (Cambridge: Cambridge University Press, 2008), 205.
19. Christian Soffel has argued that the text was to aid recall of literary knowledge and vocabulary rather than develop writing skills. However, his conclusion is based on findings of irregularities from strict parallelism and poetic form in the text, without evidence on how knowledge was transmitted or retained. Soffel, "Lesebücher aus dem späten kaiserlichen China am Beispiel des *Youxue gushi qionglin*," 224–225.
20. Cheng and Zou, *Youxue gushi qionglin*, 145.
21. Ibid.
22. Ibid., 154.

23. Ibid., 4.
24. Ibid., 14.
25. Jerry Norman, *Chinese* (New York: Cambridge University Press, 1988), 44.
26. Cheng and Zou, *Youxue gushi qionglin*, 47.
27. Ibid., 56.
28. Alan Baddeley, Michael W. Eysenck, and Michael C. Anderson, *Memory* (New York: Psychology Press, 2015), 477.
29. Fergus I. M. Craik and Robert S. Lockhart, "Levels of Processing: A Framework for Memory Research," *Journal of Verbal Learning and Verbal Behavior* 11, no. 6 (1972): 671–684.
30. Ibid., 675.
31. Ibid., 677.
32. Cheng and Zou, *Youxue gushi qionglin*, 183.
33. The first sentence is a quote from the exemplary mother of Wangsun Jia 王孫賈, while the second sentence is a line from the *Odes*. Cheng and Zou, *Youxue gushi qionglin*, 67; Lockhart, *Manual of Chinese Quotations*, 77. (With modifications.)
34. Nugent, *Manifest in Words, Written on Paper: Producing and Circulating Poetry in Tang Dynasty China*, 101–102.
35. Li, "Ming Qing mengxue jiaoyu shuping," 1540–1541.
36. Baddeley et al., *Memory*, 174.
37. See Allan Paivio, *Mental Representations: A Dual Coding Approach* (New York: Oxford University Press, 1990).
38. Ibid., 205.
39. Cheng and Zou, *Youxue gushi qionglin*, 129 and 178.
40. Ibid., 63 and 193.
41. Jerry Norman notes, "In the virtual absence of morphology, grammatical processes in Classical Chinese are almost totally syntactic." Hence, grammar and syntax in literary Chinese will be used synonymously here. See Norman, *Chinese*, 106.
42. Andrew H. Plaks, "Where the Lines Meet: Parallelism in Chinese and Western Literatures," *Poetics Today* 11, no. 3 (1990): 533.
43. Wang, "Jiao tongzi fa," 179.
44. Cheng Weijun 成偉鈞, Tang Zhongyang 唐仲揚, and Xiang Hongye 向宏業, *Xiuci tong jian* 修辭通鑑 (A comprehensive guide to rhetoric) (Beijing: Zhongguo qingnian chubanshe, 1991), 813–814; Wang Weiyong 王偉勇, *Yingyongwen* 應用文 (Writing for various occasions) (Tainan: Cheng da chubanshe, 2015), 86.

45. The four types are the verbal couplet, the factual couplet, the couplet of contrast, and the couplet of agreement. Liu, *Literary Mind and the Carving of Dragons*, 252.
46. Kūkai 空海, *Wen jing mi fu lun* 文鏡秘府論 (Bunkyō hifu ron) in *Xu xiu Siku quanshu* 續修四庫全書 (Supplement to the Complete Library of the Four Branches of Literature), vol. 1694 (Shanghai: Shanghai guji chubanshe, 2002), 59–70.
47. Lu Shengjiang 盧盛江, "*Wen jing mi fu lun* ji zhong duishu lun yanjiu" 《文鏡秘府論》幾種對屬論研究 (Study on the types of parallelism in the *Bunkyō hifu ron*), *Nankai Journal (Philosophy, Literature, and Social Science Edition)* no. 6 (2013): 137–146; James Robert Hightower, "Some Characteristics of Parallel Prose," in *Studies in Chinese Literature*, ed. John Lyman Bishop (Cambridge: Harvard University Press, 1965), 60.
48. Hightower, "Some Characteristics of Parallel Prose," 60–66.
49. Lei Qiaoyun 雷僑雲, *Zhongguo ertong wenxue yanjiu* 中國兒童文學研究 (Research on Chinese children's literature) (Taipei: Taiwan xuesheng chubanshe, 1998), 701.
50. In China, modern punctuation was introduced in the early twentieth century.
51. Cheng and Zou, *Youxue gushi qionglin*, 237.
52. Cui, "You xun," 1540–1541.
53. Lin Meihui 林美惠, "*Youxue qionglin* yanjiu" 幼學瓊林研究 (Study on the *Treasury of Elementary Learning*) (Master's thesis, Feng Jia University, 2008), 96–103.
54. Cheng and Zou, *Youxue gushi qionglin*, 143.
55. Ibid., 147.
56. Ibid.
57. Ibid., 54.
58. Ibid., 92.
59. Ibid., 89.
60. Ibid., 94.
61. Although *tailao* 太牢 can also refer to "the offerings of three livestock," the annotation in the *Treasury* glosses the term to mean "oxen" in this instance. Ibid., 183.
62. Ibid., 183.
63. Ibid., 5; Lockhart, *Manual of Chinese Quotations*, 6.
64. Nugent, "Structured Gaps," 166.
65. George A. Miller, "The Magical Number Seven, Plus or Minus Two: Some Limits on our Capacity for Processing Information," *Psychological Review* 63, no. 2 (1956): 81–97.

66. Cheng and Zou, *Youxue gushi qionglin*, 45.
67. Torkel Klingberg, *The Learning Brain: Memory and Brain Development in Children*, trans. Neil Betteridge (New York: Oxford University Press, 2013), 3.
68. Kirsten Read, "Clues Cue the Smooze: Rhyme, Pausing, and Prediction Help Children Learn New Words from Storybooks," *Frontiers in Psychology* 5 (2014): 1–10; Kirsten Read and Jacqueline Quirke, "Rhyme and Word Placement in Storybooks Support High-Level Verb Mapping in 3- to 5-Year-Olds," *Frontiers in Psychology* 9 (2018): 1–8.
69. Cheng and Zou, *Youxue gushi qionglin*, 289; Lockhart, *Manual of Chinese Quotations*, 232.
70. Cui Xuegu, "Shao xue," 92.
71. Cheng and Zou, *Youxue gushi qionglin*, 286.
72. Lockhart, *A Manual of Chinese Quotations*, 225. (With modifications.)
73. Cheng and Zou, *Youxue gushi qionglin*, 94.
74. Lockhart, *Manual of Chinese Quotations*, 121. (With modifications.)
75. Nugent, "Medieval Encyclopedias," 303; Nugent, *Manifest in Words, Written on Paper,* 123.
76. Lin, *Bagu fengguang wubai nian*, 127.
77. Bai, *Shaping the Ideal Child,* 56.
78. Nick C. Ellis and Susan G. Sinclair, "Working Memory in the Acquisition of Vocabulary and Syntax: Putting Language in Good Order," *Quarterly Journal of Experimental Psychology* 49, no. 1 (1996): 246.
79. Baddeley et al., *Memory*, 114–115.
80. Yong and Peng, *Chinese Lexicography,* 52–53.
81. See Philip B. Gough and William E. Tunmer, "Decoding, Reading, and Reading Disability," *Remedial and Special Education* 7, no. 1 (1986): 6–10.
82. Ellis and Sinclair, "Working Memory in the Acquisition of Vocabulary and Syntax: Putting Language in Good Order," 247.
83. Kit-ling Lau, "Language Skills in Classical Chinese Text Comprehension," *Journal of Psycholinguistic Research* 47, no. 1 (2018): 139–140.
84. David Kember, "The Intention to Both Memorise and Understand: Another Approach to Learning?" *Higher Education* 31, no. 3 (1996): 341–354.
85. Bo Dahlin and David Watkins, "The Role of Repetition in the Processes of Memorising and Understanding: A Comparison of the Views of German and Chinese Secondary School Students in Hong Kong," *British Journal of Educational Psychology* 70, no. 1 (2000): 80–81.
86. This is distinct from a later concept of "cultural literacy" in academia, which is defined as viewing social and cultural phenomena through the lens of

literary thinking. See Naomi Segal and Daniela Koleva, *From Literature to Cultural Literacy* (London: Palgrave Macmillan UK, 2014).

87. E. G. Hirsch Jr., *Cultural Literacy: What Every American Needs to Know* (Boston: Houghton Mifflin, 1987), 19.
88. Ibid.
89. Elman, *A Cultural History of Civil Examinations in Late Imperial China*, 375.
90. Herbert Giles, *Elementary Chinese* 三字經 *San Tzu Ching* (Shanghai: Kelly and Walsh Ltd, 1900), 78 and 81. (With modifications.)
91. Cheng, "*Dushu fen nian richeng*," 10–17.
92. Tang, *Jiashu jiaoxue fa*, 138–149.
93. Zhang Zhidong 張之洞, "Shumu dawen" 書目答問 (Answers to the reading list), in *Guoxue jiaoyu ji yao jiaofa juan* 國學教育輯要教法卷 (Essentials of traditional Chinese education: Volume on teaching methods), ed. Jun Yihao 君藝豪 and Jiao Yuhua 焦玉華 (Beijing: Minzhu yu jianshe chubanshe, 2015), vol. 3, 630–703.
94. Liang Qichao 梁啟超, "Guoxue rumen shu yao mu jiqi dufa" 國學入門書要目及其讀法 (Essential introductory books on Chinese studies and how to read them), in *Guoxue jiaoyu ji yao jiaofa juan* 國學教育輯要教法卷 (Essentials of traditional Chinese education: Volume on teaching methods), ed. Jun Yihao 君藝豪 and Jiao Yuhua 焦玉華 (Beijing: Minzhu yu jianshe chubanshe, 2015), vol. 3, 719–720.
95. Lin, *Bagu fengguang wubai nian*, 55.
96. Feng, *San song tang zixu*, 3.
97. Hirsch, *Cultural Literacy*.
98. E. G. Hirsch Jr., Joseph F. Kett, and James S. Trefil, *The Dictionary of Cultural Literacy* (Boston: Houghton Mifflin, 1988).
99. Lin, *Bagu fengguang wubai nian*, 55.
100. Ridley, "Educational Theory and Practice in Late Imperial China," 115–131.
101. Rafe de Crespigny, *A Biographical Dictionary of Later Han to the Three Kingdoms (23–220 AD)* (Boston: Brill, 2006), ix.
102. Paar, *Thousand Character Classic*, 23.
103. Cheng and Zou, *Youxue gushi qionglin*, 21.
104. Ibid., 32.
105. Ibid., 64.
106. This is likely a misattribution. The anecdote is not found in the *Shishuo xinyu* 世說新語 (A new account of tales of the world) but rather the *Shuoyuan* 說苑 (Garden of eloquence). See Liu Xiang 劉向, *Garden of Eloquence Shuoyuan* 說苑, trans. Eric Henry (Seattle: University of Washington Press, 2021), 142–143.

107. Cheng and Zou, *Youxue gushi qionglin*, 73.
108. Bernhard Karlgren, *The Book of Odes* (Stockholm: Museum of Far Eastern Antiquities, 1974), 103. (With modifications.)
109. Cheng and Zou, *Youxue gushi qionglin*, 94.
110. Ibid., 128.
111. Ibid., 145.
112. Ibid., 194.
113. Ibid., 236–237.
114. Ibid., 243–244.
115. Ibid., 257.
116. Ibid., 258.
117. Ibid., 295.
118. Ibid., 312.
119. Johnston and Ping, *Daxue and Zhongyong*, 138, 140, 158, and 168.
120. *Mencius*, 44 and 58.
121. *Analects of Confucius*, 48.
122. Johnston and Ping, *Daxue and Zhongyong*, 440–441; *Mencius*, 27.
123. "The Duke of Zhou said to the Duke of Lu: 'The gentleman does not neglect his relatives and does not cause his high officials to be resentful because he does not heed them. He does not dismiss old associates without good reason, and he does not demand perfection from one person.'" 周公謂魯公曰：「君子不施其親，不使大臣怨乎不以。故舊無大故，則不棄也。無求備於一人. *Analects of Confucius*, 131.
124. Johnston and Ping, *Daxue and Zhongyong*, 440–443.
125. *Mencius*, 44.
126. Makeham, ed., *Dao Companion to Neo-Confucian Philosophy*, xxxvii.
127. Baddeley et al., *Memory*, 182.
128. Michelene T. H. Chi, "Knowledge, Structure, and Memory Development," in *Children's Thinking: What Develops?*, ed. Robert S. Siegler (Hillsdale: Lawrence Erlbaum Associates, 1978), 80–84.
129. Robert C. Anderson, "Role of the Reader's Schema in Comprehension, Learning, and Memory," in *Theoretical Models and Processes of Reading*, ed. Robert B. Ruddell, Martha R. Ruddell, and Harry Singer (Newark: International Reading Association, 2004), 598–599.
130. Catherine A. Haden, "Interactions of Knowledge and Memory in the Development of Skilled Remembering," in *The Wiley Handbook on the Development of Children's Memory*, ed. Patricia J. Bauer and Robyn Fivush (Somerset: John Wiley & Sons, 2013), 809.

131. Klingberg, *The Learning Brain,* 36.
132. Alan Bailin and Ann Grafstein, *Readability: Text and Context* (Basingstoke: Palgrave Macmillan, 2015), 67–68.
133. Zhang Xuecheng 章學成, "Lun ke mengxue wenfa" 論課蒙學文法 (Lessons on grammar for elementary education), in *Guoxue jiaoyu ji yao jiaofa juan* 國學教育輯要教法卷 (Essentials of traditional Chinese education: Volume on teaching methods), ed. Jun Yihao 君藝豪 and Jiao Yuhua 焦玉華 (Beijing: Minzhu yu jianshe chubanshe, 2015), vol. 1, 156.
134. Zhang, *Chuantong yuwen jiaoyu jiaocai lun,* 58–60.
135. Ibid., 70.
136. Lu, *Sibian lu ji yao*, 724:5.
137. Hirsch, *Cultural Literacy,* 30.
138. Chen Fangsheng 陳芳生, "Xunmeng tiaoli" 訓蒙條例 (Regulations on instructing the young), in *Mengxue yaoyi* 蒙學要義 (Essential ideas in primary education), ed. Xu Zi 徐梓 and Wang Xuemei 王雪梅 (Taiyuan: Shanxi jiaoyu chubanshe, 1991), 174.
139. "History of the Tang dynasty" (*Tang shu* 唐書) could refer to either the *New History of the Tang Dynasty* (*Xin Tangshu* 新唐書) or the *Old History of the Tang Dynasty* (*Jiu Tangshu* 舊唐書).
140. Huang, *Xin yi Sanzi jing*, 69–78.
141. Ibid., 236–237; Lockhart, *Manual of Chinese Quotations*, 296–298. (With modifications.)
142. Huang, *Xin yi Sanzi jing*, 82.
143. Ibid., 133.
144. Kelleher, "Back to Basics," 238–239.
145. Nugent, "Structured Gaps," 159.
146. Wendy Swartz, *Reading Philosophy, Writing Poetry: Intertextual Modes of Making Meaning in Early Medieval China* (Cambridge: Harvard University Asia Center, 2018), 8.
147. Liu, *Literary Mind and the Carving of Dragons*, 271.
148. Hartman, *Han Yu and the T'ang Search for Unity*, 237.
149. Gong Duqing 龔篤清, *Zhongguo baguwen shi: Qingdai juan* 中國八股文史清代卷 (History of the Chinese eight-legged essay: Qing dynasty volume) (Changsha: Yuelu shushe, 2017), 15.
150. Wang, "Jiao tongzi fa," 164. Translation from Ridley, "Educational Theory and Practice in Late Imperial China," 7.
151. Chow, *Publishing, Culture, and Power in Early Modern China*, 98.
152. Brokaw, *Commerce in Culture,* 209.

CONCLUSION

1. Ronnie Littlejohn and Qingjun Li, "Chinese and Western Philosophy in Dialogue," *Educational Philosophy and Theory* 53, no. 1 (2021): 11.
2. Kwong-loi Shun, "Studying Confucian and Comparative Ethics: Methodological Reflections" *Journal of Chinese Philosophy* 36, no. 3 (2009): 456–457.
3. Claudia Eppert and Hongyu Wang, eds., *Cross-Cultural Studies in Curriculum: Eastern Thought, Educational Insights* (New York: Lawrence Erlbaum Associates, 2008); Cline, *Families of Virtue*; Michael A. Peters, "Socrates and Confucius: The Cultural Foundations and Ethics of Learning," *Educational Philosophy and Theory* 47, no. 5 (2015): 423–427; Oren Ergas and Sharon Todd, eds., *Philosophy East/West: Exploring Intersections Between Educational and Contemplative Practices* (New York: Wiley, 2015); Xu Di and Hunter McEwan, eds., *Chinese Philosophy on Teaching and Learning: Xueji in the Twenty-First Century* (Albany: State University of New York Press, 2016); Roland Reichenbach and Duck-Joo Kwak, *Confucian Perspectives on Learning and Self-Transformation: International and Cross-Disciplinary Approaches* (Cham: Springer International Publishing AG, 2020); Michael Peters, Tina Besley, and Huajun Zhang, *Moral Education and the Ethics of Self-Cultivation: Chinese and Western Perspectives* (Singapore: Springer Singapore, 2021).
4. Tim Murphy and Ralph Weber, "Confucianizing Socrates and Socratizing Confucius: On Comparing *Analects* 13:18 and the *Euthyphro*," *Philosophy East and West* 60, no. 2 (2010): 202.
5. Jin Li, *Cultural Foundations of Learning: East and West* (New York: Cambridge University Press, 2012), 20; Peters, "Socrates and Confucius," 423–424.
6. Peters, "Socrates and Confucius," 424–425.
7. Reichenbach and Kwak, *Confucian Perspectives on Learning and Self-Transformation,* 19.
8. Thoralf Klein, "How Modern was Chinese Modernity?" *International Journal for History, Culture, and Modernity* 2, no. 3 (2014): 281.
9. Zhang Zhigong devotes the beginning of his book to persuading Chinese readers of the importance of the educational strategies in premodern and early modern elementary textbooks for language acquisition that were previously rejected for their "feudalist" content. Zhang, *Chuantong yuwen jiaoyu jiaocai lun,* 1–5. Chen Lai has argued that the Confucian tradition is crucial for the development of contemporary China. See Chen Lai 陳來, *Tradition and Modernity: A Humanist View*, trans. Edmund Ryden (Leiden: Boston: Brill, 2009).

10. David Carr provides a concise survey of Western educational attitudes toward knowledge from Plato to Hirsch. See David Carr, "Curriculum and the Value of Knowledge," in *The Oxford Handbook of Philosophy of Education*, ed. Harvey Siegel (New York: Oxford University Press, 2009), 281–299.
11. Kai-wing Chow, "Discourse, Examination, and Local Elite: The Invention of the T'ung-ch'eng School in Ch'ing China," in *Education and Society in Late Imperial China, 1600–1900*, ed. Benjamin A. Elman and Alexander Woodside (Berkeley: University of California Press, 1994), 204–205.
12. Murphy and Weber, "Confucianizing Socrates and Socratizing Confucius," 187.
13. Ellis, *Exemplars of Curriculum Theory*, 17–23.
14. *Analects of Confucius*, 100.
15. Tu, "The Sung Confucian Idea of Education," 149.
16. Chen, *Yang zheng yi gui*, 951:3.
17. Christoph Harbsmeier, "Conceptions of Knowledge in Ancient China," in *Epistemological Issues in Classical Chinese Philosophy*, ed. Gregor Paul and Hans Lenk (Albany: State University of New York Press, 1993), 11.
18. Concluding couplets in a few chapters are a summary of the content covered rather than a literary allusion.
19. This is most evident in the criticism of Dai Zhen's philosophical elaborations of his textual research by fellow colleagues. Brokaw, "Tai Chen and Learning in the Confucian Tradition," 257.
20. Elman, "Collecting and Classifying," 152.
21. Bruce Uhrmacher, "Toward a Theory of Aesthetic Learning Experiences," *Curriculum Inquiry* 39, no. 5 (2009): 620–626.
22. Chow, "Discourse, Examination, and Local Elite: The Invention of the T'ung-ch'eng School in Ch'ing China," 204.
23. Denis Hays, *Primary Education: The Key Concepts* (New York: Routledge, 2006), 152.
24. Jennifer A. Moon, *A Handbook of Reflective and Experiential Learning: Theory and Practice* (New York: Routledge, 2004), 15.
25. Cheng and Zou, *Youxue gushi qionglin*, 132.
26. Liu, *Literary Mind and the Carving of Dragons*, 23. (With modifications.)
27. Hirsch, *Cultural Literacy*, 132.
28. Moon, *Handbook of Reflective and Experiential Learning*, 13.
29. Kanori, *Taiwan bunkashi*, 37; Dongfang Xiaoyi, *Taiwan sisu*, 300.
30. Carruthers, *Book of Memory*, 25.

31. Kember, "The Intention to Both Memorise and Understand," 341–354; Dahlin and Watkins, "The Role of Repetition in the Processes of Memorising and Understanding," 80–81.
32. Lai, "Li in the *Analects*," 71–72.
33. Chan, *Instructions for Practical Living and Other Neo-Confucian Writings by Wang Yangming*, 199.
34. Chen Shouyi, *Chinese Literature: A Historical Introduction* (New York: Ronald Press, 1961), 508.
35. Ibid., 566.
36. Stephen C. Angle, "A Productive Dialogue: Contemporary Moral Education and Zhu Xi's Neo-Confucian Ethics," *Journal of Chinese Philosophy* 38, Supp. 1 (2011): 185.
37. Duan, *Shuowen jiezi zhu*, 139.
38. Wang, "Jiao tongzi fa," 166.
39. Cheng and Zou, *Youxue gushi qionglin*, 92.
40. Bryan W. van Norden, *Taking Back Philosophy: A Multicultural Manifesto* (New York: Columbia University Press, 2017).
41. Martha C. Nussbaum, *Cultivating Humanity: A Classical Defense of Reform in Liberal Education* (Cambridge: Harvard University Press, 1997), 53.
42. See Meira Levinson, "Mapping Multicultural Education," in *The Oxford Handbook of Philosophy of Education*, ed. Harvey Siegel (New York: Oxford University Press, 2009), 428–450.
43. Littlejohn and Li, "Chinese and Western Philosophy in Dialogue," 18.

APPENDIX. TRANSLATION OF "GEMS AND TREASURES" SUPPLEMENTARY COUPLETS

1. Sima Qian 司馬遷, *Records of the Grand Historian of China, Volume 1, Early Years of the Han Dynasty, 209 to 141 B.C*, trans. Burton Watson (New York: Columbia University Press, 1971), 54–55. (With modifications.)
2. *Chi* 尺 is an ancient Chinese measure of length, often translated as "a Chinese foot." The exact measurement varied throughout Chinese history.
3. *Analects of Confucius*, 49.
4. *Zuo Tradition Zuozhuan* 左傳*: Commentary on the "Spring and Autumn Annals,"* trans. Stephen Durrant, Wai-yee Li, and David Schaberg, vol. 2 (Seattle: University of Washington Press, 2016), 1035. (With modifications.)

Bibliography

Ames, Roger T. *A Conceptual Lexicon for Classical Confucian Philosophy*. Albany: SUNY Press, 2022.

The Analects of Confucius. Translated by Burton Watson. New York: Columbia University Press, 2007.

Allan, Sarah. *The Way of Water and Sprouts of Virtue*. Albany: State University of New York Press, 1997.

Altenburger, Roland. "Appropriating Genius: Jin Shengtan's Construction of Textual Authority and Authorship in his Commented Edition of Shuihu Zhuan (The Water Margin Saga)." In *That Wonderful Composite Called Author: Authorship in East Asian Literatures from the Beginnings to the Seventeenth Century*, edited by Christian Schwermann and Raji C. Steineck, 183–215. Leiden: Brill, 2014.

Anderson, Robert C. "Role of the Reader's Schema in Comprehension, Learning, and Memory." In *Theoretical Models and Processes of Reading*, edited by Robert B. Ruddell, Martha R. Ruddell, and Harry Singer, 594–606. Newark: International Reading Association, 2004.

Angle, Stephen C. "The *Analects* and Moral Theory." In *Dao Companion to the Analects*, edited by Amy Olberding, 225–258. Dordrecht: Springer Netherlands, 2014.

Angle, Stephen C. "A Productive Dialogue: Contemporary Moral Education and Zhu Xi's Neo-Confucian Ethics." *Journal of Chinese Philosophy* 38, Supp. 1 (2011): 183–203.

Angle, Stephen C. *Sagehood: The Contemporary Significance of Neo-Confucian Philosophy*. New York: Oxford University Press, 2010.

Aristotle. *The Poetics of Aristotle*. Translated by Samuel Henry Butcher. London: Macmillan and Co, 1907.

Association for Asian Studies. "G001: 'A Rhyme for a Reason': Conceptualizing Euphony and Other Mnemonic Strategies in Pre-Modern Chinese Didactic Texts." Accessed 6 July 2021. www.eventscribe.net/2021/AASVirtual/SearchByPresentation.asp?pfp=BrowsebyTitle.

Ayers, William. *Chang Chih-tung and Educational Reform in China*. Cambridge: Harvard University Press, 1971.

Baddeley, Alan, Michael W. Eysenck, and Michael C. Anderson. *Memory*. New York: Psychology Press, 2015.

Bai, Limin. *Fusion of East and West: Children, Education, and a New China, 1902–1915*. Leiden: Brill, 2019.

Bai, Limin. *Shaping the Ideal Child: Children and Their Primers in Late Imperial China.* Hong Kong: The Chinese University of Hong Kong, 2005.

Bailin, Alan, and Ann Grafstein. *Readability: Text and Context*. Basingstoke: Palgrave Macmillan, 2015.

Ban Gu 班固. *Bai hu tong* 白虎通 [The comprehensive discussions in the White Tiger Hall]. In *Wenyuange Siku quanshu* 文淵閣四庫全書 (Wenyuange edition of the Complete Library of the Four Branches of Literature]. Vol. 850. Taipei: Taiwan shangwu yinshuguan, 2013.

Ban Gu 班固. *Food and Money in Ancient China: The Earliest Economic History of China to A.D. 25, Han Shu 24, with Related Texts, Han Shu 91 and Shih-Chi 129*. Translated by Nancy Lee Swann. Princeton: Princeton University Press, 1950.

Ban Gu 班固. *Hanshu* 漢書 [History of the former Han]. In *Wenyuange Siku quanshu* 文淵閣四庫全書 [Wenyuange edition of the Complete Library of the Four Branches of Literature]. Vols. 249–250. Taipei: Taiwan shangwu yinshuguan, 2013.

Barrow, Robin. *Giving Teaching Back to Teachers: A Critical Introduction to Curriculum Theory*. New York: Routledge, 2015.

Barrow, Robin. *Plato and Education*. New York: Routledge, 2012.

Ben ju *Da cidian* bianzuan weiyuanhui 本局大辭典編纂委員會. *Da cidian* 大辭典 [Comprehensive Chinese dictionary]. Taipei: San min shuju, 1985.

Billioud, Sébastien. "Confucianism, 'Cultural Tradition,' and Official Discourses in China at the Start of the New Century." *China Perspectives* 2007, no. 3 (2007): 50–65.

Billioud, Sébastien, and Joël Thoraval. *The Sage and the People: The Confucian Revival in China*. New York: Oxford University Press, 2015.

Bol, Peter. "Chu Hsi's Redefinition of Literati Learning." In *Neo-Confucian Education: The Formative Stage*, edited by William Theodore de Bary and John W. Chaffee, 151–185. Berkeley: University of California Press, 1989.

The Book of Lieh-tzu: A Classic of the Tao. Translated by A. C. Graham. New York: Columbia University Press, 1990.

Brokaw, Cynthia J. *Commerce in Culture: The Sibao Book Trade in the Qing and Republican Periods*. Cambridge: Harvard University Press, 2007.

Brokaw, Cynthia. "Commercial Publishing in Late Imperial China: The Zou and Ma Family Businesses of Sibao, Fujian." *Late Imperial China* 17, no. 1 (1996): 49–92.

Brokaw, Cynthia Joanne. *The Ledgers of Merit and Demerit: Social Change and Moral Order in Late Imperial China*. Princeton: Princeton University Press, 2014.

Brokaw, Cynthia J. "On the History of the Book in China." In *Printing and Book Culture in Late Imperial China*, edited by Cynthia J. Brokaw and Kai-Wing Chow, 3–54. Berkeley: University of California Press, 2006.

Brokaw, Cynthia J. "Reading the Best-Sellers of the Nineteenth Century: Commercial Publishing in Sibao." In *Printing and Book Culture in Late Imperial China*, edited by Cynthia J. Brokaw and Kai-Wing Chow, 184–234. Berkeley: University of California Press, 2006.

Brokaw, Cynthia J. "Tai Chen and Learning in the Confucian Tradition." In *Education and Society in Late Imperial China, 1600–1900*, edited by Benjamin A. Elman and Alexander Woodside, 257–291. Berkeley: University of California Press, 1994.

Cai Dongfan 蔡東藩. *Huitu xinzeng Youxue gushi qionglin* 繪圖新增幼學故事瓊林 [Supplemented *Treasury of Elementary Learning* with drawings]. Shanghai: Hui wen tang shuju, 1924.

Carr, David. "Curriculum and the Value of Knowledge." In *The Oxford Handbook of Philosophy of Education*, edited by Harvey Siegel, 281–299. New York: Oxford University Press, 2009.

Carruthers, Mary J. *The Book of Memory: A Study of Memory in Medieval Culture*. Cambridge: Cambridge University Press, 2008.

Chan, Wing-tsit, ed. *Chu Hsi and Neo-Confucianism*. Honolulu: University of Hawaii Press, 1986.

Chan, Wing-tsit. "The *Hsing-li* and *ching-i* and the Ch'eng-Chu School of the Seventeenth Century." In *The Unfolding of Neo-Confucianism*, edited by William Theodore de Bary, 543–579. New York: Columbia University Press, 1975.

Chan, Wing-tsit. *Instructions for Practical Living and Other Neo-Confucian Writings by Wang Yangming*. New York: Columbia University Press, 1963.

Chan, Wing-tsit. *A Source Book in Chinese Philosophy*. Princeton: Princeton University Press, 1963.

Chang Chung-li. *The Chinese Gentry: Studies on Their Role in Nineteenth-Century Chinese Society*. Seattle: University of Washington Press, 1970.

Chang Jinghai 常鏡海. "Zhongguo sishu mengtong suo yong keben zhi yanjiu" 中國私塾蒙童所用課本之研究 [Study of Chinese private school children's textbooks]. *Xin Dongfang* 1, no. 8 (1940): 103–114.

Chen Fangsheng 陳芳生. "Xunmeng tiaoli" 訓蒙條例 [Regulations on instructing the young]. In *Mengxue yaoyi* 蒙學要義 [Essential ideas in primary education], edited by Xu Zi 徐梓 and Wang Xuemei 王雪梅, 172–177. Taiyuan: Shanxi jiaoyu chubanshe, 1991.

Chen Hancai 陳漢才. *Zhongguo gudai you'er jiaoyu shi* 中國古代幼兒教育史 [History of pre-modern Chinese early childhood education]. Guangzhou: Guangdong gaodeng jiaoyu chubanshe, 1996.

Chen Junmin 陳俊民, ed. *Zhuzi wenji* 朱子文集 [Collected works of Master Zhu]. Taipei: De fu wenjiao jijinhui, 2000.

Chen Lai 陳來. *Tradition and Modernity: A Humanist View*. Translated by Edmund Ryden. Leiden: Boston: Brill, 2009.

Chen, Shih-Wen Sue. *Children's Literature and Transnational Knowledge in Modern China: Education, Religion, and Childhood*. Singapore: Palgrave Macmillan, 2019.

Chen Shouyi. *Chinese Literature: A Historical Introduction*. New York: Ronald Press, 1961.

Chen Xuan 陳選. *Xiaoxue jizhu* 小學集註 [Collected annotations of the *Elementary Learning*]. In *Wenyuange Siku quanshu* 文淵閣四庫全書 [Wenyuange edition of the Complete Library of the Four Branches of Literature]. Vol. 699. Taipei: Taiwan shangwu yinshuguan, 2013.

Cheng Dengji 程登吉. *Jiantang chongding Youxue xuzhi biandu gushi* 簡堂重訂幼學須知便讀故事 [A concise reader of allusions in the *Required Knowledge for Elementary Learning*, revised by the Bamboo Slip Studio]. Jianyang: Yang Xiaomin Shulin, publication date unknown. HathiTrust Digital Library. https://babel.hathitrust.org/cgi/pt?id=keio.10811743594&view=1up&seq=16&skin=2021.

Cheng Dengji 程登吉. *Xinzeng Youxue gushi qionglin* 新增幼學故事瓊林 [Newly expanded *Treasury of Literary Allusions for Elementary Learning*]. Supplemented and annotated by Zou Shengmai 鄒聖脈 and collated by Zou Tingyou 廷猷 and Xie Meilin 謝梅林, n.d.

Cheng Dengji 程登吉. *Ziwen ge chongding Youxue xuzhi ju jie* 紫文閣重訂幼學須知句解 [*Required knowledge for Elementary Learning* explained phrase by phrase revised by Ziwen ge]. Annotated by Huang Wangruo 黃汪若 and corrected by Qian Yuanlong 錢元龍. Jingjiang: Qian Yuanlong, 1881. Chinese University of Hong Kong Library's Chinese Rare Book Digital Collection: https://repository.lib.cuhk.edu.hk/en/item/cuhk-702758#page/2/mode/2up.

Cheng Dengji 程登吉 and Zou Shengmai 鄒聖脈. *Youxue gushi qionglin* 幼學故事瓊林 [Treasury of literary allusions for elementary learning]. Shanghai: Shanghai guji chubanshe, 2018.

Cheng, Dennis Chi-hsiung. "Inter-Explanation of the Classics: Qing Scholars' Methods for Interpreting the Five Classics." In *Interpretation and Intellectual Change: Chinese Hermeneutics in Historical Perspective*, edited by Ching-I Tu, 191–205. New Brunswick: Transaction Publishers, 2005.

Cheng Duanli 程端禮. "*Dushu fen nian richeng*" 讀書分年日程 [A yearly program of study at the Cheng family school]. In *Guoxue jiaoyu ji yao jiaofa juan* 國學教育輯要教法卷 [Essentials of traditional Chinese education: Volume on teaching methods], edited by Jun Yihao 君藝豪 and Jiao Yuhua 焦玉華, 2–21. Beijing: Minzhu yu jianshe chubanshe, 2015.

Cheng Weijun 成偉鈞, Tang Zhongyang 唐仲揚, and Xiang Hongye 向宏業. *Xiuci tong jian* 修辭通鑑 [A comprehensive guide to rhetoric]. Beijing: Zhongguo qingnian chubanshe, 1991.

Chi, Michelene T. H. "Knowledge, Structure, and Memory Development." In *Children's Thinking: What Develops?*, edited by Robert S. Siegler, 73–96. Hillsdale: Lawrence Erlbaum Associates, 1978.

Chi Xiaofang 池小芳. *Zhongguo gudai xiaoxue jiaoyu yanjiu* 中國古代小學教育研究 [A study on primary education in premodern China]. Shanghai: Shanghai jiaoyu chubanshe, 1998.

Chia, Lucille. *Printing for Profit: The Commercial Publishers of Jianyang, Fujian (11th–17th Centuries)*. Cambridge: Harvard Asia Center, 2002.

The Chinese Classics: Translated into English, with Preliminary Essays and Explanatory Notes. Translated by James Legge. London: N. Trubner and Co, 1869.

Chow, Kai-wing. "Discourse, Examination, and Local Elite: The Invention of the T'ung-ch'eng School in Ch'ing China." In *Education and Society in Late Imperial China, 1600–1900*, edited by Benjamin A. Elman and Alexander Woodside, 183–222. Berkeley: University of California Press, 1994.

Chow, Kai-wing. *Publishing, Culture, and Power in Early Modern China*. Stanford: Stanford University Press, 2004.

Chow, Kai-wing. *The Rise of Confucian Ritualism in Late Imperial China: Ethics, Classics, and Lineage Discourse*. Stanford: Stanford University Press, 1994.

Clark, Anthony E. *A Chinese Jesuit Catechism: Giulio Aleni's Four Character Classic.* Singapore: Palgrave Macmillan, 2021.

Cline, Erin. *Families of Virtue: Confucian and Western Views on Childhood Development*. New York: Columbia University Press, 2015.

Craik, Fergus I. M., and Robert S. Lockhart. "Levels of Processing: A Framework for Memory Research." *Journal of Verbal Learning and Verbal Behavior* 11, no. 6 (1972): 671–684.

Cui Xuegu 崔學古, "Shaoxue" 少學 [Education for youth]. In *Mengxue yaoyi* 蒙學要義 [Essential ideas in primary education], edited by Xu Zi 徐梓 and Wang Xuemei 王雪梅, 87–99. Taiyuan: Shanxi jiaoyu chubanshe, 1991.

Cui Xuegu 崔學古. "You xun" 幼訓 [Instructions for children]. In *Mengxue yaoyi* 蒙學要義 [Essential ideas in primary education], edited by Xu Zi 徐梓 and Wang Xuemei 王雪梅, 73–86. Taiyuan: Shanxi jiaoyu chubanshe, 1991.

Dahlin, Bo, and David Watkins. "The Role of Repetition in the Processes of Memorising and Understanding: A Comparison of the Views of German and Chinese Secondary School Students in Hong Kong." *British Journal of Educational Psychology* 70, no. 1 (2000): 65–84.

Dardess, John W. "Childhood in Premodern China." In *Children in Historical and Comparative Perspective*, edited by Joseph M. Hawes and N. Ray Hiner, 71–94. New York: Greenwood Press, 1991.

De Bary, William Theodore, and Irene Bloom, eds. *Principle and Practicality: Essays in Neo-Confucianism and Practical Learning*. New York: Columbia University Press, 1979.

de Crespigny, Rafe. *A Biographical Dictionary of Later Han to the Three Kingdoms (23–220 AD)*. Boston: Brill, 2006.

Dong Jianzhi 董堅志. *Huitu Youxue gushi qionglin* 繪圖幼學故事瓊林 [The *Treasury of Elementary Learning* with drawings]. Shanghai jin zhang tu shuju, 1928.

Dongfang Xiaoyi 東方孝義. *Taiwan sisu* 台灣習俗 [Taiwan customs]. Taipei: Nantian shuju, 1997.

Duan Yucai 段玉裁. *Shuowen jiezi zhu* 說文解字注 [Annotated *Explaining Simple Graphs and Analyzing Complex Graphs*]. Taipei: Yee Wen Publishing Company, 2007.

Egan, Kieran. *The Educated Mind: How Cognitive Tools Shape Our Understanding*. Chicago: University of Chicago, 1997.

Ellis, Arthur K. *Exemplars of Curriculum Theory*. New York: Routledge, 2013.

Ellis, Nick C., and Susan G. Sinclair. "Working Memory in the Acquisition of Vocabulary and Syntax: Putting Language in Good Order." *Quarterly Journal of Experimental Psychology* 49, no. 1 (1996): 234–350.

Elman, Benjamin A. "Changes in Confucian Civil Service Examinations from the Ming to the Ch'ing Dynasty." In *Education and Society in Late Imperial China,*

1600–1900, edited by Benjamin A. Elman and Alexander Woodside, 111–149. Berkeley: University of California Press, 1994.

Elman, Benjamin A. "Ch'ing Dynasty "Schools" of Scholarship." *Qing shi wen ti* 4, no. 6 (1981): 1–44.

Elman, Benjamin A. "Collecting and Classifying: Ming Dynasty Compendia and Encyclopedias (Leishu)." *Extrême-Orient, Extrême-Occident* 1, no. 1 (2007): 131–157.

Elman, Benjamin A. *A Cultural History of Civil Examinations in Late Imperial China*. Berkeley: University of California Press, 2000.

Elman, Benjamin A. *From Philosophy to Philology: Intellectual and Social Aspects of Change in Late Imperial China.* Cambridge: Harvard University Press, 1984.

Elman, Benjamin A. *On Their Own Terms: Science in China, 1550–1900*. Cambridge: Harvard University Press, 2005.

Elman, Benjamin A. "Political, Social, and Cultural Reproduction via Civil Service Examinations in Late Imperial China." *Journal of Asian Studies* 50 (1991): 7–28.

Elman, Benjamin A. "Social Roles of Literati in Early to Mid-Ch'ing." In *The Cambridge History of China: Volume 9, Part 1, The Ch'ing Dynasty to 1800*, edited by Williard J. Peterson, 360–427. Cambridge: Cambridge University Press, 1998.

Elman, Benjamin A., and Alexander Woodside. "The Expansion of Education in Ch'ing China." In *Education and Society in Late Imperial China, 1600–1900*, edited by Benjamin A. Elman and Alexander Woodside, 525–560. Berkeley: University of California Press, 1994.

Eppert, Claudia, and Hongyu Wang, eds. *Cross-Cultural Studies in Curriculum: Eastern Thought, Educational Insights*. New York: Lawrence Erlbaum Associates, 2008.

Ergas, Oren, and Sharon Todd, eds. *Philosophy East/West: Exploring Intersections Between Educational and Contemplative Practices*. New York: Wiley, 2015.

Falato, Giulia. *Alfonso Vagnone's Tongyou Jiaoyu (On the Education of Children, c. 1632)*. Leiden: Brill, 2020.

Fang, Thome H. *Chinese Philosophy: Its Spirit and Its Development*. Taipei: Linking Publishing Company, 1981.

Fang, Thome H. *The Chinese View of Life: The Philosophy of Comprehensive Harmony.* Taipei: Linking Publishing Company, 1980.

Feng Youlan 馮友蘭. *A History of Chinese Philosophy, Volume II, The Period of Classical Learning*. Translated by Derk Bodde. Princeton: Princeton University Press, 1983.

Feng Youlan. *San song tang zixu* 三松堂自序 [Self-preface by the master of the House of Three Pines]. Beijing: San lian shudian, 1984.

Fingarette, Herbert. *Confucius: The Secular as Sacred*. New York: Harper and Row, 1972.

Fish, Stanley. *Is There a Text in This Class?* Cambridge: Harvard University Press, 1980.

Freund, Elizabeth. *The Return of the Reader: Reader-Response Criticism*. London: Methuen and Co., 1987.

Galambos, Imre. "Confucian Education in a Buddhist Environment: Medieval Manuscripts and Imprints of the *Mengqiu*." *Studies in Chinese Religions* 1, no. 3 (2015): 269–288.

Galambos, Imre. *Translating Chinese Tradition and Teaching Tangut Culture: Manuscripts and Printed Books from Khara-Khoto*. Berlin: De Gruyter, 2015.

Gao Qianmin 高謙民. *Zhongguo xiaoxue sixiang pinde jiaoxue shi* 中國小學思想品德教學史 [History of moral education in Chinese primary schools]. Zhongguo xiaoxue geke jiaoxue shi congshu 中國小學各科教學史叢書 [Series on the history of Chinese primary school subjects]. Jinan: Shandong jiaoyu chubanshe, 1995.

Gardner, Daniel K. *The Four Books: The Basic Teachings of the Later Confucian Tradition*. Indianapolis: Hackett Publishing, 2007.

Gardner, Daniel K. *Learning to Be a Sage: Selections from the Conversations of Master Chu, Arranged Topically*. Berkeley: University of California Press, 1990.

Gardner, Daniel K. *Zhu Xi's Reading of the Analects: Canon, Commentary, and the Classical Tradition*. New York: Columbia University Press, 2003.

Gernet, Jacques. "L'éducation des Premières Années (du XIe au XVIIe siècles)." In *Education et Instruction en Chine. 1. L'éducation élémentaire*, edited by Catherine Despeux and Christine Tri Nguyen, 7–60. Paris-Louvain: Peeters, 2003.

Giles, Herbert. *Elementary Chinese 三字經 San Tzu Ching*. Shanghai: Kelly and Walsh Ltd., 1900.

Goodrich, Luther Carrington. *The Literary Inquisition of Ch'ien-lung*. New York: Paragon Book Reprint, 1966.

Gong Duqing 龔篤清. *Zhongguo baguwen shi: Qingdai juan* 中國八股文史清代卷 [History of the Chinese eight-legged essay: Qing dynasty volume]. Changsha: Yuelu shushe, 2017.

Gough, Philip B., and William E. Tunmer. "Decoding, Reading, and Reading Disability." *Remedial and Special Education* 7, no. 1 (1986): 6–10.

Gu, Yueguo. "Politeness Phenomena in Modern Chinese." *Journal of Pragmatics* 14, no. 2 (1990): 237–257.

Gu Yanwu 顧炎武. *Record of Daily Knowledge and Collected Poems and Essays*. Translated by Ian Johnston. New York: Columbia University Press, 2017.

Guy, Robert Kent. *The Emperor's Four Treasuries: Scholars and the State in the Late Ch'ien-lung Era*. Cambridge: Harvard University Press, 1987.

Haden, Catherine A. "Interactions of Knowledge and Memory in the Development of Skilled Remembering." In *The Wiley Handbook on the Development of Children's Memory*, edited by Patricia J. Bauer and Robyn Fivush, 809–835. Somerset: John Wiley & Sons, 2013.

Hall, David L., and Roger T. Ames. *Thinking Through Confucius*. Albany: State University of New York Press, 1987.

Han Zhongwen 韓鍾文. *Zhuxi jiaoyu sixiang yanjiu* 朱熹教育思想研究 [Research on Zhu Xi's educational thought]. Jiangxi: Jiangxi jiaoyu chubanshe, 1989.

Hao Chang. "The Intellectual Context of Reform." In *Reform in Nineteenth-Century China*, edited by Paul A. Cohen and John E. Schrecker, 145–149. Cambridge: East Asian Research Center Harvard University, 1976.

Harbsmeier, Christoph. "Conceptions of Knowledge in Ancient China." In *Epistemological Issues in Classical Chinese Philosophy*, edited by Gregor Paul and Hans Lenk, 11–30. Albany: State University of New York Press, 1993.

Harbsmeier, Christoph. "May Fourth Linguistic Orthodoxy and Rhetoric: Some Informal Comparative Notes." In *New Terms for New Ideas: Western Knowledge and Lexical Change in Late Imperial China*, edited by Michael Lackner, Joachim Kurtz, and Iwo Amelung, 373–410. Leiden: Brill, 2001.

Hartman, Charles. *Han Yu and the T'ang Search for Unity*. Princeton: Princeton University Press, 1986.

Hays, Denis. *Primary Education: The Key Concepts*. New York: Routledge, 2006.

He Jiuying 何九盈, Wang Ning 王寧, and Dong Kun 董琨, eds. *Ciyuan* 辭源 [Origins of words]. Beijing: The Commercial Press, 2017.

Henderson, John B. *The Development and Decline of Chinese Cosmology*. New York: Columbia University Press, 1984.

Hightower, James Robert. "Some Characteristics of Parallel Prose." In *Studies in Chinese Literature*, edited by John Lyman Bishop, 60–71. Cambridge: Harvard University Press, 1965.

Hirsch Jr., E. D. *Cultural Literacy: What Every American Needs to Know*. Boston: Houghton Mifflin, 1987.

Hirsch Jr., E. D., Joseph F. Kett, and James S. Trefil. *The Dictionary of Cultural Literacy*. Boston: Houghton Mifflin, 1988.

Ho, Clara Wing-chung. *Zhongguo gudai yu'er* 中國古代育兒 [Premodern Chinese children's education]. Taipei: Taiwan shangwu yinshuguan, 1998.

Ho, Ping-Ti. *The Ladder of Success in Imperial China: Aspects of Social Mobility, 1368–1911*. New York: Columbia University Press, 1964.

Hsiung, Ping-chen. *A Tender Voyage: Children and Childhood in Late Imperial China*. Stanford: Stanford University Press, 2005.

Hu Shih 胡適. *Sishi zishu* 四十自述 [An autobiographical account at forty]. Beijing: Zhongguo wenlian chuban gongsi, 1992.

Hu Yunfu 胡云富, Li Chunmei 李春梅, and Fu Delin 傅德林. *Youxue qionglin xinzhu* 幼學瓊林新注 [Newly annotated *Treasury of Elementary Learning*]. Beijing: Beijing shifan daxue chubanshe, 1992.

Huang Peirong 黃沛榮. *Xin yi Sanzi jing* 新譯三字經 [A new interpretation of the *Three Character Classic*]. Taipei: San min shuju, 2003.

Huang Zifang 黃子房. "Leishu he *Youxue qionglin*" 類書和幼學瓊林 [Encyclopedic anthologies and the *Treasury of Elementary Learning*]. *Journal of Hainan Normal University (Social Sciences)* 4 (2006): 132–135.

Hunt, Peter. *Children's Literature*. Oxford: Blackwell Publishers, 2001.

The I Ching. Translated by James Legge. New York: Dover, 1963.

In Search of the Supernatural: The Written Record. Translated by Kenneth J. DeWoskin and James I. Crump Jr. Stanford: Stanford University Press, 1996.

Ivanhoe, Philip J. *Confucian Moral Self Cultivation.* Indianapolis: Hackett Publishing Company, 2000.

Ivanhoe, Philip J. *Ethics in the Confucian Tradition: The Thought of Mencius and Wang Yang-ming*. Atlanta: Scholars Press, 1990.

Jiang Ming 蔣明 and Zhang Daqing 張大慶. *Youxue qionglin zhu du: jian fan duizhao ben* 幼學瓊林助讀: 簡繁對照本 [*Treasury of Elementary Learning* reader with simplified and traditional Chinese]. Beijing: Zhongguo guoji guangbo chubanshe, 1998.

Johnston, Ian, and Ping Wang. *Daxue and Zhongyong: A Bilingual Edition*. Hong Kong: Chinese University Press, 2012.

Ju Junong 瞿菊農. "Zhongguo gudai mengyang jiaocai" 中國古代蒙養教材 [Premodern Chinese elementary education teaching materials]. *Beijing shifan daxue xuebao* 4, (1961): 45–56.

Kanori, Inō. *Taiwan bunkashi* [A history of Taiwanese culture]. Translated by Jiang Qinglin 江慶林 et al. Taipei: Taiwan Shufang chuban youxian gongsi, 2011.

Kao, Yu-Kung, and Tsu-Lin Mei. "Meaning, Metaphor, and Allusion in T'ang Poetry." *Harvard Journal of Asiatic Studies* 38, no. 2 (1978): 281–356.

Karlgren, Bernhard. *The Book of Odes*. Stockholm: Museum of Far Eastern Antiquities, 1974.

Kecheng jiaocai yanjiusuo 課程教材研究所. *Yuwen juan* 語文卷 [Volume on language learning]. Ershi shiji zhongguo zhong xiaoxue kecheng biaozhun jiaoxue dagang huibian 二十世紀中國中小學課程標準教學大綱彙編 [Collection of curriculum standards and teaching guidelines of primary and secondary schools in the twentieth century]. Beijing: Renmin jiaoyu chubanshe, 2001.

Kelleher, Theresa. "Back to Basics: Chu Hsi's Elementary Learning (Hsiao-hsueh)." In *Neo-Confucian Education: The Formative Stage*, edited by William Theodore de Bary and John W. Chaffee, 219–251. Berkeley: University of California Press, 1989.

Kember, David. "The Intention to Both Memorise and Understand: Another Approach to Learning?" *Higher Education* 31, no. 3 (1996): 341–354.

Kennedy, George A. *On Rhetoric: A Theory of Civic Discourse*. Oxford: Oxford University Press, 2007.

Kessler, Lawrence D. *K'ang-Hsi and the Consolidation of Ch'ing Rule, 1661–1684*. Chicago: University of Chicago Press, 1976.

Kinney, Anne Behnke, "Dyed Silk: Han Notions of the Moral Development of Children." In *Chinese Views of Childhood*, edited by Anne Behnke Kinney, 17-56. Honolulu: University of Hawai'i Press, 1995.

Klein, Thoralf. "How Modern was Chinese Modernity?" *International Journal for History, Culture, and Modernity* 2, no. 3 (2014): 275–301.

Klingberg, Torkel. *The Learning Brain: Memory and Brain Development in Children*. Translated by Neil Betteridge. New York: Oxford University Press, 2013.

Ko, Dorothy. "Pursuing Talent and Virtue: Education and Women's Culture in Seventeenth- and Eighteenth-Century China." *Late Imperial China* 13, no. 1 (1992): 9–39.

Kornicki, Peter Francis. *Languages, Scripts, and Chinese Texts in East Asia*. Oxford: Oxford University Press, 2018.

Kristjánsson, Kristján. "Emulation and the Use of Role Models in Moral Education." *Journal of Moral Education* 35, no. 1 (2006): 37–49.

Kūkai 空海. *Wen jing mi fu lun* 文鏡秘府論 [Bunkyō hifu ron]. In *Xu xiu Siku quanshu* 續修四庫全書 [Supplement to the Complete Library of the Four Branches of Literature]. Vol. 1694. Shanghai: Shanghai guji chubanshe, 2002.

Lai, Karyn. "Li in the *Analects*: Training in Moral Competence and the Question of Flexibility." *Philosophy East and West* 56, no. 1 (2006): 64–83.

Lakoff, George, and Mark Johnson. *Metaphors We Live By*. Chicago: University of Chicago Press, 1980.

Lau, Kit-ling. "Language Skills in Classical Chinese Text Comprehension." *Journal of Psycholinguistic Research* 47, no. 1 (2018): 139–157.

Lee, Thomas H. C. *Education in Traditional China: A History*. Boston: Brill, 2000.

Lei Qiaoyun 雷僑雲. *Zhongguo ertong wenxue yanjiu* 中國兒童文學研究 [Research on Chinese children's literature]. Taipei: Taiwan xuesheng chubanshe, 1998.

Levinson, Meira. "Mapping Multicultural Education." In *The Oxford Handbook of Philosophy of Education*, edited by Harvey Siegel, 428–450. New York: Oxford University Press, 2009.

Leung, Angela Ki Che. "Elementary Education in the Lower Yangtze Region in the Seventeenth and Eighteenth Centuries." In *Education and Society in Late Imperial China, 1600–1900*, edited by Benjamin A. Elman and Alexander Woodside, 381–416. Berkeley: University of California Press, 1994.

Li, Chris Wen-chao. "Classical Chinese." In *The Routledge Encyclopedia of the Chinese Language*, edited by Chan Sin-wai, 408–419. New York: Routledge, 2016.

Li Fengrui 李逢蕊. *Kejia zongheng* 客家縱橫 [Research on Hakka culture]. Fujian: Minxi kejiaxue yanjiuhui, 1992.

Li Guojun 李國鈞. "Ming Qing mengxue jiaoyu shuping" 明清蒙學教育述評 [Review of elementary education in the Ming and Qing dynasties]. In *Lidai jiaoyu zhidu kao* 歷代教育制度考 [Educational systems in Chinese history], edited by Gu Mingyuan 顧明遠, 1536–1543. Wuhan: Hubei jiaoyu chubanshe, 2004.

Li Guojun 李國鈞. *Zhongguo jiaoyu sixiang tongshi* 中國教育思想通史 [Comprehensive history of Chinese educational thought]. Changsha: Hunan jiaoyu chubanshe, 1994.

Li Jin. *Cultural Foundations of Learning: East and West*. New York: Cambridge University Press, 2012.

Li Jingde 黎靖德. *Zhuzi yu lei* 朱子語類 [Classified sayings of Master Zhu]. Vol. 1. Taipei: Shi hua chubanshe, 1987.

Li Ren-yuan. "*Necessary Knowledge for Young Students* and the Commercial Publishing in 17th to Early 20th Century China." *Asia Major* 35, no. 2 (2022): 1–56.

Li, Wai-Yee. "Textual Transmission of Earlier Literature during the Yuan, Ming, and Qing Dynasties." In *The Oxford Handbook of Classical Chinese Literature (1000 BCE-900 CE)*, edited by Wiebke Denecke, Wai-yee Li, and Xiaofei Tian, 325–341. New York: Oxford University Press, 2017.

Li Xin'an 李新庵. "Chong ding xun xue liang gui" 重訂訓學良規 [Revised useful guidelines for moral education]. In *Mengxue yaoyi* 蒙學要義 [Essential ideas in primary education], edited by Xu Zi 徐梓 and Wang Xuemei 王雪梅, 115–132. Taiyuan: Shanxi jiaoyu chubanshe, 1991.

Li Yan 李艷. "Chang li ju yao" 常禮舉要 [Essentials of daily etiquette]. In *Guoxue jiaoyu ji yao jiaofa juan* 國學教育輯要教法卷 [Essentials of traditional Chinese education: Volume on teaching methods], edited by Jun Yihao 君藝豪 and Jiao Yuhua 焦玉華305–314. Beijing: Minzhu yu jianshe chubanshe, 2015.

Lianchengxian difang zhi bianzuan weiyuanhui 連城縣地方志編纂委員會. *Lianchengxian zhi* 連城縣志 [Liancheng gazetteer]. Beijing: Qunzhong chubanshe, 1993.

Liang Qichao 梁啟超. “Guoxue rumen shu yao mu jiqi dufa” 國學入門書要目及其讀法 [Essential introductory books on Chinese studies and how to read them]. In *Guoxue jiaoyu ji yao jiaofa juan* 國學教育輯要教法卷 [Essentials of traditional Chinese education: Volume on teaching methods], edited by Jun Yihao 君藝豪 and Jiao Yuhua 焦玉華, 703–726. Beijing: Minzhu yu jianshe chubanshe, 2015.

Liang Qichao 梁启超. *Qingdai xueshu gailun* 清代學術概論 [Intellectual trends in the Qing period]. Shanghai: Shanghai guji chubanshe, 1998.

Liji zheng yi 禮記正義 [Orthodox exegesis of the *Records on Ritual*]. Commentary by Zheng Xuan 鄭玄; sub-commentary by Kong Yingda 孔穎達. Beijing: Peking University Press, 2000.

Lin Desheng 藺德生. *Bagu fengguang wubai nian* 八股風光五百年 [Five-hundred-year history of the eight-legged essay]. Beijing: Yuwen chubanshe, 2011.

Lin Guobiao 林國標. *Qing chu Zhuzi xue yanjiu* 清初朱子學研究 [Early Qing period research on Master Zhu scholarship]. Changsha: Hunan renmin chubanshe, 2004.

Lin Meihui 林美惠. “*Youxue qionglin* yanjiu” 幼學瓊林研究 [Study on the *Treasury of Elementary Learning*]. Master’s thesis, Feng Jia University, 1996.

Lin Wenbao 林文寶. *Lidai qimeng jiaocai chutan* 歷代啓蒙教材初探 [Preliminary study on elementary education teaching materials throughout Chinese history]. Taipei: Wan juan lou tushu youxian gongsi, 1996.

Lin Zhijin 林治金 and Ma Zhaoming 馬兆銘. *Zhongguo xiaoxue yuwen jiaoxue shi* 中國小學語文教學史 [History of language learning in Chinese primary schools]. Zhongguo xiaoxue geke jiaoxue shi congshu 中國小學各科教學史叢書 [Series on the history of Chinese primary school subjects]. Jinan: Shandong jiaoyu chubanshe, 1996.

Littlejohn, Ronnie, and Qingjun Li. “Chinese and Western Philosophy in Dialogue.” *Educational Philosophy and Theory* 53, no. 1 [2021]: 10–20.

Liu Decheng 劉德城 and Zhou Xianying 周羨潁. *Fujian mingren cidian* 福建名人詞典 [Dictionary of eminent people from Fujian]. Fuzhou: Fujian renmin chubanshe, 1995.

Liu Hsieh 劉勰. *The Literary Mind and the Carving of Dragons*. Translated by Vincent Yu-chung Shih. Hong Kong: The Chinese University Press, 2015.

Liu, James J. Y. *The Art of Chinese Poetry*. Chicago: University of Chicago Press, 1966.

Liu, James T. C. “The Classical Chinese Primer: Its Three-Character Style and Authorship.” *Journal of the American Oriental Society* 105, no. 2 (1985): 191–196.

Liu, JeeLoo. *An Introduction to Chinese Philosophy: From Ancient Philosophy to Chinese Buddhism*. Oxford: Blackwell Publishing, 2006.

Liu Xiang 劉向. *Exemplary Women of Early China: The Lienü Zhuan of Liu Xiang*. Translated by Anne Behnke Kinney. New York: Columbia University Press, 2014.

Liu Xiang 劉向. *Garden of Eloquence Shuoyuan* 說苑. Translated by Eric Henry. Seattle: University of Washington Press, 2021.

Liu Xiusheng and Yang Yuqing. *Zhongguo Qingdai jiaoyu shi* 中國清代教育史 [History of Qing dynasty education]. Beijing: Renmin chubanshe, 1994.

Liu Yucai and Luke Habberstad. "The Life of a Text: A Brief History of the *Liji* 禮記 (Rites Records) and Its Transmission." *Journal of Chinese Literature and Culture* 1, no. 1–2 (2014): 289–308.

Liu Zhaobin 劉兆璸. *Qingdai keju* 清代科舉 [Qing dynasty civil service examinations]. Taipei: Dongda chubanshe, 1979.

Lockhart, James Haldane Stewart. *A Manual of Chinese Quotations.* Hong Kong: Kelly and Walsh, 1893.

Lu Shengjiang 盧盛江. "*Wen jing mi fu lun* ji zhong duishu lun yanjiu" 《文鏡秘府論》幾種對屬論研究 [Study on the types of parallelism in the *Bunkyō hifu ron*]. *Nankai Journal (Philosophy, Literature, and Social Science Edition)* no. 6 (2013): 137–146.

Lu Shiyi 陸世儀. "Lun dushu" 論讀書 [On learning]. In *Yang zheng yi gui* 養正遺規 [Guidelines for proper upbringing], compiled by Chen Hongmou 陳宏謀. In *Xu xiu Siku quanshu* 續修四庫全書 [Supplement to the Complete Library of the Four Branches of Literature]. Vol. 951. Shanghai: Shanghai guji chubanshe, 2002.

Lu Shiyi 陸世儀. *Sibian lu ji yao* 思辨録輯要 [Essential collected records of thinking and distinguishing]. In *Wenyuange Siku quanshu* 文淵閣四庫全書 [Wenyuange edition of the Complete Library of the Four Branches of Literature]. Vol. 724. Taipei: Taiwan shangwu yinshuguan, 2013.

Lü Xinwu 呂新吾. *Xu xiao'er yu* 續小兒語 [Further words of children]. In *Yang zheng yi gui* 養正遺規 [Guidelines for proper upbringing], compiled by Chen Hongmou 陳宏謀. In *Xu xiu Siku quanshu* 續修四庫全書 [Supplement to the Complete Library of the Four Branches of Literature]. Vol. 951. Shanghai: Shanghai guji chubanshe, 2002.

Lu Xun 魯迅. *Lu Xun quanji* 魯迅全集 [Complete works of Lu Xun]. Beijing: Renmin wenxue chubanshe, 1973.

Lufrano, Richard John. *Honorable Merchants Commerce and Self-Cultivation in Late Imperial China*. Honolulu: University of Hawai'i Press, 1997.

Ma Ziyi 馬自毅. *Xin yi Youxue qionglin* 新譯幼學瓊林 [New interpretation of the *Treasury of Elementary Learning*]. Taipei: San min shuju, 2010.

Makeham, John, ed. *Dao Companion to Neo-Confucian Philosophy*. Dordrecht: Springer Science + Business Media B.V., 2010.

Mao Lirui 毛禮銳 and Shen Guanqun 沈灌群, eds. *Zhongguo jiaoyu tongshi* 中國教育通史 [Comprehensive history of Chinese education]. Jinan: Shandong jiaoyu chubanshe, 1987.

McDermott, Joseph. "The Ascendance of the Imprint in China." In *Printing and Book Culture in Late Imperial China,* edited by Cynthia J. Brokaw and Kai-Wing Chow, 55–104. Berkeley: University of California Press, 2006.

Mencius. Translated by Irene Bloom. New York: Columbia University Press, 2009.

Michael, Thomas. "The Original Text of the *Daodejing*: Disentangling Versions and Recensions." *Religions* 13, no. 4 (2022): 325. https://doi.org/10.3390/rel13040325.

Miller, George A. "The Magical Number Seven, Plus or Minus Two: Some Limits on our Capacity for Processing Information." *Psychological Review* 63, no. 2 (1956): 81–97.

Miller, Harry. *State Versus Gentry in Late Ming Dynasty China, 1572–1644*. New York: Palgrave Macmillan, 2009.

Ministry of Education of the People's Republic of China. "Wanshan Zhonghua youxiu chuantong wenhua jiaoyu zhidao gangyao" 完善中華優秀傳統文化教育指導綱要 [Essential guidance on refining education of the excellent traditional Chinese culture]. 26 March 2014. Accessed 23 March 2022, http://www.moe.gov.cn/srcsite/A13/s7061/201403/t20140328_166543.html.

Ministry of Education of the People's Republic of China. "Zhonghua youxiu chuantong wenhua jin zhong xiaoxue kecheng jiaocai zhinan" 中華優秀傳統文化進中小學課程教材指南 [A guide on incorporating the excellent traditional Chinese culture in primary and middle school curricular materials]. 8 January 2022. Accessed 18 March 2022, http://www.gov.cn/zhengce/zhengceku/2021-02/05/content_5585136.htm.

Moon, Jennifer A. *A Handbook of Reflective and Experiential Learning: Theory and Practice*. New York: Routledge, 2004.

Munro, Donald J. *The Concept of Man in Early China*. Stanford: Stanford University Press, 1969.

Munro, Donald J. *Images of Human Nature: A Sung Portrait*. Princeton: Princeton University Press, 1988.

Murphy, Tim, and Ralph Weber. "Confucianizing Socrates and Socratizing Confucius: On Comparing *Analects* 13:18 and the *Euthyphro*." *Philosophy East and West* 60, no. 2 (2010): 187–206.

Naquin, Susan, and Evelyn Sakakida Rawski. *Chinese Society in the Eighteenth Century*. New Haven: Yale University Press, 1987.

Ng, On-Cho. "Religious Hermeneutics: Text and Truth in Neo-Confucian Readings of the *Yijing*." *Journal of Chinese Philosophy* 34, no. 1 (2021): 5–24.

Norman, Jerry. *Chinese*. New York: Cambridge University Press, 1988.

Nucci, Larry, Darcia Narvaez, and Tobias Krettenauer, eds. *Handbook of Moral and Character Education*. New York: Routledge, 2014.

Nugent, Christopher M. B. *Manifest in Words, Written on Paper: Producing and Circulating Poetry in Tang Dynasty China*. Cambridge: Harvard University Asia Center, 2010.

Nugent, Christopher M. B. "Medieval Encyclopedias." In *Literary Information in China: A History*, edited by Jack W. Chen, Anatoly Detwyler, Xiao Liu, Christopher M. B. Nugent, and Bruce Rusk, 295–305. New York: Columbia University Press, 2021.

Nugent, Christopher M. B. "Structured Gaps: The *Qianzi wen* and Its Paratexts as Mnemotechnics." In *Memory in Medieval China: Text, Ritual, and Community*, edited by Wendy Swartz and Robert Ford Campany, 158–192. Leiden: Brill, 2018.

Nugent, Christopher M. B. *Textual Practices of Literary Training in Medieval China: Evidence from Dunhuang Manuscripts*. Leiden: Brill, 2023.

Nussbaum, Martha C. *Cultivating Humanity: A Classical Defense of Reform in Liberal Education*. Cambridge: Harvard University Press, 1997.

Nylan, Michael. "Calligraphy: The Sacred Text and Test of Culture." In *Character and Context in Chinese Calligraphy*, edited by Cary Y. Liu, Dora C. Y. Ching and Judith G. Smith, 16–78. Princeton: Princeton University, 1999.

Nylan, Michael. *The Five "Confucian" Classics*. New Haven: Yale University Press, 2001.

Olberding, Amy. *Moral Exemplars in the Analects: The Good Person Is* That. New York: Routledge, 2012.

O'Neill, Timothy Michael. *Ideography and Chinese Language Theory*. Boston: Walter De Gruyter, 2016.

"On Teaching and Learning" [*Xueji* 學記]. Translated by Xu Di, Yang Liuxin, Hunter McEwan, and Roger T. Ames. In *Chinese Philosophy on Teaching and Learning: Xueji in the Twenty-First Century*, edited by Xu Di and Hunter McEwan, 9–21. Albany: State University of New York Press, 2016.

Paar, Francis W., ed. *Ch'ien Tzu Wen* 千字文 *The Thousand Character Classic: A Chinese Primer*. New York: Frederick Ungar Publishing Company, 1963.

Paivio, Allan. *Mental Representations: A Dual Coding Approach*. New York: Oxford University Press, 1990.

Pan, Yuling and Kádár, Dániel Z. *Politeness in Historical and Contemporary Chinese*. London: Continuum, 2011.

Peng, Enhua Edward. "The Role of Allusion in Classical Chinese Poetry." PhD thesis, University of California, 1994.

Peters, Michael A. "Socrates and Confucius: The Cultural Foundations and Ethics of Learning." *Educational Philosophy and Theory* 47, no. 5 (2015): 423–427.

Peters, Michael, Tina Besley, and Huajun Zhang. *Moral Education and the Ethics of Self-Cultivation: Chinese and Western Perspectives*. Singapore: Springer Singapore, 2021.

Petersen, Willard J. "Advancement of Learning in Early Ch'ing: Three Cases." In *The Cambridge History of China: Volume 9, Part 2, The Ch'ing Dynasty to 1800*, edited by Willard J. Petersen, 513–570. Cambridge: Cambridge University Press, 2016.

Peterson, Willard J. "Confucian Learning in Late Ming Thought." In *The Cambridge History of China: Volume 8, Part 2, The Ming Dynasty, 1368–1644,* edited by Denis C. Twitchett and Frederick W. Mote, 708–788. Cambridge: Cambridge University Press, 1998.

Peterson, Willard J. "Dominating Learning from Above During the K'ang-Hsi Period." In *The Cambridge History of China: Volume 9, Part 1, The Ch'ing Dynasty to 1800,* edited by Willard J. Peterson, 571–605. Cambridge: Cambridge University Press, 1998.

Plaks, Andrew H. "Where the Lines Meet: Parallelism in Chinese and Western Literatures." *Poetics Today* 11, no. 3 (1990): 523–546.

Qian Mu 錢穆. *Zhongguo jin sanbai nian xueshu shi* 中國近三百年學術史 [Chinese intellectual history of the recent three hundred years]. Taipei: Shangwu yinshu guan, 1967.

Qian Mu 錢穆. *Zhuzi xin xue an* 朱子新學案 [New compendium to Master Zhu]. Vol. 3. Taipei: San min shuju, 1971.

Qiao Weiping 喬衛平 and Cheng Peijie 程培傑. *Zhongguo gudai you'er jiaoyu shi* 中國古代幼兒教育史 [History of premodern Chinese early childhood education]. Hefei: Anhui jiaoyu chubanshe, 1989.

Qiu Jun 邱浚. *Jiaozheng Youxue xuzhi chengyu kao* 較正幼學須知成語考 [Corrected edition of the *Required Knowledge for Elementary Learning* with verification of the idioms]. Guangdong: Wei jing tang, 1872. HathiTrust Digital Library, https://babel.hathitrust.org/cgi/pt?id=keio.10811605590&view=1up&seq=3.

Quine, Willard Van Orman. "A Postscript on Metaphor." In *On Metaphor*, edited by Sheldon Sacks, 159–160. Chicago: University of Chicago Press, 1979.

Rainey, Emily C., and Scott Storm. "English Teacher Interpretive Communities: An Exploratory Case Study of Teachers' Literacy Practices and Pedagogical Reasoning." *Literacy Research and Instruction* 60, no. 4 (2021): 352–371.

Rawski, Evelyn Sakakida. *Education and Popular Literacy in Ch'ing China.* Ann Arbor: University of Michigan Press, 1979.

Read, Kirsten. "Clues Cue the Smooze: Rhyme, Pausing, and Prediction Help Children Learn New Words from Storybooks." *Frontiers in Psychology* 5 (2014): 1–10.

Read, Kirsten, and Jacqueline Quirke. "Rhyme and Word Placement in Storybooks Support High-Level Verb Mapping in 3- to 5-Year-Olds." *Frontiers in Psychology* 9 (2018): 1–8.

Reichenbach, Roland, and Duck-Joo Kwak. *Confucian Perspectives on Learning and Self-Transformation: International and Cross-Disciplinary Approaches.* Cham: Springer International Publishing AG, 2020.

Ren Shixian 任時先. *Zhongguo jiaoyu sixiang shi* 中國教育思想史 [History of Chinese philosophy of education]. Vol. 44. Shanghai: Shanghai shudian, 1992.

Richardson, Virginia, Patricia Anders, Deborah Tidwell, and Carol Lloyd. "The Relationship between Teachers' Beliefs and Practices in Reading Comprehension Instruction." *American Educational Research Journal* 28, no. 3 (1991): 559–586.

Ridley, Charles. "Educational Theory and Practice in Late Imperial China: The Teaching of Writing as a Specific Case." PhD thesis, Stanford University, 1973.

Rosemont, Henry, Jr., and Roger T. Ames. *The Chinese Classic of Family Reverence.* Honolulu: University of Hawai'i Press, 2009.

Rosemont Henry, Jr., and Roger T. Ames. *Confucian Role Ethics: A Moral Vision for the 21st Century?* Göttingen: Vandenhoeck and Ruprecht, 2016.

Rowe, William T. *China's Last Empire: The Great Qing*. Cambridge: Harvard University Press, 2009.

Saari, Jon L. *Legacies of Childhood: Growing Up Chinese in a Time of Crisis, 1890–1920*. Cambridge: Harvard University Press, 1990.

The Sacred Books of China: The Texts of Confucianism Part III: The Li Ki I–X. Translated by James Legge. Delhi: Motilal Banarsidass, 1968.

Sacred Edict Containing Sixteen Maxims of the Emperor Kang-Hi, Amplified by his Son the Emperor Yoong-Ching. Translated by William Milne. Shengzu Xuanye 聖祖玄燁, commentary by Shizong Yinzhen 世宗胤禛. Shanghai: American Presbyterian Mission Press, 1870.

Sakai, Tadao. "Confucianism and Popular Educational Works." In *Self and Society in Ming Thought*, edited by William Theodore de Bary, 331–366. New York: Columbia University Press, 1972.

Searle, John R. "Metaphor." In *Metaphor and Thought*, edited by Andrew Ortony, 92–123. New York: Cambridge University Press, 1993.

Segal, Naomi, and Daniela Koleva. *From Literature to Cultural Literacy*. London: Palgrave Macmillan UK, 2014.

Shangshu zheng yi 尚書正義 [Orthodox exegesis of the *Documents*]. Commentary by Kong Anguo 孔安國; sub-commentary by Kong Yingda 孔穎達. Beijing: Peking University Press, 2000.

Shi Chengjin 石成金. "Dushu xinfa" 讀書心法 [Attitudes for reading]. In *Guoxue jiaoyu ji yao jiaofa juan* 國學教育輯要教法卷 [Essentials of traditional Chinese education: Volume on teaching methods], edited by Jun Yihao 君藝豪 and Jiao Yuhua 焦玉華, 580–589. Beijing: Minzhu yu jianshe chubanshe, 2015.

Shi Chengjin 石成金. "Tong li zhi yao" 童禮知要 [Essential knowledge for childhood etiquette]. In *Guoxue jiaoyu ji yao jiaofa juan* 國學教育輯要教法卷 [Essentials of traditional Chinese education: Volume on teaching methods], edited by Jun Yihao 君藝豪 and Jiao Yuhua 焦玉華, 273–278. Beijing: Minzhu yu jianshe chubanshe, 2015.

Shu Ching Book of History—A Modernized Edition of the Translations of James Legge. Translated by Clae Waltham. London: George Allen and Unwin Ltd., 1971.

Shun, Kwong-loi. "Studying Confucian and Comparative Ethics: Methodological Reflections." *Journal of Chinese Philosophy* 36, no. 3 (2009): 455–478.

Sim, May. *Remastering Morals with Aristotle and Confucius.* New York: Cambridge University Press, 2007.

Sima Qian 司馬遷. *Records of the Grand Historian of China, Volume 1, Early Years of the Han Dynasty, 209 to 141 B.C.* Translated by Burton Watson. New York: Columbia University Press, 1971.

Smith, Richard J. *The Qing Dynasty and Traditional Chinese Culture*. Lanham: Rowman and Littlefield, 2015.

Soffel, Christian. "Lesebücher aus dem späten kaiserlichen China am Beispiel des *Youxue gushi qionglin*." In *Aspekte des Lesens in China in Vergangenheit und Gegenwart: Referate der Jahrestagung 2001 der Deutschen Vereinigung für Chinastudien* [Aspects of reading in China, past and present: Collected papers of the 2001 annual meeting of the German Association for Chinese Studies], edited by Bernhard Führer, 216–228. Bochum: Projekt Verlag, 2005.

Swanson, Don R. "Toward a Psychology of Metaphor." In *On Metaphor*, edited by Sheldon Sacks, 161–164. Chicago: University of Chicago Press, 1979.

Swartz, Wendy. *Reading Philosophy, Writing Poetry: Intertextual Modes of Making Meaning in Early Medieval China*. Cambridge: Harvard University Asia Center, 2018.

Tang Biao 唐彪. *Jiashu jiaoxue fa* 家塾教學法 [Teaching methods for the family school]. Shanghai: Hua dong shifan daxue chubanshe, 1992.

Tang Jian 唐鑑. *Qing xue'an xiao shi* 清學案小識 [Small records of the cases of learning in the Qing]. Taipei: Shangwu yinshu guan, 1968.

Tian, Xiaofei. "Literary Learning: Encyclopedias and Epitomes." In *The Oxford Handbook of Classical Chinese Literature (1000 BCE–900 CE)*, edited by Wiebke Denecke, Wai-yee Li, and Xiaofei Tian, 132–146. New York: Oxford University Press, 2017.

Tian Zhengping 田正平, ed. *Zhongguo xiaoxue changshi jiaoxue shi* 中國小學常識教學史 [History of general knowledge teaching in Chinese primary schools]. Zhongguo xiaoxue geke jiaoxue shi congshu 中國小學各科教學史叢書 [Series on the history of Chinese primary school subjects]. Jinan: Shandong jiaoyu chubanshe, 1996.

Tongmeng xuzhi 童蒙須知 [Essential instructions for the young]. Compiled by Zhu Xi 朱熹. In *Yang zheng yi gui* 養正遺規 [Guidelines for proper upbringing]. Compiled by Chen Hongmou 陳宏謀. In *Xu xiu Siku quanshu* 續修四庫全書 [Supplement to the Complete Library of the Four Branches of Literature]. Vol. 951. Shanghai: Shanghai guji chubanshe, 2002.

Tontini, Roberta. *Muslim Sanzijing: Shifts and Continuities in the Definition of Islam in China*. Leiden: Brill, 2016.

Tu Wei-ming. *Centrality and Commonality: An Essay on Confucian Religiousness*. Albany: State University of New York Press, 1989.

Tu Wei-ming. "The Sung Confucian Idea of Education: A Background Understanding." In *Neo-Confucian Education: The Formative Stage*, edited by William Theodore de Bary and John W. Chaffee, 139–150. Berkeley: University of California Press, 1989.

Turner, Mark, and Gilles Fauconnier. *The Way We Think: Conceptual Blending and the Mind's Hidden Complexities*. New York: Basic Books, 2002.

Uhrmacher, Bruce. "Toward a Theory of Aesthetic Learning Experiences." *Curriculum Inquiry* 39, no. 5 (2009): 613–636.

The United Nations Terminology Database (UNTERM). "Definition of Primary Education." Adopted 13 June 2013, https://dcp.unesco.org/UNTERM/Display/Record/UNHQ/NA?OriginalId=7220a2a02d079913852569fd00038002.

van Norden, Bryan W. *Taking Back Philosophy: A Multicultural Manifesto*. New York: Columbia University Press, 2017.

van Norden, Bryan W. *Virtue Ethics and Consequentialism in Early Chinese Philosophy*. New York: Cambridge University Press, 2007.

Wang Chong 王充. *Xin bian Lun heng* 新編論衡 [Newly compiled *Lun heng*]. Taipei: Taiwan guji, 1990.

Wang Dan 王丹. "*Youxue qionglin* yanjiu" 幼學瓊林研究 [A study on the *Treasury of Elementary Learning*]. Master's thesis, Northeast Normal University, 2018.

Wang Jinmin 王錦民. "Education in Schools and in Society." In *The History of Chinese Civilization (volume 4)*, edited by Yuan Xingpei 袁行霈, Yan Wenming 嚴文明, Zhang Chuanxi 張傳璽, and Lou Yulie 樓宇烈, 485–528. Cambridge: Cambridge University Press, 2012.

Wang Kaifu 王凱符. *Baguwen gaishuo* 八股文概說 [An overview of the eight-legged essay]. Beijing: Zhongguo heping chubanshe, 1991.

Wang Longlin 汪龍麟 and Zong Yanfu 踪岩夫. *Youxue qionglin* 幼學瓊林 [Treasury of elementary learning]. Beijing: Beijing shaonian ertong chubanshe, 1995.

Wang Shouren 王守仁. *Wang wen cheng gong quanshu* 王文成公全書 [Collected works of Wang Yangming]. Taipei: Shangwu yin shu guan, 1979.

Wang Weiyong 王偉勇. *Yingyongwen* 應用文 [Writing for various occasions]. Tainan: Cheng da chubanshe, 2015.

Wang Xiang 王相. *Sanzi jing xungu* 三字經訓詁 [Exegesis of the *Three Character Classic*]. Beijing: Zhongguo shudian, 1991.

Wang Xiaoping. "On *Qianzi wen* in the Sinological Literary History of Asia." *Frontiers of Literary Studies in China* 3, no. 3 (2009): 348–364.

Wang Yun 王筠. "Jiao tongzi fa" 教童子法 [Methods for teaching children]. In *Guoxue jiaoyu ji yao jiaofa juan* 國學教育輯要教法卷 [Essentials of traditional Chinese education: Volume on teaching methods], edited by Jun Yihao 君藝豪 and Jiao Yuhua 焦玉華, 164–173. Beijing: Minzhu yu jianshe chubanshe, 2015.

Wang Zichen 王咨臣. "Cheng Dengji shengping jiqi zhuzhuo *Youxue qionglin*" 程登吉生平及其著作幼學瓊林 [Life of Cheng Dengji and the *Treasury of Elementary Learning*]. In *Jiangxi lishi mingren yanjiu* 江西歷史名人研究 [Research on eminent people in Jiangxi history], edited by Chen Wenhua 陳文華, 135–137. Beijing: Zhongguo renshi chubanshe, 1995.

Weng Yanzhen 翁衍楨. "Gudai ertong duwu gaiguan" 古代兒童讀物概觀 [An overview of premodern children's books]. *Tushuguan xueji kan* 10, no. 1 (1936): 91–146.

Williams, Charles A. S. *Chinese Symbolism and Art Motifs: A Comprehensive Handbook on Symbolism in Chinese Art through the Ages*. North Clarendon: Tuttle Publishing, 2006.

Woniu fangzi 蝸牛房子, ed. *Youxue qionglin zao zao du* 幼學瓊林早早讀 [Reading the *Treasury of Elementary Learning* in the early years]. Fuzhou: Fujian shaonian ertong chubanshe, 2015.

Woodside, Alexander. "Some Mid-Qing Theorists of Popular Schools: Their Innovations, Inhibitions, and Attitudes Toward the Poor." *Modern China* 9, no. 1 (1983): 3–35.

Xiao Liangyou 蕭良有. *Longwen bianying* 龍文鞭影 [The young horse and the shadow of a whip]. Shanghai: Shanghai guji chubanshe, 2014.

Xiao Yishan 蕭一山. *Qingdai tongshi* 清代通史 [Comprehensive history of the Qing dynasty]. Taipei: Shangwu yinshu guan, 1963.

Xie Qikun 謝啓昆. *Xiaoxue kao*小學考 [A study on primary education]. Hefei: Anhui jiaoyu chubanshe, 2002.

Xie Shuishun 謝水順 and Li Ting 李珽. *Fujian gudai keshu* 福建古代刻書 [Premodern publishing in Fujian]. Fuzhou: Fujian renmin chubanshe, 1997.

Xu Di. "The Teaching and Learning Principles of Xueji in the Educational Practice of the World Today." In *Chinese Philosophy on Teaching and Learning: Xueji in the Twenty-First Century*, edited by Xu Di and Hunter McEwan, 39–60. Albany: State University of New York Press, 2016.

Xu Di and Hunter McEwan, eds. *Chinese Philosophy on Teaching and Learning: Xueji in the Twenty-First Century*. Albany: State University of New York Press, 2016.

Xu Zi 徐梓. *Mengxue duwu de lishi toushi* 蒙學讀物的歷史透視 [Perspectives on the history of reading materials for elementary studies]. Wuhan: Hubei jiaoyu chubanshe, 1997.

Yang Bojun 楊伯峻. *Liezi ji shi* 列子集釋 [Collected explanations of the *Liezi*]. Beijing: Zhonghua shuju, 1985.

Yang Bojun 楊伯峻. *Mengzi yizhu* 孟子譯註 [Annotated translation of the *Mencius*]. Beijing: Zhonghua shuju, 2015.

Yang Yung-chih 楊永智. "*Youxue qionglin* liuchuan Taiwan kao" 《幼學瓊林》流傳臺灣考 [Research on the transmission of the *Youxue qionglin* in Taiwan]. *Donghai daxue wenxueyuan xuebao* 47, no. 7 (2006): 83–116.

Yang zheng yi gui 養正遺規 [Guidelines for proper upbringing]. Compiled by Chen Hongmou 陳宏謀. *Xu xiu Siku quanshu* 續修四庫全書 [Supplement to the Complete Library of the Four Branches of Literature]. Vol. 951. Shanghai: Shanghai guji chubanshe, 2002.

Yao Xinzhong. *An Introduction to Confucianism*. Cambridge: Cambridge University Press, 2000.

Ye Guangda 葉光大. *Youxue gushi qionglin yizhu* 幼學故事瓊林譯注 [Annotated translation of the *Youxue gushi qionglin*]. Guiyang: Guiyang renmin chubanshe, 1991.

Yearley, Lee H. *Mencius and Aquinas: Theories of Virtue and Conceptions of Courage*. Albany: State University of New York Press, 1990.

Yong, Heming, and Jing Peng. *Chinese Lexicography: A History from 1046 BC to AD 1911*. Oxford: Oxford University Press, 2008.

You Zhuran, A. G. Rud, and Yingzi Hu. *The Philosophy of Chinese Moral Education: A History*. New York: Palgrave Macmillan, 2018.

Yu Li. "Character Recognition: A New Method of Learning to Read in Late Imperial China." *Late Imperial China* 33, no. 2 (2012): 12–18.

Yu Li. "A History of Reading in Late Imperial China, 1000–1800." PhD thesis, Ohio State University, 2003.

Yu, Pauline. *The Reading of Imagery in the Chinese Poetic Tradition*. Princeton: Princeton University Press, 1987.

Yu Ying-shih. "Qing Confucianism." In *Chinese History and Culture Volume 2, Seventeenth Century through Twentieth Century*, edited by Yu Ying-shih, Josephine Chiu-Duke and Michael S. Duke, 113–133. New York: Columbia University Press, 2016.

Yu Ying-shih. "Some Preliminary Observations on the Rise of Qing Confucian Intellectualism." In *Chinese History and Culture Volume 2, Seventeenth Century through Twentieth Century*, edited by Yu Ying-shih, Josephine Chiu-Duke, and Michael S. Duke, 1–39. New York: Columbia University Press, 2016.

Zagzebski, Linda Tinkaus. *Divine Motivation Theory*. Cambridge: Cambridge University Press, 2004.

Zhang Boxing 張伯行. *Xiaoxue ji jie* 小學集解 [Collected commentaries on *Elementary Learning*]. Vol. 981. Beijing: Zhonghua shuju, 1985.

Zhang He 張河 and Mu Zhi 牧之. *Zhongguo gudai mengshu jijin* 中國古代蒙書集錦 [Anthology of premodern Chinese elementary education texts]. Jinan: Shandong youyi shushe, 1989.

Zhang Hong 張洪 and Qi Bi 齊璧. *Zhuzi dushu fa* 朱子讀書法 [Master Zhu's method of reading]. *Wenjinge Siku quanshu* 文津閣四庫全書 [Wenjinge edition of the Complete Library of the Four Branches of Literature]. Vol. 235. Beijing: Shangwu yinshu guan, 2005.

Zhang Hua 張華. *Bowu zhi* 博物志 [Treatise on curiosities]. *Wenyuange Siku quanshu* 文淵閣四庫全書 [Wenyuange edition of the Complete Library of the Four Branches of Literature]. Vol. 1047. Taipei: Taiwan shangwu yinshuguan, 2013.

Zhang Jian and Chen Dandan. "Primers and Poetry in Ancient China: Shenglü Fameng and Beyond." *Journal of Chinese Literature and Culture* 1, no. 1–2 (2014): 186–215.

Zhang Mei 張梅. *Tales from the Children's Knowledge Treasury (Chinese-Japanese edition)*. Beijng: Sinolingua, 2010.

Zhang Mei 張梅 and Chang Guojie 暢國傑. *Tales from the Children's Knowledge Treasury*. Beijng: China Intercontinental Press, 2013.

Zhang Xingjian 張行簡. "Shu zhong suo yan" 塾中瑣言 [Common remarks in the private school]. In *Mengxue yaoyi* 蒙學要義 [Essential ideas in primary education], edited by Xu Zi 徐梓 and Wang Xuemei 王雪梅, 100–114. Taiyuan: Shanxi jiaoyu chubanshe, 1991.

Zhang Xuecheng 章學成. "Lun ke mengxue wenfa" 論課蒙學文法 [Lessons on grammar for elementary education]. In *Guoxue jiaoyu ji yao jiaofa juan* 國學教育輯要教法卷 [Essentials of traditional Chinese education: Volume on teaching methods], edited by Jun Yihao 君藝豪 and Jiao Yuhua 焦玉華, 155–163. Beijing: Minzhu yu jianshe chubanshe, 2015.

Zhang Youheng 張有恆. *Shijiao sanzijing baihua jieshi* 釋教三字經白話解釋 [Three character classic of Buddhism]. Tainan: Zhang Youheng, 2020.

Zhang Zhidong 張之洞. "Shumu dawen" 書目答問 [Answers to the reading list]. In *Guoxue jiaoyu ji yao jiaofa juan* 國學教育輯要教法卷 [Essentials of traditional Chinese education: Volume on teaching methods], edited by Jun Yihao 君藝豪 and Jiao Yuhua 焦玉華, 630–703. Beijing: Minzhu yu jianshe chubanshe, 2015.

Zhang Zhigong 張志公. *Chuantong yuwen jiaoyu jiaocai lun: ji mengxue shumu he shuying* 傳統語文教育教材論：暨蒙學書目和書影 [Discussion of teaching materials for language learning in traditional Chinese education including bibliography and images of the elementary education texts]. Beijing: Zhonghua shuju, 2017.

Zhao Erxun 趙爾巽. *Qing shi gao* 清史稿 [Draft history of the Qing]. Vol. 33. Beijing: Zhonghua shuju, 1999.

Zhao Jiyao 趙基耀 and Li Xu 李旭. *Qingdai baguwen yi zhu* 清代八股文譯註 [Modern Chinese translations and annotations of Qing dynasty eight-legged essays]. Shanghai: Shanghai guji chubanshe, 2011.

Zhao Xiaohuan. "Xiaoshuo as a Cataloguing Term in Traditional Chinese Bibliography." *Sungkyun Journal of East Asian Studies* 5, no. 2 (2005): 157–181.

Zhouli zhushu 周禮注疏 [Commentary and sub-commentary on the *Rituals of Zhou*]. Commentary by Zheng Xuan 鄭玄; sub-commentary by Jia Gongyan 賈公彥. In *Wenyuange Siku quanshu* 文淵閣四庫全書 [Wenyuange edition of the Complete Library of the Four Branches of Literature]. Taipei: Taiwan shangwu yinshuguan, 2013.

Zhouyi zheng yi 周易正義 [Orthodox exegesis of the *Changes*]. Commentary by Wang Bi 王弼; sub-commentary by Kong Yingda 孔穎達. Beijing: Peking University Press, 2000.

Zhu Xi 朱熹. "Bai lu dong shuyuan tishi" 白鹿洞書院提示 [Regulations of the white deer grotto academy]. In *Guoxue jiaoyu ji yao jiaofa juan* 國學教育輯要教法卷 [Essentials of traditional Chinese education: Volume on teaching methods], edited by Jun Yihao 君藝豪 and Jiao Yuhua 焦玉華, 378–379. Beijing: Minzhu yu jianshe chubanshe, 2015.

Zhu Xi 朱熹. *Jin si lu* 近思錄 [Record of reflections on things at hand]. Commentary by Zhang Boxing 張伯行. Taipei: Shangwu yinshuguan, 1996.

Zhu Xi 朱熹. *Sishu zhangju jizhu* 四書章句集註 [The four books in chapter and verse with collected commentaries]. Beijing: Zhonghua shuju, 2012. Zhu Xi 朱熹. *Zhouyi benyi* 周易本義 [The original interpretation of the *Changes*]. Beijing: Renmin chubanshe, 2009.

Zou Gang 鄒剛 and Zou Zhiyuan 鄒志瑗. *Youxue qiongling yizhu* 幼學瓊林譯注 [Annotated translation of the *Treasury of Elementary Learning*]. Nanchang: Jiangxi remin chubanshe, 1990.

Zou Shengmai 鄒聖脈 and Hu Xiazhi 胡遐之. *Youxue qionglin* 幼學瓊林 [Treasury of elementary learning]. Changsha: Yueli shushe, 1986.

Zuo Tradition Zuozhuan 左傳: *Commentary on the "Spring and Autumn Annals."* Translated by Stephen Durrant, Wai-yee Li, and David Schaberg. Vol. 2. Seattle: University of Washington Press, 2016.